Researching Children's Experience

Researching Children's Experience

Methods and Approaches

Edited by
Sheila Greene and Diane Hogan

SAGE Publications
London ● Thousand Oaks ● New Delhi

First published 2005. Reprinted 2005 (twice), 2006

 SAGE Publications Ltd
1 Oliver's Yard
55 City Road
London EC1Y 1SP

SAGE Publications Inc
2455 Teller Road
Thousand Oaks, California 91320

SAGE Publications India Pvt Ltd
B-42, Panchsheel Enclave
Post Box 4109
New Delhi 110 017

British Library Cataloguing in Publication data

A catalogue record for this book is available
from the British Library

ISBN-10 0-7619-7102-5   ISBN-13 978-0-7619-7102-3
ISBN-10 0-7619-7103-3 (pbk) ISBN-13 978-0-7619-7103-0 (pbk)

Library of Congress Control Number available

Typeset by C&M Digitals (P) Ltd., Chennai, India
Printed in Great Britain by Cromwell Press Ltd, Trowbridge, Wiltshire

Contents

Notes on Contributors

Dr Pam Alldred lectures in Childhood Studies in the School of Education at the University of Greenwich, UK. She was a member of the feminist research groups that produced *Ethics in qualitative research* (M. Mauthner, M. Birch, J. Jessop & T. Miller (Eds.), 2002, Sage) and *Feminist dilemmas in qualitative research: public knowledge, private lives* (J. Ribbens and R. Edwards (Eds.), 1998, Sage). Before that, she was part of the collectives that produced *Challenging women: psychology's exclusions, feminist possibilities* (E. Burman, P. Alldred, C. Bewley, B. Goldberg, C. Heenan, D. Marks, J. Marshall, K. Taylor, R. Ullah & S. Warner, 1996, Open University Press) and *Psychology, discourse, practice: from regulation to resistance* (E. Burman, G. Aitken, P. Alldred, R. Attwood, T. Billington, B. Goldberg, A.J. Gordo Lopez, C. Heenan, D. Marks, S. Warner, 1996, Taylor and Francis). Besides methodology, she also writes about young people's views of sex education, education policy and political activism.

Dr Marc Briod is Associate Professor of Education and Philosophy in the Department of Human Development and Child Studies at Oakland University, Rochester, Michigan, USA. His research and publications include a phenomenological approach to child development, a study of children's emerging sense of time and the clock, and an investigation of children's developing awareness of a future. His current work focuses on the essential role played by imagination for sense-making during childhood and throughout life. He is especially interested in conceptions of imagination that view it as the cognitive taproot for a wide range of thinking, meaning, and learning.

Erica Burman is Professor of Psychology and Women's Studies in the Department of Psychology and Speech Pathology at Manchester Metropolitan University, UK, where she is currently convenor of the Women's Studies Research Centre and co-director of the Discourse Unit. She has written extensively about the gendering of childhood, the critiques of developmental psychology and the projection of problematic North–South relations onto global discourses of development, as well as about the critical potential of discourse analysis. More recently she has written about power relations and difference in psychotherapy, and minoritization and racialization in service provision.

Pia Christensen is Senior Researcher at the National Institute of Public Health, Copenhagen, Denmark. She has published widely on children and health, schooling, the family, methods and research ethics, and children's time and space. Her publications include *Research with Children*, co-edited with A. James (Falmer Press, 2000) and *Children in the City*, co-edited with M. O'Brien (RoutledgeFalmer, 2002).

Tom Danaher, MA, is a therapist and psychological assessor for marginalized teenagers in shelters in Pittsburgh, Pennsylvania, USA. He has been researching these teenagers' sense of justice and injustice, which he sees as fundamental to their experience of anger/rage and their abuse of drugs. His studies in phenomenological method began in Pittsburgh at Duquesne University – one of the original centres for Existential-Phenomenology in the USA. He is currently working on his doctoral dissertation at Saybrook Graduate School and Research Center, San Francisco, California.

Judy Dunn is MRC Research Professor at the Institute of Psychiatry in London. A developmental psychologist, she has conducted extensive longitudinal research on children's close relationships, including siblings and friends, non-shared experiences within the family, the development of social understanding, and, most recently, family transitions and the impact of family change. Among honours bestowed she has recently received the Award for Distinguished Scientific Contributions to Child Development from the Society for Research in Child Development. She is a fellow of the British Academy and the Academy of Medical Sciences. She has published sixteen books and numerous papers.

Dr Ruth Emond is a social work practioner and academic. She is employed by the Department of Applied Social Science at the University of Stirling, UK, where she teaches mainly on the social work undergraduate and postgraduate programme. She also works part time as a social worker in a therapeutic project with children and families who have experienced trauma. Ruth has a keen research interest in the experiences of children who have involvement in a social welfare system and in children's experiences of friendship.

Susan Engel is Senior Lecturer at Williams College, Department of Psychology, where she is also Director of the Program in Teaching. She is co-founder and educational advisor to an experimental school, Hayground, in Bridgehampton, New York. Her research interests include narrative development, autobiographical memory, and the development of imagination. She is also interested in school reform and new models of education. She is the author of *The stories children tell* (W.H. Freeman, 1995).

Sheila Greene is Associate Professor in the Psychology Department, Trinity College Dublin (TCD). She is a co-founder of the Centre for Gender and Women's Studies and the Children's Research Centre, both at TCD, and is currently the Director of the Children's Research Centre. Her research and publications are mainly in developmental psychology, with a focus on social development and developmental theory, and she is the author of *The psychological development of girls and women: rethinking change in time*, recently published by Routledge.

Dr Caroline Heary is a lecturer in developmental psychology at the National University of Ireland, Galway. Her research interests lie in the delivery of child-centred health services, child-centred research methodology and psycho-social factors associated with health and illness. She is also involved in a collaborative research project with Eilis Hennessy on children's understanding of psychological problems. She has experience in both qualitative and quantitative research methodologies and has a particular interest in the value of focus group interviews for research with children and young people.

Dr Eilis Hennessy is a lecturer in developmental psychology in the Psychology Department in University College Dublin, Ireland. Her research interests include children's experiences of child care environments and how these have an impact on their development. In addition, she has recently been involved in studies relating to children's perceptions of mental health and their experiences of health services. She is interested in qualitative research methods that facilitate communication with children about their lives and experiences.

Professor Malcolm Hill is Director of the Glasgow Centre for the Child & Society, which was established in 1991. He has been Director of the Centre since 1996. He has a degree in Geography, a Diploma in Applied Social Studies and a PhD in Social Science. For the past twenty years he has been teaching and carrying out research, largely in relation to children and families. He has written and edited a number of books on children's services and children's lives.

Dr Diane Hogan is a lecturer in developmental psychology in the Department of Psychology, Trinity College Dublin, and a Senior Research Fellow of The Children's Research Centre, Trinity College. Her research interests are in the area of children's social development within families. She has published in the areas of sociocultural theories of child development, children's experiences of parental separation, the impact of parental drug use on children, and on methodological issues associated with conducting research on children's subjective experiences.

Dr Karen Littleton is a Senior Lecturer in Developmental Psychology in the Centre for Childhood, Development and Learning at The Open University, UK, and Visiting Professor at the University of Helsinki. She has researched children's collaborative learning, with special reference to new technologies and gender, and has published extensively in this area. Karen co-edited *Learning with computers* (Routledge, 1999) with Paul Light, and is the co-author, also with Paul Light, of *Social processes in children's learning* (Cambridge

University Press, 1999). From 1994–99 she was senior scientist in the European Science Foundation's 'Learning in Humans and Machines' programme.

Alan Prout is Professor of Sociology at the University of Stirling and was formerly Director of the Economic and Social Research Council's 'Children 5–16 Research Programme'. He is author of many works on contemporary childhood, including *Theorizing childhood* (Polity Press, 1998, with Alison James and Chris Jenks), *The body, childhood and society* (Macmillan, 2000) and *Hearing the voices of children: social policy for new century* (RoutledgeFalmer, 2003, with Christine Hallett). His latest book is *The future of childhood: towards the interdisciplinary study of children* (RoutledgeFalmer, 2004).

Annie G. Rogers, PhD, is a clinical psychologist, poet and painter. Formerly Associate Professor at Harvard University, her interests include qualitative research methods, girls' psychological development, child sexual abuse and Lacanian psychoanalysis. She has a private practice in Amherst, Massachusetts, USA. She is currently Assistant Professor of Clinical Psychology at Hampshire College, a research associate in Psychology at Trinity College Dublin, and a member of the Boston Psychoanalytic Circle of the Freudian School of Quebec.

Jonathan Tudge is a Professor of Human Development and Family Studies, at the University of North Carolina at Greensboro, USA. He was raised and educated in England (Lancaster and Oxford) before moving to the USA for his PhD (Cornell). His main interests are in peer social interactions and the relations between children's development and culture, and he has co-edited, with Jaan Valsiner and Mike Shanahan, *Comparisons in human development* (1997, Cambridge University Press), and is currently writing *The cultural ecology of young children*, also to be published by Cambridge University Press.

Angela Veale, PhD, is lecturer in Applied Psychology at the National University of Ireland, Cork. Her research and publications focus on youth in adversity, in particular asylum seekers and unaccompanied minors in Ireland, and the reintegration of war affected children and psychosocial interventions in Rwanda, Uganda, Sudan and Ethiopia. Currently, she is researching and publishing on child soldiers, youth and political involvement in conflict and post-conflict contexts.

Dr Helen L. Westcott is Senior Lecturer in Psychology at The Open University, UK. Her particular research interests lie in investigative interviewing and the evidence of children, and more recently in children's eyewitness identifications. She has also researched widely on the abuse of disabled children, and children's responses to child protection investigations. Helen writes and presents on these topics nationally and internationally, and is closely involved in projects with practitioners in the child protection and criminal justice systems.

Preface

In this book we have two main objectives. The first is to examine the theoretical and ethical issues that arise in researching children's experience and the second is to provide examples of how researchers from a variety of social science perspectives have set about carrying out research into children's experience. Our intention is to advance thinking and debate on why researching children's experience is important and on how it should be done. This book focuses on theory and practice and we hope that the reader will find within it both food for thought and very practical assistance in conducting research in this area. In the first section of the book we explore the theoretical and ethical issues and tensions that arise in researching what is inevitably a complex and sensitive topic and in the second part a range of authors discuss their approaches to accessing children's experience, outlining what they do and how they address the challenges entailed in using their particular method. We want this book to be useful to researchers embarking on research in this area and to experienced researchers who wish to explore new methods.

As editors we started this project with a number of core principles in mind. The first is that there is strength in a multi-disciplinary approach. Children's lives benefit from being considered from multiple perspectives and there is no one theoretical or methodological perspective which deserves to be dominant. The social science disciplines – sociology, anthropology, education, social work, social policy and psychology – have much to learn from each other. Children's lives are complex and multi-faceted and require an analysis that is informed by knowledge of biological, psychological and social factors and their interactions. Different theoretical standpoints can build on each other or, at the very least, be open to being challenged by an alternative viewpoint.

Second, we are convinced that children are subject to historical and cultural influences that ensure that every child has an individual and unique experience of his or her childhood. Thus we were interested in approaches and methods of research that respected this individuality and diversity in children and childhoods. As a result, the methods described in this book are mainly, although not exclusively, qualitative since qualitative methods are suited to enquiry into children's unique and individual encounters with their worlds.

Third, we were interested in exploring and promoting those approaches that are premised on a view of children as human beings who share with adults a comparable level of agency (likewise constrained) and the capacity to reflect on, and shape, their own experience.

Interest in accessing children's perspectives and views has been prompted in recent years by widespread acceptance and official endorsement of the United Nations Declaration on the Rights of the Child, in itself a consequence of social movements which recognized and sought to vindicate children's rights. From this point of view it could be argued that we have an obligation to assist children to express their perspectives and views on matters of importance to them. We leave aside inevitably vexed questions about how this should be done and with what end. In this book we are not interested exclusively in methods of eliciting children's perspectives, views and opinions. Our primary focus is on children's experience, which is a factor in the formation of their opinions, but more than that, it is about the totality of their subjective engagement with the world.

From a scientific perspective also we have much to learn about children from children. By enquiring into children's experience we will come to know more about how they interpret and negotiate their worlds, material and discursive, past, present, and future. Knowledge about children includes knowledge about children's subjectivity and requires and deserves careful analysis and the use of appropriate methods. For example, we include in this book, observational studies on young children where the focus is on activity, but the intention is to infer what the activity means to the children concerned, not to assess levels or types of behaviour. Such an approach may be seen as problematic and indeed many of the issues arising in this arena are problematic and contested, and may well remain so.

We fully recognize the multiple and sometimes, but not always, compatible perspectives that exist in this field and thus, in this book, we have brought together authors from different disciplinary backgrounds and with different theoretical standpoints. What they share is an interest in developing research methods that can tell us more about how children experience their daily lives and make sense of their position in the world.

The editors of this book are both psychologists who freely admit to a frustration with the 'objective' stance of many of our colleagues in developmental psychology. Psychology's focus on the objective is seen in both its methodology and in its choice of subject matter. There is still little acceptance of the epistemological arguments that question our capacity to measure objectively our human subjects, and there is still a wariness of relying on children's views of their own lives and therefore of their experience. Children's individual experience is typically not valued as a focus of research since it is perceived as unreliable and idiosyncratic. In its urge to assess and measure the child, some mainstream developmental psychology has sought to homogenize the experience of children. (These issues are explored in more detail by Diane Hogan, and by Sheila Greene and Malcolm Hill in their chapters.) This characterization of developmental psychology is of course incomplete and to some extent a cartoon drawing. There is, in the mainstream, more recognition of diversity and on the margins, more critique of traditional epistemology and methodology. Research on children and childhood in recent years has been strongly influenced by the emergence of the new sociology of childhood, as described by Pia Christensen and Alan Prout. More recently we have seen the emergence of childhood studies as an interdisciplinary field. While welcoming this coming together of disciplines, we would argue strongly for maintaining disciplinary diversity also. For example, while being very critical of some of the manifestations of our own discipline, we would both see it as essential to the study of children that we continue to address questions to do with psychological growth and change in time. We would therefore see a continuing place for developmental psychology in the consortium of disciplines with a shared interest in researching children and childhood.

In compiling the chapters for this book we were surprised again and again by how little explicit attention to method there is in published research on children or childhood. In journal articles, which are the main vehicle for publishing empirical research, much attention is given to describing the method, but very little attention is given to the rationale for using the method in the first place or to a critique of the method's strengths and weaknesses, including the practical and ethical problems arising when employing it. In the last (fifth, four volumes) edition of the *Handbook of Child Psychology*, we were struck by the relative neglect of attention to research methods. In looking for researchers who specialize in analysis of issues arising when using qualitative methods with children, we noted the huge expansion in the use of qualitative methods in research, but the lack of discussion about methodological issues in relation to children. We are encouraged, however, by the growth of interest in this area and note the publication of several texts in recent years that complement this one. We hope that this book will provide social science researchers with a broad conceptual framework for understanding and researching children's subjectivities and lived experiences, and equip them with a range of methods appropriate to the exploration and analysis of children's experience.

Sheila Greene and Diane Hogan
Editors

Acknowledgements

We would like to thank our colleagues in the Psychology Department and in the Children's Research Centre in Trinity College Dublin for their support. In particular we would like to acknowledge the stimulation and encouragement offered by Robbie Gilligan at an early stage in our deliberations on this topic. We are grateful for the patience of our contributors and hope that they are as pleased as we are to see the book in print. Fionnuala Dillane helped us with considerable skill in the final formatting and editing of the manuscript. We are very grateful to Michael Carmichael and Fabienne Pedroletti and all the staff we have worked with at Sage who have been more than helpful.

Finally we thank our families: Martin Fellenz, Aine, Leah and Isabel Hogan Fellenz; and Paul, Kit and Helen O'Mahony.

Diane Hogan and Sheila Greene

| Conceptual, Methodological and Ethical Issues in Researching Children's Experience | PART ONE |

| 1 | Researching Children's Experience: Methods and Methodological Issues |

Sheila Greene and Malcolm Hill

Why Research Children's Experience?

As one looks from an historical perspective at the vast field of social scientific, empirical research already conducted on and with children, it is evident that the predominant emphasis has been on children as the objects of research rather than children as subjects, on child-related outcomes rather than child-related processes and on child variables rather than children as persons.

The chapters by Hogan, and by Christensen and Prout in this book (Chapters 2 and 3 respectively) outline the assumptions held by psychologists, sociologists and anthropologists about children that shaped the approach taken by these disciplines for much of the twentieth century. Both chapters also describe the shift in emphasis and ideology which has become known as 'the new social studies of childhood'. As Hogan outlines, similar critiques of the dominant perspective on child development research have become evident amongst psychologists, although mainstream developmental psychology tends to be somewhat more wedded to traditional epistemologies than appears to be the case amongst contemporary sociologists and anthropologists, or indeed, other disciplines like geography and history (Holloway & Valentine, 2000).

This chapter is written by two people with different disciplinary backgrounds – developmental and clinical psychology (Greene) and social work and social research (Hill). Despite this difference in background and perspective, we share an interest in conducting research that helps us to understand more about children's experience of their worlds. This is not an easy task: there are many questions and pitfalls that can trouble the researcher in this area.

The impetus to set out to understand and describe children's experience may reflect one or more of a range of different commitments as a researcher. First, it may reflect an interest in experience itself. According to William James, 'individual experience defines the scope of psychology' (1990 [1890]: 361). Yet very few psychologists these days would agree with James on the centrality of experience. In fact, the idea that individual experience is central to psychology has come under siege from many quarters. For example, it does not accord with the desire on the part of twentieth-century mainstream psychology to identify itself as a science, in the very traditional sense of that term.

From the sociological perspective, experience, as a term, has been one that is relegated to the realm of the psychological. It is a phenomenon that does not fit with the sociological emphasis on social forces and factors as the causes of human activity (Giddens, 1989). Susan Oyama (1993) points out that both sociology and anthropology fought for a long time to replace psychological determinism with sociocultural determinism – although it must be said that this has been modified by the recent emphasis on the part of Giddens and others on the importance of individual agency. In fact, with a few exceptions, such as psychoanalysis, many contemporary psychologists eschew 'psychological' explanations, feeling much more comfortable with biological rather than psychological determinism. However, both socio-cultural determinism and biological determinism avoid the psychological and serve to obliterate the person as agent and as experiencing subject.

Recent movements, such as social constructionism, the social scientific wing of postmodernism, have also played their part in undermining any claim that we can or should place experience at the centre of our interests. Where there is an attack on the notion of the unitary self, an attack on the notion of individual experience cannot be far behind. If there is no self, who is the experiencer?

On the other hand, one might well argue that the nature of children's experience is of great interest to social science. It is, for example, very open to a developmental analysis. When do children begin to recognize that they have an internal representation of the world, which is private to them? Do young children experience their worlds via pictures, feelings or words? How do adults assist and shape the experiential life of young children? The active role that children play in constructing their own developmental story is increasingly recognized and calls out for a methodology that assists us in accessing and understanding children's experiential life.

Jerome Kagan has commented that, 'The person's interpretation of experience is simultaneously the most significant product of an encounter and the spur to the next' (1984: 279). It can be argued that without some kind of access to the content of a person's experience, we have a very incomplete account, from a scientific perspective, of what it is that causes any person, adult or child, to act as they do.

Second, aside from an interest in experience itself, research into children's experience can reflect an interest in the study of children as persons rather than study of the child that is carried out in order to advance our understanding of human psychology in general. Studying children as persons implies a view of children as sentient beings who can act with intention and as agents in their own lives. An interest in researching children's experience can, there-fore, be allied to a moral perspective on the role and status of children which respects and promotes their entitlement to being considered as persons of value and persons with rights. The focus shifts thereby to studying children and not child variables. The child as an experiencing subject is a person whose experience and whose response to that experience are of interest to themselves, to other children and to adults. In Chapter 3 of this volume, Christensen and Prout talk about conferring on children and childhood 'a sense of present value'. Children in most societies are valued for their poten-tial and for what they will grow up to be but are devalued in terms of their present perspectives and experiences.

The researcher who values children's perspectives and wishes to under-stand their lived experience will be motivated to find out more about how children understand and interpret, negotiate and feel about their daily lives. If we accept a view of children as persons, the nature of children's experien-tial life becomes of central interest.

In recent years, children's right to be considered as persons has been voiced publicly in a number of different fora. Vindication of this right under-pins the United Nations Convention on the Rights of the Child (1989), the Children Act (1989) in the UK and The National Children's Strategy (2000) in Ireland. The seeds were sown for the recognition of children's right to be heard in the 1960s and 1970s, a time of social upheaval in the West when the voices of marginalized groups such as women and ethnic minorities sur-faced and changed the political landscape. An interest in children as mar-ginalized people could be seen as part of this larger movement. Within the social sciences, a new interest in children's experience and perspectives was fueled by the alignment of researchers with this moral and political per-spective on children's position in the world (see for example, Qvortrup, Bordy, Sgitha, & Wintersberger, 1994). Furthermore, the demand on the part of policy makers and practitioners to have ways of accessing the child's per-spective and giving voice to children has also led to a pragmatic interest among researchers in the development of appropriate methods (Davie, 1993; Davie, Upton, & Varma, 1996).

Third, researching children's experience is premised on the view that children are not all the same. It resists the idea that what we are setting out to research is 'the child' and replaces this piece of automatic discourse – very central to the practice of developmental psychology in particular – with the recognition that children encounter their worlds in an individual and idio-syncratic manner and that their worlds are themselves all different. The longstanding lack of recognition of one major distinction, that of gender, led Ennew to comment on the existence of 'that strange ungendered isolate, the child' (Ennew, 1994). Clearly numerous other distinctions also apply. Setting out to research children's experience implies a respect for each child as a unique and valued experiencer of his or her world. It also demands the use of methods that can capture the nature of children's lives as lived rather than those that rely on taking children out of their everyday lives into a professional's office or 'lab'.

Recognition of children's diversity and individuality has implications for research methodology. Developmental psychology has had and continues to have a fascination with statistics and with attempting to draw conclusions about 'the child' by combining measures of some particular behaviour of a large group of children. In an interesting review of a book by Cairns, Bergman and Kagan, *Methods and models for studying the individual* (1998), Ingrid Josephs repeats the guiding question for the eleven chapters of the book. 'How can the richness of individual lives be captured by the objective methods and statistical analyses of developmental research?' After reviewing the book, Josephs concludes, 'the answer is simple "It cannot be captured at all!"' (p. 475). Perhaps there is an unresolvable struggle between the desire for so-called objectivity and the wish to understand children and how they lead their lives.

We both subscribe to the view that the understanding of children, their lives and their development requires a multiplicity of methodological approaches. The method selected should fit the question that is asked. If the focus of enquiry is on the quality of individual lives, statistical methods are not the method of choice since statistics serve to obliterate individuality and richness. The richness of an individual's life is very often not to be found in the surface of life but in how it is lived, in the person's experiences and reactions to the world. On the other hand, if we want to know how many children in a particular population have experienced the death of a parent we must collect the appropriate statistics.

What is Meant by 'Experience'?

At this point it might be useful to ask what one means when one uses the word 'experience'. The *Shorter Oxford English Dictionary* gives various definitions of experience. The most relevant from our perspective is perhaps the definition of experience as, 'The fact of being consciously the subject of a state or condition or of being consciously affected by an event. Also an instance of this.' By this definition, consciousness is a requisite for experience. The definition implies that those who experience are conscious of being the subject of a state/condition or the effects of an event. By this token, one might ask whether pre-verbal children can be said with confidence to have experiences since they cannot report on them in a self-conscious manner. That a young child has experiences of the world is an inference, which we make when and if we attribute consciousness to infants. This becomes relevant to the researcher who claims an interest in researching the experience of infants and young children via observation.

Sociocultural perspectives on the construction of self suggest persuasively that how we relate to the world is very largely a function of the cultural context, particularly, those discourses which are central to structuring the world and the individual's place in it. Thus, children come to think of themselves as selves and interpret their encounters with self, the world and others in very different ways depending on the discourses that are dominant in their culture. Scheiffelin and Ochs (1998) describe the radically different attributions made by the Kaluli people in Papua New Guinea and the US and British middle classes about how infants relate to the world and how they should be treated. The Kaluli people assume that babies 'have no understanding' and do not address them or treat them as communicative partners. By contrast, in the middle-class homes of the USA and Britain 'from birth on, the infant is treated as a social being and as an addressee in social interaction' (p. 51). Where in many western cultures parents spend a lot of time interpreting the baby's behaviour and their underlying mood states, preferences, and so on, the Kaluli people show 'a cultural dispreference for talking about or making claims about what another might think, what another might do, or what another is about to do, especially if there is no external evidence' (p. 56). Thus the child is socialized into a mode of relating to her/himself and others that is very specific to his or her culture. The interest that we show in some parts of the West in the inner experience of others, even of babies, is not a universal phenomenon. Interest in, and interpretation of, experience is also likely to vary in important ways from culture to culture. How we value and speak about experience is then, in large part, a function of a culturally specific process.

In western cultures the observer of children tends to assume that their activity and verbalizations are products of, or in some essential way connected to, the child's experience. However, the nature of any child's (or adult's) experience is always in part inaccessible to an outsider: this must be a fundamental premise for the researcher. This inaccessibility is even more problematic when children are as yet unable to report on their conscious encounters with the world. We will leave aside for the moment the capacity of even very young children to deceive.

The inaccessibility of experience might be assumed to be total if experience is seen as essentially private. However most contemporary understandings of experience, since the time of John Dewey at least, would see experience as socially mediated and therefore, in some essentials, shared. Experience is interpretative and the medium by which humans interpret their encounters with the world is linguistic or at least symbolic. From a discourse theory perspective, our experience is constituted by the discourses that are available to us (see, for example, Henriques, Hollway, Urwin, Venn, & Walkerdine, 1984). While recognizing the importance of discourse in creating meaning, to conclude that experience is entirely constituted by discourse is going a step too far since it negates the material and sensational foundation of some forms of experience, for example, the abscess that causes a pain in one's jaw.

Experience is about interpretation, on the part of the self to the self (as in reflexive mental processes) and on the part of the self to others (as in attempts to communicate experience) and, further, on the part of the others as they attempt to understand the original experience. The latter exchange has been encompassed in the term 'intersubjectivity', that process which occurs in exchange between two or more subjectivities. This dialectic process applies not only to the development of meaning in children's daily lives, but also to the encounters by which researchers seek to understand children's experiences.

Researching children's experience is a project that is fundamentally problematic. The process is highly inferential. We assume that it is possible to learn about children's experience *both* by enquiry into their active engagement with their material and social worlds, whether the focus is on actions or words, *and* from their own reports on their subjective world. Thus, observational studies may give us an entrée into children's experience if they show us the ways in which children make efforts to understand and negotiate their worlds.

Kagan notes that, 'The problem psychologists have been unable to solve is how to diagnose these interpretations (children's interpretations) from the actions, statements and undetected physiological reactions of children' (1984: 279). This is an ongoing issue which will remain a problem for researchers in this area but it is a problem which is intrinsic to the nature of the questions which we are asking.

Researching Experience: Some Further Limitations on What can be Known

The researcher who sets out to research experience needs not only to be aware of the limitations on his or her capacity to access the experience of another person, but also the limits of what a focus on experience can tell us about the other.

It is salutary perhaps to look at the interest in experience that characterized a certain phase of research into the psychology of women. Because women's experience had been so blatantly disregarded by the social sciences, one of the first goals of feminist researchers was to find a central place for women's accounts of their own experiences of their lives. Feminist research was also in the main committed to the view that each woman's experience was different and that each woman's experience deserved to be heard. There are many resonances in the history of feminist research with the kind of rhetoric that is produced around children, rather more recently. One might accuse such researchers of valorizing experience beyond other sources of information on human life.

Much of the early feminist work appeared to be premised on the view that the woman herself has a special knowledge about the self. The work of Freud, among others, must lead us to radically question that assumption. Most psychologists accept that we may not have access to all of our feelings and motivations at all times. Mechanisms such as denial and dissociation result in the 'forgetting' of events and thoughts that have been experienced. People can report on their motivations and emotions only to the extent that they are aware of them and only in the manner that they have come to interpret them. People are prone also to all sorts of biases in reporting their views and experiences to others. Psychometricians have spelled out the effect of unconscious response biases on the way in which people respond to surveys. For instance, the impulse to present oneself in a way that is socially acceptable to others (social desirability) can influence answers to direct questions and is likely to remain a significant factor even in extended qualitative encounters with a researcher. People can also deliberately set out to lie and deceive. Children are not exempt from any of these processes.

Accordingly, even where our focus is on the understanding of one human being's actions and motivations, his or her account of his or her own experience should be seen as but one source of information, one which may be valid as an experience but suspect as a source of complete understanding. To quote Kagan again:

> When a mother, who has just struck a child with the heavy, blunt end of a chopping block explains with sincerity to an observer that she loves her child and is only trying to make sure that her daughter learns to control her strong will, we must reflect on that subjective interpretation – but we do not have to accept it in our objectively framed explanation. (1984: 278)

Kagan contrasts the subjective frame with the objective frame, two positions that the researcher can adopt, both having a contribution to make to our knowledge. There are ways other than Kagan's of characterizing sources of information, but what is important is that we acknowledge the strengths and limitations of each source, that we do not, for example use a child's account of her reactions to a particular event as the beginning and end of our understanding of her reaction. When parents and children give differing accounts of the same events or relationships, as they often do (Sweeting, 2001; Triseliotis, Borland, Hill, & Lambert, 1995), the researcher needs to present these as complementary perspectives and not seek a single version of the 'truth'.

Given all these caveats we might ask, 'Can research access experience?' As Stainton Rogers and Stainton Rogers state, 'there is no device for inquisiting the child which can tell us what the child is like' (1992: 17). Elsewhere in this book Annie Rogers comments, 'The very notion that we might know what is in a child's head is ridiculous' (p. 162). Ultimately we would agree with these statements but believe that we can and should aim towards an increased level of understanding, albeit a partial understanding, of children's experience and the ways in which they process it, mentally, physically and behaviourally.

The subjectivity of the researcher adds a further layer of complexity to the research process. William James suggests that 'we begin our study with our own experience since other experiences can be intelligible only in these terms' (1990 [1890]: 361). Despite the fact that James wrote in this way so many years ago, it is only comparatively recently that researchers have become alert once more to the extent of their own involvement with the research process. In the social sciences, this awareness was triggered in the wake of the realization by natural scientists of the impossibility of direct perception of physical events. The lens of the observer or researcher inevitably distorts. Many social scientists, but not all, would accept that the objective researcher is a myth and that it is essential for researchers to scrutinize and take account of their own position as an enquirer. Reflexivity is therefore an essential element in any research (Davis, Watson, & Cunningham-Burley, 2000). As we set out to research children's experiences we must add analysis of this extra layer of interpretation to the interpretation that is at the heart of experience itself. As adults we bring to our encounters with children a particular package of attitudes and feelings, constructed through our own personal childhood history and our contemporary perspective on childhood, often coloured by one or more of the various prevailing ideologies of childhood.

Researching Children's Experience: What is Different about Children?

As we have attempted to argue, there are a number of difficulties that beset the researcher who embraces the aim of researching a person's experience. Are there particular difficulties and challenges in relation to researching children's experience? Some social scientists, particularly those who have identified with 'The new sociology (or social studies) of childhood' have argued strongly that there is no need for a specific set of methods to research children's lives (Christensen & James, 2000). Sociologists are critical of developmental psychology's tendency to see children as less than adult and as people in the making rather than as competent and complete social actors.

We would agree that researchers should not take for granted any adult–child distinction. The questioning of taken-for-granted assumptions about children and childhood is central to this book and to the project of enquiring into children's own perspectives on, and experience of, their worlds. However, we would suggest that the researcher must be open to the use of methods that are suited to children's level of understanding, knowledge, interests and particular location in the social world. In their discussion of children's role in research and the methods used to research their experience, Hogan, Etz, and Tudge (1999) ask 'how information can be obtained from children in developmentally appropriate ways'. This question cannot be disregarded: infants, young children and teenagers cannot be treated identically. The question of developmental differences in level of ability or understanding must arise. It is palpably ridiculous to claim that an infant has the same kind of understanding of the world as does a teenager. For example, infants and very young children cannot understand complex and/or abstract questions so it is therefore essential for the researcher to adjust their mode of enquiry accordingly.

But we need to keep open all the time our views on what 'developmentally appropriate' might mean in any particular context with any group of children. The simple equation of age with a particular level of ability or knowledge or set of attitudes should be avoided. It is easy for adults to underestimate children's abilities and to patronize them. Such attitudes to children have undoubtedly been a feature of past research endeavours. It is also the case that researchers have tended to use age in a way that disregards the wide diversity of ability and interests that can be found in any group of children of the same chronological age. At the same time, age is a powerful social marker in our society and we adults very often ensure that children go through the same kind of experience simply because they have reached a particular age (Greene, 2003). Thus, 5-year-olds in the UK will typically experience the transition to formal schooling in unison. Similarly, all 13-year-olds in Ireland will be expected to make the transition to secondary school. Other countries have different ideas about what happens at what age, but the importance of age is central in the patterning of children's life courses.

We would endorse the view that in many ways children behave and think similarly to adults. It is important, however, not to essentialize either the differences or the similarities which research might reveal, since any set of findings is very often a function of local or historical demands and discourses and may not have any significance at another time or place.

Children, like adults, may be very open to the demand characteristics of the research setting and the nature of the relationship between themselves and the researcher or interrogator. An interview is a social exchange in which the social demands may outweigh the ostensible demands of the interview itself. Thus, children may give answers that are determined more by their desire to please than their desire to be truthful. Children behave in different ways in different settings so the choice of where to carry out research is as important as how to carry it out (Morrow & Richards, 1996).

Studies have shown that children will often answer very odd questions posed to them by adults. Hughes and Grieve (1980) asked children questions such as, 'Is red heavier than yellow?' and, 'One day there were two flies crawling up a wall. Which fly got to the top first?' They found that almost all children gave answers to the questions. In a follow-up study, Waterman, Blades, and Spencer (2001) asked 5 to 8-year-old children a series of nonsensical questions in closed and open format and found that children were much more likely to try to give answers to closed format questions, that is, those requiring a 'yes' or 'no' response. These researchers suggest that children will very often answer 'no' when they do not understand a question. Seventy six percent of children gave an inappropriate 'yes' or 'no' answer to a nonsense question compared to 20 per cent of adults. Waterman et al. suggest that interviewers should be very cautious about how they interpret children's answers to closed questions and that they 'should use open questions as much as possible' (p. 477). Such caveats also extend to questionnaire and test responses. To a significant extent, children are used to being directed by adults and to doing either what they are told or what adults seem to expect of them, however baffling.

The question arises, then, whether children are particularly suggestible, that is, more suggestible than adults. Children's suggestibility had been analysed by a number of researchers, particularly those with an interest in children's reliability as witnesses in a legal setting (Spencer & Flin, 1991). Ceci, Ross, and Toglia (1987) found that children are more likely to take on board incorrect information supplied by an adult than that supplied by a child. On the other hand, it appears that there is very little difference between adults and children as regards memory loss and recall and both are helped by recognition aids (Spencer & Flin, 1991). So children are not necessarily less reliable informants than adults.

Are children less tolerant of ambiguity in language? It has been convincingly demonstrated that our language is permeated with metaphor (Gibbs, 1994). Children may show a lack of understanding of conventional metaphors frequently used by adults but equally they have a capacity to invent their own metaphorical expressions. In relation to the former, one of our research colleagues was surprised when a young child answered her question, which was one of a sequence of questions in the area of family relationships, as follows:

Q How close are you to your grandfather?
A Well, not very close really: I live in Dublin and he lives in Offaly.

This is not to say that children do not make use of metaphor in their speech. Indeed adults may often fail to understand the idiosyncratic and creative use of language that children can employ. A Finnish study of young people's text messaging revealed their high level of linguistic inventiveness, resulting in communication that was often obscure to uninitiated adults (Kaseniemi, 2001).

A question which arises when attempting to access children's experience is how one tells the difference between a child's recounting of an experience which actually happened to him or her and telling an imaginative tale concocted either to amuse or fascinate the researcher or to mislead. One might answer that it does not really matter but, again, whether it matters or not will depend upon the nature of the research question. Children start to tell lies at a young age. Studies reported by Lewis, Stanger and Sullivan (1989) show just how effectively many 3-year-olds lie about a minor transgression and how difficult it was for adults to detect whether or not they were lying from their facial expression and demeanour.

One major difference between the adult–adult research relationship and the adult–child research relationship relates to power (Alderson, 1995), although it must be noted that this is a quantitative difference since the power differential operates for adults also. Mayall argues that the subordinate position of children cannot be ignored and must be taken into account by the researcher (Mayall, 2000). Adults typically have authority over children and children often find it difficult to dissent, disagree or say things which they think may be unacceptable. Children may have difficulty in believing that any adult will take their views seriously if their daily experience of adults dictates otherwise (Cloke, 1995). At the same time children are adept at undermining the power of adults by such tactics as resistance, subversion and subterfuge. As Harris (1998) points out, children learn very early on that they are part of a 'kids versus grown-ups' dynamic. Corsaro (1997) describes the strategies by which nursery school children, aged 3 to 5, 'mock and evade adult authority'. The researcher needs to be aware in every new context about the meaning that being asked questions by strange adults has for this child or this group of children. Have they learned to give careful, 'scripted' answers? Have their lives changed in negative ways as the result of answering adults' questions? As discussed below in relation to children's involvement in the construction of the research process, researchers may be advised to think about ways of giving up some of their power in the research situation by, for example, allowing the children to choose the time and place of interviews.

In some cases it seems to be possible for adults to convince children that they are, as adults go, pretty powerless. In the course of Emond's long sojourn with young people in a residential group home (described in Chapter 7 of this volume) it became clear to her fellow residents that being a doctoral student was not too much fun and she reports being seen eventually as 'an object of pity rather than a threat'.

It is clear that the characteristics of the researcher matter. We disagree with the view, still apparently fostered in some schools of thought, that researchers can be like flies on the wall or in some way neutralize themselves. The extent to which researchers need to be like their child subjects or participant is an issue, however. Researchers, especially ethnographers and anthropologists, have long debated how far it is necessary to adopt special tactics to allow them to enter the 'separate worlds' of children and young people (see for example, Corsaro, 1985, on 'peer culture'). At an extreme, this perspective on children's worlds implies that children occupy a different world to adults and that adults can never hope to understand the world of children. One response to this view is not to try and another is to become like children. The former seems to be an unnecessarily gloomy and probably invalid conclusion and the second unwise and doomed to failure. Our view would be that children would generally be quick to detect any contrivances that an adult may adopt to be more like them. There are, however, examples in the literature of researchers who have successfully negotiated a space somewhere between adult figures of authority and the children themselves (Christensen, 2004). Barrie Thorne describes how she attempted to negotiate a role as 'least adult', somewhere between the children she observed and their adult authority figures, and how complicated such a negotiation must be. Her chapter, 'Learning from kids' in *Gender Play* (1993) stands as a very thoughtful reflection on the relationship of the researcher to the children whom they engage in research. A further matter about which there can be little dispute is the importance of being familiar with the 'local cultural practices of communication' used by the children and young people involved in the research (Christensen & James, 2000: 7). This extends to establishing a familiarity with children's routines, timetables and expectations.

Finally we wish to touch briefly on children's role in research. We assume that children are actively engaged in making sense of the research process once they are engaged in it and that this effort after social understanding is present even in very young children (Dunn, 1988). In this sense it is always appropriate to see children as participants in the research process. Researchers' terminology has changed in recent years in line with the view that the people who are the focus of research are participants not subjects (Woodhead & Faulkner, 2000). The extent of children's participation in the research process can vary beyond this basic level. One of us (Hill) discusses ethical issues surrounding consent and involvement in research in Chapter 4 of this volume. From the perspective of methodology, it is still the case that most of the research carried out into children's experience of their worlds is prompted, designed, analysed and disseminated by adults. Involving children in research design and data handling is unusual but a number of researchers are beginning to explore when and how this can be done (Alderson, 2000; Hill, 1997 and see Veale, Chapter 14 of this volume). Interesting examples of how children can be more fully drawn into the design and analysis of research are beginning to emerge in the literature. Children have been involved in advisory groups that work with researchers to identify appropriate methods and procedures for answering research questions (see for example, Edwards & Alldred, 1999; Emond, 2002), a practice which seems to hold a lot of potential. Checking back with child participants that the researcher's attempts at understanding make sense to them is also a very useful practice, which is in line with the goal of keeping faith with children's own perspective and voice. Some researchers have gone much further in assisting children in becoming involved to some extent at all stages of the research process (Emond, 2002). Ultimately, however, it is adults who control the world of publishing, policy making, the universities, the social services and so on, so children's independence and autonomy as researchers are fundamentally and intrinsically constrained.

Methods Suited to Researching Children's Experiences and Perspectives

There is a long but not very influential tradition of research on children's experience and experiences of their worlds. We might start with research where children are the informants on their own lives. Margaret Mead provides an early example in her interviews of children as reported in conversations with children and young people in New Guinea and Samoa (1930; 1961). A further early example is the work of Charlotte Bühler (1930) and her use of diaries as a mode of accessing the experience of teenage girls.

Over the twentieth century an immense range of different methods was developed and employed in research on and with children. This section focuses on methods that involve children themselves reporting on, or in some way revealing or displaying, their experience.

The approach to collecting data of this kind can be both qualitative and quantitative, or involve a mixture of both. Quantitative methods can be informative on children's experience but our emphasis here will be on qualitative methods since they tend to be open-ended, narrative and holistic. They are more able to capture the full richness of experience whereas using numbers provides a means of summarizing some essential features of experience, as they relate to either single individuals or groups.

This is not to say that there is no place for measurement or statistics in researching children's experience (Alanen, 2003). Qvortrup (2000) argues, for example, that large-scale statistical surveys are important in capturing the diversity of childhood and of children's daily life experience. Such data may describe the parameters of experience but not the subjective content. Meaning and content can be accessed through standardized questionnaires, but in many ways use of such tools conflicts with the goal of arriving at an understanding of how children themselves construe and negotiate their worlds.

Some of the wide range of possible methods that can be useful in accessing children's experience are listed below. At this stage, there will be no attempt to describe or discuss methods in detail. Several of them are discussed in full in succeeding chapters and further information can be found in recent texts referenced in this book, such as that of Grieg and Taylor (1999).

Observation

The use of observation is discussed in two of the chapters in this volume: those of Dunn (Chapter 5) and Tudge and Hogan (Chapter 6: participant observation, as used by Emond, is discussed in Chapter 7).

Observational methods can take a variety of forms. In terms of content, they can be naturalistic or contrived. The possibilities in terms of recording are even more various, involving paper and pencil, audio, video and filmed records. The data may include children's actions and verbalizations. Sampling methods also dictate what is recorded. For example, time sampling methods result in frequency counts, whereas event sampling typically produces descriptive narratives.

In relation to children's experience, the analysis and interpretation of observational records of behaviour (including speech) necessitate a level of inference beyond that which is required when the child is in some way reporting directly on his or her experience.

Interviews – individual and group

Interview methods are discussed and described in several chapters in this volume, (Wesctott & Littleton (Chapter 8); Rogers (Chapter 9); Hennessy & Heary (Chapter 13)).

Interviews may involve single children with a single interviewer or groups of children responding to one or more interviewers, as in the focus group method. The interviewer may ask children standardized questions or allow the nature of the questions to flow with the conversation. Between a totally prescribed set of questions and a totally unstructured exchange lies the more frequently occupied territory of the semi-structured interview. Within an interview setting, there is scope for the use of a variety of linked methods such as brainstorming on a theme or an object, or interspersing the question and answer format with pencil and paper or other tasks.

The possible data generated through interviews are rich and varied. Depending on the focus of the interview the data may extend from straightforward facts about the child's life to data which require a great deal of interpretation, perhaps guided by psychoanalytic or other depth psychologies. Interviewers need not be human! Measelle, Ablow, Cowan and Cowan, for example, have used puppets successfully as 'interviewers' of 4- to 7-year-old children (The Berkeley Puppet Interview, 1998).

Creative methods

Reference to the use of creative methods can be found in the chapters by Veale (Chapter 14) and by Rogers (Chapter 9) in this volume.

Creative methods are those that explicitly give reign to the child's imagination. They would include creative writing, such as telling or writing stories (as opposed to giving a factual account of one's past experiences), writing poems, drawing or painting, taking photographs, making videos or films and drama and role play (Christenson & James, 2000; Levin, 1995).

Elicited self-reports and children's spontaneous narratives

Self-report methods include those which rely on verbal reports but which involve children in writing or recording their views, feelings, and so on without direct and ongoing interaction with an interviewer. Other methods include asking children to respond to scenarios and vignettes (see Barter and Renold, 2000, for an interesting discussion on the use of vignettes with children), questionnaires, sentence completion tasks, recording children's naturally occurring narratives and asking children to record their commentaries in diaries. Simple but effective verbal prompts such as asking children to tell or write down their 'three wishes' fall somewhere between this category and the interview category.

The analysis of autobiography and life stories represents a growing area of interest in social science research (for example, Josselson & Lieblich, 1993). Work with children is very much less common than work with adults and is represented in this book by the chapter by Engel (Chapter 11).

New forms of computing technology offer considerable scope for use in research. Children are often more familiar than adults with these media and can use them readily to communicate with others about their lives (Borland, Hill, Laybourn, & Stafford, 2001; Holloway & Valentine, 2001).

Use of material props and visual prompts

Under this heading, one might place mapping and graphical methods (such as ecomaps, life story charts, genograms), the use of dolls, puppets and other toys or games and using pictures, cartoons or photographs as triggers or prompts.

Projective techniques

These techniques rely on children's responses to ambiguous stimuli. Their responses are assumed to reveal their unconscious orientations and feelings. Examples include the Blacky Drawings and the Children's Thematic Apperception Test.

Methods that can capture the ongoing interactions and transactions of children's lives

Many of the methods listed above have been developed within the traditional positivist model of the child and how the child should be researched (Hogan et al., 1999). Contemporary perspectives on children's lives that characterize children as social actors and that place emphasis on seeing children as embedded in a rich sociocultural context demand methods that can address these conceptualizations. In many ways, our repertoire of methods is inadequate to the task. They speak to the isolated child in a fixed and universalized context.

Ethnographic methods can often be well suited to capturing the ongoing flow and complexities of children's daily lives (see Emond, Chapter 7 of this volume). Ethnographic approaches involve spending extended time with children in their everyday environments, such as a school or play space (Christensen, 2004; James, 1993; Moore, 1986). They often combine participant observation with key informant interviews, informal group discussions and creative exercises. For pre-school children an interesting mix of methods has been developed in the Mosaic Model (Clark & Moss, 2001).

All of the above methods generate data that may be recorded in a variety of different ways (audiotaped, videotaped, filmed, photographed, and written down contemporaneously or after the event). The potential of online recording and analysis is huge and varied (Holloway & Valentine, 2001). The data, however collected, must be analysed and here again a number of choices can be made depending on the focus of the study and the theoretical commitments of the researcher. For example, the discourse analyst would see all data sets as potential texts, which are open to discourse analysis (see Alldred & Burman, Chapter 10 of this volume).

Choosing a Method

The choice of method or methods should depend on its appropriateness to the purpose and nature of the research. If the researcher's work is embedded in a particular theoretical framework, the choice of method may flow seamlessly from the researcher's prior commitments. So, for example, a commitment to discourse theory demands a focus on discourse analysis (see, for example, Chapter 10 by Alldred & Burman in this volume). Phenomenological theorists use methods that have been developed by adherents of that theoretical viewpoint (see Chapter 12 by Danaher & Briod in this volume).

Although most researchers have a theoretical commitment of some kind, even if they choose not to make it very explicit, some methods are essentially pragmatic and do not connect either historically or logically to any one theoretical orientation. It is often argued, furthermore, that there is an advantage to using more than one method of data collection since this may provide the opportunity for triangulation of data (Brannen, 1992) and variety can in itself stimulate and maintain the interest of participants (Thomas & O'Kane, 2000). For example, Hill, Laybourn and Borland (1996) describe the use of a sequence of mixed methods geared to elicit children's feelings and perspectives on their own wellbeing. Woodhead (1999) used an eclectic but carefully chosen mix of quantitative and qualitative methods in his study of child workers in Bangladesh, Ethiopia, the Phillipines and Central America. The methods making up his 'Children's Perspectives Protocol' include drawing, mapping, games and role-play as well as interviews. If the aim is to provide rich and comprehensive accounts of experience, some would say the more sources the better. For example, Garbarino and Stott state: 'The more sources of information an adult has about a child, the more likely that the adult is to receive the child's messages properly' (1992: 15).

Triangulation should not open the doors to an 'anything goes' approach to method choice. Even if method choice is not a direct consequence of theoretical perspective, there should be a clear rationale for choosing a particular method or selection of methods. It is also important to remain alert to some of the implications of promoting triangulation as a methodological doctrine rather than simply as a practice. Triangulation can imply that there is a reality to which one can come closer by combining multiple perspectives. Richardson (1994) questions 'the assumption that there is a "fixed point" or "object" that can be triangulated' (p. 522) and suggests that the metaphor of the crystal might be more useful than the metaphor of the triangle to the qualitative researcher. Each representation in research can be seen as a facet of a crystal, and crystals 'reflect externalities and refract within themselves, creating different colors, patterns, arrays, casting off in different directions. What we see depends on the angle of our repose' (Richardson, 1994: 523). The researcher's epistemological theories and commitments will shape his or her choices throughout the research process and will fundamentally influence what claims the researcher makes.

It is not always possible to discover and take account of each individual child's preferences but there should be some awareness of the desirability of matching child to method. Individual contacts with children are generally preferable for the private exploration of personal issues. Many children will be reluctant to share sensitive matters in a group, unless the groups consist of children who are in similar circumstances (for example, who are in residential care, whose parents have divorced). On the other hand, on some subjects, children seem to be fortified by the presence of others, and prefer to meet the strange researcher in the company of their supportive peers (Hood, Kelley, & Mayall, 1996). Other group members may also stimulate memories and remind them of things they otherwise would not think to say. Differences in viewpoint can be discussed. (These and other issues relating to the use of focus groups in research with children are discussed by Hennessy and Heary in Chapter 13 of this volume). Children with different attributes will require different methods. The same children may behave quite differently when interviewed individually and when in focus groups and may give different types of answers to similar questions (Stanton, Aronson, Borgatti, Galbraith, & Feigelman (1993). West and Mitchell (1998) found that 'lower status girls' who had been slow to reveal their views in a group setting were much more forthcoming in one-to-one interviews. Differences to do with their age, physical and mental ability, ethnicity and culture will all be crucial in determining the appropriateness of any method (see, for example, Stalker, 2002; Woodhead, 1999).

Time is an important and sometimes forgotten aspect of the research process. The research literature on children is replete with examples of what might be called snapshot or smash and grab approaches to collecting data. There are situations or research questions that will make such an approach desirable or necessary. We do not always have the resources that we would like to have in order to spend extended time with children. Given the consideration discussed above in terms of the child participant's need to understand what is going on in the research encounter or to establish trust in the researcher, even the one-stop research encounter should not be a rushed affair. However, giving time to research becomes a more important consideration if the research question is one that demands getting to know the child or the child getting to know the researcher. Emond (Chapter 7 of this volume) set out to find out what it was like living in a children's home. It was one of the young people who suggested to her that the only way to find out was to move into the children's home and find out how they live by becoming a resident. Living in the home for a year gave Emond insights into their way of life that would not have been possible at a distance or without such a major time commitment.

Prospective, longitudinal studies of children's daily lives and experience are rare but they offer great potential in capturing the dynamic and changing nature of life experience and place less reliance on children's inevitably selective memories of past events. Contact with children over time should not only be seen as justifiable in a developmental design since it is clear that time is sometimes needed for children to relax enough with a researcher to reveal their thoughts, feelings and concerns. Time and trust can go hand in hand, particularly with those children who have learned not to trust.

The choice of method or combination of methods should be made in the light of the need to establish the rigor and credibility of the research project. Choice of method is but one consideration among a variety of methodological considerations that cannot be neglected. Thus, the researcher must pay attention to issues to do with sampling, design, replicability of procedures, reliability of interpretation, range of applicability of the findings, and so forth. There are, of course, many textbooks dealing with theses issues (for example, Denzin & Lincoln, 1994). As mentioned earlier in relation to triangulation, different epistemological frameworks will result in different expectations about how knowledge and understanding can be achieved and how it can be authenticated. There is no particular reason to think that these broader epistemological and methodological issues demand separate and specific reappraisal when the research participants are children.

Conclusion

Attempting to access and understand children's experience of their worlds presents researchers with a range of challenges. Our understanding will always be partial and imperfect. Our experience of the world is constantly unfolding and in flux. It is complex, multi-layered and not fully accessible to us let alone to others. For an adult researcher to understand the experience of a child (or children) as a stranger is in many ways an impossible task. Yet it is an important one because for too long we have assumed that children have nothing of interest or importance to tell us about their lives and that we adults understand much better than they what is good for them and how events impact on them.

There are many reasons – scientific, moral, political and pragmatic – for researching children's experience. Children's perspectives on, or views about, issues and events can be seen as a subset of the wider enterprise that is aimed at understanding children's experience of the world. As the National Children's Bureau's 'Highlight' states on including children in social research: 'Recent decades have witnessed an increasing interest in listening to children's views' (Harker, 2002). It is the task of the social researcher to provide the methods to enable this interest to become a worthwhile reality and the ongoing methodological analysis and critique that ensure that we can listen to children in ways that faithfully represent their views and their experiences of life. It is important that we avoid merely paying lip-service to the idea of listening to children or exploiting what we learn from children about their lives in ways that meet adult agendas only. We should contextualize our own research activities, not just the lives of the children we study. Thus, researchers are obligated to examine their reasons for carrying out research and the ends that their research might serve. It is important also that we do not fall into the trap of thinking that listening to children and understanding their experience of the world is a simple matter, either methodologically or politically.

References

Alanen, L. (2003). Children: the generational ordering of social relations. In B. Mayall & H. Zeiner (Eds.), *Children in generational perspective* (pp. 27–45). London: Institute of Education.

Alderson, P. (1995). *Listening to children: Children, ethics and social research*. London: Barnado's.

Alderson, P. (2000). Research by children. *International Journal of Research Methodology, 42*, 139–153.

Barter, C. & Renold, E. (2000). 'I wanna tell you a story': Exploring the application of vignettes in qualitative research with children and young people. *International Journal of Social Research Methodology, 3*, 307–323.

Borland, M., Hill, M., Laybourn, A., & Stafford, A. (2001). *Improving consultation with children and young people in relevant aspects of policy-making and legislation in Scotland*. Edinburgh: The Scottish Parliament.

Brannen, J. (Ed.). (1992). *Mixing methods: Qualitative and quantitative research*. Aldershot: Avebury.

Bühler, C. (1930). *Das Seelenleben des Jugendlichen*. Jena: Fischer.

Cairns, R.R., Bergman, L.R., & Kagan, J. (1998). *Methods and models for studying the individual*. Thousand Oaks, CA: Sage.

Ceci, S.J., Ross, D.F., & Toglia, M.P. (1987). Suggestibility of children's memory: Psychological implications. *Journal of Experimental Psychology: General, 116*, 38–49.

Christensen, P. (2004). Children's participation in ethnographic research: Issues of power and representation. *Children & Society, 18*, 2, 165–176.

Christensen, P. & James, A. (2000). *Research with children: Perspectives and practices*. London: Falmer Press.

Clark, A. & Moss, P. (2001). *Listening to young children: The Mosaic approach*. London: National Children's Bureau.

Cloke, C. (1995). Forging the circle: the relationship between children, policy and practice in children's rights. In C. Cloke & M. Davies (Eds.), *Participation and empowerment in child protection* (pp. 265–285). London: Pitman Publishing.

Corsaro, W. (1985). *Friendships and peer culture in the early years*. Norwood, NJ: Ablex.

Corsaro, W.A. (1997). *The sociology of childhood*. Thousand Oaks, CA: Pine Forge Press.

Davie, R. (1993). Listen to the child: A time for change. *The Psychologist, 6*, 252–257.

Davie, R., Upton, G., & Varma, V. (Eds.). (1996). *The voice of the child*. London: Falmer Press.

Davis, J., Watson, N., & Cunningham-Burley, S. (2000). Learning the lives of disabled children: Developing a reflexive approach. In P. Christensen & A. James (Eds.), *Research with children: Perspectives and practices* (pp. 201–224). London: Falmer Press.

Denzin, N.K. & Lincoln, Y.S. (Eds.). (1994). *Handbook of qualitative research*. London: Sage.

Dunn, J. (1988). *The beginnings of social understanding*. Oxford: Blackwell.

Edwards, R. & Alldred, P. (1999). Children and young people's views of social research: The case of research on home–school relations. *Childhood, 6*, 261–281.

Emond, R. (2002). *Learning from their lessons: A study of young people in residential care and their experiences of education*. Dublin: The Children's Research Centre.

Ennew, J. (1994). Time for children or time for adults. In J. Qvortrup, M. Bardy, G. Sgitta, & H. Wintersberger (Eds.), *Childhood matters* (pp. 125–144). Aldershot: Avebury.

Garbarino, J. & Stott, F. (1992). *What young children can tell us: Eliciting, interpreting and evaluating critical information from children*. San Francisco: Jossey-Bass.

Gibbs, R.W. (1994). *The poetics of mind: Figurative thought, language and understanding*. Cambridge: Cambridge University Press.

Giddens, A. (1989). *Sociology*. Cambridge: Polity Press.

Greene, S. (2003). *The psychological development of girls and women: Rethinking change in time*. London: Routledge.

Grieg, A. & Taylor, J. (1999). *Doing research with children*. London: Sage.

Harker, R. (2002). *Including children in social research*. Highlight No.193. London: Children's Research Bureau.

Harris, J.R. (1998). *The nature assumption: Why children turn out the way they do*. New York: The Free Press.

Henriques, W., Hollway, W., Urwin, C.,Venn, C., & Walkerdine, V. (1984). *Changing the subject: Psychology, social regulation and subjectivity*. London: Methuen.

Hill, M. (1997). Participatory research with children. *Child and Family Social Work, 2*, 71–183.

Hill, M., Laybourn, A., & Borland, M. (1996). Engaging with primary-aged children about their emotions and well-being: Methodological considerations. *Children and Society, 10*, 129–144.

Hogan D., Etz, K., & Tudge, J. (1999). Reconsidering the role of children in research. In F. M. Berado & C. Shehan (Eds.), *Through the eyes of the child: Revisioning children as active agents of family life* (pp. 93–105). Stanford, CT: JAI Press.

Holloway, S. & Valentine, G. (2000). *Children's geographies: Playing, living and learning*. London: Routledge.

Holloway, S. & Valentine, G. (2001). 'It's only as stupid as you are': Children's and adults' negotiation of ICT competence at home and at school. *Social and Cultural Geography, 2*, 25–42.

Hood, S., Kelley, P., & Mayall, B. (1996). Children as research subjects: A risky enterprise. *Children and Society, 10*, 117–128.

Hughes M., & Grieve, R. (1980). On asking children bizarre questions. *First Language, 1*, 149–160.

James, A. (1993). *Childhood identities*. Edinburgh: Edinburgh University Press.

James, W. (1990 [1890]). *Psychological principles*. Chicago: Encyclopaedia Britannica.

Josselson, R. & Lieblich, A. (Series Eds.). (1993). *The narrative study of lives*. Vol. 1. London: Sage.

Kagan, J. (1984). *The nature of the child*. New York: Basic Books.

Kasesniemi, E.-L. (2001). Finnish teenagers and mobile communication: Chatting and storytelling in text messages. In A. Furlong & I. Guidikova (Eds.), *Transitions of youth citizenship in Europe* (pp. 157–180). Strasbourg: Council of Europe.

Levin, I. (1995). Children's perceptions of their family. In J. Brannen & M. O'Brien (Eds.), *Childhood and parenthood* (pp. 281–293). London: Institute of Education.

Lewis, M., Stanger, C., & Sullivan, M. W. (1989). Deception in three-year-olds. *Developmental Psychology, 25*, 439–443.

Mayall, B. (2000). Conversations with children: Working with generational issues. In P. Christensen & A. James (Eds.), *Research with children: Perspectives and practices* (pp. 120–135). London: Falmer Press.

Mead, M. (1930). *Growing up in New Guinea*. New York: Mentor Books.

Mead, M. (1961). *Coming of age in Samoa*. Harmondsworth: Penguin.

Measelle, J.R., Ablow, J.C., Cowan, P.A., & Cowan, C.P. (1998). Assessing young children's views of their academic, social and emotional lives: An evaluation of the self-perception scales of the Berkeley Puppet Interview. *Child Development, 69*, 1556–1576.

Moore, R.C. (1986). *Children's domain: Play and space in child development*. London: Croom Helm.

Morrow, V. & Richards, M. (1996). The ethics of social research with children: An overview. *Children and Society, 10*, 90–105.

Oyama, S. (1993). How shall I name thee? The construction of natural selves. *Theory and Psychology, 3*, 471–496.

Qvortrup, J. (2000). Macroanalysis of childhood. In P. Christensen & A. James (Eds.), *Research with children: Perspectives and practices* (pp. 77–97). London: Falmer Press.

Qvortrup, J., Bardy, M., Sgitta, G., & Wintersberger, H. (Eds.). (1994). *Childhood matters*. Aldershot: Avebury.

Richardson, L. (1994) Writing: a method of inquiry. In N.K. Denzin & Y.S. Lincoln (Eds.), *Handbook of qualitative research* (pp. 516–529). London: Sage.

Schieffelin, B.B. & Ochs, E. (1998). A cultural perspective on the transition from prelinguistic to linguistic communication. In M. Woodhead, D. Faulkner, & K. Littleton (Eds.), *Cultural worlds of early childhood* (pp. 48–63). London: Routledge and the Open University.

Spencer, J.R. & Flin, R. (1991). *The evidence of children*. London: Blackstone Press.

Stainton-Rogers, R. & Stainton-Rogers, W. (1992). *Stories of childhood: Shifting agendas of child concern*. Hemel Hempstead: Harvester Wheatsheaf.

Stalker, K. (2002). *Children's experiences of disability*. Edinburgh: Scottish Executive.

Stanton, B., Aronson, R., Borgatti, S., Galbraith, J., & Feigelman, S. (1993). Urban adolescent high risk sexual behavior: Corroboration of focus group discussions through pile-sorting. *AIDS Education and Prevention, 5*, 162–173.

Sweeting, H. (2001). Our family, whose perspective? An investigation of children's family life and health. *Journal of Adolescence, 24*, 229–250.

Thomas, N. & O'Kane, C. (2000). Discovering what children think. *British Journal of Social Work, 30*, 819–835.

Thorne, B. (1993). *Gender play: Girls and boys in school*. Buckingham: Open University Press.

Triseliotis, J., Borland, M., Hill, M., & Lambert, L. (1995). *Teenagers and the social work services*. London: HMSO.

Waterman, A., Blades, M., & Spencer, C. (2001). Is a jumper angrier than a tree? *The Psychologist, 14*, 474–477.

West, P. & Mitchell, L. (1998). Smoking and peer influence. In A. Goreczny & M. Hersen (Eds.), *Handbook of pediatric and health psychology*. Needham Heights: Allyn and Bacon.

Woodhead, M. (1999). Combatting child labour: Listening to what the children say. *Childhood, 6*, 27–49.

Woodhead, M. & Faulkner, D. (2000). Subjects, objects or participants: Dilemmas of psychological research with children. In A. James & P. Christensen (Eds.), *Research with children: Perspectives and practices* (pp. 9–35). London: Falmer Press.

2 Researching 'the Child' in Developmental Psychology

Diane Hogan

Study of 'the child' has been, for more than a century, the territory of developmental psychology. In recent decades, the hegemony of developmental theory and methods has been challenged by critics within the now well-established field of the sociology of childhood that has emerged primarily in Europe in the course of the last two decades (see for example, Corsaro, 1997; James & Prout, 1997; James, Jenks, & Prout, 1998; Qvortrop, 1987). Within developmental psychology, some critical voices also emerged (for example, Alldred and Burman, Chapter 10 of this volume; Burman, 1994; Bradley, 1989; Morss, 1996) but these have been few, and mainstream research in developmental psychology has taken little note of the criticisms posed from either outside or inside the discipline. Some of these criticisms centre around the perception that developmental psychology has failed to adequately describe and understand children's ordinary lives and their active participation in their social worlds, or in other words, to research their subjective experience. As I have argued elsewhere (Hogan, 1998; Hogan, Etz, & Tudge, 1999), most research with children conducted over the last century of developmental psychology has not sought to understand children's subjective experience.

In the present chapter I aim to shed some light on developmental psychology's apparent lack of interest in learning about the content and personal meaning of children's everyday lives. The chapter reflects on the models of children and child research that dominate the field, and explores how assumptions about children manifest themselves in specific research practices. The chapter also describes some of the challenges that the field faces, especially in Europe, as new assumptions about children and research, and a growing regard for understanding children's worlds from their perspectives, takes hold in related fields of child study and in the policy domain. It explores opportunities for pursuing dual goals of researching both children's development and their personal experience of events, relationships and culture, independent of adult perspectives. The chapter begins with an overview of the criticisms that developmental psychology has received for its approach to the study of children, both from within and outside the field.

Critiques from Outside and Inside the Field

More than ten years ago, psychologist John Flavell (1992), in a review of advances in cognitive developmental psychology, conceded that the field of developmental psychology had learned little about children's subjective experience although it had made impressive advances in the empirical study of children's cognitive growth. He concluded that learning about children within the discipline had been limited to age-linked competencies and knowledge acquisition, and the effects of these cognitive accomplishments on some aspects of social and nonsocial behaviour:

> we have seldom tried to infer what it is like to be them and what the world seems like to them, given what they have and have not achieved cogni- tively. When knowledge and abilities are subtracted from the totality of what could legitimately be called 'cognitive', an important remainder is surely the person's subjective experience: how self and world seem and feel to that person, given that knowledge and those abilities. (Flavell, 1992: 1003)

Flavell's comments are important because they resonate so well with the views of critical developmental psychologists, and with the principal critics of the field within the sociology of childhood, yet appear to have gained little purchase within developmental psychology itself.

Christenson and Prout (Chapters 3 of this volume) describe the approach to the study of children and childhood as emerging under the banner of the sociology of childhood, or the 'new social studies of childhood', but it is use- ful here to briefly outline the perspective on developmental psychology that has emerged from that quarter. Sociologists of childhood criticize psychol- ogy for its focus on documenting age-related competencies at the expense of investigating what it means to be a child. They argue that the developmental approach leads to a detached and impoverished understanding of children's needs. Indeed, the sociology of childhood has, at least in part, defined itself in reaction to the approach to the study of children in developmental psy- chology; it is concerned with presenting an alternative view of children and childhood to that which it perceives developmental psychology as repre- senting and promoting. The ontological and epistemological basis for this approach lies mainly in constructivist and critical theory paradigms. The methodologies are primarily case studies with children conceptualized as active participants of the research endeavour, and the favoured methods of data collection are interviews and participant observations. There is a strong emphasis on reflexivity, and on interpretative approaches to analysis.

Much of sociology's dissatisfaction with psychology centres around a few core issues: the perception that a focus on development has led to the neglect of the quality and meaning of children's present lives, the search for 'univer- sal' laws of child development, the assumption that child development is 'natural' (biologically based), a view of children as passive, and a focus on age- related competency/deficits rather than on subjective experience. Some of the arguments that have emerged from the sociology of childhood are also to be found in the writings of developmental psychologists who have adopted a critical perspective on their discipline (Bradley, 1989; Burman, 1994; Greene, 1999; 2003; Hogan, 1998; Hogan et al., 1999; Morss, 1996; Westcott & Littleton, Chapter 8 of this volume; Woodhead & Faulkner, 2001).

Kuzcynski and his colleagues (Kuzcynski, Harach, & Bernardini, 1999), believe that most developmental psychologists are somewhat concerned about the emergence of the sociology of childhood and, by implication, by its critical position on theory and methods. Evidence to support this claim is not readily evident; rather, it appears that developmental psychology, especially in North America, where the majority of research and publishing in the field takes place, is largely unaware of these challenges either to territory or to its vision of children. It may indeed be the case, as Damon (1998) attests in a preface to the most recent *Handbook of Child Psychology*, that the field has undergone a period of self-reflection in recent years; that it has debated the notion of development and has grappled with the possibility of reconciling itself with ideological principles of diversity and equality. Notwithstanding these developments, the field has not engaged in reflection and self-appraisal at other levels. Indeed, Valsiner (1998: 189) also writing in the *Handbook*, has characterized the field as being immersed in 'hyperactive data collection' to the neglect of reflection and development at the meta-theoretical level. Bennett (1999: 11) has observed that developmental psychology, unlike some other areas of psychology, has not engaged in 'a period of self-scrutiny prompted by post-modern critiques' where the fundamental goals and methods of the field have been debated. Critical developmental psychology exists only on a small scale, and mainly outside North America. As a result, many of the field's guiding assumptions remain unchallenged and research agendas remain unchanged. The search for a greater understanding of how children experience their lives in particular, a question that has captured the attention of policy makers and social research funders in the UK and Ireland, remains a minor research issue for the field.

'The Child' as Research Object in Developmental Psychology

If there is a core mission in the field of developmental psychology, it is to understand the processes of change, with age, in the psychological functioning of individuals. Most of the field's efforts to understand these processes have targeted the childhood years and a large proportion of the research on children involves documenting children's age-related competencies, with a view to discovering the factors most likely to predict a passage to competency and positive functioning in adulthood. The epistemological basis for the majority of this work is in positivist and post-positivist paradigms. The

Table 2.1   'Mainstream' model of research with children in developmental psychology

Ontology *Assumptions about children*	Epistemology *Assumptions about research with children*	Methodology *Applications in research with children*
Context-free • Universal • Timeless • Isolable	Leads to information about 'the child'	Efforts to 'control' or to neutralize effects of context; reliance on standardized tests

Predictable
• Standard
  development
• Progressive
  development
	Leads to universal laws
	of child development
		Exclusion of atypical children,
		variation beyond norms
		interpreted as deviance

Irrelevant • Unformed • Passive- dependent • Unreliable	Adult reports receive higher value than children's, emphasis on 'objective' measurement	Adult reports more widely used, treated as benchmark

principal methodologies are experimental, survey and objective testing and although the methods are varied, they largely favour collection of quantifiable data. The use of qualitative methods is rare, and self-report is less trusted than observation.

Critics have argued that 'the child' of research in developmental psychology, as the common use of the definite article suggests, is an object rather than subject of scientific research, in that researchers expect to come to know its essential qualities through rigorous examination of its properties, under controlled circumstances. There is some merit to this argument, in that this approach to children is evident at multiple levels within the overall research endeavour in developmental psychology; in its research agenda, dominant meta-theory, theories and methodologies (Greene, 1999; 2003; Hogan, 1998; Hogan et al., 1999; Woodhead & Faulkner, 2000). It must also be acknowledged, however, that developmental psychology is a large and variable field, within which several paradigms of development co-exist. Yet it can certainly be argued that there is a mainstream model that wields a powerful influence over research practice and publishing on children's issues.

As new conceptualizations of children and their role in research attract increasing attention in other disciplines, and also from policy makers and research funders, it is important for the field to reflect on what could be called the 'mainstream model' and its influence over research activity. Here I will first briefly describe the approach to developmental psychology that is reflected in much of the criticism that has been targeted at the field in respect of claims that children have been treated as 'objects' of research, to the neglect of their subjective experiences, before considering the merits of such a characterization of research within the field. These criticisms suggest that there is a mainstream ontology of childhood (assumptions or premises about the nature of children and childhood) and an associated epistemology (attendant beliefs about the kind of knowledge it is possible to gain about children, about the role of researchers, and about the role of children in research) that have given rise to accepted methodologies with prescribed design and sampling options, and to a set of methods used to conduct research.

The context-free child

The first broad criticism of the field is that children are conceptualized, and therefore researched, as though they have an existence that can be divorced from the context in which they live. Universal laws governing development continue to be sought and the findings of research are explicitly or implicitly held to be globally applicable across both place and historical time. Furthermore, the context-free child is assumed to function at a mainly individual level, with abilities and behaviours that are *isolable*, to use Kessen's (1979) term, from the social world in which he or she lives. These ontological assumptions, critics argue, are reflected in certain epistemological positions and methodological approaches. One fundamental epistemological premise is that context, be it culture, community, research setting, time in history, or relationships, can be 'controlled' and that the 'true' child will emerge. Those who adopt this standpoint, it is argued, do not consider it to be important to find out what is going on between children and the world in which they live. It follows that their psychological characteristics can be recorded and understood by the detached and neutral observer. Most importantly for the issues under consideration in the present volume, children's personal responses to the research process and the implications these might have for data gathering and data interpretation are rarely considered.

The predictable child

A second area of criticism is that developmental psychology is based on a view of childhood as a phenomenon already known to adults. This can be broken down into two strands: first, the view of child development as regulated or *standard*, with children behaving and developing within predictable age parameters; and second, the view of child development as *progressing* naturally in a linear fashion. The field is considered to be uncomfortable with an image of childhood as fragmented, multi-directional, and idiosyncratic. Instead, there is a search for universal age parameters and strivings to establish normative models of child development. Walkerdine (1984), for example, argues that developmental psychology has produced a vision of childhood, one that is reflected in pedagogic practice, which insists that there is 'an actual sequence of development' (p. 163).

The irrelevant child

Another strand of criticism directed at developmental psychology is that it has viewed children as having less to offer to research, even about children themselves, than adults. This view encompasses three arguments. The first is that children are viewed as *unformed persons* within the field. This perception of children as adults-in-the-making, not so much as persons in their own right in whom researchers should be interested, is reflected in the way in which tenses are used, according to Morss (1996). He argues that adults are commonly represented as existing in the present and children in the future. By positioning children as 'becomings' rather than as 'beings,' Morss maintains, adulthood defines itself in a territorial way – 'it commands the present, and hence legitimizes the denial of rights to non-adults' (Morss, 1996: 158). It is for this reason, he argues, that so much emphasis is placed on the long-term effects of early experiences, perhaps to the detriment of adequate attention to immediate effects and needs.

The second argument concerning irrelevance is that children are represented within developmental psychology as being *passive and dependent* and therefore that agency is viewed as being located not internally but externally. Thus, while children are viewed as distinct from adults, there is also an expectation that their views will be interchangeable with those of adults if their reports are to be deemed valid and reliable, since parent reports are typically used as the 'gold-standard' to judge the accuracy and value of the child report (Hodges, 1993).

The third argument in this set is that children are viewed within developmental psychology as being *unreliable informants*; that it is assumed that they cannot credibly and consistently provide information about events or experiences for research purposes. The knowledge that they can provide is viewed with skepticism, particularly when there is evidence of inconsistency, and especially when it is presented by very young children. Children are viewed as living in an ephemeral fantasy world, as being highly suggestible, prone to making up stories, and as having limited age-dependent competencies. Taking these three premises together, an image emerges of children as unequipped for the task of describing themselves, at least until they are approaching adulthood, when they can offer an adult-like perspective in adult language.

In summary, the various strands of argument about the shortcomings of the field presented together above suggest that developmental psychology has produced a mainstream model of research with children that reflects a vision of childhood as important and distinct, but also universal and essentially known or predictable. That image has material consequences for research methodology used with children. An important element of that research model is that it supports the exclusion of children from assuming the role of expert and validates adults instead as expert informants on children. If childhood is a highly regulated and universal experience, unrelated to historical time and to social context, then adults, with their superior capacity for objectivity and more sophisticated understanding, who themselves have been children, can claim to possess expertise on the experience of any given child. Children's personal experience of events, relationships and everyday life receive little attention, with the result that knowledge about what it is to be a child can scarcely be described within the literature. How valid is this characterization of developmental psychology's approach to research with children, and especially to research on children's experience?

It can be argued that all of the criticisms laid out above have some merit and can be easily substantiated. Assumptions of universality are reflected in the use of standardized tests and measures across time and place, often normed on the dominant cultural group in a given society, such as white middle-class Americans, and in the testing of children in 'strange situations' such as university laboratories (Bronfenbrenner, 1979: 19). Such assumptions are also reflected in expectations by some psychologists that research will yield the 'true score' of each child. This image of 'the child' reflects a core assumption of the positivist paradigm – the assumption of a real, rather than a socially constructed, world.

Assumptions about predictability also have some merit; in support of this criticism it can be argued that individual differences in behaviours, thought, and emotion that transgress established norms are often viewed as deviance, while the methods most commonly used in research with children involve standardized testing (where children's performance is compared to a standard or norm). Meanwhile, little effort has been expended in the development of research tools to examine such issues as young children's perspectives on their relationships (Sturgess, Dunn, & Davies, 2001). Above all, however, criticisms regarding assumptions of the irrelevance of children in research are warranted (Hogan et al., 1999). While claims that children are portrayed as passive by the mainstream of developmental psychologists are open to question, and especially if the increasingly influential models proposed by theorists such as Bronfenbrenner (Bronfenbrenner, 1979; Bronfenbrenner & Morris, 1998) and Vygotsky (Vygotsky, 1978; 1987) are taken into account, the tendency of the field to disregard children's perspectives on the nature and meaning of their lives is easily evidenced. There is clearly a scarcity of research asking children, especially young children, to describe their own feelings and behaviours or to evaluate the services and care provided to them. As Langsted has asked with respect to the paucity of research on children's perspectives on early childhood services: 'Is anyone interested in the kind of daily life the *children* want? Does anyone regard children as experts when it comes to their own lives?' (Langsted, 1994: 29).

While the criticisms outlined above do have merit, however, the characterization of developmental theory and research that is typically presented in critiques of the field by sociologists of childhood has often been unduly simplistic, overlooking the complexity of ideas about children and their development within the field both historically and currently, and especially theories and research in which children have been represented as agentic and development as culturally and historically located. It is fair to say that such ideas have not, historically, dominated the field (Tudge, Gray & Hogan, 1996), but their influence on contemporary research and theorizing is considerable and is increasing (Lerner, 1998). In the remainder of this chapter. I will examine the ideas and events that have shaped developmental psychology's approach to research with children, and especially its neglect of subjective experience. I will also outline both historical and emerging ideas that can contribute to creating an impetus within the field for developing models of research with children that are compatible with gaining knowledge about both children's development and their lived experience.

Constructing 'the Child' of Developmental Psychology

It has often been argued that perceptions of the nature of childhood are socially constructed. Such arguments have occasionally been made by psychologists such as Kessen (1979), who famously argued that the child of developmental psychology was a 'cultural invention'. So too are our approaches to research with children. The research studies we conduct reflect choices; we select issues to research, questions to ask and participants deemed worthy as informants. We then select which aspects of our findings to believe and which to doubt, and we chose which findings to reiterate and reinforce in our discourse about research, so that a certain finding becomes 'well-established' or 'widely accepted'. Through this ongoing process, sets of assumptions about the nature of children are constructed, as are assumptions about their role, their capacities, and their needs. These in turn create the basis for research methodologies. The extent to which those assumptions and methodologies are accepted, implicitly or explicitly, by the community of researchers in the field, determines which research approaches become dominant and which remain marginal. To understand the present state of research with children, it is helpful to examine the historical origins of research in child development, as well as the events that have recently contributed to interest in children's experience of their lives and indeed to participation in research.

Early philosophies of childhood

There is a danger in this type of brief historical analysis of bringing twentieth-century western values to bear on evaluations of the treatment of children in another historical period, as is evidenced in the work of some historians of childhood (Aries, 1962; DeMause, 1974) and to conclude that societal treatment of children has improved in a unilinear fashion across time. The history of childhood does, however, provide compelling evidence that there were *different* orientations to childhood in other centuries than exist today.

Modern histories of childhood suggest that the concept of childhood as distinctive may not have emerged until the eighteenth century and that the seventeenth-century ideas of philosopher John Locke contributed significantly to this new thinking. In his popular book *Some Thoughts Concerning Education* (1693), which offered advice on the physical and psychological development of children, Locke presented a vision of childhood as a phase of life worthy of attention in its own right, a formative period of heightened vulnerability. He is generally credited as being among the earliest to perceive children as individuals in their own right, with particular abilities, with impulses that were governed by reason and restraint, and with their own point of view. His ideas of childhood have become assimilated into mainstream thinking about the nature of childhood (Borstelmann, 1983). In many respects these ideas had positive consequences for the understanding and treatment of children in society but may also be seen as shaping an image of children as unformed persons who are passive and dependent.

Rousseau's image of childhood in the eighteenth century, portrayed in works such as *Emile*, also cast childhood in terms of distinctiveness and value (Borstelmann, 1983). Yet his belief that children did not reach what he termed 'the age of reason' (implying adult reason) until age 12 contributed to the common image of children as incapable of making meaningful judgments, and perhaps contributed to the idea of children as 'becomings' rather than 'beings', as described by Morss (1996).

What can be seen as romantic views of childhood innocence and purity, which were strong at the turn of this century, can be traced back to these ideas, and forward to contributing to the creation of a moral imperative to improve the lives of children and to vindicate their rights (Kessen, 1979). They may also, paradoxically, have laid the foundation for a view of children as passive, inexpert, and lacking valuable knowledge, while at the same time placing agency and knowledge in the realm of adults. Hendrick (1990) argues that the historical positioning of children as helpless was part of an attempt at social control and accompanied by efforts to control young people's activities, particularly in the wake of the industrial revolution which brought parents' work out of the home, and separated children from parents. Moves to establish a system of public education were backed with arguments that children, especially those from the working classes, were ignorant and in need of education and socialization. The denial of the street knowledge of working-class children, in Hendrick's view, arose out of the fear of children as a potentially powerful group in society.

By the end of the nineteenth and the start of the twentieth century, children and their education and development had gained the interest of both academic researchers and governments, evidenced by the establishment of institutes for the study of children (Burman, 1994) and in the intervention by state, private, and religious agencies into family life to protect children (Hart, 1991). By the 1890s a journal of human development had been established in the USA and the questionnaire method had been used with children in Germany to 'investigate the contents of children's minds', providing the precursor to aptitude tests (Cairns, 1983).

The institutionalization of child study

Early institutes for the study of the child in the USA and in Europe continued to pursue methods to objectively study children; so too did the first academic departments conducting research on children, principally developmental psychology, education and home economics. Interest in research on children grew at a time of widespread enthusiasm for science and scientific progress and in these early research activities the roots of ideas about 'the child' as context-free and predictable can be seen.

One of the founders of child study in the USA, G. Stanley Hall, was committed to Darwinian ideas of evolution and by extension to the notion that childhood follows a natural, regulated pathway (Cairns, 1983). Such biological progressivist ideas were widely accepted in these new institutes where a primary goal was to discover the origins and processes of the adult mind (Burman, 1994) as they were in the new discipline of developmental psychology. They continued to be articulated in the theories of Baldwin in the USA, and of Freud and Piaget in Europe (Greene, 1999). These ideas were well received by western society and universities as they were entirely compatible with the philosophy of science to which the social sciences and especially psychology were turning.

The hegemony of positivism in social science

Positivism originated in the natural sciences, its defining assumptions being that there is an objective reality that researchers can accurately measure. Ironically, this paradigm was embraced by social scientists at a time when the natural sciences were calling into question its usefulness as a single investigative framework (Suppe, 1977). As child study became established, the child of research became increasingly objectified throughout the 1940s and 1950s. A certain level of variation was considered normal, but beyond this, individual differences were interpreted as deviance or alternatively as 'outliers' in data sets and were duly ignored. The basis for this was a desire to produce data that were scientifically rigorous, which in the positivist paradigm is equated with objectivity (Guba & Lincoln, 1994). In the context of a western culture enamored by science, folk knowledge about children was denigrated as 'old wives tales' and children were brought into laboratories to be weighed, measured, tested, and contrasted to norms. In institutes of child study, women's reports of child behaviour were discouraged, since mothers were viewed as incapable of providing impartial, objective information on children (Burman, 1994). Early adherence to the positivist paradigm strengthened with successive generations of researchers in the twentieth century supported, at least in part, by emergent theories of child development and models of human functioning. Among these were the 'grand theories' of child development in psychology, a small number of which have guided research on children throughout the century, directly or indirectly.

Theories of child development

The scientific model provided a basis for the emergence of individualistic stage theories of child development. The 'grand' theories, those that offered the most comprehensive explanations of human functioning and that gained the most attention, contributed to the creation and maintenance of a number of assumptions about children and their place in research. Freudian theory, for example, promoted the idea of predictable stages, and the notion of a regulated child. Freud's work was aimed primarily at understanding the adult mind by tracing the experiences of children and can be seen as contributing to the notion of the unformed child. Piaget's theory of cognitive development, which has been so influential in education systems and other domains, also assumed a natural basis for development. It set parameters around the age at which certain tasks could be accomplished and the stages through which children were thought to move progressively. Piagetian revisionists over the last two decades have shown that under different research conditions from those used by Piaget, children can display competencies at substantially earlier ages than he had believed (Donaldson, 1978; McGarrigle & Donaldson, 1974). Bradley (1989) argues that they retain, however, the notion of quite specific age parameters around certain competencies, and by implication, the notion of a universal or standard child.

Interpretations of Piaget's work as a model of biologically-based and predictable developmental patterns permeate societal structures such as the education system, the juvenile justice system, organized religion, welfare provision, and, of course, research across all of these domains. Piaget's work, however, is often incorrectly interpreted as placing children in isolation from the social world (Tudge & Winterhoff, 1993) and therefore as supporting the image of the context-free or isolable child, a criticism that has continued to be aimed at many successive cognitive theorists. Although Piaget was a constructivist, believing that children's cognitive development was shaped both by biological influences and social experiences, his ideas have come to represent, for sociologists of childhood, much of what is unacceptable about developmental psychology's approach to the study of children (cf. James et al., 1998).

There is some irony in this: Piaget's principal method of inquiry, the clinical interview (Piaget, 1928; 1932), and his close observations of the minutiae of the everyday lives of his own children, have much in common with the methodologies espoused by the new social studies of childhood, and indeed with an ethos of respect for children's perspectives (Woodhead & Faulkner, 2000). Furthermore, Piaget emphasized children's agency in constructing their understanding of their worlds. Thus the typical representation of Piaget's work by some critics provides a good example of over-simplification of concepts of child development, and constitutes another example of what Woodhead and Faulkner refer to as 'throwing the baby out with the developmental bathwater' (2000: 31). Unfortunately, this tendency to concentrate on relatively narrow aspects of theories of child development, both by psychologists and non-psychologists, serves to unduly dichotomize theoretical positions within developmental psychology itself and between developmental psychology and other fields of child study.

Challenges to Mainstream Models of Research in Developmental Psychology

The principal contemporary challenge to the theories and methods of developmental psychology originate outside the discipline, in the sociology of childhood, as described above. Perhaps the most important developments within the field itself, those most likely to precipitate the adoption of alternative models of children and research, are those that challenge specific theoretical and methodological assumptions. These include, on the one hand, the growth in social-contextual models of child development, and on the other, new research findings that bring into question notions of limitations in children's ability to contribute meaningfully, through their own accounts of events, to scientific knowledge.

Old and new ideas about meaning in research

Investigating children's contextually situated development is not a new or even recent activity. For at least a century there has been dissatisfaction with an approach to studying children that separates them from context and tries to reduce their experiences to a numerical code (Tudge et al., 1996). Sociologist James Mark Baldwin (1895), psychologist Lev Vygotsky (1978, 1987), and educator John Dewey (1896, 1902), advocated investigating the everyday meaning of children's lives. They were among a number of researchers and theorists across several disciplines and fields who, at the outset of the century, rejected the notion that children are isolated and timeless. Mid-twentieth century, the gestalt movement added to the call for research to have greater relevance to the real world of individuals. Roger Barker and Herbert Wright (1951), were among the first to document all of the activities, of which there were thousands, in which one boy was engaged in the course of single day.

Yet research activity and theorizing of this kind were at the fringes of mainstream research in the field for most of this century. It gained acceptance by a critical mass of researchers in the late 1980s with an enthusiastic welcome for the rediscovered work of Lev Vygotsky and for the ideas of Urie Bronfenbrenner (1979) marking an awareness of the importance of context for child development itself (Greene, 1994) and for the practice of research. Both Vygotsky and Bronfenbrenner argued that children grow up in a social world in which both social and temporal context plays a critical role but that they are active agents in shaping their own lives. They also insisted that research in laboratories cannot alone represent the real worlds and everyday experiences of children. Vygotsky (1978, 1987) brought attention to the value of observing children's routine activities in the social world as a source of knowledge about their social and intellectual development. Bronfenbrenner (1979) argued convincingly that research must be *ecologically valid*, that is, it must take place in real life settings and aim to capture the experiences of children that have relevance to their lives. There is increasing evidence of research that takes such an approach (see Tudge & Hogan, Chapter 6 of this volume).

Interest in contextual/ecological ideas has grown, and theoretical models have advanced (Bronfenbrenner & Morris, 1998; Lerner, 1998), contributing to a shift away from the model of 'the child' as research object, in theory, if not fully in practice. It has been bolstered by, and in turn contributed to, the emergence of social-contructionism and a turn to qualitative methods across the social sciences. In response, in part to criticism that research on children's social and cognitive competencies bore little relevance to their experiences in the real world, researchers have increasingly taken into account the context in which research takes place and the different meanings children might assign to research questions, depending on how, and by whom, they are posed.

New research findings

Recent findings about children's abilities challenge the premise that children cannot contribute meaningfully to research. They help to shed light on some of the developmental limitations on children that are imposed by age and the implications for researchers of doing research with children that facilitates their providing meaningful accounts of their subjective experiences. It should be noted that there is also a substantial history of criticism of the assumption that young children are not sufficiently competent to report on their own experiences. Margaret Donaldson (1978), for example, argued that we often confuse children's language ability with their general intellectual ability, and that when we attempt to make ourselves understood to children we find them to be more competent than we expected. Recent research supports this view.

It is typically assumed, for example, that the younger the children, the less they are to be believed. Furthermore, when young children make errors in remembering an event, we are inclined to allow that to reinforce our prejudices about their (lack of) credibility more than we do when older children make errors (Lieppe, Mannion, & Romancyck, 1991). However, researchers are now finding that young children can give accurate accounts of personally experienced events (Ceci & Bruck, 1993; Steward & Steward, 1996). Younger children remember less than adults and they are more susceptible to external cues from the interview process itself, such as the suggestibility of questions (Bruck, Ceci, & Hembrooke, 1998). They are also influenced by question format. Waterman, Blades, and Spencer (2002) found that the use of ambiguous closed questions may lead to the researcher misunderstanding what the child means to communicate in his or her response to a question. But children can remember accurately, especially when they are freely allowed to recall the details of events they have personally experienced (Baker-Ward, Gordon, Ornstein, Larus, & Clubb, 1993; Peterson & Bell, 1996). Pre-schoolers have been found to be the most suggestible age group (Bruck et al., 1998). School-aged children are better able to recall, although they are still very sensitive to contextual suggestion and particularly to their interpretation of the investigator's expectations (Garbarino & Stott, 1992). Children *are* capable of providing reliable responses, but the researcher must be aware of the most appropriate ways to phrase questions (Waterman et al., 2002). The research setting is also important, in that real-life settings lead to greater validity than research conducted in artificial research contexts, such as university laboratories (Ceci & Bronfenbrenner, 1991)

Challenges from the Practice and Policy Domains

In the practice domain, the issue of child abuse has gained growing attention and has contributed to interest in appropriate methods for interviewing children. Indeed it has contributed to the upsurge in research on children's memory for personally experienced events, or autobiographical memory. Williamson and Butler (1995) connect an increased commitment by professionals to hearing what children themselves have to say about their treatment to a rise in social work activity in the area of child protection and welfare domain as it relates to child sex abuse. They attribute this shift in perceptions of appropriate professional practice in part to a greater public scrutiny of services arising from a number of high-profile child abuse cases involving care staff in residential child care settings. In several cases, claims were made that children had complained about abusive treatment but had not been attended to – they had either been ignored or not believed.

The perception that children's subjective experiences should be better valued and understood is reflected in recent international policy changes and particularly in the United Nations Convention on the Rights of the Child. There is considerable consensus that the convention, adopted in 1989, reflects an unprecedented value for the subjective worlds of children and for their right to be consulted and taken seriously (Cohen & Naimark, 1991; Davie, 1996, Hart, 1991; Melton, 1991). Children's right to hold and express personal beliefs is contained in Articles 12, 13, and 14. For research purposes, however, Article 12 bears the greatest relevance since it reflects the principle that the child's own views should be respected and should in the first case be listened to:

> State parties shall assure to the child who is capable of forming his or her own views freely in all matters affecting the child, the views of the child be given due weight, in accordance with the age and maturity of the child.

It is open to individual states to decide the appropriate age at which to consult children, and there has been variation in the breadth with which this principle has been applied. Some states consider it relevant only to issues such as custody, rather than an approach that is inclusive of a broad range of children's experiences, such as school, family, or research (Franklin, 1995). Legislative and policy changes have occurred at the national level in both the Irish and UK contexts, and are reflected in recent initiatives. In Ireland, for example, an expressed goal in government policy, captured in *The national children's strategy: our children, their lives* (Ireland, 2000), is to afford children more and better opportunities to 'have their voices heard' in matters that affect them, and to 'understand their lives'. The material consequence of this initiative has been the channeling of resources, in the form of research funding, into studies that will meet this goal. Thus there is now a financial as well as a moral imperative to orient research towards child-centreed questions and methods.

Reconciling Competing Approaches to Research with Children

It is tempting to portray developmental psychologists and sociologists of childhood as occupying separate universes, with one group focusing on 'the child' as the object of study and the other group interested exclusively in sociostructural factors in society. Such dichotomies are, however, overly simplistic. Sociologists have long been interested in the ways in which broad social forces exert their impact on large groups, but there is also a long tradition in psychology, stretching back over a century, of more 'ecological' approaches in which individual and broader sociocultural factors are viewed as being mutually constitutive (Tudge et al., 1996).

I have argued in this chapter that developmental psychology has come under increasing criticism from other fields of child research about the marginal position afforded to children in research. I have also argued that such criticism, while having some merit, is too often based on a simplistic analysis of a complex field of inquiry. This type of analysis creates the foundation for the polarization of ideas, and supports unnecessary divisions between disciplines of child study. At the same time, the growth of interest in contextual models of child development within developmental psychology holds promise of the emergence of alternative research models grounded in constructivist paradigms. These moves increase the likelihood that developmental psychologists will pay more attention to the ways in which children experience their lives.

To date, however, developmental psychology has not been particularly successful in matching conceptual advances with methodological progress, and much research carried out using contextual theories continues to be based within positivist and post-positivist paradigms, emphasizing objective knowledge of 'the child'. The fault may lie, at least in part, with the culture of publishing within developmental psychology, which values such models and shows considerably less interest in alternative models of research on or with children. The upshot of this perspective on what constitutes worthwhile research is that those researchers who are interested both in children's development *and* their experiences find themselves in a difficult position. There are few avenues available for publishing qualitative research that adopts inter-pretative approaches to data analysis in the leading developmental journals, although it is worth noting that highly ranked journals such as *Child Development* have lately attempted to include more studies that reflect diversity in samples and recognize the importance of context for development.

What then is the role for developmental psychology in the study of children's subjective experience, and can the goals of developmental research agendas and the underlying meta-theories be reconciled with those of sociologists and other researchers of children and childhood? In my view, the study of children's experiences of their worlds, focusing on their perspectives, and the study of their development, need not be mutually exclusive. To adopt a developmental approach is to ask in what ways, and through what processes, individuals change with age. The approach to developmental psychology found objectionable by sociologists of childhood and critical developmental psychologists is not the whole story of developmental psychology, as I have argued above. There is ample scope for research with children about their lives within developmental frameworks, and for collaboration across relevant disciplines for the following reasons:

1. A developmental perspective can be retained while some traditional assumptions and research practices are forfeited. For example, assump-tions about biological determinism and universally invariant stages of change (insofar as these actually drive research agendas) can be exchanged with a view of child development as a series of transactive processes, involving child and environment, moving through time, assumptions contained in the work of theorists such as Bronfenbrenner (Bronfenbrenner, 1979; Bronfenbrenner & Morris, 1998), Lerner (1998), Sameroff (1975; 1983), Valsiner (1997a, 1997b, 2000) and Vygolsky (1978, 1987).

2. Developmental psychology need not ignore the present lives of children and disregard or ignore the material, relational and temporal contexts in which they are located – and indeed there are many examples of research that does not ignore these phenomena (see for example, Dunn (Chapter 5), Tudge & Hogan (Chapter 6), and Westcott & Littleton (Chapter 8, this volume).

3. Developmental psychology need not focus on measurement of compe-tencies at the expense of exploring the nature and meaning of the activ-ities, events, and relationships that make up life experiences.

4. The goal of understanding processes of change in individual functioning is not intrinsically incompatible with a perspective on children as active agents in their own worlds. Accepting a role for chronological age as one of many factors potentially shaping human experience does not neces-sarily pose a threat to a valid exploration of children's experiences. Neither is it necessary to entirely ignore or discount biological forces in order to learn about children's experiences.

Rather than dismissing developmental approaches, then, as being antithetical to the study of children's lived experiences, it is important to consider what might be lost if we attempt to understand children's experience without reference to their development. Greene (2003) argues that a developmental perspective crucially anchors individual experience in time, both individual and historical:

> The outright rejection of a developmental perspective can lead to an approach to psychology that fails utterly to take on board the significance of our dynamic existence in time, of our specific location in the life course, and of the crucial influence of our personal interpretation of time and age. (Greene, 2003: 143)

To conclude, there is much of interest to developmental psychologists that need not be forfeited in the interest of studying children's experiences. A developmental perspective on children's experience within psychology is both possible and valuable. The tasks ahead are to garner the interest of developmental psychologists to ask questions about children's experience, and to develop the methodological tools that will allow such questions to be answered. Greater reflexivity about research models would help to advance the field and to facilitate inter-disciplinary research.

References

Aries, P. (1962). *Centuries of childhood: A social history of family life.* New York: Knopf.

Armstrong, J. & Sugawara, A.I. (1989). Children's perceptions of their day care experiences. *Early Childhood Development and Care, 49,* 1–15.

Baker-Ward, L., Gordon, B., Ornstein, P.A., Larus, D., & Clubb, P. (1993). Young children's long-term retention of a pediatric examination. *Child Development, 64,* 1519–1533.

Baldwin, J.M. (1895). *Mental development in the child and the race: Methods and processes* New York: Macmillan.

Barker, R.G. & Wright, H.F. (1951). *One boy's day.* New York: Harper.

Bennett, M. (1999). Introduction. In M. Bennett (Ed.), *Developmental psychology: Achievements and prospects* (pp. xv–xvi). London: Psychology Press.

Borstelmann, L.J. (1983). Children before psychology. In P.H. Mussen (Ed.), *Handbook of child psychology: History, theory and methods* (Vol. 1, pp. 1–40). New York: Wiley.

Bradley, B.S. (1989). *Visions of infancy: A critical introduction to child psychology.* Cambridge: Polity Press.

Bronfenbrenner, U. (1979). *The ecology of human development: Experiments by nature and design.* Cambridge, MA: Harvard University Press.

Bronfenbrenner, U. & Morris, P.A. (1998). The ecology of developmental processes. In W. Damon (Series Ed.) & R.M. Lerner (Vol. Ed.), *Handbook of child psychology, Vol. 1. Theoretical models of human development* (5th ed., pp. 993–1028). New York: Wiley.

Bruck, M., Ceci, S.J., & Hembrooke, H. (1998). Reliability and credibility of young children's reports: From research to policy and practice. *American Psychologist, 53*(2), 136–151.

Burman, E. (1994). *Deconstructing developmental psychology.* London: Routledge.

Cairns, R.B. (1983). The emergence of developmental psychology. In P. Mussen (Ed.), *Handbook of child psychology: History, theory, and methods* (Vol. 1, pp. 41–102). New York: Wiley.

Ceci, S. & Bronfenbrenner, U. (1991). On the demise of everyday memory: 'The rumors of my death are much exaggerated' (Mark Twain). *American Psychologist, 46,* 27–31.

Ceci, S.J. & Bruck, M. (1993). The suggestibility of the child witness: A historical review and synthesis. *Psychological Bulletin, 113,* 403–439.

Cohen, C.P. & Naimark, H. (1991). United Nations Convention on the Rights of the Child: Individual rights concepts and their significance for social sciences. *American Psychologist, 46*(1), 60–65.

Corsaro, W.A., (1997). *The sociology of childhood.* Thousand Oaks, CA: Pine Forge Press.

Damon, W. (1998). Preface to the handbook of child psychology, fifth edition. In W. Damon (Series Ed.) & R. M. Lerner (Vol. Ed.), *Handbook of Child Psychology, Vol. 1. Theoretical models of human development* (5th ed., pp. xi–xvii). New York: Wiley.

Davie, R. (1996). Partnership with children: The advancing trend. In R. Davie, G. Upton, & V. Varma (Eds.), *The voice of the child: A handbook for professionals.* (pp. 1–12). London: Falmer Press.

DeMause, L. (1974). *The history of childhood.* NY: The Psychohistory Press.

Dewey, J. (1896). The reflex arc concept in psychology. *The early works of John Dewey, 1882–1897* (Vol. 5, pp. 96–109). Carbondale, IL: Southern Illinois University Press.

Dewey, J. (1902). The child and the curriculum. *The middle works of John Dewey, 1899–1924* (Vol. 2, pp. 271–292). Carbondale, IL: Southern Illinois University Press.

Donaldson, M. (1978). *Children's minds.* Glasgow: Fontana Press.

Flavell, J. (1992). Cognitive development: Past, present, and future. *Developmental Psychology, 28*(6), 998–1005.

Franklin, B. (Ed.) (1995). *The handbook of children's rights.* London: Routledge.

Garbarino, J. & Stott, F.M. (1992). *What children can tell us: Eliciting, interpreting, and evaluating critical information from children.* San Francisco, CA: Jossey Bass.

Greene, S. (1994). Growing up Irish: Development in context. *The Irish Journal of Psychology, 15*(2–3), 354–371.

Greene, S. (1999). Child development: Old themes, new directions. In M. Woodhead, D. Faulkner, & K. Littleton (Eds.), *Making sense of social development* (pp. 250–268). London: Routledge and the Open University Press.

Greene, S. (2003). *The psychological development of girls and women: Rethinking change in time.* London: Routledge.

Guba, E.G. & Lincoln, Y.S. (1994). Competing paradigms in qualitative research. In N.K. Denzin & Y.S. Lincoln (Eds.), *Handbook of qualitative research* (pp. 105–117). Thousand Oaks, CA: Sage.

Hart, S. (1991). From property to person status: Historical perspectives on children's rights. *American Psychologist, 46*(1), 53–59.

Hendrick, H. (1997). Constructions and reconstruction of British childhood: An interpretative survey, 1800 to the present. In A. James & A. Prout (Eds.), *Constructing and reconstructing childhood: Contemporary issues in the sociological study of childhood* (pp. 34–62). Basingstoke: Falmer.

Hodges, K. (1993). Structured interviews for assessing children. *Journal of Child Psychology and Psychiatry, 34*(1), 49–68.

Hogan, D.M. (1998). Valuing the child in research: Historical and current influences on research methodology with children. In D.M. Hogan & R. Gilligan (Eds.), *Researching children's experiences: Qualitative approaches* (pp. 1–11). Dublin: The Children's Research Centre, Trinity College Dublin.

Hogan, D.M., Etz, K., & Tudge, J.R.H. (1999). Reconsidering the role of children in family research: Conceptual and methodological issues. In C. Shehan (Ed.), *Contemporary perspectives on family research, Vol. 1. Through the eyes of the child: Re-visioning children as active agents of family life* (pp. 93–105). Stamford, CT: JAI Press.

Ireland (2000). *The National Children's Strategy: Our children, their lives.* Dublin: Stationery Office.

James, A. & Prout, A. (Eds.) (1997). *Constructing and reconstructing childhood* (4th ed.). London: Falmer Press.

James, A., Jenks, C., & Prout, A. (1998). *Theorizing childhood.* Cambridge: Polity Press.

Kessen, W. (1979). The American child and other cultural inventions. *American Psychologist, 34*(10), 815–820.

Krahn, G.L., Hohn, M.F., & Kime, C. (1995). Incorporating qualitative approaches into clinical child psychology research. *Journal of Clinical Child Psychology, 24*(2), 204–213.

Kuczinsky, L., Harach, L., & Bernardini, S.C. (1999). Psychology's child meets sociology's child: Agency, influence and power in social relationships. In C. Shehan (Ed.), *Contemporary perspectives on family research, Vol. 1. Through the eyes of the child: Re-visioning children as active agents of family life* (pp. 21–52). Stamford, CT: JAI Press.

Langsted, O. (1994). Looking at quality from the child's perspective. In P. Moss & A. Pence (Eds.), *Valuing quality in early childhood services* (pp. 28–40). London: Paul Chapman.

Lerner, R. (1998). Theories of human development: contemporary perspectives. In W. Damon (Series Ed.) & R.M. Lerner (Vol. Ed.), *Handbook of Child Psychology, Vol. 1. Theoretical models of human development* (5th ed., pp. 1–24). New York: Wiley.

Lieppe, M.R., Mannion, A.P., & Romancyck, A. (1991). Eyewitness testimony for a touching experience: Accuracy differences between child and adult witnesses. *Journal of Applied Psychology, 76,* 367–379.

McGarrigle, J. & Donaldson, M. (1974). Conservation accidents. *Cognition, 3,* 341–350.

Mead, M. (1928). *Coming of Age in Samoa.* William Morrow & Co.

Melton, G.B. (1991). Socialization in the global community: Respect for the dignity of the child. *American Psychologist, 46,* 66–71.

Morss, J.R. (1996). *Growing critical: Alternatives to developmental psychology.* London: Routledge.

Peterson, C. & Bell, M. (1996). Children's memory for traumatic injury. *Child Development, 67,* 3045–3070.

Piaget, J. (1928). *Judgment and reasoning in the child.* London: Routledge and Kegan Paul.

Piaget, J. (1932). *The moral judgment of the child.* New York: Harcourt Brace.

Qvortrop, J. (1987). Introduction to the sociology of childhood. *International Journal of Sociology, 17*(3), 3–37.

Sameroff, A.J. (1975). Early influences on development: Fact or fancy? *Merrill Palmer Quarterly, 21,* 269–294.

Sameroff, A.J. (1983). Developmental systems: Contexts and evolution. In W. Kessen (Ed.), *Handbook of child psychology: Vol. 1. History, theory, and methods* (pp. 237–294). New York: Wiley.

Steward, M.S. & Steward, D.S. (1996). *Interviewing young children about body touch and handling.* Monographs of the Society for Research in Child Development, 61(4–5, Serial No. 248).

Sturgess, W., Dunn, J., & Davies, L. (2001). Young children's perceptions of their relationships with family members: Links with family setting, friendships, and adjustment. *International Journal of Behavioral Development, 25*(6), 521–529.

Suppe, F. (1977). *The structure of scientific theories* (2nd ed.). Urbana, IL: University of Illinois Press.

Tudge, J.R.H. & Winterhoff, P. (1993). Vygotsky, Piaget, and Bandura: Perspectives on the relations between the social world and cognitive development. *Human Development, 36*, 61–81.

Tudge, J., Gray, J., & Hogan, D. (1996). Ecological perspectives in human development: A comparison of Gibson and Bronfenbrenner. In J. Tudge, M. Shanahan, & J. Valsiner, (Eds.), *Comparisons in human development: Understanding time and context* (pp. 72–105). New York: Cambridge University Press.

Valsiner, J. (1997a) *The guided mind: A sociogenetic approach to personality.* Cambridge, MA: Harvard University Press.

Valsiner, J. (1997b). *Culture and the development of children's action* (2nd ed.). New York: Wiley.

Valsiner, J. (1998). The development of the concept of development: Historical and epistemological perspectives. In W. Damon (Series Ed.) & R.M. Lerner (Vol. Ed.), *Handbook of Child Psychology, Vol. 1. Theoretical models of human development* (5th ed., pp. 89–232). New York: Wiley.

Valsiner, J. (2000) *Culture and human development.* London: Sage.

Vygotsky, L.S. (1978). *Mind in society.* Cambridge, MA: Harvard University Press.

Vygotsky, L.S. (1987). *The collected works of L.S. Vygotsky Vol. 1. Problems of general psychology.* New York: Plenum.

Walkerdine, V. (1984). Developmental psychology and the child-centered pedagogy: The insertion of Piaget into early education. In J. Henriques, W. Holloway, C. Urwin, C. Venn, & V. Walkerdine (Eds.), *Changing the subject: Psychology, social regulation and subjectivity.* London: Methuen.

Waterman, A., Blades, M. & Spencer, C. (2002). How and why do children respond to nonsensical questions? In H. Westcott, G. Davies, & R. Bull (Eds.), *Children's testimony: Psychological research and forensic practice* (pp. 147–159). Chichester: Wiley.

Whiting, B.B. & Edwards, C.P. (1988). *Children of different worlds: The formation of social behavior.* Cambridge, MA: Harvard University Press.

Williamson, H. & Butler, I. (1995). No one ever listens to us: Interviewing children and young people. In C. Cloke & M. Davies (Eds.), *Participation and empowerment in child protection* (pp. 61–79). London: Pitman Publishing.

Woodhead, M. & Faulkner, D. (2000). Subjects, objects or participants: Dilemmas of psychological research with children. In A. James & P. Christensen (Eds.), *Research with children: Perspectives and practices* (pp. 9–35). London: Falmer Press.

Anthropological and Sociological Perspectives on the Study of Children

Pia Christensen and Alan Prout

During the last fifteen years the social study of children has undergone a fundamental change of perspective. Sometimes called the 'new sociology' or 'new social studies' of childhood, this new perspective accords children conceptual autonomy, looking at them as the direct and primary unit of study. It focuses on children as social actors in their present lives and it examines the ways in which they influence their social circumstances as well as the ways in which they are influenced by them. It sees children as making meaning in social life through their interactions with other children as well as with adults. Finally, childhood is seen as part of society not prior to it and it is subject to the same type of influences that shape other social phenomena. In this chapter we explore this perspective, examining why it came about, how social scientific ideas about children are embedded in wider social and cultural ideas about childhood and outlining the main features of the new approaches. Finally we point to some of the debates and issues that are arising in the field, especially the concept of generational order.

The Paradox of Sameness and Difference

Writing almost thirty years ago Hardman (1973) identified two general problems about children in social and cultural studies: their lack of visibility and their muteness. The situation she described can be seen as similar in some respects to that of women in society and their representation in earlier social science (see for example, Ardener, 1975a, 1975b; Moore, 1988). The critique of this, pioneered by feminists, brought the particular perspectives of women, their social position and everyday experiences to the attention of social scientists (Alanen, 1988) and led to changes in their representation. In contrast, the similar need to make children 'visible' in the social sciences may seem superfluous in view of children's apparent centrality in western cultures, exhibited, for example, in the highly staged material and symbolic worlds of modern childhood. However, what may be challenged are those traditional perspectives that neglect the fact that children have little or no influence over their own social representation. The importance of this is highlighted by Dyer's statement that 'how we are seen determines in part how we are treated, how we treat others is based on how we see them; such seeing comes from representation' (1993: 1). If the child can now be thought of as a subject who is both acted upon and acts in the world, then most earlier anthropological and sociological studies emphasized the former. Their focus left the child as a social person in his or her own right and his or her perceptions and actions in the social and cultural world more or less unaddressed.

Changing the position of children in the social and cultural sciences, then, requires a re-examination of the conceptual frameworks that influence children's representation. A starting point for this is to explore the ways that children are constituted in social and cultural theory. For Jenks (1982) an examination of how children are dealt with in social theory reveals a ceaseless paradox. Jenks writes:

> The child is familiar to us and yet strange, she/he inhabits our world and yet seems to answer to another, she/he is essentially of ourselves and yet appears to display a different order of being. (p. 9)

The child cannot be imagined in the absence of an idea about what an adult is, just as it is impossible to picture the adult and his or her society without positing the child. The ambiguity in the relationship between the child and the adult is encapsulated in the notion of 'difference'. This perception of difference, Jenks suggests, may be attributed to a conventional theoretical focus on the social processes of overcoming it – that is, socialization. It is an underlying western cultural premise that people are made, not born (Riesman, 1990). In this view people are made what they become through the influence of their parents and through education, with both being seen as essential for their successful development and future life. The emphasis is therefore put on understanding children in terms of 'becoming' rather than as 'being' a social person (Qvortrup, 1991; Qvortrup, Bardy, Sgritta, & Wintersberger, 1994).

At the same time as child and adult are seen to form a continuum, there is an implication of a socially and culturally constituted opposition. This marking of boundaries between the categorical positions of child and adult forms a part of cultural ideas about their fundamental separateness. This point is well evidenced in popular culture that addresses generational and familial problems. Films such as *Look Who's Talking Too* and TV soap operas such as *Cosby* all employ a central plot device that works by making a constant contrast between the world of children (and young people) and the adult world. Traditional (op)positions and commonly perceived conflicts of everyday family life are highlighted by inverting 'child' and 'adult' power, control, competence and responsibility and by exaggerating elements of these dichotomous relationships. Such depictions often portray the embarrassing, weak and preposterous adult in relation to the lively, clever and smart child or demonstrate the adults' shortcomings when confronted with children's manipulative powers and alternative worldviews. Eventually, however, the storyline finds its equilibrium when children and adults are again reinstated into their 'usual' and 'proper' roles and positions.

These examples demonstrate how 'child' and 'adult' are seen as culturally and socially inseparable but at the same time as equally constituted in terms of 'difference'. Crawford's (1994) suggestion that stigmatizing images of the 'other' are founded in a social self that needs this other may, with regard to children, suggest that establishing the norm of the 'adult' in terms of an independent, responsible and active person necessarily constitutes its opposite, which at the same time is its complement. This can be seen through dominant notions of children as essentially dependent, incompetent and vulnerable (Christensen, 2000a; Hutchby & Moran-Ellis, 1998).

Fabian's (1983) notion of coevality serves to summarize these points. Adults are coeval with children; that is, they live and share with them the same historical moment. However, at the same time, emphasis is given to childhood as a phase of development and preparation for future adult life that establishes an 'other-time-worldliness' in which the child's present tends to disappear. This implies that the *present* value of childhood is to be read off (in relation to) a *future* in terms of a *past*. This particular temporal constitution of childhood is, Jenks (1996a: 15) proposes, connected to the core features of modernity. The modern family, he suggests, enabled the state to invest in children, constituting them not as beings but as 'promising' material for the future.

The Development of Western Ideas of Childhood

The propensity to contextualize children through the past or future rather than the present can, however, be understood as consistent with the historical and ideological development of the idea of childhood first noticed by Aries (1962). The child in the Middle Ages, he argues, did not occupy a particular social status and the idea of childhood did not exist. Archard (1993) criticizes this conclusion, suggesting one cannot infer that European medieval societies had no notion of childhood from the premise that they did not share the modern concept of it. Rather they must be seen as having a different idea of childhood. Children formed a part of society and participated in work and other social activities as soon as they did not need constant maternal care and attention. The word 'child' implied a structured lineage, that is, a relationship and position in the family, and did not refer to a hierarchy of age. Children from the age of 6- or 7-years-old were regarded as adults – little adults or deficient ones – with relevant rights and responsibilities. During the seventeenth and eighteenth centuries, there was a shift in values and childhood became constituted through a notion of the intimate and private family and the value placed on learning. These ideas developed into a number of practices and schedules of child care and training. Childhood became a 'quarantine' period where particular protective care was necessary. The child prepared and learned for a future adult life and developed to become a full and accepted member of society. Aries concludes that the care and control thus enacted by family, church, moralists and trustees deprived children of the freedom that they had previously enjoyed among adults.

This constitution of modern childhood was associated with the formation of other features of contemporary European society: motherhood, the early mother–infant relationship and the separation of play, school and work (Alanen, 1988). This furthered the development of professional expertise in relation to children that was based on observing this new social world and viewed children as different from adults. Two sets of ideas may thus be suggested as forming the basis of the general European and North American cultural view of children and the structuration of childhood (Ennew, 1986: 20). One set of ideas separates children from adults and defines the ideal family as a nuclear unit that is seen as the appropriate setting for children's socialization. The family as social institution became the locus for undertaking the proper development and sustenance of both child and parental health (Crawford, 1994). Within the family these perceptions implied the positioning of adults as responsible providers and carers of the child, while the child, as 'not as yet part of society', received care, protection and training. The other set of ideas separated children from adults in production processes, that is, work. Perceptions of children meant that they were formally protected from work. The child had the status of a 'non-worker', was not expected to work and in fact, children (depending on their age) were gradually becoming legally excluded from it. Contemporaneously the child must not and is not expected to work, but has instead the right to play, learning and knowledge.

Dominant perceptions of childhood in European and North American cultures can then be summarized as follows: childhood is ascribed special meaning as a phase in human life; the child is surrounded with care and concern which endeavour to prepare and protect the child; at the same time these perceptions attribute value to childhood and the child mostly in relation to a future adult life through the status of 'non-adult'; the child is more valued as a being in process, that is, being socialized towards a goal through which to take his or her place in society, than in his or her present state.

These views form a remarkable contrast to the position of the child in cultures that are dependent on, and emphasize, children's contributions to family economy in the form of work, support of the elderly or care-taking for younger siblings (see for example, Rodgers & Standing, 1981; Qvortrup et al., 1994). However, even in industrial societies these understandings of modern childhood actually underestimate and render children's contributions to the economy invisible (Morrow, 1996). They deprive children's actions and contributions of any genuine and 'serious' impact or importance for societal life. That the contribution children make may be considerable but still not be properly valued, was demonstrated by a British study which showed that about 10,000 children under the age of 16 were carers of an adult family member (Fallon, 1990). The invisibility of this work carried out by children was underlined by the fact that, unlike adults doing the same work, persons of this age cannot claim a care allowance from the state. Consequently, the exact figure of children involved could only be estimated. The social nonrecognition of their work was accompanied by a frustration on their part because, as children, they were frequently excluded from having any part in negotiations and decisions. The professionals believed that they were too young to be involved.

Socialization: The Mechanical Reproduction of Society and Culture

Despite such examples, the value of children in contemporary society remains largely invested in their future, a view emphasized in the concept of 'socialization'. This designates the social processes by which the child internalizes cultural values and, through learning and development, prepares for adult life. However, within sociology the concept of socialization originally referred to the social forces that drew people together in a society (Durkheim, 1950 [1903]). Socialization was perceived as a primarily collective process, which had as secondary the individual psychological process of internalization. By shifting its meaning towards internalization, socialization has now come to imply a fundamental polarity between an uncivilized and asocial 'human nature' and a civilized and 'social being', a distinction that places the child at the uncivilized pole.

This reinterpretation of socialization as a psychological process has proven to have particular conceptual power. In psychology, socialization is redefined as an individual process of internalization reducing social reality to externally given conditions or milieu. In contrast to earlier understandings of the term, socialization became understood as involving a passive recipient (almost always a child) instead of an active social person in their relations and interactions with others. The child was more or less seen as an empty vessel with 'potential sociality' that would develop through the influences and guidance of significant others (such as the parents and the school). Even though later theories incorporated ideas of socialization as an interactional process, the main concern for socialization research remained to determine the processes by which the social and material environment and the cultural system that the child grows up with (and which are treated as an external given) are internalized by the child and thus reproduced (Denzin, 1977; MacKay, 1973). Socialization processes are thus held to provide a seemingly convincing, but in fact, misleadingly partial framework for understanding children in the social world (Alanen, 1988).

Within anthropology, the interest in children has, until recently, often merely served as 'part of the decoration' in ethnography. The life of children and children's play are used more or less only to colour the background or sketch the atmosphere for what the anthropologist sees as of main concern – namely the adults, their relations and the culture at large. Insofar as children have been present in ethnographies, it has also largely been through an interest in socialization, in anthropology most notably through the work of the Culture and Personality School during the period 1930–60 (see for example, Benedict, 1946; Mead, 1968 [1930], 1955; Whiting & Child, 1953). This school of thought was influenced by Freudian psychoanalysis and focused on cultural child-rearing practices as the basis for the formation of the adult personality and the nature of adult social life. The emphasis was also on children as those who would ensure the continuity of the community, and thus the Culture and Personality School was concerned predominantly with how children were enculturated or socialized and how cultural values, traditions and social organization were maintained. The prevalent idea of children was thus as persons who were molded and shaped into social beings. In this perspective anthropologists observed adults, and especially mothers, caring for and training children as part of society. Adults were interviewed about their perceptions and ideas and, eventually, the anthropologist supplemented his or her interpretations by observing children's behaviour in play and other social activities. It should be noted, however, that in Mead's work children were recognized as informants and child thinking is seen as interesting in its own right.

By the late 1970s, however, Culture and Personality studies began to be criticized for their mechanistic and deterministic model which assumed that events at one point would produce a given result at a later time. In an important review paper, Shweder (1979) concluded that a clear and consistent relation could not be found between child rearing practices in the first years of the child's life, and the adult personality prevalent in a certain culture. Nevertheless, studies still continued to inscribe themselves in this tradition, suggesting the persuasive power of the idea of a cultural connection between the socialization of the small child and adult life (see for example, Levine, Levine and Leiderman, 1994).

Reconstructing the Social Study of Children

So far we have argued that ideas about the determinant character of socialization processes, especially of early childhood in relation to adult life and the constitutive effect for social relations among adults in a society, tend to obscure important aspects of children's lives. In relieving childhood from these presumptions, we are able to ascribe to the idea of childhood and of children's relationships a sense of present value. We wish to argue against seeing childhood only as related to a future goal, as part of a relationship of cause and outcome, but rather to take a perspective that emphasizes the current value for children of their lives and relationships. Related to this is Thorne's (1987) argument that the sociological study of children requires their 'conceptual autonomy'. Through this, children become the direct focus of the analysis rather than necessarily being seen through their link to other social institutions such as family and schooling. This both reconceptualizes childhood and broadens the range of its referents, contexts and meanings.

Recent theoretical advances, especially those derived from ethnographic and qualitative studies that view children as actively participating in the interpretation and reproduction of cultural knowledge, form an essential background to the task of focusing on children's lives in the present. In order to explain this current thinking it is necessary to sketch the argument made by contemporary sociologists of childhood. They have suggested that the notion of 'development' is a dominant discourse of children within European and North American thought (Jenks, 1982; James, Jenks, & Prout, 1998; Prout & James, 1997 [1990]). Although fostered within psychology, the developmental approach has until recently formed an implicit basis for most sociological and anthropological work on childhood (James et al., 1998). Central to this mode of thought are three elements: 'naturalness', 'universality', and 'rationality'. This trio has until recently been thought to tie the biological facts of infancy and growth with the social aspects of childhood. As a consequence, Jenks (1982, 1996b) suggests, the child is seen as progressing from simplicity to complexity, from irrational to rational behaviour, from a stage of biological immaturity, passing through a developmental process and moving into a fully developed human status as adult. Although a harsh judgement on developmental psychology, one that does not adequately acknowledge its diversity and more positive contributions (see Woodhead & Faulkner, 2000), the new sociology of childhood mounted a challenge to it on every point (for a programmatic statement of the new paradigm of the sociology of childhood see Prout & James, 1997 [1990]). The key theoretical move was that of social constructionism. Rather than seeing childhood as a natural or biological phenomenon, it was understood as a product of history, society and culture. This was a highly productive development (albeit one that contains its own dangers, see Prout, 2000) that allowed children to be seen as active, competent beings dealing with complex social worlds.

In the sociology of the 1950s, however, current ideas about child development were directly transferred into theories of socialization. At a time when the social sciences were greatly influenced by positivist and functionalist thinking 'socialization' offered a convincing account of how children 'become social' (Prout & James, 1997 [1990]). The theoretical preoccupation of sociology with the reproduction of the social order replicated the individual–society dualism presupposed by the psychological view of children. The individual was seen as a pre-existing 'cogito' outside of society (Ingleby, 1986); children were seen as immature, irrational, incompetent, asocial, and acultural while adults were regarded as 'mature, rational, competent, social and autonomous' (MacKay, 1973: 27–28). As suggested above, children and adults were thus made to appear as two different instances of the same species. Socialization was seen as the process that transformed the one into the other (for an excellent account and critique see Frønes, 1995).

In this model, children were the passive representatives of the future generation and, in the social processes involved in socialization, adults were, as Elkin (1960: 101) critically describes it, the active and constituent end. In such traditional views the notion of children as 'outcomes' became the principal concern at the expense of attending to the socialization process in itself or even of exploring the possible contradictions and conflicts involved in such processes. In the 1970s, however, the work of socialization theorists was undergoing critical appraisal. Shildkrout, for example, argued that:

> Child culture is seen as a rehearsal for adult life and socialization consists of the processes through which, by one method or another, children are made to conform in cases of 'successful' socialization or become deviants in cases of failed socialization. (1978: 109–110)

These critiques pointed to the overarching determinism characteristic of socialization studies, a point echoed by Shildkrout's contemporaries and challenged in much of the newer work on socialization that employed an interactional perspective and aimed to investigate children's own part in the processes (see for example, Denzin, 1977; MacKay, 1973). Contemporary research has also recognized the increasing complexity of socialization processes, talking for example of the 'double socialization' that occurs when young children begin to spend a large part of their daily life at school, in after-school clubs or in day-care institutions. The German educationalist Giesecke (1985) goes further, arguing that we also have to acknowledge that children, like adults, live in a pluralist society and thus are confronted by a range of competing, complementary and divergent values and perspectives from the media, the consumer society and their peer relations. He suggests parents, teachers and other people with responsibility for the care of children have less power to control and steer these different factors as a whole. It becomes important, therefore, to understand how children make coherence and sense of the world they live in. The new sociology of childhood has offered a solution in this respect. It has moved the perspective away from seeing the child–adult relationship as necessarily the most important factor to seeing children's interrelationships and interactions with others – children as well as adults – as equally important. In doing so, it has allowed a focus on the work that children themselves do to socialize each other (including the way they socialize adults) and how these activities contribute to, and produce, change.

On the basis of these critiques, children came to be seen as much more active in the process of cultural learning as interpreters and creators of meaning rather than simply absorbing the meanings of adults. Contemporary approaches in the ethnography of children depart from this point by seeing socialization as a collective rather than an individual process, by emphasizing the importance of children's peer relations, and by placing socialization in the public rather than the private domain. Corsaro (1992, 1997) has theorized this approach as 'interpretive reproduction'. He emphasizes children's active participation in both interpreting and reproducing culture through three particularly important elements: (1) language and language use; (2) cultural routines that provide actors with a shared understanding of belonging to a social group and supply the frames within which a wide range of sociocultural knowledge can be produced, displayed and interpreted; and (3) by seeing development as reproductive rather than linear.

Taken together these dispense with the idea of seeing the child as outside of society and societal institutions (Cook-Cumperz, Corsaro, & Streek, 1986). As Corsaro puts it:

> children do not simply imitate or internalize the world around them. They strive to interpret or make sense of their culture and to participate in it. In attempting to make sense of the adult world, children come to collectively produce their own peer worlds and cultures. (1997: 24)

Here, then, both children and adults are seen as part of culture and both make contributions to its reproduction and (re)interpretation. This happens both through children's negotiations with adults and through the creative production of a series of peer cultures with other children. Individual development thus becomes embedded in children's collective weaving of their places in the webs of significance that constitute their culture. The social study of children and childhood must, therefore, acknowledge the interplay between adults' and children's perspectives on social relations and culture.

Based on these perspectives, often arrived at separately by researchers working in different contexts, the last two decades have seen an upsurge in such ethnographic and qualitative sociological investigations of children's lives in many different settings. These include children in hospital (Alderson, 1993; Bluebond-Langner, 1978); children's self care at school and after-school clubs (Christensen, 1993, 1999); school sickness absence (Prout, 1986, 1989); identity and chronic illness (James, 1993); ethnicity and gender identity (Connolly, 1998); children's daily life in school (Mayall, 1996); school career and learning identity (Pollard, 1985; Pollard & Filer, 1996); paid work (Nieuwenhys, 1994; Reynolds, 1996; Solberg, 1994) and play (Thorne, 1993). Special mention must also be made here of the ESRC Children 5–16 Research Programme in the UK in which twenty-two linked projects focused on children as social actors in many different contexts of their lives (for an overview see Prout, 2001).

Looking at children as social actors in this way, they are far from being seen as passive subjects in social structures and processes. Instead they are seen as active in the construction and determination of their social lives, active in the lives that other people lead around them and the societies in which they live. Rather than looking only at how children are formed by social life, children are seen as social actors whose actions can both shape and change social life. Giddens (1979: 69) argues that an action that serves to reproduce structure is a productive action, and, as such, it may initiate social change by transforming structure at the same time as it reproduces it. Thus, to acknowledge the simultaneous reproductive and transformative relations between human conduct and culture, one must perceive the person as not only a 'product' of his or her own culture, but also as a co-writer of reality (Hastrup, 1988: 137) and the interpreter as well as mechanical reproducer of society and culture (Cosaro, 1992, 1997). It is important to recognize children as *both* restricted or encapsulated by social structures and as persons acting within or towards the structure (Prout & James, 1997 [1990]).

Childhood as Social Structure

The idea of children as co-constructors of society links studies of children, their peer cultures and their interactions with adults to another important strand in the sociological rediscovery of childhood. This work focuses less on *children* and more on understanding *childhood* as a feature of the social structure. The argument here is that, although its membership may be constantly changing, childhood forms a permanent part of the social structure. The key sociological question in this perspective becomes relating 'the childhood' of a society to the wider social forces operating in and on society. From this perspective Qvortrup has argued that the sociologist can subject childhood to the same sort of analysis as any other social phenomenon, placing it alongside longstanding topics of social analysis such as class and gender (Qvortrup et al., 1994: 5).

Such a perspective encourages the comparative analysis of childhood along a number of dimensions. First, it allows comparison of children with other population groups such as youth, adults and the elderly. For example, it suggests a need to understand the distribution of resources such as income and welfare spending among these different groups. The importance of this is clear when one remembers that trends in the industrialized countries mean both that children are a declining proportion of the population and that the proportion of households including children is also declining (Clarke, 1996; European Commission, 1996; Office for National Statistics, 1991). This, combined with the emergence of political lobbies for the older generation, must provoke questions about who is to speak for children in decisions about resource allocation and how inter-generational distributive justice is to be achieved and maintained (Sgritta, 1994: 361). It is well known, for example, that child poverty in the UK rose sharply during the 1980s and 1990s. Children as a group, however, saw a disproportionate rise in poverty compared to the rest of the population; in effect, as a group, they moved down the income distribution (Adelman & Bradshaw, 1998). This example also illustrates a second type of comparative analysis, that between countries. This shows that poverty among children in the UK rose sharply at a time when it remained more or less stable in most other similar countries. This suggests that, unlike these other countries, the UK did not protect children against worsening economic conditions through welfare and social policy measures (Adelman & Bradshaw, 1998). This type of international comparative approach is also implicit in the reports produced by UNICEF that compare how children in different countries fare according to a series of indicators.

Finally, considering childhood as a structural form has led sociologists to examine how it changes over time, and especially its contemporary trends. On this front, sociologists in the industrialized world have suggested three somewhat contradictory processes that may be going on alongside each other. These have been referred to as: 'institutionalization'; 'familialization' and 'individualization' (Brannen & O'Brien, 1995; Nasman, 1994). These are thought to operate in tension with each other, pushing and pulling childhood in rather different directions. The first of these, institutionalization, reflects that in the Nordic countries especially, but increasingly elsewhere too, children's everyday lives are spent more and more within day-care institutions (such as nurseries and playgroups), school and after-school clubs. Even leisure time is framed in this way for many children because participation in activities, such as sport or music, takes place within some kind of institutional setting. Public debates express the views of professionals, parents and politicians about the possible effects of this increasing institutionalization and fragmentation on children and the potentially undesirable outcomes of growing up in such diverse social environments. Fears are expressed that it may hinder children in forming and developing stable and coherent worldviews and relationships. The highly institutionalized schooling and professional day-care system for children is suspected of creating and sustaining generational divisions in society and, in particular, of creating a gap between children and their parents (who spend most of their everyday lives apart).

Clearly, the trend towards institutionalization is related to wider social changes, especially the increased participation of women in the labour market, of which it is both a consequence and an enabling mechanism. This in turn can be located as part of the breakdown of what has been called the 'male breadwinner model' of society (Creighton, 1999). Although the implications for children of these changes are under-researched, and in many discussions displaced by adult concerns, it remains important for the new social studies of childhood to address them. One way of approaching this is from the institutional perspective as exemplified by researchers such as Smith (2000) who have investigated what children in the UK like and dislike about after-school clubs, leading to a number of suggestions for their improvement. Christensen (2000b), however, has approached it from the family side of the institutionalization process by examining children's views about, and experience of, 'quality time', a frequently promoted solution to the problem of the time squeeze brought about by conflicting parental and employment obligations. She notes that quality time is simply assumed to be a solution from children's point of view without there being any evidence for it. In fact, her ethnography suggests that time in the family is understood by children in much more complex ways than allowed for by the notion of quality time.

The trend towards 'familialization' refers to the tendency for children to be increasingly seen as dependent on, and contained within, their families (Brannen & O'Brien, 1995) and can be seen to be in partial conflict with institutionalization. It is evident, for example, in the international trend towards parental involvement in schools (Edwards, 2002), which, in the UK at least, was accompanied by a parallel decline in the participation of children in school governance (Wyness, 1999). Familialization has corollaries across the range of services directed towards children and young people. In the UK policy environment of the 1980s, the family increasingly replaced the identification of young people as a group. The family became the government's preferred route to policy interventions and recent policy statements confirm this trend (Home Office, 1998).

It also seems that the trend begun in the 1970s (Hillman, Adams, & Whitelegg, 1990) towards the sequestration of children in the family and the decline of children's autonomous movement around their neighbourhood may have continued into the 1990s (O'Brien, 1999). This suggests a double effect: the first is an incipient exclusion of children from public space, where they are seen increasingly as causing problems, as 'out of place' and there-fore becoming more subject to regulation and control (see Matthews & Limb, 2000; Valentine, 1996). The second is a simultaneous proliferation of special locations that concentrate groups of children together for activities taking place under more or less adult surveillance and supervision (Furedi, 1997). The effect would seem to be the construction of a way of life for many children that consists of moving from one 'island' of childhood to another. In this sense, the space of childhood, literally as well as metaphorically, may be becoming more specialized and more localized. From this point of view, the institutionalization of childhood is in some senses quite compatible with familialization. Indeed, it is well caught in the contemporary image of the middle-class parent as chauffeur to children whose week is packed with different activities, to and from which they are ferried by car.

Finally, the notion of individualization refers to the tendency for contempo-rary children to be seen as having a voice in determining their lives and shap-ing their identity. It is immediately apparent that this resonates with ideas associated with the new social studies of childhood. It is arguable, for exam-ple, that sociology's discovery of children as actors and agents is caught up in the individualization of childhood, parallel with, for example, the participa-tion rights promulgated by the United Nations Convention on the Rights of the Child. Beck (1992, 1998) argues that such developments are part of a 'second modernization', central to which is a recent societal propensity towards people – adults and children alike – coming to think of themselves as unique individu-als with chosen rather than prescribed or standard identities. A concatenation of factors, rather than a single cause, is said to be responsible for this shift. The emergence of consumption (especially leisure) as a source of identity, the plu-ralization of family forms, the decline in the authority of expert knowledges, the distribution of norms about the value of democracy and so on, all con-tribute to a process that has become self-propelling.

Problems and Perspectives

The above discussion has shown how successful the new social studies has been, and we trust will continue to be, in producing new insights about both children as social actors and childhood as a component of social systems. However, it is also evident that the division of the field into these two parts, roughly the division between a focus on children or one on childhood, is not really satisfactory. This is an ongoing debate within the sociology of child-hood (see James, Jenks, & Prout, 1998) that has yet to be resolved. It is impor-tant not to over-emphasize this problem because by focusing on a particular empirical area, researchers often manage to move productively between these two modes of analysis. Christensen (1993, 1999), for example, in her study of children's self-care around illness and accidents at home, school and at the after-school club, linked large-scale trends in the constitution of Danish childhood, the local interactions of children and adults in these settings and the personal experiences of particular children. She accomplished this by applying Nader's (1981) notion of the 'horizontal' and 'vertical' slices (or perspectives) in social analysis. The former is the processual or interactional level, while the latter refers to the relation between the person and society. Nader argues that ethnographic studies tend to focus on a horizontal level, leaving out of the analysis the vertical perspective. In relation to studies of children, this has resulted in a lack of attention to the complex relation between children and institutions and the formal and informal hierarchies that influence children's lives. Christensen argues that it is important to substantiate both the nature of the relationships between persons and social institutions *and* to understand the structure and meaning of these relationships in the lives of children and their families. Starting at the interactional level, but with a theoretically informed understanding of contemporary childhood as a social phenomenon, she traces through the ideological and material connections to these societal and institutional phenomena.

Nevertheless, there are conceptual inconsistencies between thinking of childhood as a socially constructed phenomenon that varies in time and space and the attempt to characterize childhood as a social structure or form. The former tends towards seeing many different 'childhoods' within a given society, while the latter tends to put different children together into a more unitary entity. Clearly there is a danger of disaggregating children to the extent that every child represents only their own childhood (Qvortrup, 2000). This, however, is paralleled by the danger that in unifying children into a notional 'childhood', significant differences (of gender, class, ethnicity, disability, and so on) between children are underplayed. Frønes for example argues: 'There is not one childhood, but many, formed at the intersection of different cultural, social and economic systems, natural and man-made physical environments. Different positions in society produce different experiences' (1993: 1). A good example of this is found in O'Brien's (1999) study of children's autonomous mobility in cities. While they found an overall decline in this over time, it was also the case that it varied widely according to social class, gender, ethnicity and neighbourhood. There was a differentiation between children that should not be ignored. Nor is this simply a problem of differentiation within a given society. Frønes (1997) has argued that one effect of globalization is that childhoods similar to those of the Euro-American middle classes are being produced and distributed around the world. These often appear within the protected enclaves of elites in developing countries such that the childhoods of privileged children in New York and Delhi may have more in common with each other than with the majority in either location. The nation state may be becoming less salient as a point of comparison. Research on 'transnational childhoods' raises similar questions about the complexity of childhood in a rapidly changing world that in certain respects may be dissolving national boundaries (Orelleana, Thorne, Chee, & Lam, 2001).

Finally, it is important to ask, as Christensen (1999: 30) does, whether the concept of childhood is really an analytical category. She argues that it is better thought of as a focus for empirical enquiry, a field of study to which the analytical and explanatory resources of the social sciences should be brought. Childhood, she suggests, can only be understood in relation to adulthood because both are constituted in the same set of social and cultural practices. Such a relational idea of childhood has been systematically expounded by Alanen (2001), who argues that the central organizing concept of the sociology of childhood should be that of the 'generational order': that is, the systematic pattern of social relationships in which children are located as a social group. Its parallel is with other key dimensions of social differentiation such as class and gender order. It is suggested that theorizing children through generational relationships would enable the sociological analysis of children to find a place alongside such key sociological concepts.

There are real advantages in this: the notion of generational order constitutes childhood not as an essential entity but as one produced within a set of relations. Within these, childhood and adulthood are simultaneously produced in relation to each other. How adulthood is constructed thus always has implications for childhood and vice versa. This also reminds us that adulthood itself is not the finished product towards which children are headed, but a phenomenon constantly in process, review and change (Lee, 1998). The distinction between adulthood as 'being' and childhood as 'becoming' is therefore questioned and destabilized.

However, there are also some dangers and much depends, we would suggest, on how the idea of generational order is developed. In the first place, we suggest that generation should be though of as a verb not a noun (Curt, 1994: 15). In other words, we need to look at generational order*ing* as an active, open-ended and unfinished process. The central analytical task would then be not only to describe relationships between children and adults but to discover how (and when) they are given a generational aspect or meaning. Second, the process of generationing should be seen as plural. Building on the discussion above about whether there can be a single childhood of a society, it seems unlikely to us that there could be a single practice of making or maintaining a generational order. Rather, at any one time there may be several competing, cross-cutting ways of ordering that jostle uneasily alongside each other. Perhaps, too, these are distributed unevenly between contexts such that the generational orderings of school, state, family, and so on, are different and vary through time and space. Nor should it be assumed that adults are the active pole of this process, whereas children are always passive in the face of a power hierarchy that always subordinates them.

Third, there should be a constant guard against re-rendering children invisible in generational orders. As we suggested above, there is a kind of generational politics around and about societal resources in which the presence, rights and needs of children may be overshadowed as their demographic weight declines. This could be reflected easily in the human sciences as ageing becomes a more readily funded and more popular topic of investigation.

Lastly, there is a danger of counterposing the generational perspective to that of life-course. Rather, we suggest that a better analytical purchase could be achieved by combining them and looking for points of intersection. There is still much to be learnt by asking what it means to be, for example, a 5-, 8-, 10-, or 12-year-old child and how these points on a trajectory of growing up are similar yet different. The notion of generational ordering could complement this by highlighting how growing up is constructed within sets of shifting generational relations. Nevertheless, growing up remains crucially important not just for future adulthood outcomes, but also for the experience of childhood itself. As we have argued above, significant relationships in children's life projects include not only those with parents and other adults, but also those with other children, including but not confined to their age peers. Overcoming children's invisibility and muteness in sociology and anthropology, with which we began this chapter, has involved attempting to construct a more detailed and complex account of the social life of children and adults. It has required suspending taken-for-granted notions about the differences and similarities between children and adults and the adoption of more open-minded questioning about how these are constructed in different contexts. This, in turn, has produced an appreciation of the importance of relationships between children and a greater sensitivity to the differences and similarities between them. A sociology that replaced this complex web of shifting relationships with a sole, or even a primary, focus on the generational relationships between adults and children would not necessarily be a step forward.

References

Alderson, P. (1993). *Children's consent to surgery*. Milton Keynes: Open University Press.

Adelman, L. & Bradshaw, J. (1998). *Children in poverty in Britain: An analysis of the family resources survey 1994/5*. York: Social Policy Research Unit, University of York.

Alanen, L. (1988). Rethinking childhood. *Acta Sociologica, 31*(1), 53–67.

Alanen, L. (2001). Childhood as a generational condition. In L. Alanen & B. Mayall (Eds.), *Conceptualising child–adult relationships* (pp. 129–43). London: Falmer Press.

Archard, D. (1993). *Children: Rights and childhood*. London: Routledge.

Ardener, E. (1975a). Belief and the problem of women. In S. Ardener (Ed.), *Perceiving Women* (pp. 1–17). London: J.M. Dent.

Ardener, E. (1975b). The 'problem' revisited. In S. Ardener (Ed.), *Perceiving women* (pp. 19–27). London: J.M. Dent.

Aries, P. (1962). *Centuries of childhood: A social history of family life*. London: Jonathan Cape.

Beck, U. (1992). *Risk society: Towards a new modernity*. London: Sage.

Beck, U. (1998). *Democracy without enemies*. Cambridge: Polity Press.

Benedict, R. (1946). *The chrysanthemum and the sword: Patterns of Japanese culture*. Boston, MA: Houghton Mifflin.

Bluebond-Langner, M. (1978). *The private worlds of dying children*. Princeton, NJ: Princeton University Press.

Bluebond-Langner, M., Perkel, D., & Goertzel, T. (1991). Paediatric cancer patients' peer relationships: The impact of an oncology camp experience. *Journal of Psychosocial Oncology, 19*(2), 67–80.

Brannen, J. & O'Brien, M. (1995). Childhood and the sociological gaze: Paradigms and paradoxes. *Sociology, 29*(4), 729–738.

Christensen, P. (1993). The social construction of help among Danish children: The intentional act and the actual content. *Sociology of Health and Illness. A Journal of Medical Sociology, 15*(4), 488–502.

Christensen, P. (1999). *Towards an anthropology of childhood sickness: An ethnographic study of Danish school children.* Unpublished doctoral dissertation, University of Hull

Christensen, P. (2000a). Childhood and the cultural constitution of vulnerable bodies. In A. Prout (Ed.), *The body, childhood and society* (pp. 38–59). Basingstoke: Macmillan Press/New York: St Martin's Press.

Christensen, P. (2000b). *Why more quality time is not on the top of children's lists: The qualities of time, content and context.* Paper presented at a meeting at the National Family and Parenting Institute, London, October.

Clarke, L. (1996). Demographic change and the family situation of children. In J. Brannen & M. O'Brien (Eds.), *Children in families: Research and policy* (pp. 66–83). London: Falmer Press.

Connolly, P. (1998). *Racism, gender identities and young children.* London: Routledge.

Cook-Cumperz, J., Corsaro, W., & Streek, J. (Eds.) (1986). *Children's worlds and children's languages.* Berlin: Mouton de Gruyter.

Corsaro, W. (1992). Interpretive reproduction in children's peer cultures. *Social Psychology Quarterly, 55,* 160–177.

Corsaro, W. (1997). *The sociology of childhood.* Thousand Oaks, CA: Pine Forge Press.

Crawford, R. (1994). The boundaries of the self and the unhealthy other: Reflections on health, culture and AIDS. *Social Science and Medicine, 38*(10), 1347–1365.

Creighton, C. (1999). The rise and decline of the male breadwinner family in Britain. *Cambridge Journal of Economics, 23,* 519–542.

Curt, B. (1994). *Textuality and tectonics: Troubling social and psychological science.* Buckingham: Open University Press.

Denzin, N. (1977). *Childhood socialization.* San Francisco, CA: Jossey-Bass.

Durkheim, E. (1950[1903]). *The rules of sociological method.* Chicago: Free Press.

Dyer, R. (1993). *The matter of images: Essays on representations.* London: Routledge.

Edwards, R. (2002). *Children, home and school: Regulation, autonomy or connection?* London: RoutledgeFalmer.

Elkin, F. (1960). *The child and society.* New York: Random House.

Ennew, J. (1986). *The sexual exploitation of children.* Cambridge: Polity.

Ennew, J. (1994). *The environmental health of working children.* Paper presented at the Sociology of Childhood Seminar, Brunel, University of West London.

European Commission. (1996). *The Demographic situation in the European Union – 1995.* European Commission: Brussels.

Fabian, J. (1983). *Time and the other: How anthropology makes its object.* New York: Columbia University Press.

Fallon, K. (1990). An involuntary workforce. *Community Care, 4*(January), 12–13.

Frønes, I. (1993). Changing childhoods. *Childhood, 1,* 1.

Frønes, I. (1995). *Among peers: On the meaning of peers in the process of socialization.* Oslo: Scandanavian University Press.

Frønes, I. (1997). *Children of the post-industrial family* (mimeo). Oslo: Department of Sociology and Human Geography, University of Oslo.

Furedi, F. (1997). *The culture of fear: Risk taking and the morality of low expectations*. London: Cassell.

Giddens, A. (1979). *The central problems of social theory*. London: Macmillan.

Giesecke, H. (1985). *Das Ende der Erziehung (The End of Education)*. Stuttgart: Kiett-Cotta-Verlag.

Hardman, C. (1973). Can there be an anthropology of children? *Journal of the Anthropology Society Oxford*, 4(1), 85–99.

Hastrup, K. (1988). Kultur som analytisk begreb (culture as an analytical concept). In H. Hauge & H. Horstbøll (Eds.), *Kulturbegrebets kulturhistorie* (The cultural history of the concept of culture) (Kulturstudier 1), (pp. 120–139). Aarhus: Aarhus Universitetsforlag.

Hillman, M., Adams, J., & Whitelegg, J. (1990). *One false move: A study of children's independent mobility*. London: Policy Studies Institute.

Home Office. (1998). *Supporting parents: A consultation document*. London.

Hutchby, I. & Moran-Ellis, J. (Eds.) (1998). *Children and social competence: Arenas of action*. London: Falmer Press.

Ingelby, D. (1986). Development in a social context. In M. Richards & P. Light (Eds.), *Children of social worlds* (pp. 297–317). Cambridge: Polity Press.

James, A. (1993). *Childhood identities: Self and social relationships in the experience of the child*. Edinburgh: Edinburgh University Press.

James, A. & Prout, A. (1990/97). *Constructing and reconstructing childhood: Contemporary issues in the sociological study of childhood*. London: Falmer Press.

James, A., Jenks, C., & Prout, A. (1998). *Theorizing childhood*. Cambridge: Polity Press.

Jenks, C. (1982). *The sociology of childhood. Essential reading*. London: Batsford.

Jenks, C. (1996a). The postmodern child. In J. Brannen, & M. O'Brien (Eds.), *Children in families: Research and policy* (pp. 13–25). London: Falmer Press.

Jenks, C. (1996b). *Childhood*. London: Routledge.

Lee, N. (1998). Towards an immature sociology. *Sociological Review*, 46(2), 459–482.

Levine, R., Levine, S., & Leiderman, P.H. (1994). *Child care and culture: Lessons from Africa*. Cambridge: Cambridge University Press.

Mackay, R. (1973). Conceptions of children and models of socialization. In H.P. Dreitzel (Ed.), *Childhood and socialization* (pp. 27–43). London: Macmillan.

Matthews, H. & Limb, M. (2000). *Children and the street*. (ESRC Children 5–16 Research Programme Briefing). Retrieved 29 June 2001 from: http://www.esrc.ac.uk/curprog.html.

Mayall, B. (1996). *Children, health and the social order*. Buckingham: Open University Press.

Mead, M. (1968[1930]). *Growing up in New Guinea*. Harmondsworth: Penguin.

Mead, M. (1955). Theoretical setting. In M. Mead & M. Wolfstein (Eds.), *Childhood in contemporary culture* (pp. 3–20). Chicago: University of Chicago Press.

Moore, H. (1988). *Feminism and anthropology*. Cambridge: Polity Press.

Morrow, V. (1996). Rethinking childhood dependency: Children's contributions to the domestic economy. *Sociological Review*, 44(1), 58–77.

Nader, L. (1981). The vertical slice: Hierarchies and children. In G.M. Britain & R. Cohen (Eds.), *Hierarchy and society: Anthropological perspectives on bureaucracy* (pp. 31–44). Philadelphia, PA: Ishi.

Nasman, E. (1994). Individualization and institutionalization of children. In J. Qvortrup, M. Bardy, G. Sgritta, & H. Wintersberger (Eds.), *Childhood matters: Social theory, practice and politic* (pp. 165–188). Aldershot: Avebury.

Nieuwenhuys, O. (1994). *Children's life worlds: Gender, welfare and labor in the developing world*. London: Routledge.

O'Brien, M. (1999). *Chaperoned and autonomous childhoods: Difference and diversity in children's families.* Paper presented to the ESRC Seminar on Postmodern Kinship, Leeds University, December.

Office for National Statistics (1991). *Social Trends 29.* London: The Stationery Office.

Orellana, M.F., Thorne, B., Chee, A., & Lam, W.S.E. (2001). Transnational childhoods: The participation of children in processes of family migration. *Social Problems, 48*(4), 572–91.

Pollard, A. (1985). *The social world of the primary school.* London: Holt, Rhinehart and Winston.

Pollard, A. & Filer, A. (1996). *The social world of children's learning.* London: Cassell.

Prout, A. (1986). 'Wet children' and 'little actresses': Going sick in primary school. *Sociology of Health and Illness, 8*(2), 111–136.

Prout, A. (1989). Sickness as a dominant symbol in life course transitions: An illustrated theoretical framework. *Sociology of Health and Illness, 11*(4), 336–359.

Prout, A. (2000). Childhood bodies: Construction, agency and hybridity. In A. Prout (Ed.), *The body, childhood and society* (pp. 1–18). Basingstoke: Macmillan Press/ New York: St Martin's Press.

Prout, A. (2001). Representing children: reflections on the Children 5–16 Programme, *Children and Society, 15,* 193–201.

Prout, A. & James, A. (1997 [1990]). A new paradigm for the sociology of childhood? Provenance, promise and problems. In A. James & A. Prout (Eds.), *Constructing and reconstructing childhood* (pp. 7–33). London: Falmer Press.

Qvortrup, J. (1991). *Childhood as a social phenomenon: An Introduction to a series of national reports* (Eurosocial Reports, Vol. 36). Vienna: European Centre.

Qvortrup, J. (2000). Macroanalysis of childhood. In P. Christensen & A. James (Eds.), *Research with children: Perspectives and practice* (pp. 77–97). London: Falmer Press.

Qvortrup, J., Bardy, M., Sgritta, G., & Wintersberger, H. (1994). (Eds.). *Childhood matters: Social theory, practice and politics.* Aldershot: Avebury.

Reynolds, P. (1996). *Traditional healers and children in Zimbabwe.* Athens, Ohio: Ohio University Press.

Rodgers, G. & Standing, G. (Eds.). (1981). *Child work, poverty and underdevelopment.* Geneva: International Labor Organization.

Sgritta, G. (1994). The generational division of welfare: Equity and conflict. In J. Qvortrup, M. Bardy, G. Sgritta, & H. Wintersberger (Eds.), *Childhood matters: social theory, practice and politics* (pp. 335–362). Aldershot: Avebury.

Shildkrout, E. (1978). Roles of children in urban Kano. In J.S. La Fontaine (Ed.), *Sex and age as principles of social differentiation* (pp. 109–39). London: Academic Press.

Shweder, R.A. (1979). Rethinking culture and personality theory. Part 1: A critical examination of two classical postulates. *Ethos, 7*(3), 255–278.

Smith, F. (2000). *Out of school care* (ESRC Children 5–16 Research Programme Briefing). Retrieved 29 June 2001 from: http://www.esrc.ac.uk/curprog.html.

Solberg, A. (1994). *Negotiating age: Empirical investigations and textual representations of children's everyday lives.* Stockholm: Nordic Institute for Studies in Urban and Regional Planning.

Thorne, B. (1987). Re-visioning women and social change: Where are the children? *Gender and Society, 1,* 85–109.

Thorne, B. (1993). *Gender play: Girls and boys in school.* Piscataway, NJ: Rutgers University Press.

Valentine, G. (1996). Children should be seen and not heard? The role of children in public space. *Urban Geography, 17*(3), 205–220.

Whiting, J.W.M. & Child, I. (1953). *Child training and personality: A cross-cultural study.* New Haven, CT: Yale University Press.

Woodhead, M. & Faulkner, D. (2000). Subjects, objects or participants: Dilemmas of psychological research with children. In P. Christensen & A. James (Eds.), *Research with children: Perspectives and practice* (pp. 9–35). London: Falmer Press.

Wyness, M.G. (1999). Childhood, agency and educational reform. *Childhood, 6*(3), 353–368.

4 Ethical Considerations in Researching Children's Experiences

Malcolm Hill

Despite the wealth of research that has been carried out in relation to children, until very recently surprisingly few publications were available that discussed research methods with children, though individual papers usually provide considerable details about the studies concerned. Ethical issues have been even more rarely reported, outside the specialist area of medical research involving invasive or painful procedures (Grodin & Glantz, 1994).

At last the dearth of written guidance for the budding or experienced researcher is coming to an end (see Alderson & Morrow, 2004[1]). At the same time, approaches to children's research are diversifying. The public prominence given to children's rights and the fast-developing social studies of childhood have challenged conventional adult thinking about children, in the process placing children's perspectives in the foreground (Christensen & James, 2000; Holloway & Valentine, 2000; Jenks, 1996; Mayall, 1994, 2000; Qvortrup, Bardy, Sgritta, & Wintersberger, 1994). This entails a reappraisal of appropriate ways of carrying out research with children. Understanding children's own priorities and interpretations of what is important to them in their everyday lives is no longer a narrow, isolated alleyway, but is becoming part of the main avenue of empirical study (Hill, Davis, Prout & Tisdall, 2004; Morrow & Richards, 1996). Therefore, this chapter reviews ethical and other considerations that are particularly relevant to qualitative research on children's subjective experiences in natural contexts. In the process, it examines dilemmas as much as providing clear guidelines.

This review concentrates on research that involves children themselves reporting or displaying their experiences in some way. This should not be taken to devalue other methods and data sources. Understanding is enhanced by triangulation of theoretical orientations, methods and perspectives (Brannen, 1992; McKendrick, 1996), although it is important to be clear about the distinctive assumptions and purposes of different approaches. Nevertheless, the United Nations Convention on the Rights of the Child and children's legislation emphasize the importance of enabling children to express their opinions on important matters and decisions affecting themselves.

Also several studies have shown how adult perceptions of what children think, do or need may differ from what children themselves say (Clarke, Craig, & Glendenning, 1996;. Sweeting, 2001; Triseliotis, Borland, Hill, & Lambert, 1995).

Until the mid-1990s, children's research was dominated by the positivist paradigm with its emphasis on measurement, abstraction and statistical relationships. By contrast, studies involving adults had for a long time been influenced by social constructivist and qualitative approaches (see, for example, Bell & Newby, 1977; LaRossa & Wolf, 1985). This links to a theme that will permeate this chapter – how far are ethical considerations in research with children different from or the same as those which apply to adults? A wider debate has been taking place concerning how different – or not – children are from adults anyway. The question is given edge by recent critiques of developmental psychology by sociologists analysing childhood. They have asserted that, for too long, the developmental paradigm has portrayed children as deficient adults rather than competent human beings in their own right (Hill & Tisdall, 1997; James & Prout, 1990; Qvortrup et al., 1994).

How Different is Researching Children's Experiences?

The question of how far researching with children is different from or similar to researching with adults relates to wider perceptions of childhood and adulthood and the relations between generations (Mayall, 2002). So-called 'child-centreed' approaches, which emphasize the distinctiveness of children, have been criticized for devaluing and patronizing children (Bury, 1993; Mauthner, 1993; Mayall, 1994). In recent years, common developmental assumptions about children have been questioned in both sociology and psychology. In particular children's capacities for understanding have been re-evaluated upwards and some of the problems identified in adult–child communication laid more at the door of adults for failing to adapt to children's perspectives (Donaldson, 1978; Garbarino, Stott, & The Erikson Institute, 1992). Adults may have difficulty in empathizing and taking account of children's priorities and sense of time:

> Is there any one who can recover the experience of childhood, not merely with the memory of what he did and what happened to him, what he liked and disliked … but with an intimate penetration, a revived consciousness of what he felt like then – when it was so long from one Midsummer to another. (George Eliot, 1903: 2)

It is an important tenet among some researchers that they should constantly question preconceptions of children in general or particular 'categories' of children, in order not to impose these ideas on the study (Christensen, 2004; Davis, Watson, & Cunningham-Burley, 2000). While there are dangers of overemphasizing differences between adults and children, some do need to be recognized.

Differences

The main relevant differences between children and adult
to ability and power. There are well-demonstrated distin
obvious differences between young children and adolesce
competence and their capacity to express and understand
systemic interactions (Berti & Bombi, 1988; Matthews, 1!
qualification, though, is that children vary greatly at any _
widely in their development between one age and another. The language
used between adults and younger children needs to be adapted to the
linguistic understandings of the latter, including checks and repetition
(Brodzinsky, Singer, & Braff, 1984). This has implications for explanations
about research and obtaining consent, for instance.

A second factor is that of power, which is closely linked to status. Adults
are ascribed authority over children, who often find it difficult to dissent,
disagree or say things which they fear may be unacceptable. Except for large
adolescents, children are physically weaker and usually have a limited range
of coping repertoires. Many children are not used to being asked their views
or may feel that their views are often disregarded by key adults like parents,
teachers or others (Cloke, 1995). This may be particularly true of certain
children, such as those who have been abused or who have disabilities.
Consequently some practitioners and writers have depicted children as an
oppressed social group. In order to empower children, it is argued that
research should start from the perspective of the children and involve them
actively in the whole research process. Parallels have been drawn with participatory and emancipation approaches to research with poor, marginalized
adults (Hall, 2000; O'Kane, 2000). However, it is an oversimplification to
suggest that all power resides with a researcher and none with respondents,
even when the latter are children (Humphries & Martin, 2000).

The combination of perceived incompetence and weakness means that
children are seen as especially *vulnerable* to persuasion, adverse influence
and indeed harm – in research as in the rest of life. Hence it is particularly
important that children are not pressurized into taking part in studies whose
implications have not been clearly explained to them. The interpersonal style
adopted by researchers and the settings for research should aim to reduce
and not reinforce children's inhibitions and desire to please, which will otherwise limit the amount, value and validity of what they say. Researchers
can seek to minimize the authority image they convey, for instance, by
using informal language or sitting in a position and at a level comfortable
for the child (Alderson, 1995). Nevertheless the differences in social status
(see Table 4.1) cannot be avoided, so Mayall (2000) and Christensen (2004)
argue that the influence of children's subordinate position should be taken
into account, rather than ignored or disguised. Seiber (1992) points out that
while younger children are more vulnerable in most respects (for example,
as regards coping with stress), older children tend to have heightened sensi-
tivities about self-image, social evaluation and privacy.

.1   **Possible bases for differentiating children from adults**

npetence	Power	Vulnerability
nderstanding	Size and strength	Physical and cognitive weakness
Memory	Social status	Openness to influence
Language skills	Legal status	Dependence
Use of nonverbal communication	Institutional position	Trust

Similarities

There are many similarities between children and adults, though sometimes these may express themselves differently. Adults too can feel incompetent and powerless, because of the language and status of researchers or because of characteristics of the adult, including learning difficulties. Like any adult informants, children are the best informed people about their own lives and cultures, so have an expert role in that respect (James, Jenks, & Prout, 1998).

There is little difference between adults and children as regards memory loss and recall. Both are helped by recognition aids (Garbarino et al., 1992; Spencer & Flin, 1991). The competence of older children in research is as good as adults (Scott, 1997, 2000). Modes of communication do not always need to be specifically child-oriented, since many children can verbalize as articulately as adults, provided the context allows them to do so. Some child respondents, like some adult respondents, can encapsulate effectively in a few words what it might take researchers several paragraphs to convey. Thus one discussion group in our study of children's wellbeing (Hill, Laybourn, & Borland, 1995) borrowed a phrase from the British Highway Code to sum up what they wanted from adults: *Stop; look; and listen.*

Children and adults have similar rights to be informed about the nature and purpose of the research; understand researchers' intentions; to feel confident that the study is worthwhile; and to know what will happen to the findings. The need to motivate participation applies to everyone – both children and adults are more likely to participate if they feel respected and interested.

In many ways the similarities between children and adults are greater than the differences, so that much of this chapter could apply equally well to adults, though in some respects requiring modification for children.

Differentiation of Children

At the risk of stating the obvious, children are not all the same. They include babes in arms and teenagers who may tower over some researchers; girls and boys; children from different social, ethnic and religious backgrounds; able-bodied children and those with physical and sensory impairments; a wide range of intellectual abilities and educational competence; children living with their families, in substitute care or on the streets. Moreover, children with a shared characteristic like disability or being excluded from school have diverse and fluid contexts and experiences (Davis et al., 2000). As we shall see later, this diversity has ethical as well as methodological implications, particularly with regard to the danger that sampling and method choices may exclude the viewpoints of certain groups. Davis (1998) argues that it is important for researchers to be reflexive, question their own assumptions about children and adapt to each individual, rather than assume there are universal answers to the ethical and methodological issues of researching with children.

Ethical Principles and Research

Ethical issues in nonmedical research with children have received very little attention until recently. Training in this area is usually minimal and, partly as a result, few researchers (including myself) could claim to be ethically pure in the sense of always following all the good guidelines. Limited time, personnel and money can also constrain researchers' capacity to act as ideals suggest, but are perhaps too easily used as excuses to cut corners. Morrow and Richards (1996) emphasized that ethical considerations need to be borne in mind throughout the research process. They are not simply a preliminary stage or hurdle to be got out of the way at the beginning.

A small number of key principles underpin an ethical approach to research. These include respect for persons, equity, nondiscrimination and 'beneficence', that is, avoiding harm and protecting the weak (Butler, 2000; Eby, 2000; Graue & Walsh, 1998; Seiber, 1992). These principles can be developed and expressed as a set of rights: to self-determination, privacy, dignity, anonymity, confidentiality, fair treatment and protection from discomfort or harm. A useful framework incorporating these rights was devised by Alderson (1995) with respect to research that involves listening to children. Based on discussion with many researchers, she identified ten ethical topics. She also formulated eighty associated questions – rather too many to be considered here, so a simplified version is provided in Table 4.2.

These may be grouped for more detailed consideration, as follows:

1. involvement of children in the research;
2. consent and choice;
3. possible harm or distress;
4. privacy and confidentiality.

Involvement of Children in the Research

Children as active participants

Children's role as researchers can take a number of forms (Alderson, 2000; West, 1999), where the children:

Table 4.2   Key ethical issues in research with children (Based on Alderson, 1995)

	Topic	Sample questions
1.	Research purpose	Is the research in children's interests?
2.	Costs and benefits	What are the costs and risks for children of doing or not doing the research? What are the potential benefits?
3.	Privacy and confidentiality	What choices do children have about being contacted, agreement to take part, withdrawing, confidentiality?
4.	Inclusion and exclusion	Who is included, who is excluded? Why? What efforts are made to include disadvantaged groups (e.g. those with physical impairments, homeless young people)?
5.	Funding	Are funds 'tainted'? Are resources sufficient? In what circumstances should children be recompensed?
6.	Involvement and accountability	To what extent can children or carers contribute to the research aim and design? What safeguards and checks are in place?
7.	Information	Are the aims and implications clearly explained? Is written documentation available in other languages?
8.	Consent	How well are rights to refuse cooperation explained and respected? Are informal 'pressures' used? What is the correct balance of parental and child consent?
9.	Dissemination	Do participants know about and comment on the findings? How wide is the audience for the research – academics, practitioners, policy makers, the public, research participants, etc.?
10.	Impact on children	How does the research affect children through its impact on thinking, policy and practice? Are children's own perspectives accurately conveyed?

1. conduct interviews from schedules developed by adults;
2. are involved in developing research questions and schedules;
3. help determine issues to be researched;
4. participate in analyzing and presenting findings;
5. decide on action to be taken.

It should be borne in mind that very few studies enable adult users to contribute to the research aims, design, fieldwork, analysis or reporting. Examples

with children are even rarer. Both the UN Convention on the Rights of the Child and current thinking about participatory research and consultation suggest researchers should seek to maximise opportunities for children's input at each stage.

Nearly all research on children is initiated by adults, with aims set by adults. Increasingly, though still exceptionally, children are asked to be co-researchers. Sometimes 'children' have carried out surveys as part of a formal research project, but these are usually young adults of 16–17 years (Alderson, 1995; West, 1999). Davies and Dotchin (1995) described how children helped identify key categories and develop questionnaires in their study of services offered by the NSPCC in England. Ennew (1994) gave examples of children helping other children to produce data and assist in the interpretation of drawings and maps produced by street children. In a study of children looked after in public care, a group of young people assisted with the selection and processing of audiotaped comments (Thomas & O'Kane, 1998b). Alderson (2000) observed how many young people are nowadays more skilled at data gathering and analysis than in the past as a result of involvement in investigations for school or neighborhood projects. A striking example of assuming a role that is normally confined to adults occurred when a 9-year-old presented a paper to the Royal Geographical Society, giving her interpretation of maps drawn by her school friends (Valentine, 1999).

On a more restricted scale, research may give children as respondents choices about which themes to explore, within a pre-set research topic. In this limited way, children may contribute to the research agenda. Our study of children's wellbeing sought to explore children's own definitions of wellbeing and to pursue with them what particular groups or individuals they themselves stated were the most important aspects (Borland, Laybourn, Hill, & Brown, 1998). A study of decision-making for looked after children shifted its focus from formal meetings to everyday situations, in response to what children said (O'Kane, 2000).

Sampling, representativeness and inclusion

Qualitative research rarely aims at statistical representativeness. Nevertheless, qualitative studies do often concern 'typical' children with a view to offering some kind of generalization about childhood in general or children in particular circumstances. Many young people themselves believe that research aiming to tap their views should be as inclusive as possible. For this reason, some favour use of questionnaires over apparently more engaging methods (Borland, Hill, Laybourn, & Stafford, 2001). Commonly the practical ease of access to some children rather than others may mean that the voices of certain categories are undervalued or overlooked, such as those with communication difficulties.

School is a convenient point of access, but this means that school-based studies may omit those who are excluded or absent. The viewpoints of minority ethnic children may be downplayed when their numbers are small or they hesitate to be open with white researchers (Barn, Sinclair, & Ferdinand, 1997). Despite increasing policy and practice efforts to deal with disabled children more inclusively, they are often absent from research other than that focusing on disability. Additional efforts may be needed to locate or communicate with children with certain disabilities (Alderson & Goodey, 1996; Begley, 2000; Detheridge, 2000; Stalker, 2002), though Davis and Watson (2000) suggest that spending time with them is the most vital requisite. Much of the currently popular trend to consult with young people and set up school and youth councils largely ignores younger children.

Consent and Choice

Choice about taking part

Good practice and the Helsinki Declaration about biomedical research indicate that the informed consent of children should be obtained, provided they have the understanding to do so. Having the opportunity to give or deny informed consent is not only a right in relation to research which children share with adults, but also contributes to their wellbeing, through giving respect for their sense of control (Weithorn & Sherer, 1994). It is helpful to regard obtaining and giving consent not as a once only event, but as a continuous process, with opportunities to withdraw at any stage, either temporarily or permanently (Harker, 2002). Children may also require reassurance that they or their family will not lose access to a service if they decline to cooperate with research (Cree, Kay, & Tisdall, 2002).

At what age are children able to give informed consent? This will vary from child to child, though clearly a tiny baby cannot and nearly all 17-year-olds can. An assessment of children's appraisals of the implications of medical research revealed that 14-year-olds were as able as adults to make judgments. This was less true of 9-year-olds in certain respects (for example, they took account of only some of the significant factors), but they were still able to show 'a surprising degree of competence' (Mason & McCall Smith, 1994: 372). Younger children may well need more careful explanation and discussion of potential outcomes. It is wrong to assume that even young children are incompetent to assent (treating them as a class). Instead an individual assessment should be made (Weithorn & Sherer, 1994). It is generally accepted that a child or adult should give positive consent, not simply fail to register dissent.

Ideally consent should be obtained in person from the child following the presentation of written and verbal information about the research and its implications, and after opportunities to discuss queries and concerns by the child. In time-limited research, it may not be practicable to visit children twice, first to discuss consent and then to carry out the research. Then it may be necessary to rely on written consent, which can be confirmed when the researcher arrives to see the child or group (Hill, Laybourn, & Borland, 1996).

An inherent tension exists between the desire to give maximum information and ensure choice is freely given, and the wish to maximize participation in the research. As with adults, there are often sizeable numbers of people who are willing to take part in research or are at least accepting of it, but who will not necessarily take active steps (like returning a consent form). This can raise dilemmas about how often and how persuasively to send reminders or use intermediaries, which are familiar ways of reducing the 'refusal' rate.

To be valid, consent needs to be appropriately informed. Thus children should be told such things as:

1. the aims of the research;
2. what time and commitment is required;
3. who will know the results;
4. whether there will be feedback;
5. whether confidentiality is promised.

A recent trend has been to develop attractively presented and illustrated leaflets or packs, with a distinctive logo that can also be used in other communications, such as 'thank you' letters or summary findings for the children. A tape-recorded explanation of the study and photos of researchers can help prepare children for direct contact. These are also accessible for children who have difficulties with reading (Thomas & O'Kane, 1998b; Thomas, Beckford, Lowe & Murch, 1999). Even pre-school children may be given very simple explanations, for example, that the researcher is going to play with and watch them to see what they do and like (Fine & Sandstrom, 1988). Information about the research and consent forms may need to be translated into other languages or forms of communication, for example, Braille (Alderson & Goodey, 1996).

A core ethical issue for both adults and children is the extent to which it is permissible to hide or disguise part or even the whole purpose of the research. Covert or semi-covert research is often seen as unethical because it goes against the principle of informed consent, but some researchers in some circumstances feel this is justified either to avoid pre-judging or over-influencing data provided by children or to avoid upsetting children. For example, James (1993) wished to explore processes of stigma and rejection among children as part of a wider study of their relationships and cultures, but felt it was unfair to the children to make this aspect explicit. Fine and Sandstrom (1988) distinguish between explicit explanation, shallow cover (partial explanation) and deep cover (secrecy about the research purpose) in relation to participant observation. They point out the dangers arising from explicit explanation that children will tell the researcher what they think he or she wants to hear (social expectancy effect) and the risk of putting the children on guard. The ethical problem with shallow cover is that it can gain consent from people who would decline if they realized the full implications of the study.

It is usually seen as legitimate to point out potential benefits arising from the research – indeed Alderson (1995) suggests that one requirement for giving consent is being reassured that the research is worthwhile. The benefits may not accrue directly to the participants, but to other children. It is common to claim that research will help improve services for children. When does explanation shade over into pressure? As we have seen, it can be hard to say 'no' to a more powerful adult. A few researchers have rehearsed with children how they can say 'no' (Farmer & Owen, 1995). It is also valuable as adults to make clear to children, that they can decline to answer and can withdraw at any time or from any part of the research (Marchant, Jones, Julyan, & Giles, 1999; Morrow, 2000; Thomas & O'Kane, 1998a).

It may be appropriate for a child to have an independent adviser or advocate to help decide (Nicholson, 1986). If a child gives consent but seems uncertain, then researchers may explore the matter further or even suggest the child does not take part (Ireland & Holloway, 1996; Mahon, Glendenning, Clarke, & Craig, 1996).

Adult gatekeepers

Often an adult is the first point of contact to gain access to ask children's consent. Agreement by parents or other relevant adults is usually seen as necessary. This results partly from a recognition of the legal status of children as dependants and partly from concern about children's vulnerability. In practical terms, it may be hard to make contact with children unless parents, schools or local authority departments authorize this (Borland et al., 1998; Heptinstall, 2000).

Although statutory and case law are available in the UK about children and young people's consent to medical treatment, uncertainty remains about if and when parental consent is needed for involvement in research (Alderson, 1995; Nicholson, 1986). Based in part on medical parallels, it is suggested that competence is a more important factor than age. Drawing on the Human Rights Act 1998, Masson (2000) argued that a child who is able to understand the nature and consequences of the research has the capacity to decide about participation without the need for parental permission. More cautiously the British Psychological Society recommended that parental consent should be sought in relation to children aged under sixteen (Morrow & Richards, 1996). In the USA, federal regulations similarly embody expectations that the consent of both parents and child should be sought and obtained separately (King & Churchill, 2001). Parental permission may be waived in two sorts of situation: first, when parents have acted irresponsibly or abusively towards the child and, second, when it is impractical to locate parents and the research will not adversely affect the child (Seiber, 1992).

The meaning of parental consent is not always clear. Are parents exercising their judgment to act in their child's interests? Might they simply substitute their own wishes for that of the child? Should they give guidance to the child but leave the choice up to the child? Should or can the researcher affect the processes by which the parent forms a judgment? It can be particularly difficult to obtain agreement to talk with children about subjects that are sensitive and potentially stigmatizing for their parents or other significant adults, as in studies of children affected by parental mental health problems or HIV (Cree et al., 2002).

When a parent refuses to give permission for their child to take part in research, that is usually seen as the end of the matter, at least for children up to their mid-teens. Yet legislation in many countries indicates that children of any age should be able to express their views, provided they are mature enough to do so, and to have their opinions taken into account. Is it fair that a parent can debar a child who might wish to take part? Likewise, some researchers have questioned the entitlement of teachers, health professionals and others to prevent access to children who may themselves be willing to assist (Alderson & Goodey, 1996; Hood, Kelley, & Mayall, 1996), though Masson (2000) acknowledged the protective duties of caring professionals.

Conversely if an adult has given prior approval, it may be hard for a child to say no, as when a parent agrees for an individual child or a teacher is willing for his or her class to participate. Children may then take part reluctantly or contribute in a minimal way (Hill and Morton, 2003; Morrow, 2000). When a child is noncommunicative in interview, it can be hard to know whether this represents shyness, intimidation or simply resentment at having to take part in the research.

Gifts, payments and favours

Opinions differ about the desirability of giving children money or small presents. Some view this negatively as inducement or bribery. Alternatively it can be seen as fair recompense. If adults in the same study are given payment for this reason, then treating children likewise shows that they are equally valued (Scott, 2000). Sometimes researchers make a payment after the event as a token of thanks, but give no prior warning to avoid the danger of this affecting consent (Mahon et al., 1996). Unannounced rewards do not count as incentives for the individuals receiving them, but if the practice becomes general and well known, then others may be swayed to take part by material considerations. On occasion, gifts have been provided as an explicit encouragement to take part. Punch (2002) observed that the prospect of a reward was useful in gaining the cooperation of young people in residential care.

For participant observers and practitioner researchers, the researcher may give practical help or provide fun activities to gain trust and cooperation. This raises questions about manipulation and unfairness, since those not involved in the research do not get treats (Fine & Sandstrom, 1988).

Choice about researcher, location and methods

We know from research on ethnic identity and child protection, that children often have a preference as regards the gender and ethnic background of adults they wish to confide in. They may unwittingly be more forthcoming with someone they identify as being more similar and empathic. Not many studies have the resources to offer such choice. Williamson and Butler (1995), both white men, checked with female and black or Asian children in their study. All made it clear, apparently, that they wanted to proceed, since they believed the main consideration was to know if the researcher could grasp their perspective.

Sometimes children can be offered a choice of location, methods and whether or not they are accompanied (Jones, 2000). For example, some young carers preferred to be interviewed in settings like a burger bar rather than be seen at home (Mahon et al., 1996). Interviews at home allow for more informality and give the child an element of control over the interview environment (Laybourn, Brown, & Hill, 1996; Mayall, 2000), though it may seem more intrusive to some children than contact at school or a clinic. A neutral territory may be desirable and offer the researcher more scope to adapt to different children (McAuley, 1996). Prior contact with children can also help ensure that interviews are made at suitable times (Ireland & Holloway, 1996). It is customary to ask children about the use of tape-recorders and to offer to play back any part they wish (Bentley, 1987).

'Resistance'

Probably most people who have carried out research with children will recall a group where one individual contributed nothing despite repeated invitations or an individual interview when almost every answer was monosyllabic. Were such young people expressing their wish not to be involved, which should be respected? How far is the researcher entitled to probe, to change tack in an attempt to gain interest, to reflect on the communication difficulties? Are these appropriate mechanisms for facilitating communication or pressures which contravene the child's rights? As Williamson and Butler remarked 'Quite how one copes with the "dunnos", "all rights", "not sures" and "Oks", *we* dunno' (1995: 69).

Possible Harm or Distress

There is a considerable medical research literature which deals with the potential for physical damage to adults or children from research. This is not likely to apply in social research, although consideration may need to be given to the possibility of accidents. What are the ethical or insurance implications if a child falls down stairs or has an accident with research equipment during fieldwork?

Sadly, an important consideration has to be – might *an adult with abusive intentions* use research as a means of access to children, as have for instance a small minority of residential carers and youth workers. The literature gives examples of apparently bona fide researchers putting themselves in situations which did or might invoke suspicion. Fine and Sandstrom (1988) cited the case of Horan (1987) who invited two boys to his house to watch a break-dancing video. One of the boys' parents called the police, who investigated and so he abandoned his 'folklore' study. Certain geographers have asked children to show them secret play areas and routeways, as far as I know with the legitimate aim of understanding children's use of space and territorial range (Hart, 1979; Moore, 1986). Many will be familiar with the fascinating insights obtained into children's culture by hanging around playgrounds and talking with children there (for example, Opie, 1993). With current high public consciousness about risk and child protection, many would have qualms about the potential for children in such circumstances to be initiated into abuse. The risk of exploitation exists in any context where an adult researcher is alone with a child. Commonly, researchers are not allowed to be alone with an individual child in schools. Only recently have British universities begun to require all new research staff to have a criminal records check.

It is to be hoped that the chances of physical harm are slight, but *emotional harm* is a more likely risk. Only rarely does research that sets out to upset children, as in the 'Strange Situation' used in the development of attachment theory (Roberts & Wellard, 1997; Woodhead & Faulkener, 2000). In some experimental research children have been deceived and distressed, for example, asked to take care of kittens then distracted and the kitten removed (cited in Koocher & Keith-Speigel, 1994). More commonly, research on sensitive topics like divorce may lead to distress, even resulting in a child crying. Citing examples of this, Levin (1995) stressed the need for care and skill on the part of the researcher not to press a child too far.

Some research studies aim to understand children's experiences of traumatic situations – for example, their intra-familial abuse (Roberts & Taylor, 1993; Westcott & Davies, 1996). Since the children may well have already experienced multiple interviews and examinations as part of a child abuse investigation, such research might subject some children to further distress by having to recall events yet again with a stranger. Other young people will simply be fed up with another repeat of previous accounts. Sometimes key adults can form helpful appraisals of which children may be at risk and so should not take part, but they may be over-protective and exclude children who would like to take part in a study. Children themselves should be involved in the decision but may not anticipate the repercussions. Whatever may be the processes for obtaining agreement for children to take part in research, the children who eventually participate may not be typical. The presence of a parent or other attachment figure may be desirable to reassure a child (Koocher & Keith-Speigel, 1994), but this may inhibit the child or influence their account in a particular direction. Alternatively it may give the child confidence to speak freely.

Several studies have found it useful to adapt *therapeutic techniques* for research purposes, especially for pre-teen children. It is important to heed the warning by Fratter (1996) that researchers should be careful not to 'open up painful or distressing areas' (p. 75), especially in one-off contacts, unless it is clear that follow-up support is available to a child. For some children it may be beneficial to talk over areas of concern, but others may be very upset by having otherwise suppressed emotions disturbed.

If a child becomes upset, the researcher is beholden to offer immediate comfort, but it would not be appropriate to offer longer-term help or counseling. It may be valuable to have available a specialist, though in most instances it is likely that a child can identify a person known to them that they would rather confide in or seek help from. It may be appropriate to give details of ChildLine or equivalent confidential telephone helplines. Some ethical committees insist on the availability of a specialist.

A further possibility is that a child will *disclose an incident of abuse* during the course of an interview, resulting in a need to inform parents or other adults. Opinions differ on whether revelations of abuse should automatically lead to reporting the situation to the relevant authorities (Runyan, 2000), but it is generally agreed that the implications should be carefully discussed with the child before any action is taken. This links with the issue of confidentiality, considered in the next section.

An issue in naturalistic research concerns the obligations of the researcher when children do things unprompted by the research which may *harm themselves or others*. Researchers studying violent gangs have generally refrained from joining in, but have not sought to stop the incidents (Fine & Sandstrom, 1988). Many people might think that the researcher should intervene to stop a fight or avert an accident, but what about examples of verbal abuse? A researcher wishing to understand discrimination will probably close up the subject if he or she tells children off for stereotyping insults (for example, related to gender or race).

Risk of harm may apply not only to research participants, but to people affected by the *research findings*. As a result researchers have been urged to take control of dissemination (Robson, 1993). There is an onus to try and present findings in ways so that they cannot be used or misused by others against children's interests. Many will know that findings that get into the hands of the media can easily be misrepresented in order to make a 'good' story. Research on parental alcohol misuse stressed that some families and children coped well in adverse circumstances (Laybourn et al., 1996), but the media concentrated on the horror stories and most extreme accounts. Research evidence that many young people prefer residential care to foster care has been often used to support blanket statements that disregard the fact that just as many prefer foster care to residential care (Hill, 1995).

Privacy and Confidentiality

Feedback from children about professionals indicates that many are very concerned about actual or potential breaches of confidence (Thoburn, Lewis, & Shemmings, 1995; Triseliotis, Borland, Hill, & Lambert, 1995; Westcott & Davies, 1996). There are at least three elements:

1. public confidentiality – not identifying research participants in research reports, presentations and so forth;
2. social network confidentiality – not passing on information to family members, friends or others known to the child;
3. third-party breach of privacy – where a group or household member reveals something personal about another.

Public confidentiality

It is a commonplace of nearly all research that participants are promised that they will not be named or identifiable in any written or verbal dissemination of the findings. This is not always unproblematic. What if some children actually want to have their contribution acknowledged? This is even more tricky if some do and some don't. This was the case in a US study of Little League players. The author decided to use pseudonyms for everyone, partly in order not to differentiate and also because he thought that the children who wanted to be named did not necessarily see how they might come across in a bad light or feel ashamed later (Fine & Sandstrom, 1988). Thus, in the end an adult view of the children's best interests prevailed over the expressed wishes of some of the children.

Care also needs to be taken in the more general presentation of research findings. Compared with quantitative research where individuals become 'lost' within statistics, in qualitative research illustrative narratives, examples and quotes are often integral to the presentation of the data. Therefore ensuring that participants are not identified is more difficult and requires particular attention. Drawings used as data may be especially hard to make anonymous (Levin, 1995). In one study, my colleagues and I had the opportunity to obtain feedback from children on a booklet based on some health promotion research they had contributed to. One child asked for her quote to be taken out, as she was concerned she might be recognizable. Such opportunities to check take time and money, so are not common. In the absence of feedback, it is tempting to include vivid examples, which may reveal too much about an individual, even though referred to anonymously. Whenever there is doubt, it may be necessary to omit or disguise certain details of a situation so that the persons involved are not identifiable.

Network confidentiality

In some studies, information is gathered from children and other members of their household, for example, parents, carers, siblings. In order to facilitate honesty, it may be necessary to reassure that none of the others will be told. In some instances, different interviewers have been used to help demonstrate that nothing will be conveyed by the research team to other parties (for example, Clarke et al., 1996). Even then, other household members or significant others cannot necessarily be relied on not to pressurize each other after the researcher has gone. Parents sometimes do seek information about what their children have said, apparently out of concern for their children, and it is important to remain firm about not sharing what a child has said. Likewise, some teachers believe they are entitled to know about any activity in the school. France, Bendelow and Williams (2000) found that certain teachers agreed to research confidentiality but interpreted this as including themselves within the circle of privacy. The researchers concluded that it is necessary to explain and discuss what is meant by confidentiality when seeking assurances about it.

In group situations, it is not just the researcher who has to keep confidences from nonparticipants, but other members of the group. This possibility makes it especially important to agree the boundaries of confidentiality with the group. In some contexts, including schools, it may be unrealistic to expect that nothing will be said about what went on, but agreement can be reached at the outset not to describe anything that can be connected with a particular individual.

Third-party breach of privacy

This refers to disclosure of private information within a group or research participants, as opposed to revelations by participants to people outside the research, which has just been discussed. Joint or group interviews 'enable one or more of the participants to rupture – either deliberately or accidentally – another's rights to privacy by disclosing "sensitive" information about them' (Valentine, 1999: 147). An example given by Valentine was a girl mentioning her brother gaining access to pornography on the internet. It is difficult to prevent this entirely without inhibiting spontaneous discussion, which is a benefit of shared interviews. As with network confidentiality, however, discussion of ground rules at the beginning can include asking children to be careful not to say personal things about another which that person would probably object to.

Limits to confidentiality

It may be impossible to offer absolute confidentiality, since research contacts may reveal that a child is being abused or seriously harming others. In such cases the researcher may feel they should report what is happening. In the USA, various persons are obliged to report any suspected child abuse: researchers are not explicitly included among the mandated categories, but some people believe they should be (Steinberg, Pynoos, Goenjian, Sossenabadi, & Sherr, 1999). Guidelines issued by the National Children's Bureau (n.d.) in London insist that the researcher has a duty to pass on information about abuse to a relevant professional.

This seemingly straightforward advice ignores the difficulty that may arise in judging whether an incident is serious enough to count as abuse and also takes no account of the child's wishes. In our study of alcohol misuse, a prior commitment to report any abuse revealed was asked for by some agencies as a condition for access to families (Laybourn et al., 1996). In order not to build up false expectations of complete confidentiality, this needed to be explained in advance, but that ran the risk of deterring participation. In this particular study, the proviso about confidentiality was explained thus: 'For example, if we went into a family and discovered that someone's life was in danger, or a child was at serious risk' (Laybourn et al., 1996: 31). This seemed to be acceptable and no family withdrew after hearing this. Similarly in a study of young people about the Child Support Agency, children were told that confidentiality was guaranteed, unless it emerged that someone was at risk, but 'nothing would be done without consulting or informing them' (Mahon et al., 1996: 151). Furthermore, blanket injunctions to report abuse may ignore the wishes of the children themselves. Good advice is to talk over with the child what strategy they would like to pursue (Butler & Williamson, 1994; Thomas & O'Kane, 1998a).

Ethical Committees, Codes and Policies

The need for formal controls over research was shown in devastating fashion during the Third Reich in Germany. This led to the Nuremberg Code in the late 1940s, which applied particularly to experimental research, but also has wider relevance. Among the key points covered in the code are voluntary consent, freedom to retract consent and avoidance of unnecessary pain or harm (Greig & Taylor, 1999; Troher, Reiter-Teil & Herych, 1998). In medical research it is now standard practice for all research proposals to be scrutinized for approval or disapproval by an ethics committee (Medical Research Council, 2000). Medical committees vary greatly in size from a few members to over 50. Most have at least one lay person. The procedures and protocols are thought by some to have become excessively complex (Greig & Taylor, 1999). A survey carried out in the mid-1980s found that the main reasons for suggesting modifications in proposals were, in order:

1. inadequate arrangements for obtaining consent;
2. ethical unacceptability;
3. poor research design.

For the most part, the committees insisted on children's consent only from 15-years-old upwards (Nicholson, 1986).

Psychologists, too, increasingly use research ethics committees (Morrow & Richards, 1996). These have been less common in sociological and social welfare research, although many local authorities in the UK have their own research application forms, requiring approval by individuals. Many universities now have a Research Ethics Committee, though their nature and scope varies (Butler, 2000). While such committees are welcome as safeguards for research participants, including children, there are dangers that they become too bureaucratic and restrictive, more focused on protecting the organization (van den Hoonard, 2002).

Among the advantages of local or national research ethics committees are that they can safeguard the rights of potential research participants, act as a check on poor research and remind researchers about issues they may have overlooked. However, they often leave much scope for discretion, while monitoring and sanctions may be weak (Humphries & Martin, 2000).

When research is not subject to external scrutiny, it is suggested that researchers should use checklists of questions about ethical considerations (Barker, Pistrang, & Elliott, 1994; Robson, 1993). Academic and professional bodies have developed a range of codes and standards. These mainly focus on the responsibilities of individual researchers or projects, although arguably it is just as important to consider the collective operations and effects of research (Rossiter, Prilletensky & Walsh-Bowers, 2000). In particular, research studies often divide into those that focus on children in general and those that are concerned with particular types of child or situation. This may result in an undifferentiated and oversimplified image of 'ordinary' children, while understanding of minority perspectives is confined to the specialized margins (see, for example, Davis & Watson, 2000, with regard to disabled children).

Several codes suggest that an ethical approach to research is embodied in appropriate attitudes as much as in attention to a checklist of considerations. On the whole, codes produced by academic and professional disciplines do not single out children for special consideration. This may be because children have not been considered or because the same standards are thought to apply to adults and children alike. Occasionally vague reference is made to the need for 'special care' when 'research participants are vulnerable' (SLSA, 2000: see also Butler, 2000). The Ethical Guidelines of the Social Research Association (2002) refer briefly to children as one of a range of vulnerable groups who may have particular difficulty in resisting cooperation. The guidelines acknowledge that gatekeepers can protect and assist vulnerable people, but stress that researchers should 'not devolve their responsibility to protect the subject's interests on to the gatekeeper' and should beware not to disturb the relationship between subject and gatekeeper (Section 4.2). The Norwegian ethical guidelines for social sciences, law and humanities exceptionally have a short section on 'Regard for Children' (National Committee for Research Ethics in the Social Sciences, Law and the Humanities', n.d.: 8). This argues that children require extra protection and support, because compared with adults they are more open to risk, 'more willing to obey authorities', and less able to foresee longer-term consequences of taking part in research.

In the main research, ethical codes refer to principles and issues that are similar to those outlined earlier in this chapter. For instance, the American Psychological Association (APA, 1992) includes among its general principles respect for people's rights and dignity, concern for others' welfare and social responsibility. It also stresses the importance of technical competence and other professional duties such as maintaining records. Several codes (like that of the APA (1999) and the Psychological Society of Ireland, (1991)) include a duty to report ethical violations by other researchers. Most codes deal with confidentiality in some detail. Thus the British Psychological Society (1991) states that identities should not be revealed without consent (apart from exceptional circumstances of possible harm) and that records should be kept securely. The Socio-Legal Studies Association (n.d.) proposes that ideally, research participants should have the opportunity to see and comment on interview transcripts and conclusions.

Several children's organizations (for example, Barnardo's and the National Children's Bureau in the UK) have developed codes that apply general principles specifically to children (Alderson, 1995). Barnardo's, for instance, puts stress on making sure that samples do not exclude certain groups (for example, those with learning difficulties). The National Childrens Bureau (n.d.) also emphasizes equal opportunities, the centrality of including children's perspectives in any research and taking a holistic view of the child. The National Children's Bureau accepts the ethical standards of the British Sociological Association, but sees the need for research with children 'to go further' with respect to:

1. informed consent – special care must be taken to ensure that all children participating have been asked (for example, in school) and they understand the implications of the research;
2. confidentiality – it should be acknowledged openly with children that confidentiality may be breached if risk of significant harm is divulged;
3. payment – children ought to be compensated for their time and effort;
4. the impact on children – researchers should 'conclude with a careful debriefing' (p. 5), observe or discuss any adverse effects and, if necessary, assist the child to obtain help.

Interestingly, some ethical standards accept that deviation from ideals may be acceptable in some circumstances. For instance, the Society for Research in Child Development (1991) prioritizes the child's welfare as regards non-harmful procedures, informed consent, anonymity and so on. However, it accepts that 'assent' by the child rather than 'consent' may be sufficient, that is, the child 'shows some form of agreement to participate without necessarily comprehending the full significance of the research necessary to give informed consent' (p. 1). Deception is seen to be sometimes justifiable, provided that the rationale has been checked with colleagues and the investigators 'make an effort' to employ methods with no known negative consequences. The British Psychological Society (1991) similarly notes that much psychological research would be impossible if participants were aware of the guiding hypothesis in advance. Here the principle of honesty runs up against the danger of research participants modifying what they do or say, influenced by what they think is expected. Some argue that the pursuit of 'scientific' truth does not justify or outweigh the negative consequences on participants of having been 'duped' (Guba & Lincoln, 1989). While accepting that covert investigations may occasionally be in the public interest, the Socio-Legal Studies Association (n.d.) states unequivocally that such research methods 'violate the principle of consent and invade the privacy of those studied' (p. 7).

Several codes include substantial sections on duties to funders, peers, governments and/or to society as a whole (for example, APA, 1992; Association of Social Anthropologists of the Commonwealth, 1999; Medical Research Council, 2000; SLSA, n.d.). The Society for Research in Child Development (1991) advocates care in the reporting of findings and taking appropriate action if there are any undesirable consequences.

Contexts and Constraints

Alderson (1995) sets high ideals, but also notes the constraints under which research operates. Professional researchers often have little choice over the nature of the funding or even the broad research remit, when responding to a program. Restrictions on grant levels and competitive tendering often mean that costings have to be pared to the bone, necessitating a quick start and an abrupt end as the researcher moves to a new project or job.

Some, though not all, good practices require time and this is often in short supply. For example, ideally individuals or groups should be seen on separate occasions to discuss the nature of the research; express concerns and give consent; take part in the research. The time required may be multiplied when consent is needed from child and parent and possibly other adults (for example, teachers, foster carers). In reality this is often collapsed into two stages or one, perhaps with written communication only to establish consent.

Research timetables are often so tight that analysis, drafting and writing of final reports reach right up to or beyond the end of the study period, leaving no formal time for wider dissemination or personal feedback to participants. Student researchers are often expected to do their research to tight timescales with precise academic requirements. Workplace researchers may be struggling to fit their research in around other commitments. However, limited time and money do not exclude certain good practices, and in any case perhaps these are too readily used as alibis for taking the easy path.

Even when researchers have time for careful negotiation and planning, they can still be very dependent on the uncertain commitment of other adults, who have different priorities (Cree et al., 2002).

Conclusions

To summarize ethical issues I shall adopt a rights perspective. In considering children's rights in general, many distinctions have been made (for example, Archard, 1993; Freeman, 1983) but four broad kinds are commonly identified. These are the:

1. right to satisfactory development and wellbeing (welfare rights);
2. right to protection from harm (protective rights);

3. right to appropriate services (provision rights);
4. right to express opinions which are taken account of (choice or participatory rights).

Research which aims to appreciate children's experiences qualitatively
should be guided by similar considerations:

1. welfare – the purpose of the research should contribute to children's
   well-being, either directly or indirectly (for example, through increasing
   adult's understanding of children so that their interactions or interventions are more sensitive to children's wishes and needs);
2. protection – methods should be designed to avoid stress and distress;
   contingency arrangements should be available in case children become
   upset or situations of risk or harm are revealed;
3. provision – children should whenever possible feel good about having
   contributed to research as a service which can inform society, individuals,
   policy and practice;
4. choice and participation – children should make informed choices about
   the following:

   a. agreement or refusal to taking part;
   b. opting out (at any stage);
   c. determining the boundaries of public, network and third-party
      confidentiality;
   d. contributing ideas to research agendas and processes, both for indi-
      vidual research projects and to the research enterprise as a whole.

As with children's rights more generally, research with children has entered
an exciting new phase. We are only at the beginning of a challenging but
fascinating process.

Note

1 Regretfully the Alderson and Morrow book was published just after this chapter went to
  press, so its contents could not be taken into account.

References

Alderson, P. (1995). *Listening to children*. London: Barnardos.
Alderson, P. (2000). Children as researchers: the effects of participation rights on
  research methodology. In P. Christensen & A. James (Eds.), *Research with children:
  Perspectives and practices* (pp. 241–257). New York: Falmer Press.
Alderson, P. & Goodey, C. (1996). Research with disabled children: How useful is
  child-centered ethics? *Children & Society, 10*(2), 106–117.
Alderson P. & Morrow, V. (2004). *Ethics, social research and consulting with children and
  young people*. Barkingside: Barnardos.

American Psychological Association. (1992). Ethical principles of psychologists and code of conduct. *American Psychologist, 47*(12), 1597–1611.

Archard, D. (1993). *Children: Rights and childhood.* London: Routledge.

Association of the Social Anthropologists of the Commonwealth. (1999). *Ethical guidelines for good research practice.*

Barker, C., Pistrang, N., & Elliott, R. (1994). *Research methods in clinical and counseling psychology.* Chichester: Wiley.

Barn, R., Sinclair, R., & Ferdinand, D. (1997). *Acting on principle.* London: BAAF.

Begley, A. (2000). The educational self-perceptions of children with Down's Syndrome. In A. Lewis & G. Lindsay (Eds.), *Researching children's perspectives* (pp. 98–121). Buckingham: Open University Press.

Bell, C. & Newby, H. (Eds.) (1977). *Doing sociological research.* London: Allen & Unwin.

Bently, D. (1987). Interviewing in the context of non-verbal research. In J. Powney & M. Watts (Eds.), *Interviewing in educational research* (pp. 94–99). London: Routledge & Kegan Paul.

Berti, A.E. & Bombi, A.S. (1988). *The child's construction of economics.* Cambridge: Cambridge University Press.

Borland, M., Laybourn, A., Hill, M., & Brown, J. (1998). *Middle childhood.* London: Jessica Kingsley.

Borland, M., Hill, M. Laybourn, A., & Stafford, A. (2001). *Improving consultation with children and young people in relevant aspects of policy-making and legislation in Scotland.* Edinburgh: The Scottish Parliament.

Brannen, J. (Ed.) (1992). *Mixing methods.* Aldershot: Avebury.

British Psychological Society. (1991). *Code of conduct ethical principles and guidelines.* Leicester: BPS.

Brodzinsky, D.M. Singer, L.M., & Braff, A.M. (1984). Children's understanding of adoption. *Child Development, 55,* 869–876.

Bury, A. (1993). *Researching children: The same or different?* Paper presented to the BSA Conference on Research Imaginations: Practical, personal, philosophical and political. University of Essex.

Butler, I. (2000). *A code of ethics for social work and social care.* Keele: University of Keele.

Butler, I. & Williamson, H. (1994). *Children speak: Children, trauma and social work.* London: NSPCC/Longman.

Christensen, P. (2004). Children's participation in ethnographic research: Issues of power and representation. *Children and Society, 18,* 2, 165–176.

Christensen, P., &. James, A. (Eds.) (2000). *Research with children: Perspectives and practices.* London: Falmer Press.

Clarke, K., Craig, G., & Glendinning, C. (1996). *Children's views on child support.* London: The Children's Society.

Cloke, C. (1995). Forging the circle: the relationship between children, policy, research and practice in children's rights. In C. Cloke & M. Davies (Eds.), *Participation and empowerment in child protection* (pp. 265–284). London: Pitman.

Cree, V.E., Kay, H., & Tisdall, K. (2002). Research with children: Sharing the dilemmas. *Child and Family Social Work, 7,* 47–56.

Davies, M. & Dotchin, J. (1995). Improving quality through participation: An approach to measuring children's expectations and perceptions of services. In C. Cloke & M. Davies (Eds.), *Participation and empowerment in child protection* (pp. 248–264). London: Pitman.

Davis, J.M. (1998). Understanding the meanings of children: A reflexive process. *Children & Society, 12*(5), 325–335.

Davis, J.M. & Watson, N. (2000). Disabled children's rights in everyday life: Problematising notions of competency and promoting self-empowerment. *International Journal of Children's Rights, 8*(5), 211–228.

Davis, J., Watson, N., & Cunningham-Burley, S. (2000). Learning the lives of disabled children: Developing a reflexive approach. In P. Christensen & A. James (Eds.), *Research with children: Perspectives and practices* (pp. 201–224) London: Falmer Press.

Detheridge, T. (2000). Research involving children with severe learning difficulties. In A. Lewis & G. Lindsay (Eds.), *Researching children's perspectives* (pp. 112–121). Buckingham: Open University Press.

Donaldson, M. (1978). *Children's minds.* London: Fontana.

Eby, M.A. (2000). Producing evidence ethically. In R. Gomm & C. Davies (Eds.), *Using evidence in health and social care* (pp. 108–128). London: Open University Press/Sage.

Eliot, G. (1903). *The Mill on the Floss.* Oxford: Oxford University Press (original publishers Blackwood & Son, Edinburgh).

Farmer, E. & Owen, M. (1995). *Child protection practice: Private risks and public remedies.* London: HMSO.

Fine, G.R. & Sandstrom, K.L. (1988). *Knowing children.* Newbury Park, CA: Sage.

Fratter, J. (1996). *Adoption with contact.* London: BAAF.

France, A., Bendelow, G., & Williams, S. (2000). A 'risky' business: Researching the health beliefs of children and young people. In A. Lewis & G. Lindsay (Eds.), *Researching children's perspectives* (pp. 150–162). Buckingham: Open University Press.

Freeman, M. (1983). *The rights and wrongs of children.* London: Pinter.

Garbarino, J., Stott, F.M. & The Erikson Institute. (1992). *What children can tell us.* San Francisco, CA: Jossey-Bass.

Graue, M.E. & Walsh, D.J. (1998). *Studying children in context.* Thousand Oaks, CA: Sage.

Greig, A. & Taylor, J. (1999). *Doing research with children.* London: Sage.

Grodin, M.A. & Glantz, L.H. (1994). *Children as research subjects.* New York: Oxford University Press.

Guba, E.G. & Lincoln, Y.S. (1989). *Fourth generation evaluation.* Newbury Park, CA: Sage.

Hall, B.L. (2000). I wish this were a poem of practices of participatory research. In P. Reason & H. Bradbury (Eds.), *Handbook of action research.* Thousand Oaks, CA: Sage.

Harker, R. (2002). Including children in social research: practical, methodological and ethical considerations. *Highlight* (Research Summary Leaflet). London: National Children's Bureau.

Hart, R. (1979). *Children's experience of place.* New York: Irvington.

Heptinstall, E. (2000). Gaining access to looked after children for research purposes: Lessons learned. *British Journal of Social Work, 30,* 867–872.

Hill, M. (1995). Young people's views of social work and care services. *Child Care in Practice, 2*(1), 49–59.

Hill, M. (1997). Participatory research with children. *Child and Family Social Work, 2*(3), 171–183.

Hill, M., Davis, J., Prout, A., & Tisdall, K. (2004). Moving the participation agenda forward. *Children and Society, 18,* 77–96.

Hill, M., Laybourn, A., & Borland, M. (1995). *Children's well-being.* University of Glasgow: Report to the Health Education Board for Scotland.

Hill, M., Laybourn, A., & Borland, M. (1996). Engaging with primary-aged children about their emotions and well-being: Methodological considerations. *Children & Society, 10*(2), 129–144.

Hill, M. & Morton, P. (2003). Promoting childern's interests: An evaluation of the child health profile. *Children and Society, 17,* 291–304.

Hill, M. & Tisdall, K. (1997). *Children and society.* Harlow: Longman.

Holloway, S.L., & Valentine, G. (Eds.) (2000). *Children's geographies.* London: Routledge.

Hood, S., Kelley, P., & Mayall, B. (1996). Children as research subjects: A risky enterprise. *Children & Society, 10*(2), 117–129.

Humphries, B. & Martin, M. (2000). Disrupting ethics in social research. In B. Humphries (Ed.), *Research in social care and social welfare* (pp. 69–85). London: Jessica Kingsley.

Ireland, L. & Holloway, I. (1996). Qualitative health research with children. *Children & Society, 10*(2), 155–165.

James, A. (1993). *Childhood identities.* Edinburgh: Edinburgh University Press.

James, A. & Prout, A. (Eds.) (1990). *Constructing and reconstructing childhood.* London: Falmer Press.

James, A., Jenks, C., & Prout, A. (Eds.) (1998). *Theorising childhood.* Cambridge: Polity Press.

Jenks, C. (1996). *Childhood.* London: Routledge.

Jones, A. (2000). Exploring young people's experience of immigration controls: The search for an appropriate methodology. In B. Humphries (Ed.), *Research in social care and social welfare* (pp. 31–47). London: Jessica Kingsley.

King, N.M.P. & Churchill, L.R. (2001). Ethical principles guiding research on child and adolescent subjects. *Journal of Interpersonal Violence, 15,* 710–724.

Koocher, G.P. & Keith-Speigel, P. (1994). Scientific issues in psychosocial and educational research with children. In M.A. Grodin & L.H. Glanz (Eds.), *Children as research subjects: Science, ethics and law* (pp. 47–80). New York: Oxford University Press.

LaRossa, R. & Wolf, J. (1985). On qualitative family research. *Journal of Marriage and the Family, 47*(3), 531–541.

Laybourn, A., Brown, J., & Hill, M. (1996). *Hurting on the inside: Children, families and alcohol.* Aldershot: Avebury.

Levin, I. (1995). Children's perceptions of their family. In J. Brannen & M. O'Brien (Eds.), *Childhood and parenthood* (pp. 281–293). London: Institute of Education.

Mahon, A., Glendenning, C., Clarke, K., & Craig, C. (1996). Researching children: Methods and ethics. *Children & Society, 10*(2), 145–155.

Marchant, R., Jones, A., Julyan, A., & Giles, A. (1999). *Listening on all channels.* Brighton: Triangle Publications.

Mason, J.K. & McCall Smith, R.A. (1994). *Law and medical ethics.* London: Butterworths.

Masson, J. (2000). Researching children's perspectives: Legal issues. In A. Lewis & G. Lindsay (Eds.), *Researching children' perspectives* (pp. 34–45). Buckingham: Open University Press.

Matthews, M.H. (1992). *Making sense of place.* Hemel Hempstead: Harvester Wheatsheaf.

Mauthner, M. (1997). Methodological aspects of collecting data from children: Lessons from three research projects. *Children & Society, 11*(1), 6–28.

Mayall, B. (Ed.). (1994). *Children's childhoods.* London: Falmer Press.

Mayall, B. (2000). Conversations with children: Working with generational issues. In P. Christensen & A. James (Eds.), *Research with children: Perspectives and practices* (pp. 120–135). London: Falmer Press.

Mayall, B. (2002). *Towards a sociology of childhood*. Buckingham: Open University Press.

McAuley, C. (1996). *Long-term foster care*. Aldershot: Avebury.

McKendrick, J. (Ed.) (1996). *Multi-method research in population geography*. Manchester: University of Manchester Press.

Medical Research Council. (2000). *Good research practice*. London: MRC.

Moore, R.C. (1986). *Children's domain: Play and place in child development*. London: Croom Helm.

Morrow, V. (2000). 'It's cool … cos' you can't give us detentions and things, can you?': Reflections on research with children. In P. Milner & B. Carolin (Eds.), *Time to listen to children* (pp. 203–215). London: Routledge.

Morrow, V. & Richards, M. (1996). The ethics of social research with children: An overview. *Children & Society, 10*(2), 90–105.

National Children's Bureau (n.d.). *Guidelines for research*. London: National Children's Bureau.

National Committee for Research Ethics in the Social Sciences, Law and the Humanities. (n.d.). *Guidelines for research ethics in the social sciences, law and humanities*. Oslo: Research Council of Norway.

Nicholson, R.H. (1986). *Medical research with children: Ethics, law and practice*. Oxford: Oxford University Press.

O'Kane, C. (2000). The development of participatory techniques: Facilitating children's views about decisions which affect them. In P. Christensen & A. James (Eds.), *Research with children: Perspectives and practices* (pp. 136–159). London: Falmer Press.

Opie, I. (1993). *The people in the playground*. Oxford: Oxford University Press.

Psychology Society of Ireland. (1991). *Code of ethics*. Dublin: PSI.

Punch, S. (2002). Interviewing strategies with young people. *Children & Society, 16*, 45–56.

Qvortrup, J., Bardy, M., Sgritta, G., & Wintersberger, H. (Eds.) (1994). *Childhood matters*. Aldershot: Avebury.

Roberts, H. & Wellard, S. (1997). Hear my voice. *Community Care, 16*(22 January), 24–25.

Roberts, J. & Taylor, C. (1993). Sexually abused children and young people speak out. In L. Waterhouse (Ed.), *Child abuse and child abusers* (pp. 13–37). London: Jessica Kingsley.

Robson, C. (1993). *Real world research*. Oxford: Blackwell.

Rossiter, A., Prilleltensky, I. & Walsh-Bowers, R. (2000). A postmodern perspective on professional ethics. In B. Fawcett, B. Featherstone, J. Fook, & A. Rossiter (Eds.), *Practice and research in social work* (pp. 83–103). London: Routledge.

Runyan, D. (2000). The ethical, legal and methodological implications of directly asking children about abuse. *Journal of Interpersonal Violence, 15*, 675–681.

Scott, J. (1997). Children as respondents: Methods for improving quality. In L. Lyberg, P. Biemer, M. Collins, E. DeLeeuw, C. Dippo, N. Schwartz, & D. Trewin (Eds.), *Survey measurement and process quality* (pp. 331–350). New York: Wiley.

Scott, J. (2000). Children as respondents: The challenge for quantitative methods. In P. Christensen & A. James (Eds.), *Research with children: Perspectives and practices* (pp. 98–119). London: Falmer Press.

Seiber, J.E. (1992). *Planning ethically responsible research*. Newbury Park, CA: Sage.

Society for Research in Child Development. (1991). *Guidelines for research*. Michigan: Society for Research in Child Development.

Socio-legal Studies Association (n.d.) First re-statement of research ethics. Bristol: SLSA.

Spencer, J.R. & Flin, R. (1991). *The evidence of children*. London: Blackstone Press.

Stalker, K. (2002). *Children's experiences of disability*. Edinburgh: Scottish Executive.

Steinberg, A.M., Pynoos, R.S., Goenjian, A.R., Sassenabadi, H., & Sherr, L. (1999). Are researchers bound by child abuse reporting laws? *Child Abuse & Neglect*, 23(8), 771–777.

Sweeting, H. (2001). Our family, whose perspective? An investigation of children's family life and health. *Journal of Adolescence*, 24, 229–250.

Thoburn, J. Lewis, A., & Shemmings, D. (1995). *Paternalism or partnership? Family involvement in the child protection process*. London: HMSO.

Thomas, C., Beckford, V., Lowe, N., & Murch, M. (1999). *Adopted children speaking*. London: BAAF.

Thomas, N. & O'Kane, C. (1998a). The ethics of participatory research with children. *Children & Society*, 12(5), 336–348.

Thomas, N. & O'Kane, P. (1998b). *Children and decision-making*. Swansea: University of Wales.

Triseliotis, J., Borland, M., Hill, M., & Lambert, L. (1995). *Teenagers and the social work services*. London: HMSO.

Troher, U., Reiter-Theil, S., & Herych, E. (1998). *Ethics codes in medicine*. Aldershot: Ashgate.

Valentine, G. (1999). Being seen and heard: The ethical complexities of working with children and young people at home and school. *Ethics, Place and Environment*, 2(2), 141–155.

van den Hoonard, W.C. (2002). *Walking the tightrope*. Toronto: University of Toronto Press.

Weithorn, L.A. & Sherer, D.G. (1994). Children's involvement in research participation decisions: Psychological considerations. In M.A. Grodin & L.H. Glantz (Eds.), *Children as research subjects* (pp. 133–180). New York: Oxford University Press.

West, A. (1999). Children's own research: Street children and care in Britain and Bangladesh. *Childhood*, 6(1), 145–155.

Westcott, H.L. & Davies, G.M. (1996). Sexually abused children's and young people's perspectives on investigative interviews. *British Journal of Social Work*, 26, 451–474.

Williamson, H. & Butler, I. (1995). No one ever listens to us: Interviewing children and young people. In C. Cloke & M. Davies (Eds.), *Participation and empowerment in child protection* (pp. 61–79). London: Pitman.

Woodhead, M. & Faulkner, D. (2000). Subjects, objects or participants? Dilemmas of psychological research with children. In P. Christensen & A. James (Eds.), *Research with children: Perspectives and practices* (pp. 9–35). London: Falmer Press.

5

Naturalistic Observations of
Children and their Families

Judy Dunn

Three key principles make naturalistic studies of children of special significance for those who wish to understand development in childhood. The first is that children grow up in *social* worlds – complex networks of relationships with others. It is within these social worlds that they develop their powers of understanding, their ability to communicate, their sense of self, their adjustment and powers of coping with stress and change (Dunn, 1993). If we are to describe and understand young children's abilities, and the influences on their development, we need to include in our research strategies the careful and rigorous study of their behaviour, talk and expression of emotion *within their close relationships*, and observation plays a central role in such investigations.

The second, related, principle is that naturalistic observations enable us to study children in situations that have real emotional significance to them. By studying children within the daily dramas of their lives with family and friends, we gain a very different perspective on the nature of their capacities and how these change than the picture from other more formal, standardized experimental strategies, in part because of the emotional importance of those interactions to the children – an argument that is illustrated below with a focus on their understanding of others. The emotional significance of these relationship settings means that naturalistic observations give us a window on the links between emotion and cognition that would simply be unavailable otherwise.

The third principle that gives special significance to naturalistic observations is that such observations provide invaluable evidence on children's real-life experiences and their reaction to those experiences. If we are to document the salient influences on children's development, we need to know not only how they respond to standardized experimental procedures or situations, but what actually happens to children in their family and school lives. We can, of course, ask children about such experiences, and their perceptions are of enormous interest and importance; even children as young as 4-years-old can be interviewed and can tell us about their perceptions of their lives and those of their family and friends (Dunn & Hughes, 1998). However, for young children especially direct observation greatly enriches the answers we gain, employing other techniques, to the question 'what happens to this child in her family, or with her friends, and how does it affect her development'.

The examples we will take to illustrate the power of naturalistic observations as research strategies are: first, the nature and development of children's close relationships with other children – their siblings and friends; second, their understanding of other people; third, the link between their emotional experiences and their social understanding – illustrated with evidence on the significance of their conversations about feelings and mental states. In the final section of the chapter some of the limitations of naturalistic studies are considered. We begin with children's relationships with other children.

Relationships

The ways in which naturalistic observation can inform our understanding of children's relationships is particularly clearly shown by research on siblings and friends.

Siblings

From early infancy, children's interest in their siblings is evident to even a casual observer. Careful systematic observation methods have now documented for a wide range of cultures (Weisner, 1993) the attention children pay to their siblings from their first year on. The emotional salience of the relationship is strikingly clear frame in both the amusement and delight children show in their siblings, and in the other side of that coin – the uninhibited hostility, aggression and frustration between young siblings. What is absolutely clear is the dramatically wide range of individual differences in the quality of sibling relationships. For some sibling pairs, almost every interaction is warm, friendly, cooperative and supportive. For others, hostility and aggression characterize almost all interactions. No one who is interested in development can fail to be impressed by the potential impact of such experiences on children's individual development (Dunn, 2000).

These individual differences, and the daily experiences of siblings with one another, raise questions about the developmental significance of the early relationships between the children. Do these patterns of interaction relate to later differences in the children's outcomes? Is there consistency over time in the quality of the relationships? And why do some brothers and sisters get along well and others so badly (a question that looms large for many parents)?

Observational studies have been very important in documenting the extent of individual differences in sibling relationships in the early years, when children are too young to be interviewed or 'tested' to document the nature of their relationships. These observational studies have highlighted first, the key special features of the relationship – high levels of conflict, shared cooperative play, shared fantasies that can continue for months, and rivalry for parental attention. Second, they have documented the links between the quality of early sibling relationships and children's later adjustment. Clear evidence for the 'shaping' role of experiences at the hands of an aggressive sibling – leading to aggression from the 'victim' child – was first obtained from Patterson's detailed home observations, (see for instance, Patterson, 1986). With younger children, one longitudinal study that included direct observations of pre-school-aged siblings at home, and then follow-up assessments of the children in adolescence, showed that both externalizing and internalizing problems in young adolescents were related to their experiences in the pre-school years with their siblings, connections that remained significant when the mothers' own relations with the children were controlled for (Dunn, Slomkowski, Beardsall, & Rende, 1994).

The close connections between child–sibling and child–parent relationships are, of course, developmentally of great importance, however, and this is a third feature of family relationships that direct observations have documented, extending the findings of interview and self-report studies (Dunn & Plomin, 1990). The salience for babies and toddlers of what is happening between mother and sibling has been highlighted in observational studies of babies from the end of the first year on. Two studies in Cambridge documented that both firstborn and later born children reacted very promptly to a high proportion (as many as three in four) of the interactions between their mothers and siblings (Dunn, 1993). They were especially attentive to interactions in which emotions were expressed (whether disputes, attentive cuddles, or playful games). A third study which focused on talk in the family showed that pre-schoolers monitored closely the talk between their mothers and siblings, and interrupted such conversations to draw attention to themselves with growing effectiveness during the third year (Dunn & Shatz, 1989). The *only* way such evidence for children's growing powers as conversationalists, and indeed as family members, could have been collected is through naturalistic observations. The general principle, that we should not consider children's relationships with their parents, or indeed their relations with their siblings, as those of dyads isolated from the other relationships within the family is powerfully highlighted in such observational data. The processes of monitoring and social comparison implicated in these links between sibling–child and parent–child relationships are operating very early in siblings' lives. Deciphering what the mechanisms may be that link these relationships – and the evidence suggests that a variety of social processes are implicated – depends importantly on naturalistic observations.

Friendships

The idea that children's early close relationships with other children are developmentally very important has a key place in the writings of Piaget

(Piaget, 1965 [1932]) and Sullivan (Sullivan, 1953). Over the last decade or so, there has been a huge increase in studies of children with their peers (for review, see Rubin, Bukowski, & Parker, 1998). Much of this research has focused on children's relations with others in their group – on popularity and rejection, the sociometrics of the classroom – rather than on friendship. It has been assumed that children younger than 6 or 7 were simply not able to relate in an intimate way to other children, and that their relationships with other children were inevitably fleeting and transitory (Selman, 1980). However, recently, a new perspective on these early friendships, which shows that some children bring considerable powers of understanding, sensitivity and intimacy to their relationships with other children even in the toddler and pre-school years, is gaining increasing support. And it is naturalistic observation of children with their friends that has changed our views of the nature and significance of these relationships.

Landmark research here is the work of Howes (1983, 1988, 1996), who established through her observational evidence two central principles. The first was that closeness and intimacy – expressed not verbally but through subtle cooperation in shared fantasy and activities – were shown remarkably early between 2- and 3-year-old friends. The second was that contrary to received opinion, young children's friendships were *not* unstable and transitory. On average, in her 1987 study, friendships lasted two years and some considerably longer. In our own study of 4-year-olds in Pennsylvania we found that, on average, the friends we were studying had already been close for more than two years (Dunn, 1993). Park and colleagues also provide evidence on stability of young children's friendships (Park, Lay, & Ramsay, 1990), drawing on observations.

Of course, very young children do not articulate elaborately what they value in their friendship. If they are asked directly about their friendships, they are very likely to say simply 'she's my friend because we play together'. But as Gottman and his colleagues have argued, this should not be taken as evidence against the importance or subtlety of their friendships (Parker & Gottman, 1989). Rather, as they show, the naturalistic observational studies have shown that the establishment of a shared world of play is in itself an achievement that depends on a close attuning of interests, aims and intellectual excitement, and this depends on a child subduing his or her own wishes in the interests of joint play. Parker and Gottman point out that basing conclusions about mutuality and stability of relationships solely on self-report data from young children does a serious disservice to these relationships.

Probably the most revealing studies of young friends have included audiotape or videotape recording of friends without parents or observers present (Dunn & Cutting, 1999; Gottman & Parker, 1986; Kramer & Gottman, 1992). These 'eavesdropping' studies have revealed, first, the concern children show for their friends (for example, Blum, 1987), second, the connectedness of communication between them, (Slomkowski & Killen, 1992), and third the extent of shared fantasy – which Gottman sees as the central core of close friendships, reflecting the 'willingness to go on an adventure with someone else, to influence and accept influence' (Gottman, 1986). A convincing case has been made for this shared fantasy as a context in which children first begin to explore intimacy, trust and self-disclosure (for example, Howes, Unger, & Matheson, 1992). None of this evidence on the nature of early friendships would be available without naturalistic observation, and a focus on naturally occurring conversations – which show us not only these dimensions of friendships, but also the extent of shared humour, gossip, self-disclosure, joint amusement, and ways of managing conflict that distinguish friendship from acquaintance.

Understanding Others

A second domain of children's development that has been illuminated by naturalistic observations concerns their understanding of others' emotions, intentions, and their appreciation of the connections between others' thoughts, beliefs and goals, and their actions. The nature of children's understanding of why people behave the way they do, and of what they think and feel – their 'discovery of the mind' – has become the 'hottest' topic of cognitive developmental psychology over the past decade. And naturalistic observations have played a central part in raising questions about the nature of the early stages of understanding others. This understanding is, clearly, of great significance for children's social and emotional relationships. However, paradoxically, the study of its development has been primarily conducted in settings far removed from children's 'real-life' social behaviour, and their familiar relationships. Investigations have centred on children's grasp of what puppets, storybook characters or toys might do in hypothetical situations. The manipulation of the false beliefs held by the protagonists in these 'stories' has illuminated both the limitations and capacities of very young children (Astington, 1993). But there are two reasons why naturalistic observations need to be included in the investigation of children's mind reading, and have indeed transformed the account of their understanding.

First, the experimental techniques, and the inferences we make about children's understanding of the mind from these strategies, depend largely on questioning children about these hypothetical situations, and such approaches present obvious difficulties with children in their first two or three years of life. Second, we are only likely to gain insights about the contexts in which these capacities develop and the salient influences on them from observations of children in their real-life settings. Without such observations we are limited to accounts of the development of mind reading that are couched solely in terms of cognitive elaboration, and make no reference to the social impetus that may drive children to understand others. There are clearly hazards in drawing inferences about children's ability to mind read from naturalistic observations alone, which we consider in the final section. It would be foolish to draw conclusions from isolated incidents of behaviour, or on tallies of the words about feelings or the mind that children use, without paying attention to the context in which they are using them. Our own strategy has been to study a range of aspects of children's behavior and their conversations, in different emotional settings and with different social partners – with parents, siblings, and friends. The evidence on which we draw comes from observations of children's cooperative play, their discussion of other people, their response to the interactions between others, their fantasy play, their disputes, their attempts at deception, and their empathetic actions.

The nature of young children's understanding of psychological states in others

The evidence from this broad range of features of children's behaviour, accumulated in four longitudinal studies carried out in the USA, Cambridge and London highlights children's growing grasp of others' psychological states, over the second, third and fourth years of life. Four categories of this evidence stand out clearly. First, there are children's actions that relate to their attempts to alter others' psychological states: *teasing,* comforting, and *helping* provide clear examples, as do the topics of children's *jokes*. Second there are children's explicit discussions of other people's *feelings*, and their *mental and intentional states* (for instance, thinking, remembering, knowing, meaning to, forgetting). The clear developmental increase in children's use of these terms and their curiosity about such internal states are particularly powerfully documented in *Children talk about the mind* (Bartsch & Wellman, 1995).

A third category of behaviour that naturalistic observations reveal, which is of particular importance in theories of mind reading, is *deception*. In the context of their families, observations show children in their second and third year are already anticipating the intentions of their mothers and siblings, and attempting to manipulate the beliefs of others, and to mislead others, in their denial of wrongdoing and their attempts to shift blame on to others. Excuses made by children attempting to avoid trouble include denial of possible future psychological states, reference to what other people intended or liked, and reference to transgressions as *made in pretend*.

Pretend is the fourth category of children's behaviour that provides evidence of their early understanding of other minds. In our observations of young siblings we found that as early as 18 months old, in the context of an affectionate supportive relationship, children were able to participate in, and contribute to, the shared world of make-believe. During the third year of life, such play increasingly involved discussion of the inner state of pretend characters. And studies of young friends playing alone together amply document how the context of a shared pretend game provides a framework for extensive discussion of mental states (Hughes & Dunn, 1998).

The observational evidence, then, gives us ample evidence for children's growing understanding of the emotional and mental states of others. Importantly, the developmental account from these investigations is in notable contrast to that derived from testing children in standard procedures with hypothetical characters, such as the widely used 'false belief' tests. The capabilities that

2- and 3-year-old children demonstrate in their real-life conflicts and play and their interventions between mother and sibling are striking, and discrepant with their lack of ability to make correct judgements about the hypothetical characters in the false belief task procedures. And it must be emphasized that naturalistic observations are the *only* source of the information on these very young children's skills as a teaser, joker, or as a deceitful evader of parental disapproval.

Developmental processes and social influence

Naturalistic observations of children in the daily dramas of their lives with family and friends have, then, provided us with rich evidence for the capacities of children, and it is a picture that contrasts notably with the accounts that are based on conventional standardized tests. But naturalistic observations of young children in their families do much more. They draw our attention to the processes that may influence the development of such understanding, both in terms of normative development, and in terms of the individual differences between children that are so marked, in their understanding of others. As an example, consider the significance of *talk* in the development of understanding feelings and mental states.

Talk and the development of social understanding

The study of children's naturally occurring talk has played a major role in clarifying the nature of children's capacity for understanding others and the social world (see Bartsch & Wellman, 1995 and, for instance, the special issue of *Merrill-Palmer Quarterly*, 1992, *38*(1)). Talk is likely to play a major role too in the *development* of children's understanding of others. Children grow up in a world in which people's feelings, wants, behaviour and intentions are frequently discussed, and, from their second year onwards, they are participants in such discussions. What we have learned from observations and records of such family talk is that well before they are able to successfully complete psychologists' 'theory of mind' tasks, they are exposed to discussion about why people behave the way they do, what they are feeling and for what reason, what they remember and forget, and so on. The connection between differences in children's experience of participation in such discourse and their own developing powers of understanding has now been established in several longitudinal studies (Brown & Dunn, 1991; Dunn, Brown, & Beardsall, 1991; Dunn, Brown & Slomowski, 1991; Hughes & Dunn, 1998). Children who are frequent participants in such conversations in their second and third years are better able to understand others' feelings and mental states, when tested years later. The naturalistic observations have taken us further than simply demonstrating this association; they have enabled us to investigate what situations and social settings precipitate such talk, which is so potentially rich as a forum for learning about others. And this investigation highlights the significance of the emotional and pragmatic context of the interactions between family members and between friends.

Links between Emotional Context and Social Understanding

With observational research, we can begin to ask questions about the contexts in which children's early powers of understanding are demonstrated, and in which conversations about emotions and mental states take place. The answers to these questions have highlighted the significance of the emotional context – both for the demonstration of children's capacities and for the cognitively rich discourse about why people behave the way they do. The contexts in which children's understanding of others' psychological states is first demonstrated – their teasing, comforting, deception, excuses and blame-shifting – are rarely emotionally neutral. They are situations in which children are intensely involved: the child's self-interest is threatened, or in which the child is absorbedly involved in pretend, or is intensely amused or concerned about another person's state. For instance, deception is most common when children are embattled in disputes with their parents (Newton, 1994); causal talk about others' psychological state is much more common when children are attempting to manipulate others in their own interest (Brown & Dunn, 1991; Dunn & Brown, 1993); talk with friends about mental states is most common in settings of joint pretend play (Hughes & Dunn, 1998). At least in the early years of childhood, it appears, understanding psychological states is not only revealed but also fostered in such settings.

Our argument is not that understanding others is *only* fostered in contexts of heightened emotion. Clearly by 4- and 5-years-old, children's intellectual search into the social world often takes place in calm, reflective conversations with familiar others (Tizard & Hughes, 1984). There may, however, be particular potential for learning in the emotional settings within family life. And the key point, as regards naturalistic research, is that these are the situations so rarely studied by cognitive psychologists, but which are notably common within the daily dramas of family life, as unstructured observation of children at home makes clear.

Further evidence for the significance of the emotional setting of children's interactions comes from observations of the same child interacting with different social partners. Studies of children in conflict with their mothers, siblings and friends, of their pretend play with mothers and siblings, and of their causal talk with different companions all highlight a key point. The children *used* their powers of understanding differently within these various relationships (Dunn, 1996). A child who took account of the perspective and intentions of her mother when in dispute with her rarely did so when in conflict with her sibling. A child who shared an elaborate world of make-believe with her close friend rarely did so with her sibling or mother. The point here is that the emotional dynamics of particular relationships and interactions profoundly affects the use children make of their powers – again a point that could only be established through the use of naturalistic observation of the children with the different familiar partners who formed their social worlds.

Methodological principles and limitations of naturalistic studies

There are obvious problems and limitations involved with a reliance on naturalistic observational methods, which we will consider in this section. But first, two general methodological principles about naturalistic studies need to be made explicit.

Observation systems

The first is that any observational system reflects the theoretical ideas of the investigator: there is no such thing as an 'objective' record of behaviour that is independent of the observer's ideas and hypotheses. As Bakeman and Gottman put it in their very useful book on observational methods (Bakeman & Gottman, 1986), creating a coding system for observations is stating a set of hypotheses, and it is a crucial stage of planning a piece of research which they urge should not be hurried. If we are interested in, for instance, the quality of the relationship between a mother and her child, we might choose to rate the interactions we observe in terms of broad global categories which our theoretical background leads us to think are important – warmth, criticism, hostility, for example. If we are conducting our research from an attachment background, we would want to focus in particular on the 'security' aspects of the relationship, and to include the baby's response to separation and reunion with the parent, rated on broad dimensions of emotional response.

In contrast to such rating systems, designed to categorize the qualities of a relationship in broad terms, we might think that it is relevant to try to code the interactions we observe at a more 'micro' level, focussing on smaller 'units' of interaction (for instance, coding who initiated each interaction, and how did each respond?). Alternatively, systems that focus on particular *events* in the interactions between people can be very useful for some research questions. For instance, when we were interested in investigating babies' responses to what is happening between other people (as in the Cambridge studies described earlier (Dunn, 1993; Dunn & Munn, 1985)), we decided to include an 'event' system in our observational recording. Each time mother and sibling interacted in particular ways (disputes, affectionate exchanges) these interactions were recorded as events, and we coded the baby's response to each event (did the baby watch, laugh, ignore, imitate either participant, or act in support of either participant?) Our particular interest was in whether it was the affect expressed by the family members, or the topic of the dispute or joke that was of special interest to the baby, so we focussed on both these aspects of the events (see Dunn & Munn, 1985).

The general point is that there is no single 'best' way of observation coding. The advantages and what can be learned from any particular system chosen depend crucially on the research question at issue. The relative merits of particular types of observation for predicting outcome can of course be assessed and compared empirically. Thus in a study of sibling interaction we compared the picture we gained from different levels of description (rating scales, detailed interaction units, and so on) and different settings (which varied in the extent to which they were structured) (Dunn, Stocker, & Plomin, 1990). The results showed that the less structured settings gave us a wider range of individual differences in the interactions between the sibling pairs (in which we were especially interested in that study), and the more global rating systems were more reliable in terms of their predictive power. This issue of reliability and representativeness is considered further, below.

Limitations of Naturalistic Studies

Drawing inferences from behaviour in particular contexts

We have already noted that making inferences from their naturally occurring actions about what children understand presents problems. It is clearly important to plan to sample a broad range of different kinds of behaviour in a variety of social situations, before drawing conclusions about children's capacities or indeed their relationships. The evidence that how children use their differing understanding with mothers, siblings and friends makes this plain. In our studies of children's conversations involving causal reasoning, their handling of disputes and their pretend play, for instance, we tape-recorded their conversations when they were with their mothers, their siblings and their friends. The same child behaved very differently in the context of interacting with each of these social partners, and made quite different use of his or her capacity to take the other person's point of view, or to cooperate in shared imaginative play.

The limitation applies not only to naturalistic studies, however. Drawing inferences about cognitive capacity from experimental settings alone also present serious problems, as the naturalistic data on mind reading has shown. How should we interpret most 3-year-old children's apparent incapacities in the 'false belief' test situations, when we see the same children deceiving their parents in naturalistic observations? It is just as difficult to make inferences from failures in experimental situations as it is to do so in observations.

Clearly the kind of context in which we choose to observe will depend on the research question we are investigating. If we are interested in how children manage conflict, and the use they make of their understanding of others in dispute, then we would plan our observations to include situations that are potentially the settings in which child and parent or child and sibling typically confront one another. If we are interested in a child's cognitive capacity in the more private world of shared pretence and imaginative play, we might well chose to audiotape or videotape them without an observer present. Gottman, for instance, found that the frequency and sophistication of shared pretend between young friends, which he tape-recorded as they played alone in a room, dropped significantly *even when the mother entered the room* (Gottman, 1986).

Lack of control in naturalistic observations

The most obvious limitation of unstructured observations when compared with experimental approaches is that with experimental studies the researcher can delineate much more precisely what aspects of the situation are significant in relation to the outcome of interest, and can manipulate these aspects systematically. The possibility of drawing causal inferences is much more powerful than with completely unstructured observations. With observations we lack the power to define and standardize the features of experience or performance we hypothesize are important.

Is the behaviour we observe a representative sample of what usually happens?

Another problematic issue is that of representativeness of the samples of behaviour or talk selected for study. Observational studies and analyses of talk are expensive and labour-intensive, yet if the investigator hopes to draw very general conclusions, the issue of representativeness is a centrally important one. This is an issue that can be seen as a series of intriguing research questions, rather than as a hopeless barrier to research. How does children's understanding of emotion, for instance, differ in various cultural or community settings? How similar are the arguments and alliances between different family members at mealtimes and at other times? How reasonable is it to draw conclusions about the quality and nature of family relationships from brief observations in particular settings? These are all important questions, but questions that can be investigated (for a discussion of such methodological issues see Vuchinich, Vuchinich, & Coughlin, 1992). Careful piloting before choosing which settings to study is important. But questions of length of observation and level of observational description also remain important. How long should observations be to capture the characteristics of a social relationship, or an individual's characteristic behaviour? Although it seems obvious that this is centrally important, it is striking that the reliability of a sample of observed behaviour in this sense is rarely assessed. In the great majority of published studies of parent–child relationships, for instance, in which observations are employed, inter-observer agreement is reported, but no assessment is made of whether the time and setting of the sample of interaction chosen for study reflect what usually happens between the interactants. Yet students of animal behaviour standardly assess the findings of *different* samples of time (Martin & Bateson, 1986). The ethnologists know that you can test empirically how long you need to observe an animal to gain a representative picture of its behaviour, and this is a lesson that would usefully be learned by those who observe children. Obviously if what happens in families with children varies very much from day to day, and the researcher is interested in capturing a representative sample of family interaction from which to generalize, he or she will have to make observations on different days and assess empirically what will provide a sample that reflects how the families typically interact.

Similar issues arise with the choice of how to code children's behaviour. How do you choose what is an appropriate 'unit' of behaviour to analyse? We have already noted that choice of coding method crucially depends on the hypothesis the observer holds about the behaviour or relationship in which he or she is interested, but the usefulness of different coding methods can be compared empirically.

Problems with the naturalistic study of talk and emotion

The study of talk and of emotion both present particular problems for the investigator using observational approaches. Conversations, for example, by definition involve two people; how then can we use conversational data to draw conclusions about an individual child's capacities? Thus, as Scholnick and Wing (1992) point out in their study of children's powers of logical inference, it is not evident that the children could make the deductions they effectively draw in conversation, *on their own*. We return to the point made at the start of this chapter – that it is in social contexts that children's powers are often first demonstrated. One lesson for researchers has already been emphasized: that we have to patiently amass evidence from a variety of social settings, and be very cautious about making inferences of any generality. A second lesson is that this very difficulty presents a key issue for further research: what are the developmental changes that enable children, by middle childhood, to think abstractly and cope with questions and logical problems without the support of a conversational partner?

The analysis of emotional context and children's emotional involvement presents further problems. How do we investigate the subtle nuances of emotion that may be important? How do we describe and measure the pragmatics and what is intended by speakers – for instance, in terms of irony, mockery, puzzlement, provocation, embarrassment? Measuring the 'paralinguistic' aspects of children's talk precisely and reliably is difficult, intensive and expensive. Videotaping can help, but also can seriously interfere with the naturalistic freedom of the observation. Luckily audiotape recording can be used to great effect in the description of emotion in the voice, and is less intrusive than videotaping. The acoustic properties of speech that reflect the emotion expressed by the speaker can be assessed by playing the recorded speech through a machine that will 'iron out' certain paralinguistic features (Fernald, Tauschner, Dunn, Papousek, & deBoyssib-Bardies, 1989).

Finally, it must be acknowledged that, as they grow up, children become much more aware of the presence of observers, and more explicit about issues of social desirability. It is difficult to achieve a 'natural' situation in which children of 8 years and above can be videotaped; frequently, they exploit this situation by clowning for the camera! Luckily, by this age, of course, they are wonderful interview subjects, and so other strategies are available for the researcher. The great strengths of naturalistic observation are more evident with young children, with the key advantages that we can see what the *children* themselves are interested in, curious about and amused by, study their abilities in settings that are of emotional significance to them, and monitor what happens to them in their daily lives without depending solely on the 'filter' of the accounts and perceptions of others. It is an invaluable tool.

Acknowledgement

Research by the author discussed in this chapter was funded by grants from NIH, the Medical Research Council and the ESRC.

Recommended Reading

Dunn, J. (1988). *The beginnings of social understanding*. Oxford: Blackwell.
Dunn, J. & Hughes, C. (1998). Young children's understanding of emotions within close relationships. *Cognition and emotion, 12*(2), 171–190.
Dunn, J. & Kendrick, C. (1982). *Siblings: Love, envy and understanding*. Cambridge, MA: Harvard University Press.

References

Astington, J.W. (1993). *The child's discovery of the mind*. Cambridge, MA: Harvard University Press.
Bakeman, R. & Gottman, J.M. (1986). *Observing interaction: An introduction to sequential analysis*. Cambridge: Cambridge University Press.
Bartsch, K. & Wellman, H.M. (1995). *Children talk about the mind*. Oxford: Oxford University Press.
Blum, L. (1987). Particularity and responsiveness. In J. Kagan & S. Lamb (Eds.), *The emergence of morality in young children* (pp. 306–337). Chicago: University of Chicago Press.
Brown, J.R. & Dunn, J. (1991). 'You can cry, mum': The social and developmental implications of talk about internal states. *British Journal of Developmental Psychology, 9*(2) (Special issue: perspectives on the child's theory of mind: II), 237–256.

Dunn, J. (1993). *Young children's close relationships: Beyond attachment*. Newbury Park, CA: Sage Publications.

Dunn, J. (1996). The Emanuel Miller Memorial Lecture 1995: Children's relationships: Bridging the divide between cognitive and social development. *Journal of Child Psychology and Psychiatry, 37*(5), 507–518.

Dunn, J. (2000). State of the art: siblings. *The Psychologist, 13*(5), 244–248.

Dunn, J. & Brown, J.R. (1993). Early conversations about causality: Content, pragmatics and developmental change. *British Journal of Developmental Psychology, 11*(2), 107–123.

Dunn, J. & Cutting, A. (1999). Understanding others, and individual differences in friendship interactions in young children. *Social Development, 8*(2), 201–219.

Dunn, J. & Hughes, C. (1998). Young children's understanding of emotions within close relationships. *Cognition and Emotion, 12*(2), 171–190.

Dunn, J. & Munn, P. (1985). Becoming a family member: Family conflict and the development of social understanding in the second year. *Child Development, 56*, 764–774.

Dunn, J. & Plomin, R. (1990). *Separate lives: Why siblings are so different*. New York: Basic Books.

Dunn, J. & Shatz, M. (1989). Becoming a conversationalist despite (or because of) having an older sibling. *Child Development, 60*(2), 399–410.

Dunn, J., Brown, J., & Beardsall, L. (1991). Family talk about feeling states and children's later understanding of others' emotions. *Developmental Psychology, 27*(3), 448–455.

Dunn, J., Brown, J., & Slomkowski, C. (1991). Young children's understanding of other people's feelings and beliefs: Individual differences and their antecedents. *Child Development, 62*(6), 1352–1366.

Dunn, J., Stocker, C., & Plomin, R. (1990). Assessing the relationship between young siblings. *Journal of Child Psychology and Psychiatry, 31*, 983–991.

Dunn, J., Slomkowski, C., Beardsall, C., & Rende, R. (1994). Adjustments in middle childhood and early adolescence: Links with earlier and contemporary sibling relationships. *Journal of Child Psychology and Psychiatry and Allied Disciplines, 35*(3), 491–504.

Fernald, A., Tauschner, T., Dunn, J., Papousek, M., & deBoyssib-Bardies, B. (1989). A cross-language study of prosodic modifications in mothers' and fathers' speech to preverbal infants. *Journal of Child Language, 16*, 477–501.

Gottman, J.M. (1986). The world of coordinated play: same- and cross-sex friendship in young children. In J.M. Gottman & J.G. Parker (Eds.), *Conversations among friends* (pp. 139–191). Cambridge: Cambridge University Press.

Gottman, J.M. & Parker, J.G. (1986). *Conversations among friends*. Cambridge: Cambridge University Press.

Howes, C. (1983). Patterns of friendship. *Child Development, 54*(4), 1041–1053.

Howes, C. (1988). Peer interaction of young children. *Monographs of the Society for Research in Child Development, 53*(1, Serial No. 217.)

Howes, C. (1996). The earliest friendships. In W.M. Bukowski, A.F. Newcomb, & W. W. Hartup (Eds.), *The company they keep: Friendship in childhood and adolescence* (pp. 66–86). New York: Cambridge University Press.

Howes, C., Unger, O.A., & Matheson, C. (1992). *A collaborative construction of pretend: Social and pretend play friends*. Albany, NY: SUNY Press.

Hughes, C. & Dunn, J. (1998). Understanding mind and emotion: Longitudinal associations with mental-state talk between young friends. *Developmental Psychology, 34*(5), 1026–1037.

Kramer, L. & Gottman, J.M. (1992). Becoming a sibling: 'With a little help from my friends'. *Developmental Psychology, 28*, 685–699.

Martin, P., & Bateson, P. (1986). *Measuring behavior: An introductory guide.* Cambridge: Cambridge University Press.

Newton, P. (1994). *Preschool prevarication: An investigation of the cognitive prerequisites for deception.* Unpublished PHD dissertation. Portsmouth University.

Park, K.A., Lay, K., & Ramsay, L. (1990). *Stability and change in preschoolers' friendships.* Paper presented at the Conference on Human Development, Richmond, VA, March.

Parker, J.G. & Gottman, J.M. (1989). Social and emotional development in a relational context: Friendship from early childhood to adolescence. In T.J. Berndt & G.W. Ladd (Eds.), *Peer relationships in early development* (pp. 95–131). New York: Wiley.

Patterson, G.R. (1986). The contribution of siblings to training for fighting: A microsocial analysis. In D. Olweus, J. Block, & M. Radke-Yarrow (Eds.), *Development of antisocial and prosocial behavior* (pp. 235–261). New York: Academic Press.

Piaget, J. (1965 [1932]). *The moral judgement of the child.* New York: Academic Press.

Rubin, K., Bukowski, W., & Parker, J.G. (1998). Peer interactions, relationships and groups. In W. Damon & N. Eisenberg (Eds.), *Handbook of child psychology* (pp. 619–700). New York: Wiley.

Selman, R. (1980). *The growth of interpersonal understanding: Developmental and clinical analysis.* New York: Academic Press.

Scholnick, E.K. & Wing, C.S. (1992). Speaking deductively: Using conversation to trace the origins of deductive thought in children. *Merrill-Palmer Quarterly, 38*, 1–20.

Slomkowski, C.L. & Killen, M. (1992). Young children's conceptions of transgressions with friends and nonfriends. *International Journal of Behavioral Development, 15*, 247–258.

Sullivan, H. (1953). *The interpersonal theory of psychiatry.* New York: Norton.

Tizard, B. & Hughes, M. (1984). *Young children learning.* London: Fontana.

Vuchinich, S., Vuchinich, R., & Coughlin, C. (1992). Family talk and parent–child relationships: Towards integrating deductive and inductive paradigms. *Merrill-Palmer Quarterly, 38*, 69–94.

Weisner, T. (1993). Overview: Sibling similarity and difference in different cultures. In C. Nuckolls (Ed.), *Siblings in South Asia: Brothers and sisters in cultural context* (pp. 1–17). New York: Guilford Press.

6 An Ecological Approach to Observations of Children's Everyday Lives

Jonathan Tudge and Diane Hogan

In spite of a long tradition of scientific study of children and their development, little is known about the fabric of children's everyday lives – the activities, social partners, and interactions that form part of everyday experiences. This perhaps sounds a strange way to begin the chapter, given the wealth of attention given to children by scholars in the fields of developmental psychology and sociology. However, the vast bulk of psychologists have conducted their research on children in laboratory or laboratory-like situations or have relied on parents' reports rather than examining children's typically occurring everyday activities (Tudge, Hogan, & Etz, 1999). Sociologists, on the other hand, when they have been interested in children have been primarily concerned with the socializing functions of the family, educational systems, and other major institutions of society rather than with children's experiences (James, Jenks, & Prout, 1998). This is certainly true of the 'over-socialized conception of man' as Wrong (1961) termed Parsonian structural-functionalist sociology.

Some scholars, particularly those in the relatively new field of the sociology of childhood (Corsaro, 1997; James et al., 1998; Jenks, 1996), have been critical of the 'dominant paradigms' in both psychology and sociology. In our opinion, what is needed is an approach to children's experience that is systemic, acknowledging the multi-directional synergistic aspects of numerous factors that combine to influence the ways in which children develop. To do this one must move beyond an approach that is narrowly based within a single discipline, but find ways to bridge disciplinary boundaries (Kuczysnki, Harach, & Bernadini, 1999). Fortunately ecological theories, with roots reaching back over the past century (Tudge, Gray, & Hogan, 1997) can help us not only integrate psychological and sociological perspectives, but also provide methods that allow us to focus on children's experiences.

In this chapter we describe and evaluate an ecological approach to naturalistic observations that we believe is a valuable tool for researching children's experiences. The method rests on two premises: first, that children are embedded within social and cultural contexts and that the relationship between child and context is transactional; second, that we can learn a great deal about children's lives by following and observing them within these contexts. As in any ecological approach no attempt is made to separate individual and context. As the focus of observation, children take the observer through the myriad activities and interactions, as well as their inaction and solitude, in the various contexts in which they are situated. In this way information is gathered about the physical environment, activities, social partners and roles that are available to children, through the influence of key adults and through their own actions and choices. Children's agency thus becomes visible and children are given a means of expression through their actions.

We make an assumption here that we can gain some access to children's experiences, that is, to both the content and meaning of everyday life, through observation. Observational methods are typically seen as a means to describe content rather than meaning: the types of activities in which children engage, their social interactions, and characteristics of the settings. The domain of understanding or meaning is more often associated with interview methods. The observational method we describe here, however, is one that permits us to gain insight into the meaning for children of the various activities going on around them and the ways of interacting with others in those activities. It is a relational method that pays as much attention to how children behave *in relation to others and their environments* as it does to cataloguing their activities and the characteristics of their environments. For example, we can infer from observations of interactions between children and parents the kinds of expectations that children have formed and that are guiding their choices of action. However, we also recognize that the method has certain limitations as a means of accessing children's experience, and we address these in the latter part of the chapter.

Before describing these methods in detail, we discuss the paradigmatic and theoretical basis for them. This is important, because the worth of methods cannot be judged independent of their theoretical context. We argue that there needs to be a clear and consistent connection between the basic worldview being used, the theory that constitutes the study's foundation, the methods that are employed and the analytical tools that are used to make sense of the data.

Paradigms

As early as the 1920s, Vygotsky realized that the development of new theories in psychology required the development of new methods. This is because theories have links to different conceptions of the world, the way the world works and how to understand that world: in short, different worldviews or paradigms (Kuhn, 1962; Pepper, 1942). As Guba and Lincoln (1994) argued, a paradigm refers to 'the basic belief system or worldview that guides the investigator, not only in choices of method but in ontologically and epistemologically fundamental ways' (p. 105).

Deriving from Pepper's initial discussion, a number of scholars (Goldhaber, 2000; Guba & Lincoln, 1994; Overton, 1984; Winegar, 1997) have discussed the ontological, epistemological, and methodological consequences of taking seriously a contextualist paradigm. Rather than revisit this discussion, here we will limit ourselves to the consideration of two contextualist theories and the consequences their adoption has for the methods that must be used.

Contextualist Ecological Theories

Contextualist theories are *not* theories which hold that context is the main explanatory variable. Instead, they are theories in which individuals and the contexts in which they are situated are explicitly linked. In this sense they are perhaps better termed ecological theories. We have found two such theories particularly useful in our own work – those of Lev Vygotsky and Urie Bronfenbrenner. Both theories, in addition, help us to bridge the divide that exists between psychology and sociology, providing the crucible in which context and individual undergo dialectical transformation.

Vygotsky's theory, as we have written elsewhere (Hogan & Tudge, 1999; Tudge, Putnam, & Valsiner, 1996; Tudge & Scrimsher, 2003), involves the mutual consideration of individual characteristics, interpersonal factors, and the broader historical and cultural context. Individual characteristics involve age, gender, temperament, motivation, prior understanding, and so on – in other words, those things that necessarily influence the ways that an individual acts in the course of any activity. Interpersonal factors are those involving the individual, the particular symbolic means and tools being used in the activity, and any other individuals involved in the activity. Most attention has focused on these interpersonal factors, with particular attention paid to Vygotsky's concept of the zone of proximal development, but it is important to remember that this concept is far from the cornerstone of his theory. It is not for nothing that the theory is known as a cultural-historical theory, for it is the broader social and cultural context, as it has developed over historical time, that influences, in conjunction with the individuals involved, the nature of the interpersonal interactions. Experience, in other words, cannot be viewed as something that is an attribute purely of the individual, but involves the individual and the interpersonal and broader cultural and historical context in which that individual is situated.

Children, in Vygotsky's theory, are not simply the passive recipients of cultural or social forces. Although all higher mental functions, in Vygotsky's terms, were social prior to being individual, social does not mean divorced from individual; rather, children learn from actively participating in practices involving them with others. Children experiencing, in different social and cultural contexts, is thus at the heart of Vygotsky's theory.[1] Moreover, new skills, concepts, and knowledge appropriated during the course of collaborative activities are never simply internalized as straight copies from the other person or persons involved, but are transformed on the basis of the individual's own characteristics, experiences, skills and knowledge.

Bronfenbrenner's theory also requires paying simultaneous attention to aspects of individuals, interactions, and the broader context, both spatial and temporal. This may be something of a surprise to those who continue to refer only to his 1979 book, *The ecology of human development*. Those who only know this book may think of Bronfenbrenner as a theorist who primarily is interested in various layers of context (the microsystem, mesosystem, exosystem, and macrosystem). From a sociological point of view, the macro-system is the most important layer of context. Bronfenbrenner defined context as any group whose members share value or belief systems, 'resources, hazards, lifestyles, opportunity structures, life course options and patterns of social interchange' (Bronfenbrenner, 1993: 25). For most psychologists, however, the microsystem is the most important context, as the immediate context in which children are situated and where they can both influence and be influenced by others. From an ecological perspective, both aspects of context have to be considered.

However, it is clear from his later writings (1993, 1995; Bronfenbrenner & Morris, 1998) that context, while important, is only one of four interrelated aspects of what he has termed a Process–Person–Context–Time model of development. Proximal processes (termed the 'engines of development') are the core of his theory and constitute the interactions 'between an active, evolv-ing biopsychological human organism and the persons, objects, and symbols in its immediate environment' (Bronfenbrenner, 1995: 620). Examples cited by Bronfenbrenner (1995) include parent–child and child–child activities, group or solitary play, reading, and so on. In other words, proximal processes are the essence of what occurs in the course of everyday activities between individuals, their social partners, and the other important objects and symbols in their environments. A focus on proximal processes necessarily involves dealing with individuals' typically occurring experiences.

The activities and interactions that comprise proximal processes may be the engines of development, but to understand interactions it is necessary to know something about the particular individuals (the 'person') involved in the interactions. Clearly, although studies of socialization often focus on what parents do with or for their children, it is also necessary to account for the fact that children are the agents of their own experiences. They clearly influence their own environments, for example by initiating new activities, drawing others into them, while at the same time being influenced by those around them.

It is therefore necessary to identify the 'developmentally instigative' char-acteristics of individuals, such as their directive beliefs, their activity level, their temperament, and their goals and motivations, described by Bronfenbrenner and Morris (1998) as 'force' characteristics, and which are clearly involved in child agency. All of these have an impact on the way in which the context is experienced by the individual as well as the types of con-texts to which the individual is drawn. It is also important to consider 'personal stimulus' or 'demand' characteristics, such as gender, that have an influence on the ways in which other people deal with the developing individual and the goals, values, and expectations they have for that individual.

Finally, because Bronfenbrenner's theory is developmental, it is necessary to also consider the element of time, both by studying development over time (by doing longitudinal studies that allow one to examine development in process) as well as by locating these developmental processes within their historical setting (termed 'the chronosystem'). Bronfenbrenner (1995) approvingly cites studies such as Elder's (1974), that clearly show that developmental processes are not only influenced by the spatial context (the particular setting where the study is being carried out), but also by their temporal context (the historical setting).

Scholars interested in children's experiences do not always look kindly on developmental approaches, believing that the study of development necessarily involves the assumption of progress and that it devalues children as beings still developing and thus not full members of the species (James et al., 1998; Woodhead & Faulkner, 2000). This critique does not, however, take account of views of *human* development, in which development is a process that occurs from birth to death and is thus neither inherently progressive nor restricted to childhood.

Nonetheless, researchers who are not interested in studying development per se would not, of course, conduct longitudinal studies designed to examine the effects of particular types of experiences at one age on children's experiences, feelings, or competence at another age. However, given that social and cultural contexts are continually changing (partly thanks to the individuals within them), all researchers working within a contextual or ecological framework should specify the temporal as well as the social context of their research.

The argument that we wish to make is that these two contextualist ecological theories serve a number of important functions. First, they may provide a bridge between sociological and psychological conceptions of children. Second, they provide a systemic approach to children, one that acknowledges their active role in their own development while at the same time showing that development is also influenced by broader social and cultural forces, as they have developed over historical time. In this sense, children's development is truly a co-constructive process (Valsiner, Branco, & Dantas, 1997). Third, these theories support attention being paid to the everyday experiences of children.

Meta-method

What types of methods are appropriate to use with a contextualist theory? Drawing on the insights of Winegar (1997), among others, we want to use the term 'meta-method' (Tudge, 2004) for the explicit consideration of the types of methods that need to be used given the theory of choice. Researchers whose theories can generally be described as positivist use methods that are essentially experimental and manipulative in an attempt to falsify hypotheses. By contrast, researchers working within a contextualist framework use methods that are dialogical, hermeneutic, or dialectical. Furthermore, the aims of positivist researchers are those of explanation, prediction, and control, whereas the aims of contextualist researchers have more to do with arriving at greater understanding, both for researcher and participants.

What, then, should be the methods that are used by those whose worldview is contextualist? They have to be methods that do not artificially separate the individuals from the contexts in which they are situated. It would thus make little sense to attempt to try to understand individuals better by carefully controlling everything except the one variable to be manipulated, whether that control were to occur in a laboratory or in a 'naturalistic' setting. Instead, as we have argued elsewhere (Tudge, Hogan, & Etz, 1999), use of an ecological theory requires use of ecological methods.

Instantiation of Theory into Method

As we argued above, ecological theories force researchers to pay simultaneous attention to aspects of the individuals who are the focus of the study, aspects of the context (immediate, cultural, and historical), and the interactive processes that are central in Vygotsky's and Bronfenbrenner's theories. It may seem a daunting prospect to think about designing a research project that captures each of these important aspects. The research that the first author has been conducting with various colleagues over the past 10 years, the Cultural Ecology of Young Children (CEYC) project, is one way in which to illustrate the ways in which these theories can be applied.

Observations and proximal process

Naturalistic observations are key for the study of experiences, and fit well within an ecological, contextual paradigm as a way to study proximal processes. However, there are many different types of approaches to observation, from very short observations of what occurs in experimental research to very lengthy observations in natural settings. Within psychology there is a long tradition of observational methodology used in natural settings. We therefore want to discuss briefly some of the different types of approaches to observation prior to talking about the naturalistic observational methods used in the CEYC project.

Among the best-known early studies using detailed observations are Darwin's studies of his own son, and Piaget's research with his own and other children (Piaget, 1928, 1932). Ethologists (Blurton-Jones, 1972; Hinde, 1989) adopted observations of children in natural settings from methods more typically used with animals. Barker and Wright (1951) devised an ecological method that involved the systematic documentation of everything that occurred in a single day in one boy's life.

Most observations in developmental psychology have not been so extensive, however, and have been restricted to a limited number of settings, whether child-care centre (Carew, Chan, & Halfar, 1976; Clarke-Stewart, 1973) or home (Dunn, 1988, Chapter 5 of this volume; Hart & Risley, 1995; Richards & Bernal, 1972). There have also been some excellent observational studies of young children's naturally occurring play (Gaskins, 1999; Göncü, Tuermer, Jain, & Johnson, 1999; Haight & Miller, 1993).

Interestingly, the one area that has seen the greatest amount of naturalistic observation of young children is the field of cultural anthropology, or among developmental psychologists who have been heavily influenced by cultural anthropology. Ethnography is the primary method of cultural anthropology, with its goal of trying to understand how others make sense of their social and cultural worlds (Emond, Chapter 7 of this volume; Weisner, 1996). Cultural anthropologists have spent a great deal of time following and observing children, but largely in rural non- or semi-schooled groups (Super & Harkness, 1986; Weisner, 1989; Whiting & Edwards, 1988), leading some scholars to state that far more is known about children's everyday lives in the non-industrialized world than in the industrialized west (Bloch, 1989; Richards, 1977).

Some sociologists, like their counterparts in developmental psychology, have adopted ethnographic methods, in part under the influence of Becker (1971), Denzin (1977), and Goffman (1968). In particular, they have used participant observation as the main way in which to come to understand the group under consideration. Corsaro's work in pre-schools in the USA and in Italy is the foremost example of this method being applied to understanding the experiences of young children (Corsaro, 1985; Corsaro & Molinari, 2000).

In the CEYC project, we are interested in the typical everyday experiences of children. Our approach to observations is that we simply follow the children, putting no restrictions on where the child goes or on the people who interact with the child. We follow each of the children in our study (who are all between 28 and 48 months of age when the study begins) for twenty hours over the course of a week. We do this in such a way that we cover the equivalent of a complete day in their lives, observing on one day when the child wakes up, another day the hours before he or she goes to bed, and on other days during the hours in between. Using this technique, we get a good sense of the types of activities in which the child is typically involved, the partners in those activities, the roles taken, and so on.

Our aim is to gather data over periods of time long enough to ensure, as much as possible, that the participants in the research behave as naturally as they can. We therefore collect the data in blocks of two and four hours, spread over the course of one week. During the first two days of observation, we collect data for just two hours each day. This is a period during which the participants can become acclimatized to the observer's presence and we are prepared, if we see major changes in behaviour, to throw out these four hours of data. Data are gathered on the remaining days during four-hour sessions.

Although each observer observes for twenty hours, data are only gathered during a thirty-second period every six minutes. The remainder of the time is spent coding and writing field notes, while continually tracking what the participants are doing. Time is signalled in such a way that the participants are unaware of when their behaviours are being coded, and the child who is the focus of attention wears a wireless mike so that the observer can hear what is being said while staying at a distance from the activity.

The last two hours of observation are videotaped. We do this for a number of reasons, the most important of which is that the live coding every six minutes does not allow us to study closely the ways in which children are drawn into activities (or how they draw in others) or how the activities and roles change over time. The videotapes allow us to attend to these processes of initiation and engagement. Although videotapes clearly have their uses, we do not film the entire twenty hours and base our codes on the taped activities. There are a number of reasons for this. One is that the presence of a camera is likely to change people's behaviour more than does the simple presence of an observer. Equally important, however, is the fact that the camera's field of vision is so much more limited than the human eye. Our interest is mostly on the child, but we also need to know what activities are going on that the child is not currently involved in. These are the activities that are available to the child, and it is important to know what these activities are, regardless of the child's participation. Moreover, because we are interested in knowing who initiated the activities in which the child participates, and how the child became involved, we cannot ignore activities in which the child is not yet engaged. We also need to know whether others are watching (or eavesdropping on) the child or whether the child is eavesdropping on an activity out of the camera's field of view. All of these things are accomplished much more easily without a camera.

Our approach captures children's activities in an ecologically appropriate way (children are not separated from context) and it does so over enough time to give, we believe, a reasonable sense of the types of activities that typically occur in these children's lives. The approach also allows us to examine the types of activities that are going on in which the children do not participate, or those in which they would like to participate but are discouraged from so doing. The major activities in which we are interested are displayed in Table 6.1, and are divided into five major groups (each of which is subdivided into numerous subgroups): lessons, work, play, conversation, and 'other' (sleeping, idleness, eating, bathing, and so on). For more details about the coding scheme, see Tudge, Sidden, and Putnam (1990).

Observations and child agency

Our observational method also allows us to examine some key aspects of what the children themselves do to start activities, involve others in those activities, and try to get out of activities that those around them would like them to engage in. In other words, it allows us to focus on the type of developmentally instigative characteristics that Bronfenbrenner believes so important, and that are the essence of child agency. Children are involved in

Table 6.1   Activities

Lessons	Defined as deliberate attempts to impart or elicit information relating to:
Academic	school (spelling, counting, learning shapes, colours, etc.);
Skill/Nature	how things work, why things happen;
Interpersonal	appropriate behaviour with others, etiquette, and so on;
Religious	religious or spiritual matters.
Work	Household activities (cooking, cleaning, repairing, etc.), shopping, and so on.
Play, entertainment	Activities engaged in for their own enjoyment, including:
Academic	play with academic object (looking at a book, playing with a calculator, etc.), with no lesson involved;
Role-play	play involving evidence that a role is being assumed, whether prosaic (mother shopping), mythical (super-hero), or object (animal);
Toys	objects designed specifically for children, such as toys;
Other play	objects designed not for children, such as household objects, natural objects, or no object at all (rough and tumble, chase);
TV, entertainment	watching TV, listening to radio, going to a ball-game, circus, and so on.
Conversation	Talk with a sustained or focused topic about things not the current focus of engagement:
Adult	conversation involving at least one adolescent or adult (someone clearly much older than the focal child);
Child	conversation only involving children.
Other	Activities such as sleeping, eating, bathing, and so on, and those that were uncodable.

activities not simply because others get them involved; they initiate activities themselves, and try to recruit others to be their social partners.

If a child is involved in a specific activity during our thirty-second coding 'window', we code whether the child (alone or with someone else) initiates the activity, and whether the child or another person gets the child involved in the activity. For example, imagine a situation in which the girl's father is preparing dinner and the child is helping to cook by stirring the contents of the frying pan while her father helps by holding the pan steady. If the father starts the cooking and asks his daughter to help, we code that the father initiated both the activity and the child's involvement in that activity. However, if the child comes over and asks to help we code that the father initiated the activity and the child initiated her involvement in it.

We are also able to examine differences in other types of person characteristics, such as gender. We can examine, for example, whether girls are involved in different types of activities from boys and, if so, whether that stems from differences in encouragement to get involved in different activities or differences in the extent of initiation. We therefore code how the activities started and how the child became involved in them. We are thus able to see, for example, the extent to which boys and girls differentially start (instigate) the activities themselves, and draw others into those activities, compared to the extent to which boys and girls are drawn into activities that others start.

Observations and context

Context is necessarily implicated when examining children's activities in the locations in which they are situated. We therefore observe in any of the settings in which the children are situated, and observe any of the social partners with whom the children interact. This means that we observe in the home, child-care centre if a child goes to one, with friends or relatives, at the park, in the streets, or at the shops if the child goes there. The data are gathered in any setting in which the child spends time because we believe that it is important to know more than what goes on in the home or child-care centre, the most usual locations where observational data are gathered. We therefore not only follow the child wherever he or she goes during the observational session, but also find out where the child is scheduled to be for the next session, so as to be in that place at the appointed time.

Observations and roles

These observations allow us to view more than the activities in which children are involved and the settings in which these activities take place. We also are able to see the roles played by the children and their partners in these activities, revealing both the interactions and the expectations for interactions that the children (and their typical partners) have developed. In the example given earlier the child is *participating* in cooking and her father is *facilitating* his daughter's engagement. Other roles include trying to *manage or direct* the activity (actively trying to make the activity occur in a certain way), trying to *resist or stop* the activity (telling the child that she can no longer help cooking because of the mess she's making), and *observing* the activity (if the child were closely watching what her father was doing, but not involved in a more active way). We also include as a role *eavesdropping*, similar to observing but from a greater distance and with no assumption that the person being watched is aware of being watched. Through these codes we create a chronicle of the actions and responses of children and their social partners. The chronicle contains the details of the ongoing adjustment and negotiation of relationships that form the fabric of children's everyday experiences. A shortened version of the coding sheet used in the project is provided in Figure 6.1.

However, in both Vygotsky's and Bronfenbrenner's theories, context involves not only the immediate setting, but also the broader sociocultural context. It is at this level that we hope to see culture-relevant differences in the types of activities in which children engage, differences in the extent to which children are encouraged to, and discouraged from, participating in different activities and in initiation of those activities.

	Lessons	Work	Play	Conv.	Other
Time/activity					
Child's role					
Initiat. of activ.					
Initiat. of involv.					
Partner #1					
Partner's role					
Attention					
(Similar spaces for partners 2–5)					
Age and number of available partners	Field notes here				
Mother in locale					
Father in locale					
Location					

Figure 6.1   **A shortened version of the coding sheets used in the Cultural Ecology of Young Children project**

How do we instantiate culture using this methodology? In part this depends on the definition of culture; we define culture as any group that can be differentiated on the basis of its values, beliefs, and practices, its social institutions, and its access to resources. Furthermore, the members of the group should identify themselves as being part of that group, and should attempt to pass on the values, beliefs, and practices to the next generation. By this definition different societies constitute different cultural groups, and we gather data in different societies. Data were initially collected in the USA, where the first author works. Because of his experience in the former Soviet Union, it made sense to gather comparative data in Russia and Estonia, two distinct cultures in which the parents had been raised in a single society. We also were able to gather data in Finland, culturally and linguistically similar to Estonia but without the Soviet experience, and in South Korea, Kenya and Brazil. In each case, the first author trained members of the respective countries to collect these data. These societies, of course, vary on many dimensions. Our goal was therefore to choose a single city in each society, of medium size by the standards of that society, with a range of cultural, educational, and professional possibilities.

Culture and society are not synonymous, however, and within any society can be found a variety of different cultural groups, given our definition of culture. Different ethnic groups may therefore constitute separate cultural groups, and so may members of different social classes. In this study we examined, in every city, children from two groups – those who were defined as either working or middle class on the grounds of their parents' education and occupation. In the city in the USA, in addition, we examined children from black and white families, equally divided by social class.

Observations and time

If one wishes to study development one has to study individuals over time. In our research we gather the types of observational data discussed above when the children are of pre-school age, and then gather follow-up data once the children have entered school. We are interested in examining the relations, if any, between 3-year-old children's initiation of and engagement in different types of activities and their parents' and teachers' perceptions of them during the early years of school (Tudge, Odero, Hogan, & Etz, 2003).

However, as noted earlier, we believe that we need to situate our children not simply in their physical context (both microsystem and macrosystem, in Bronfenbrenner's terms) but also in their temporal context. The way in which even young children experience their environments depends in part on what is happening, in historical time, in the culture of which that child is a part. This is true for children in a society that is rapidly industrializing, in an industrialized society in the midst of recession or boom or, as in the case of our research, in societies struggling to adapt to the changes wrought by the collapse of the Soviet Union.

Even if one is simply interested in trying to capture a sense of children's experiences one should not ignore time, however. The beauty of observations, rather than interviews or questionnaires, is that researchers are necessarily examining those experiences as they happen, over time, rather than getting a retrospective accounting of what has already happened. Only with observations is it possible to examine the ways in which a child draws a friend into an activity with her or to examine the changes in roles as a father first insists that his daughter reads with him, only to have her completely take over the process.

Some Results of Naturalistic Observations

This method allows us to capture, as much as possible, the types of activities in which children engage, their manner of engagement, their extent of initiating the activities and getting others to engage with them, and the roles taken by them and by their social partners. The value of the method as a means of describing children's experience through recording the activities and social partners they encounter in everyday life is illustrated by some key findings (Tudge, 2004). For example, in each of the societies work was going on around the children in about 25–30 per cent of our observations, but the children varied greatly in the extent to which they were involved in it (those in Kenya, particularly the working-class children, were most heavily involved in work). Play occupied the bulk of the time (between 50 per cent and 70 per cent of the observations featured the children in play), but there were clear variations in the types of play, with Korean children far more likely than those from other groups to play with school-related objects as well as with toys. By contrast, the Kenyan children were more likely to play with objects that were not specifically designed as toys (found objects, no objects at all, or things from the adult world). The children in Estonia and Russia were far more likely than other children to be involved in lessons about how things work and about the natural world.

But within each group we also found differences as a function of social class. For example, in most of the groups, middle-class pre-schoolers were more likely to be involved in lessons about how things worked and about things related to schooling than were their working-class counterparts, and girls were more likely to be involved in lessons about how to get along with others than were boys (Tudge, Hogan, Lee et al., 1999).

In part, these variations reflect the ways in which the adults around the children arrange their social worlds for them. But it is also clear that the children themselves are highly involved in the process, not simply as actively engaging in the activities, but initiating them and getting other people to join in the activities that they started. It is interesting to note that in many of the communities, children from middle-class backgrounds were more likely to initiate the activities in which they were involved than were children from working-class backgrounds (Tudge, Hogan, Lee et al., 1999). However, the relations between initiation of activities and subsequent competence at school varied dramatically across the different societies. In the city in the USA, children from both working-class and middle-class backgrounds who were more likely to start conversations with adults were perceived by their teachers as being more competent, three and four years later, than were children who were less likely to initiate (Tudge et al., 2003). By contrast, Estonian children who were more likely to initiate conversation were actually perceived as being less competent. Only by understanding the differing cultural backgrounds is it possible to make sense of what otherwise might be viewed as contradictory findings.

Methodological Challenges

Much of this chapter has been devoted to showing that the approach that we use to research children's experience fits well within a contextualist paradigm, and specifically within the theories of Vygotsky and Bronfenbrenner.

As such, the method allows us to treat children as active agents in their own experiences and development, co-constructing reality with others in a world that provides sociocultural meaning, developed over historical time. The method may thus be one that helps bridge the divide between psychological and sociological approaches to children and their development.

We do not think that the method we have described is the only appropriate ecological or contextual method. Ethnographic approaches, including participant observation, and interviews, particularly with the children themselves, may also qualify to the extent that they are able to deal adequately with the interrelations among individual, interpersonal, and cultural-historical factors. There remain, however, a number of challenges that should be addressed. One is that this method is extremely time-consuming, not simply because of the fact that each child is observed for twenty hours. Learning to observe in this way also takes a good deal of time and effort; observers have to be able to identify the various activities going on around the child, how the activities were started, how the child became involved, the various partners involved with the child, and the roles of the various individuals involved. The process takes well over a month of daily training sessions, using a mixture of live observation and observation of previously coded videotapes of naturally occurring activities. We acknowledge that this is a somewhat daunting prospect but one that, we believe, is well worth the expenditure of time and effort.

Is twenty hours enough time? We cannot deny that the longer one spends with the participants in one's research the more one may be accepted, the more one knows of the relevant contexts and the participants' roles in those contexts, and the more one is likely to understand the meaning to the participants of the experiences in which they engage. We can only say, weakly perhaps, that we believe that observations over the course of twenty hours may be sufficient to get a reasonable sense of the types of activities and interactions that are important in children's lives.

Another challenge has to do with the extent to which observations of children necessarily treat children as passive objects, specimens under the scrutiny of the scientist (Greene, 1999; Hogan, Etz, & Tudge, 1999; Woodhead & Faulkner, 2000). But what is important in the determination of whether the child is treated as object is the position that the researcher takes vis-à-vis the child and context. Putting the child into a contrived situation to see how the child responds to that particular variation in context may indeed imply that the child is simply the object of investigation. However, observing children engaging, in as natural a way as can be arranged, in the types of activities that would be a typical part of their everyday lives, is surely a way for those children to be participants in the study rather than objects of study. They, after all, control what it is that they do, when they do it, and with whom – at least to the extent that they are allowed by their social partners and the pre-existing constraints of the setting.

Nonetheless, the children themselves are clearly not the people who are constructing the meaning of their experiences. Instead, the observer, using a coding scheme that has already been developed, in essence provides the meaning from what it is that the children and their social partners are doing. In this sense there is not only a distancing of observer and children, but a privileging of the former. This separation is something that may only be partially overcome by participant observation or open-ended interview. We are mindful of the fact that the use of preset coding categories might disenfranchise children, since experiences important to them might not fit within our categories and therefore be excluded. In the CEYC project this potential does exist, but we deal with it through the use of field notes that always accompany the more formal coding of activities. These notes allow for the inductive creation of codes (we were able to expand our codes for types of work, for example, from the field notes), as well as for use in more qualitative analyses.

There is an assumption among some who are interested in children's experiences that the only valid route to understanding children's inner worlds is to study the language that they use to describe and explain them, usually in direct conversation with the researcher. It is not clear to us, however, why interviews should necessarily be viewed as being a more valid way of understanding children's experiences than observations. As Westcott and Littleton's chapter (Chapter 8 of this volume) makes clear, interviewing children involves a host of difficulties, not least of which is the fact that the talking about what one does is not the same as the doing thereof. It is our view that, although when observed children are not being given a voice through language directed at researchers, they are given a voice – a means of conveying a description of their lives and how they live them – through action observed.

Is it the case, however, that interviews, particularly with children themselves, are the only way to learn about the inner world of children, to find out what they are thinking and feeling? Interviews can certainly focus on these things in a way that observations never can. Gifted interviewers who have established the trust of the interviewees, whether children or adults, can certainly gain remarkable insights (Bearison, 1991; Westcott & Littleton, Chapter 8 of this volume). However, most of us (and here we mean 'us' not simply as researchers but as people) do not spend our time interviewing children as a way to find out what they are thinking and feeling. We talk to them, listen to them, watch them, engage with them, listen to them talking to other people. As people, we make sense of those around us by attending to both verbal and nonverbal cues, and if our interpretations are incorrect we are likely to get clear feedback when we act on those interpretations.

Observers do not lose these skills when observing young children. More important, by observing children in their natural settings with their typical social partners, we (as researchers) can be privy to the understandings and misunderstandings demonstrated by those we are observing. Interviews about experiences require a removal from engagement in the very experiences in which we are interested; observations of children experiencing allow us, as observers, to get insight into the minds and feelings of those we are observing via the children themselves and via the behaviours of those with whom they are engaged.

Woodhead and Faulkner criticize observational approaches in which the aim of the observers,

> is to render themselves invisible to the immature members of the human species they want to observe. Observers may be found backed-up against the corner of the classroom or playground, trying to ignore children's invitations to join in the game, and kidding themselves that they can appear like the metaphoric 'fly on the wall'. (2000: 15)

The aim may not be invisibility, however, but a desire to change children's regularly occurring behaviour in as minimal a way as is possible – to allow them the freedom to behave without the expectation that the observer will intervene to change what they are doing (which is not quite the same as doing exactly as they would were the observer not present). Corsaro's (1985) participant observations with pre-schoolers (in which the children define him as 'big Bill', an 'untypical adult') similarly allow the children the freedom to behave without concern that Corsaro will act like a teacher. And if we are interested in not separating children from context (the essence of an ecological-contextual approach) the type of observations we do are extremely helpful.

As with any ethnographic approach, time is important to help children know that the adult's role is *not* to alter, in any deliberate fashion, what they might otherwise do. This is the main reason that we observe for twenty hours over the course of a week, in lengthy blocks of time.

Because the children are approximately three years of age, they appear to adapt quickly to the observer. For the most part, they do not treat the observer as someone with whom they could interact (the observer has earphones in both ears and often is writing on a clipboard), and to help ensure this the observer chats with the child prior to the start of the observational session and then says that it is now time to 'work', and puts on the earphones. The length of time of observation makes it easier for the children to ignore the observer's presence, and to behave as normally as possible.

We are under no illusions that the other participants (particularly adults) could 'forget' the observer's presence so easily. Indeed, as children become more self-aware, observations may become more problematic; we do not think, for example, that we could have observed adolescents and expected them to have gone about their typical activities with as little evidence of influence as with young children. However, there are reasons to believe that even the behaviours of the adults that we observed with the children were not totally untypical. First, with observational sessions lasting so long, typically occurring activities (getting the child up, preparing meals, taking the child to a child-care provider, for example) have to happen. Second, if the parents behaved in ways that were not at all typical it seems reasonable to suppose that their children might signal that fact. Finally, if parents behave differently from their normal behaviours, it is likely that they do so in the direction of the things that they value. In other words, if they think that it is important to help their children behave independently they may do so more often than is typical; if they believe that it is important to discipline their children, they might do this more often. Since we assume that parents' activities may bear some relation to their values, their exaggerated behaviours, if these were what we were observing, were interesting in themselves.

In summary, this approach to naturalistic observations has a number of methodological challenges, but we do not believe that any of them are sufficient to discredit this method as an important way in which to understand children's experiences and development.

Conclusions

We had four main goals in this chapter. The primary goal was to describe an observational method that we have used to gather data on young children's everyday experiences in the typical settings they inhabit and with their typical social partners. This method allowed us to focus on the ways in which children, in conjunction with the sociocultural world, actively create their own world. However, the worth of a method can only be judged by reference to the theoretical and metatheoretical framework within which it is set. For this reason, a second goal was to describe the contextualist paradigm, and two ecological theories that fit within that paradigm. This allowed us to show the metamethodological connection between metatheory, theory, and method. The theoretical frameworks that we have found useful may serve to allow us to fulfil a third goal, namely that of bridging the divide between sociological and psychological approaches to children. A focus on child-in-activity allows us to examine both what the child brings to the setting as well as what the social world provides for that setting, with social world including both culture, as developed over historical time, and interactions with social others as well as the objects and symbols that are full of sociocultural meaning.

The fourth goal was to examine some of the methodological challenges of this method. There are, of course, some serious challenges – although the criticisms of naturalistic observations may not be as great as some might think. We do not wish to imply that this method is the only method appropriate to these types of contextualist theories. Nor do we wish to say that the method is problem-free. There may be other methods that are better suited to an understanding of the meaning that children give to their own experiences; with this method, we are restricted by what the children do and by what they say to others, their typical social partners, rather than directly to us as researchers. The mere fact of being observed may well change children's behaviours, too – although given our age group of interest and the length of time that we spend with the children we feel that the changes may be minimized.

Despite these challenges, we believe that this theoretically driven observational method lets children speak to us via their actions and interactions, uncovering for us their experiences of the worlds they inhabit.

Note

1. The importance of stressing 'experiencing' as a continuing action rather than 'experiences' as a noun is similar to the change of title of Vygotsky's best known book from *Thought and language* in the 1962 and 1986 translations to *Thinking and speech* in the most recent translation (Vygotsky, 1987). Only the latter translation accurately captures the dynamic nature of the words used in Russian.

Acknowledgements

We wish to thank all the participants (particularly the children) who gave so generously of their time, and our observers and data gathers: Sarah Putnam, Judy Sidden, Fabienne Doucet, and Nicole Talley (USA); Natalya Kulakova and Irina Snezhkova (Russia); Marika Meltsas and Peeter Tammeveski (Estonia); Marikaisa Kontio (Finland); Soeun Lee (Korea); Dolphine Odero (Kenya); and Giana Frizzo, Fernanda Marques and Rafael Spinelli (Brazil). The coding scheme benefitted from early collaboration with Barbara Rogoff and Gilda Morelli, to whom we express our thanks. We also gratefully acknowledge the financial support of the Spencer Foundation, the International Research and Exchanges Board, and the University of North Carolina at Greensboro. The views expressed are solely those of the authors.

Recommended Readings

Corsaro, W.A. & Molinari, L. (2000). Entering and observing in children's worlds: a reflection on a longitudinal ethnography of early education in Italy. In P. Christensen & A. James (Eds.), *Research with children: Perspectives and practices* (pp. 179–200). London: Falmer Press.

Graue, M.E. & Walsh, D.J. (1998). *Studying children in context: Theories, methods and ethics.* Thousand Oaks, CA: Sage.

Miles, M. & Huberman, A.M. (1994). *Qualitative data analysis: An expanded sourcebook.* (4th ed.). Thousand Oaks, CA: Sage.

Pelligrini, A.D. (1996). *Observing children in their natural worlds: A methodological primer.* Hillsdale, NJ: Lawrence Erlbaum Associates.

References

Barker, R.G. & Wright, H.F. (1951). *One boy's day.* New York: Harper.

Bearison, D.J. (1991). *'They never want to tell you:' Children talk about cancer.* New York: Cambridge University Press.

Becker, H. (1971). *Sociological work.* London: Allen Lane.

Bloch, M.N. (1989). Young boy's and girl's play at home and in the community: A cultural-ecological framework. In M.N. Bloch & A.D. Pellegrini (Eds.), *The ecological context of children's play* (pp. 120–154). Norwood, NJ: Ablex.

Blurton-Jones, N. (1972). (Ed.). *Ethological studies of child behavior*. Cambridge, UK: Cambridge University Press.

Bronfenbrenner, U. (1979). *The ecology of human development: Experiments by nature and design*. Cambridge, MA: Harvard University Press.

Bronfenbrenner, U. (1993). The ecology of cognitive development: Research models and fugitive findings. In R. Wozniak & K. Fischer (Eds.), *Development in context: Acting and thinking in specific environments* (pp. 3–44). Hillsdale, NJ: Erlbaum.

Bronfenbrenner, U. (1995). Developmental ecology through space and time: A future perspective. In P. Moen, G.H. Elder, Jr., & K. Luscher (Eds.), *Examining lives in context: Perspectives on the ecology of human development* (pp. 619–647). Washington, DC: American Psychological Association.

Bronfenbrenner, U. & Morris, P.A. (1998). The ecology of developmental processes. In W. Damon (Series Ed.) & R.M. Lerner (Vol. Ed.), *Handbook of child psychology: Vol. 1. Theoretical models of human development* (5th ed., pp. 993–1028). New York: Wiley.

Carew, J.V., Chan, I., & Halfar, C. (1976). *Observing intelligence in young children: Eight case studies*. Englewood Cliffs, NJ: Prentice-Hall.

Clarke-Stewart, K.A. (1973). Interactions between mothers and their young children: Characteristics and consequences. *Monographs of the Society for Research in Child Development, 38*(6–7, Serial No. 153), 1–109.

Corsaro, W.A. (1985). *Friendship and peer culture in the early years*. Norwood, NJ: Ablex.

Corsaro, W.A. (1997). *The sociology of childhood*. Thousand Oaks, CA: Pine Forge Press.

Corsaro, W.A. & Molinari, L. (2000). Entering and observing in children's worlds: A reflection on a longitudinal ethnography of early education in Italy. In P. Christensen & A. James (Eds.), *Research with children: Perspectives and practices* (pp. 179–200). London: Falmer Press.

Denzin, N.K. (1977). *Childhood socialization*. San Francisco, CA: Jossey-Bass.

Dunn, J. (1988). *The beginnings of social understanding*. Cambridge, MA: Harvard University Press.

Elder, G.H., Jr. (1974). *Children of the great depression*. Chicago: University of Chicago Press.

Gaskins, S. (1999). Children's daily lives in a Mayan village: A case study of culturally constructed roles and activities. In A. Göncü (Ed.), *Children's engagement in the world: Sociocultural perspectives* (pp. 25–61). New York: Cambridge University Press.

Goffman, E. (1968). *Asylums: Essays on the social situation of mental patients and other inmates*. Harmondsworth: Penguin.

Goldhaber, D.E. (2000). *Theories of human development: Integrative perspectives*. Mountain View, CA: Mayfield Publishing.

Göncü, A., Tuermer, U., Jain, J., & Johnson, D. (1999). Children's play as cultural activity. In A. Göncü (Ed.), *Children's engagement in the world: Sociocultural perspectives* (pp. 148–170). New York: Cambridge University Press.

Greene, S. (1999). Child development: Old themes, new directions. In M. Woodhead, D. Faulkner, & K. Littleton (Eds.), *Making sense of social development* (pp. 250–268). London: Routledge and the Open University.

Guba, E.G. & Lincoln, Y.S. (1994). Competing paradigms in qualitative research. In N.K. Denzin & Y.S. Lincoln (Eds.), *Handbook of qualitative research* (pp. 105–117). Thousand Oaks, CA: Sage.

Haight, W.L. & Miller, P.J. (1993). *Pretending at home: Early development in a sociocultural context*. Albany, NY: SUNY Press.

Hart, B. & Risley, T.R. (1995). *Meaningful differences in the everyday experiences of young American children*. Baltimore: Brookes Publishing.

Hinde, R.A. (1989). Ethological and relationships approaches. In R. Vasta (Ed.), *Annals of child development* (Vol. 6, pp. 251–285). Greenwich, CT: JAI Press.

Hogan, D.M. & Tudge, J.R.H. (1999). Implications of Vygotsky's theory for peer learning. In A.M. O'Donnell & A. King (Eds.), *Cognitive perspectives on peer learning* (pp. 39–65). Mahwah, NJ: Erlbaum.

Hogan, D., Etz, K., & Tudge, J. (1999). Reconsidering the role of children in family research: Conceptual and methodological issues. In F.M. Berardo (Series Ed.) & C. Shehan (Vol. Ed.), *Contemporary perspectives on family research, Vol. 1. Through the eyes of the child: Re-visioning children as active agents of family life* (pp. 93–105). Stamford, CT: JAI Press.

James, A., Jenks, C., & Prout, A. (1998). *Theorizing childhood.* New York: Teachers College Press.

Jenks, C. (1996). *Childhood.* London: Routledge.

Kuczysnki, L., Harach, L., & Bernadini, S.C. (1999). Psychology's child meets sociology's child: Agency, influence and power in parent–child relationships. In F.M. Berardo (Series Ed.) & C. Shehan (Vol. Ed.), *Contemporary perspectives on family research, Vol. 1. Through the eyes of the child: Re-visioning children as active agents of family life* (pp. 21–52). Stamford, CT: JAI Press.

Kuhn, T.S. (1962). *The structure of scientific revolutions.* Chicago: The University of Chicago Press.

Overton, W.F. (1984). World-views and their influence on psychological theory and research: Kuhn–Lakatos–Laudan. In H.W. Reese (Ed.), *Advances in child development and behavior* (Vol. 18, pp. 191–226). New York: Academic Press.

Pepper, S.C. (1942). *World Hypotheses: A study in evidence.* Berkeley, CA: University of California Press.

Piaget, J. (1928). *Judgment and reasoning in the child.* London: Routledge and Kegan Paul.

Piaget, J. (1932). *The moral judgement of the child.* New York: Harcourt Brace.

Richards, M.P.M. (1977). An ecological study of infant development in an urban setting in Britain. In P.H. Leiderman, S.R. Tulkin, & A. Rosenfeld (Eds.), *Culture and infancy: Variations in the human experience* (pp. 469–493). New York: Academic Press.

Richards, M.P.M. & Bernal, J.F. (1972). An observational study of mother–infant interaction. In N. Blurton-Jones (Ed.), *Ethological studies of child behavior* (pp. 175–197). Cambridge: Cambridge University Press.

Super, C.M. & Harkness, S. (1986). The developmental niche: A conceptualization at the interface of child and culture. *International Journal of Behavioral Development, 9,* 545–569.

Tudge, J.R.H. (2004). *The everyday lives of young children: Culture, class, and child-rearing in diverse societies.* Manuscript in preparation.

Tudge, J.R.H. & Scrimsher, S. (2003). Lev S. Vygotsky on education: A cultural-historical, interpersonal, and individual approach to development. In B.J. Zimmerman & D.H. Schunk (Eds.), *Educational psychology: A century of contributions* (pp. 207–228). Mahwah, NJ: Lawrence Erlbaum Associates.

Tudge, J.R.H., Gray, J., & Hogan, D. (1997). Ecological perspectives in human development: A comparison of Gibson and Bronfenbrenner. In J. Tudge, M. Shanahan, & J. Valsiner (Eds.), *Comparisons in human development: Understanding time and context* (pp. 72–105). New York: Cambridge University Press.

Tudge, J.R.H., Hogan, D., & Etz, K. (1999). Using naturalistic observations as a window into children's everyday lives. An ecological approach. In F.M. Berardo (Series Ed.) & C. Shehan (Vol. Ed.), *Contemporary perspectives on family research, Vol. 1. Through the eyes of the child: Re-visioning children as active agents of family life* (pp. 109–132). Stamford, CT: JAI Press.

Tudge, J.R.H., Putnam, S.A., & Valsiner, J. (1996). Culture and cognition in developmental perspective. In B. Cairns, G.H. Elder, Jr., & E.J. Costello (Eds), *Developmental science* (pp. 190–222). New York: Cambridge University Press.

Tudge, J.R.H., Sidden, J., & Putnam, S.A. (1990). *The cultural ecology of young children: Coding manual.* Unpublished manuscript, Greensboro, NC.

Tudge, J.R.H., Odero, D., Hogan, D., & Etz, K. (2003). Relations between the everyday activities of preschoolers and their teachers' perceptions of their competence in the first years of school. *Early Childhood Research Quarterly, 18,* 42–64.

Tudge, J.R.H., Hogan, D.M., Lee, S., Meltsas, M., Tammeveski, P., Kulakova, N.N., Snezhkova, I.A., & Putnam, S.A. (1999). Cultural heterogeneity: Parental values and beliefs and their preschoolers' activities in the United States, South Korea, Russia, and Estonia. In A. Göncü (Ed.), *Children's engagement in the world* (pp. 62–96). New York: Cambridge University Press.

Valsiner, J., Branco, A.U., & Dantas, C.M. (1997). Co-construction of human development: Heterogeneity within parental belief orientations. In J.E. Grusec & L. Kuczynski (Eds.), *Parenting and children's internalization of values: A handbook of contemporary theory* (pp. 283–304). New York: Wiley.

Vygotsky, L.S. (1987 [1934]). *The collected works of L.S. Vygotsky: Vol. 1, Problems of general psychology* (R.W. Rieber & A.S. Carton, Eds., N.Minick, trans). New York: Plenum. (Written between 1929 and 1934.)

Weisner, T.S. (1989). Cultural and universal aspects of social support for children: Evidence from the Abaluyia of Kenya. In D. Belle (Ed.), *Children's social networks and social supports* (pp. 70–90). New York: Wiley.

Weisner, T.S. (1996). Why ethnography should be the most important method in the study of human development. In R. Jessor, A. Colby, & R.A. Shweder (Eds.), *Ethnography and human development: Context and meaning in social enquiry* (pp. 305–324). Chicago: University of Chicago Press.

Whiting, B.B. & Edwards C.P. (1988). *Children of different worlds: The formation of social behavior.* Cambridge, MA: Harvard University Press.

Winegar, L.T. (1997). Developmental research and comparative perspectives: Applications to developmental science. In J. Tudge, M. Shanahan, & J. Valsiner (Eds.), *Comparisons in human development: Understanding time and context* (pp. 13–33). New York: Cambridge University Press.

Woodhead, M. & Faulkner, D. (2000). Subjects, objects or participants? Dilemmas of psychological research with children. In P. Christensen & A. James (Eds.), *Research with children: Perspectives and practices* (pp. 9–35). London: Falmer Press.

Wrong, D. (1961). The over-socialized conception of man in modern sociology. *American Sociological Review, 26,* 183–193.

Ethnographic Research Methods with Children and Young People

Ruth Emond

In the early stages of my PhD research, I asked a group of young people to share their views on an interview schedule that I had piloted with them, concerning their experiences of living in a children's home. During the course of this debate, one young man suggested that interviews would only allow a 'snapshot' of his experience. If I really wanted to know what it was like to live in a children's home, he argued, I would have to live in one. The others in the group agreed. Enthusiastically, they went on to suggest that indeed that was what I ought to do; I ought to move in with them. The more the issue was debated, the more convinced we became that living alongside the young people would give the insight and richness of data that I was seeking to achieve. This was my initiation into ethnographic research! Indeed, from this discussion I went on to live in the children's home for a year-long period. Like the young people I had my own bedroom and was expected to follow the same rules and routines.

The research study that resulted from this exchange focused on the experiences of young people living together as a group and was concerned with how such groups were formed, maintained and ordered. In other words how did the young people view the resident group and how did they gain position within this group? The study took place in a children's home in the north-east of Scotland, which had been allocated six medium- to long-term placements for young people aged between 12 and 18.

This chapter explores ethnography as a methodological approach. It identifies some of the issues that require consideration when undertaking ethnography with children and draws on my experiences as a novice ethnographer in the above-mentioned research project on children in residential care.

What is Ethnography?

Ethnography, as a research approach, was originally developed by anthropologists as a means to understand and describe 'other' cultures. It became adopted, and adapted, by sociologists in their investigations of 'other' cultures within western societies. 'Modern' sociology's early use of this method was undertaken particularly in relation to deviance and marginalized social groups (see, for example, Goffman, 1968; Whyte, 1955). In relation to children and young people, ethnographic studies have been successfully used in the study of education (Burgess, 1985; Delamont, 1984), play (Thorne, 1993) and transitions to work (Willis, 1977) and more recently in the exploration of dance culture (Thornton, 1995) and female friendship (Hey, 1997).

Increasingly, ethnography has been regarded as one of the key research methods in exploring the social worlds of children (James, Jenks, & Prout, 1998). It may be argued that this has resulted from the interplay of a variety of factors. For example, one of the most prominent changes within the sociology of childhood has been the acceptance that children are not passive receptors of socialization but are active social agents managing their own experiences and negotiating around adult controls (Buckingham, 1994; Jackson & Scott, 2000). Furthermore, over the last few decades academic research concerning children and childhood has embraced the notion of social construction; that childhood is socially, culturally and temporally specific (Edwards, 1996; Ennew, 1994; Mayall, 1994; Punch, 1998). Ethnographic research with children requires that the researcher moves away from their (adult-centred) understanding of a group or phenomena and instead seeks to understand the ways in which children's social worlds are shaped and controlled by them (Emond, 2000). Ethnography allows for researchers to get alongside children in their environment to undertake this task.

Ethnography is a generic term for a set of research tools which places emphasis on uncovering participants' understanding of their social and symbolic world (Denzin, 1970; Goffman, 1968). Crucially, ethnography does not set out to 'test' hypotheses or to establish a relationship between variables. Rather, ethnographic researchers set out to be 'taught' the ways, language and expectations of the social group they seek to study. Children become the instructors and we, as researchers, become the pupils. We may have 'hunches' or ideas about the ways in which this world works but in the course of our instruction these ideas may be thrown aside or adapted (Emond, 2000). Ethnographers do not aim to construct generalizable theories. Indeed as outlined by Hammersley and Atkinson (1995), this is 'downplayed in favour of detailed accounts of the concrete experience of life within a particular culture and of the beliefs and social rules that are used as resources within it' (p. 10).

Ethnographic research embraces a number of methodological tools including interviewing and observation (Fielding, 1993). It is perhaps most well known for its observation of groups within their 'natural' environment. There are, however, a wide range of observational positions to choose from. In simple terms, these can be seen as a continuum with a wholly observational role at one end and complete participation at the other (Hessler, 1992). The pure observer would remain detached from any interaction or activity while the complete participant will choose to immerse him/herself in the world of the researched, becoming unidentifiable as a researcher.

The researcher has to decide which approach might yield the best reward. This decision must be considered in light of the research site and those who are being sought as 'subjects'. I would argue that it may be problematic to undertake ethnographic research with children from the extremes of this continuum. A purely observational role where the researcher sits outside the activity and does not interact with the subjects under study can be experienced as deeply unsettling to children and in some ways can count against the 'expert' role that must be given to them if ethnography is to be successful. Equally, to become fully participant (a role which requires the researcher to take on all elements of the participants' daily life/interaction and so on) would require the researcher to behave in such a way as to significantly disturb the 'natural' state of those he or she seeks to research. Indeed, it is debatable whether an adult researcher can fully take on the 'part' of a child (James et al., 1998). Ethnographic research, by its very nature, does not happen within a laboratory or protected environment. Rather, the researcher enters the world of the participants – for example, a classroom, a youth club, a dance class – and therefore to take on a wholly participatory role with a group of children will be open to scrutiny, not only by the children themselves, but also by a wider society in the form of parents, teachers, social workers, passers by and so on.

A further decision that ethnographic researchers must take is whether to 'declare' themselves as undertaking research. In other words, ethnographic research can be covert or overt. It is rare for researchers to take a covert position. However, covert research has been undertaken, for example, with members of the UK National Front, football hooligans and religious sects. Such researchers argue that to be open about the research would prevent access to such groups or would only allow for limited access (see, for example, Fielding, 1981). Thus in its most prevalent form, ethnographic research involves the researcher being present in the social world under study as a semi-participant observer.

Ethnography remains a method befitting the exploration of the meanings and constructions held by research participants of their social world. Fundamental to this approach is the need to move away from typical adult/ child positions (Leonard, 1990; Walsker, 1991). Rather, in using this technique the researcher, as a person, must negotiate and develop relationships with children which acknowledge that they can control the extent to which the researcher is allowed in (Emond, 2000). There is no blanket means of attaining this position and while social science is beginning to acknowledge the diversity of childhood (Backett, 1982) we must also acknowledge the diversity of researchers. Therefore, it is argued that we must as researchers look to our own skills, abilities and resources and seek to use these to establish a worthwhile research relationship.

In the research project that I undertook with young people in residential care, I took on the role of overt, participant observer. I had been invited by the children into the children's home to conduct the research. This obviously helped me to gain access to the site but, more significantly, it immediately created a research environment where these children were taking an active role in the methodological design. Through our post-pilot discussions, it was clear that they understood the area that I was interested in exploring and had themselves identified the best method of undertaking this task. Such negotiations also served to differentiate me from other adults in the unit, that is, the staff. As a result it was agreed that I would only spend time with the young people in the unit itself. In this way I could readily avoid taking on adult responsibilities and responses, safe in the knowledge that staff were ever present. Such avoidance was not possible in the community, where as an adult, I would have been seen as having responsibility for the care and behaviour of the young people I was with.

Role of reflexivity

> Whether we like it or not, researchers remain human beings complete with the usual assembly of feelings, failings and moods. All of these things influence how we feel and understand what is going on. Our consciousness is always the medium through which research occurs; there is no method or technique of doing research other than through the medium of the researcher. (Stanley & Wise, 1983, p. 157)

As the above quotation illustrates, the research process and more specifically data collection and analysis cannot be considered as independent of the researcher. A prominent challenge to the idea that researchers can be dislocated from qualitative research came from feminist writers in the 1970s and 1980s and centred on the notion of reflexivity (for example, Smith, 1988). Many feminist methodologists stressed the importance of accepting the subjective nature of research, whatever the methodological approach. Data, they argued, are always presented through the 'lens' of the researcher and therefore, in order to address subjectivity, the impact of the researcher on the data gathered must be highlighted rather than ignored.

Not only does the researcher shape the interpretation of the data, as Stanley and Wise (1983) suggest, he or she also impacts on the production of that data. Reflexivity, as a sociological concept, allows for this dialectic to be embraced. Thus, the reader is granted insight into the ways in which the data are interpreted and, furthermore, is provided with a sense of how the data are gathered. Reflexive practice stresses the point that social researchers are not 'other' from those they research. Indeed such researchers share the social world with those they study. It implies that the researcher's own social biography and relationship with the field constructs the 'lens' through which the researcher views the field. As such, rather than attempting to disregard or eliminate the impact that the researcher has on the field and on his or her interpretation of the data, reflexivity acknowledges and gives it prominence (Gouldner, 1971).

The need for a reflexive approach is particularly felt when reading ethnographic accounts of research with children and young people. Often researchers provide a detailed description of the initial stages of getting access to children (see, for example, Mandell, 1991). However, what is more often lacking is a discussion of children's perception of the adult researcher, the extent to which they were accepted and the impact this research has upon the children's world. Further, if we accept that childhood is socially constructed, then this construction is dominated by adult discourses around childhood and notions of the 'normal' child (Qvortrup, 1994). Children as subordinate to adults may well seek to negotiate around these constraints, however, they do so within a social world that is dominated by adult surveillance (Brannen & O'Brien, 1995). It is the difficult task of the ethnographer therefore to help children and young people understand that ethnography, in the form of observation of, or participation in, their inter-actions and activities is a different form of surveillance.

Getting in

Due to its aim of getting 'alongside' research participants, ethnography tends to be undertaken with small groups of individuals (Fielding, 1993). Theoretically, there is no restriction on sample size. However, the aim of understanding and providing a 'richness' of data results in large numbers of individuals or research sites being unmanageable (Hessler, 1992).

Despite the challenges of conducting ethnographic research with children it is in many ways no different from 'doing' research with adult participants. Children require the same level of freedom to refuse participation (Stanley & Sieber, 1992), to be treated with respect (Alderson, 1993) and to be offered confidentiality. However, as with research into any social group, these issues are not always simplistically determined. Researchers are required to ensure that participants have a full understanding of the research process if informed consent is to be attained and this, while not impossible with children, requires time and flexibility on the part of the researcher. Research aims need to be articulated in a way that is accessible to children. Account must be taken of the perceived 'freedom' to refuse the researcher or from real or perceived pressure from an institution, whether that be a family, school or children's home, to participate or not (Grisso, 1992).

I take as axiomatic that young people's experiences, abilities and practices are not homogeneous, that there are, indeed, many different childhoods (Grisso, 1992). It follows that the approach taken to explore the research process and the terms of gathering data will vary from child to child. Significantly, this must not be assumed to relate to an age-dominated perspective on childhood. Age cannot be used solely to define a child's ability to participate in the research process or understand the research problem. Indeed it is the job of the researcher to make the research meaningful for all participants. For some children, this may mean talking to them alone about the research while others may prefer such discussion to be held in a group setting or with an adult or friend present (Emond, 2000). Children and young people have varying levels of knowledge about research and academia and therefore language and use of terminology should be altered accordingly. Children may want or need to be informed of the research on more than one occasion and should be given the opportunity to ask questions about the research, both formally and informally.

The majority of studies involving children and young people seek consent for participation in the research not only from the participants themselves but also from their parents (Alderson, 1993). Hammersley and Atkinson (1995) state that there is 'an assumption that children's private lives are legitimately open to scrutiny in a way that adults are not, especially professional, middle-class adults' (p. 267). Therefore, despite the notion of social agency and researchers working hard to create a position of informed consent, it may be adults who ultimately decide whether or not a child will take part in research. Furthermore, the researcher must also take into account the intra-group power dynamics that may exist. Children and young people may feel compelled to allow a researcher to become part of their group as a result of the feelings of the other group members. In many ways this is a methodological issue particular to ethnography. This issue may become particularly pertinent when a new group member/classmate/ resident joins the group. If the ethnography is already underway, how easy is it for a child/young person to not participate?

In my study, I decided to spend some time in the unit prior to moving in. Informal discussions with young people about the project were held and I was able to respond immediately to any misunderstandings about the research and my role within it. I was able to talk individually to the children about the research and their views on my moving in. I wanted to be clear that they were all making an informed decision about their participation. They therefore had to be clear about the level of my involvement, the collection of data, the length of my stay and what would happen to the information that was recorded.

It is vital if ethnographic research is to be successful with children that the adults who are responsible for their care and protection (for example, parents, teachers, youth leaders, social workers) have a clear understanding of the research process and the researcher's role as participant observer (Williamson & Butler, 1995). An established level of trust with these adults allows the researcher to spend all of his or her time with the children and avoids the expectation that they will undertake an 'adult' role in their daily lives.

In relation to my research, I wanted the staff to understand that I would not be evaluating their practice nor was I to be thought of as an additional staff member. I suggested that I could be regarded either as 'invisible' or as another young person and, in order to achieve this, I attempted to outline examples of where this might come into play prior to my moving in. I was anxious that I would be seen as troublesome or untrustworthy for failing to intervene in situations involving the children and that staff requests for my assistance in matters of care would compromise my position and the research itself. This time also provided the opportunity to work with the staff on the reality of 'hosting' ethnographic research and the potential impact my role as participant observer and not an adult member of staff might have on them. To be convincing as a non-staff member I felt that I needed to be given permission by staff to opt out of all adult responsibility.

A further aspect of gaining informed consent that is rarely mentioned in literature is the exploration of participants' motivation to be involved in the research. This is particularly important as ethnographic researchers are, in the majority of cases, required to build relationships, establish a level of trust and impinge on an individual's life to a far greater extent than is required in many other research approaches (see, for example, Polsky, 1962). In the negotiation of consent that took place in my research project each young person involved was asked why he or she wished to take part. A small number stated that they thought the project was interesting and still more said that the subject had been one that they had thought deserved reflection. The most significant number of young people, however, stated that they wished to participate because of their belief that research would 'change things' and 'make things better for the next lot of kids'. This motivation concerned me. I wanted to make clear to the young people the likely impact that the project would have in terms of policy or practice. I explained that ultimately this was an examination that would result in a further qualification for me (the study was undertaken as my doctoral thesis). I went on to say that I would be keen to talk at conferences, publish papers and feedback to their local authority but that I could not *guarantee* that the research would have any direct effect. I felt that, in order to give informed consent, it was essential that the young people needed to know not only what the research process would involve, but also what the likely outcomes would be. This view was compounded by what I regarded was a misplaced belief that my research would 'make a difference'. On reflection, I would argue that this 'honest' approach to the likely impact of the research made clear to the young people that their views were being taken seriously and that the notion of informed consent was one which was meaningful.

A further outcome of this discussion was the way that the clear outcome – a PhD qualification – supported the construction of me as 'student'. A number of researchers have argued the importance of taking on the role of an atypical, less powerful adult (Corsaro & Molinari, 2000; Fine & Sandstrom, 1988). I found that by having this student role as my initial reference point the young people were more open to being asked questions and more willing to volunteer information. They also rightly regarded me as someone who needed their help. As a result, in the early stages of the project I was seen as something of an object of pity. I did not have a clear understanding of the rules and routines of the unit, I was struggling to take field notes and balance this with an acceptable level of participation with the group and I missed my home and family. Many of the young people took on a supporting role at this stage. As Hilary stated:

> It's a shame for you really … I mean to be away from your family and all just to find out about us … I dinnae think we've anything worth finding out about … och well it'll get you to be a doctor and then you'll get loads of cash … I'm going to go to university an a …

Confidentiality

With regard to research with children there are significant considerations to be given to the issue of confidentiality and these concerns increased for me after the decision was taken to proceed with an ethnographic study. The context and extent of contact while undertaking ethnographic research may result in observing behaviours that could cause concern. Alternatively, children may choose to disclose information relating to their safety or protection. However, researchers have to balance this with the concern that by not offering total confidentiality their role as participant observer can become confused with that of parent or 'responsible' adult and in turn might mean a limited access to the children's group.

In relation to my research, a compromise position was reached. Central to this confidentiality bargain was its emphasis on discussion. It was agreed that participants would be aware of any information that I would be passing on and would have the opportunity to negotiate this with me first. Crucially, it appeared that it was not the level of confidentiality that was necessarily the issue, it was the sense that the young people felt involved in the problem solving on this point and that they would be made aware of potential 'breaches' of confidentiality *before* they happened.

Long discussions were also held in relation to anonymity. Many of the children wanted their names to be included in the thesis and resulting publications. I was uncomfortable with this, not only because people outside the unit may have been able to identify them but also because they would be identifiable to each other and to the staff. I explained that I would be an almost constant presence and it was likely that, at times, they would forget that I was a researcher. I also voiced my concern that their relationships with each other might change over time and that they may well make comments about each other that they would be unhappy to have repeated at a later date. The compromise we reached was that they would make up their own pseudonyms. I felt pleased with this, until I realized that they had told each other what these names were. This was one of the few points in the research process where I overruled the opinion of the participants and took control of anonymizing the data.

Establishing good research practice

It is vital for researchers using an ethnographic approach to consider what is 'good research practice' within the context of their research study. Useful codes of ethical practice are provided by the majority of scholarly bodies (for example, the British Sociological Association) and are helpfully addressed in a number of research manuals (see also Hill, Chapter 4 of this volume). Despite this, researchers must also consider the ethical issues that are particular to their setting or research context. In the case of ethnographic research with children, one of the paramount issues relates to that of physical and emotional 'safety'. As previously mentioned, researchers must put in place strategies to manage disclosure or dangerous practices by children and potentially other adults. They must also seek to protect themselves from 'risky' situations and again take time to develop strategies for managing their own behaviour, stress, and so on (Lee-Treweek, 2000). For example, I made the decision to always have my bedroom door locked; this protected me from children bursting in and also ensured the safety of the data. However, if a young person visited me in my bedroom I would always keep the door open.

It is crucial, if participant observation is to be undertaken, that relationships are built with children. Adults, especially adults within institutions whether that be families, schools, youth clubs residential homes and so on, are there in an authoritative capacity (Jackson & Scott, 2000). Fine and Sandstrom (1988) argue that ethnographic researchers should attempt to construct a 'friendship' relationship with participants, suspending their beliefs as to appropriate behaviour and putting aside value judgements that are in conflict with those of the children. However, the researcher needs to consider the practicalities of managing and/or maintaining this position, for example, if one child is being bullied by others. In my case, because there were staff on hand at all times and we had agreed that I would not go out of the unit with the young people, I was able to move away from an adult role. However, this did not stop me from reacting to events nor did it prevent children looking for my response to, or opinion on, matters or events.

Central to establishing a relationship with children is a reflection on the researcher's use of language and presentation. Ethnographic researchers must develop a style which is comfortable to them and which reflects their 'true self'. Indeed young people have argued against a style which they find patronizing or 'false' (Cottle, 1973). As I had spent the previous ten years in the north-east of Scotland where the research was conducted, my own Scottish accent had become more integrated with the local dialect, incorporating some of the indigenous words and phrases. I therefore understood many of the Doric words and was comfortable with the speed at which the young people spoke. This 'shared' language had further impact in that it helped me to be regarded with less fear and distrust. I also dressed casually and chose, like many of the children, not to wear shoes in the house. This acted as another way of marking me as a different type of adult.

This style must also be considered within the context of the research being undertaken. I was aware that young people who have been in the care system have been asked biographical details and views on their care on numerous occasions and I was concerned to get beyond the arguably scripted disclosures that the young people were used to producing. Not only is the asking of questions reinforcement of an 'adult' role but, for these young people, such interviews have often led to changes in circumstances. I was also concerned that these children were likely to have experienced a number of changes in carers and indeed in many of their relationships. It was therefore vital that the ending of the project, and our relationship, were as planned and structured as the earlier parts of the work.

From Planning to Practice

Into the field

Ethnographic research can be seen as comprising a number of different stages as the fieldwork progresses. Often, researchers have reported on the earlier stages of the research and provided little information relating to the middle and end sections of the fieldwork. All elements of the process are essential, however, if the reader is to gain a real insight into how the data were gathered.

Ethnographers need to be aware that getting access does not mean getting in! In my case, while the idea for an ethnographic study had been put forward by the children, this did not result in my being wholeheartedly welcomed into the group. Indeed, moving into the unit was a daunting experience. I was unsure of the way to behave in the unit, how it worked and my role as researcher. While many of the participants, especially the young women, gave me practical help with settling in – (they gave me posters for my wall and showed me around) – there were also times when I would walk into a room and other residents would walk out. I made the decision to sit back and wait to be asked to be involved; I concentrated on gaining confidence by using field notes and actively participating with the group whenever I was asked to join in.

Ethnographers have generally used written recording of events, observations and interactions. Predominately, these are categorized into field notes and field dairies (Lofland & Lofland, 1984). Field notes are what Schatzman and Strauss (1973) refer to as 'observational notes'. They argue that these should record 'events experienced principally through watching and listening. They contain as little interpretation as possible and are as reliable as the observer can construct them' (p. 110). In essence, they consist of a record of the date, time and location of the situation being observed as well as the physical location and description of the main characters. It is in these notes that any verbal and nonverbal communications are logged. 'Theoretical notes' (Schatzman & Strauss, 1973) by contrast, may be written daily in a field diary. This diary can serve as a record of the researcher's thoughts and feelings as well as any theoretical ideas that emerge. Diaries can also be a helpful tool to explore the ways in which the researcher's presence may have impacted on the environment.

In relation to my study, after the first month of fieldwork I met formally with the young people to discuss how they were experiencing my involvement. From this discussion the young people stated that they were unhappy with my use of field notes, finding my continual disappearances distracting. From my own perspective I had found it problematic to participate fully in the life of the group and was concerned that without this participation, especially in this initial phase, I would not be granted group membership. I had further been concerned by the awareness the young people had of my need to write down their interactions. This was highlighted when, during a verbal disagreement between two of the young men, they had paused, mid-fight, and said: 'Sorry Ruth, are we going too fast? Will we do it again?' This was not 'naturalistic' research! We concluded that tape-recording interactions would allow all members to feel less aware of research being conducted and would free me to participate more fully. The young people did, however, agree to my writing brief supporting notes.

In retrospect, the change in data collection techniques was extremely positive. The notebook that I carried became a doodle pad with the front and back covered in drawings and messages from the young people. I also used the notebooks to indicate my own growing levels of trust, leaving them on the table rather than clutching them. As the fieldwork progressed the young people took increasing control over the dictaphone, switching it off and on and checking that it was recording. I found that the more established I became in the group the longer the machine remained on and therefore more data were collected. This empowerment of the young people served to guide the research at a pace that they were comfortable with and, in turn, assisted the establishment of trust. That young people have a level of control over the pace of the research appears to make a significant impact on the success of the ethnographic relationship. It can provide a real opportunity to allow children and young people to take control. Indeed Polsky (1962) argued that, with hindsight, he had rushed the young men in his study to understand his interest in them and that this initial focus on research aims, rather than on building relationships, had slowed down the research process.

The success of the change in recording technique was illustrated when two of the young women suggested that they keep recorded diaries of events while I was on home leave. This idea spread among the group and during the last seven months of fieldwork the majority of the group took turns at keeping recorded diaries. They gave me an interesting insight into what the young people valued in day-to-day interactions and the meanings that they attributed to them. It also provided data regarding the differences in the material young men and young women chose to record. Significantly, it provided the opportunity for the group to 'own' the research and to participate in problem solving. This level of active participation not only empowered the young people but also served to remind them and me that they were indeed the experts in the field.

This change in recording technique allowed for me to become a much more active participant in the group. The tape-recorder was initially seen as a novelty and something which was fun. Their control of it also meant that they could switch it off as a means of 'ending' the research period without having to physically move away from me or exclude me. I also found that the period of time that I had waited to be invited had served me well and had been seen by the participants as a 'smart move'. As Gregor explains:

> Just try to be friendly … if you dinnae they get the wrong idea … like that you think that you're better than them or something … It's the same when folk come

in and they think they're hard ... like they rule the place ... it's mostly cos they think they have to be like that cos we're hard.

The next stage in the ethnographic process was very much concerned with being 'tested out'. I was not alone in this experience, indeed I would later become involved in testing out other residents. Central to these tests was my loyalty to the group and my ability to keep information to myself. This was even more pertinent to me as a researcher as it was centrally concerned with confidentiality and my capacity to keep the promises I had made in this regard. I was later to find out that the group had got together and con-structed a story which one young woman later told me. They then waited to see if I would tell the other residents or the staff. That I had not done so, not only strengthened the research relationship, but resulted in my being allowed to become more involved in the group.

After this period of being tested, the next stage was dominated by building relationships. By this point, the children were used to my presence, had tested my loyalty to them, and were in control of the data collection techniques. The building of relationships was very much helped by my own home visits and calls from home. Like the other residents, I was always anxious to go home and at the same time desperate not to miss anything in the unit. I was asked questions about my home life (as were my fellow residents) and took part in the testing out and management of new admissions. This period was the most extensive, lasting for about five months. In many ways this was the time that the greatest amount of data were collected and recorded by the group.

The last stage, of leaving the site, was again helped by the research following the care patterns of many of the residents. This period was also marked by a number of changes in the group. Many of the young people that I had lived with were being returned home or were moving on to their own flats or different forms of care. Endings with these young people were therefore instigated by them and took place before the fieldwork was over. These were often difficult endings for everyone, as Bryony explained after she had left the unit:

> it just isnae hame anymare ... Every time I come back, ken ate visit, it's different ... new staff, new kids, new cups and a'thing ... but then I still come do I?

I had extended periods of time at home, only coming to the unit once a month. I had lost my bedroom to a new resident and was therefore sleeping on the couch. During these visits I was keen to discuss the findings and the analytical and conceptual ideas that I had. In all these ways I was becoming more like an adult researcher and less like a resident.

Analysis

One of the major strengths of using an ethnographic approach is the richness and quantity of data generated. However, when it comes to analysis the volume of data can feel overwhelming. There are a number of approaches used in the analysis of ethnographic data. In general terms such analysis seeks to establish patterns or themes emerging from the data (Agar, 1986). Such themes may relate to forms of interaction, physical movement, styles of negotiation and so forth. From these themes a theoretical framework is developed in an attempt to order these accounts (McCall & Simmons, 1969).

One of the most helpful ways of approaching ethnographic data is sequential analysis (Becker, 1971). The initial stage of analysis involves gaining an understanding of the setting and identifying the ways in which that understanding has come about. Second, focus is given to the frequency and typicality of each observation and the characters that are involved. Finally, researchers are required to move from a substantive focus to a more theoretical approach. In terms of my own research, I decided to transcribe all the tape-recordings and to incorporate them into my diary. While highly time-consuming, this approach allowed me to gain a real sense of the emerging themes, the structures and patterns of interactions and the characters involved. After the fieldwork was completed, I read through the transcripts to identify the themes that were in play and constructed files of material that related to each. These themes were then broken down into subthemes. I also compiled a file consisting of data that were relevant to the experience of admission to the unit in an attempt to reflect on and support my own experience of admission.

The resultant analytical framework was then explored during my fieldwork at a second research site. While this is not common in ethnographic work, it allowed me the opportunity to consider the applicability of the analytical framework to other settings. The findings were debated with the young people and staff at both a textual level and in relation to the suggested analytical framework. It was felt that the young people had been so heavily involved in the design of the research and the collection of the data that their views on the resultant analytical framework should be taken into account. I presented my thoughts during the final few months of fieldwork at an informal level and included the young people's feedback as data. I also gave a formal presentation to the young people and staff after the analysis was completed (Emond, 2000).

Discussion

Ethnographic approaches require us to suspend any ideas we might have as to our adult notions of childhood. Indeed, Solberg (1996) states: 'I recommend instead a certain ignorance of age. This implies greater emphasis on the situational contexts within which children act and that we move our attention away from "being" to "doing"' (p. 54). While Solberg accepts that the way in which ethnography is *approached* may differ dependent on the child's age, it is vital that age does not restrict how we understand the social worlds that children experience. Ethnography allows the researcher to gain insight into *what factors are significant* to those children under study rather than assuming *what we as researchers see as significant* in childhood.

Fundamental to this is the need to listen to and respect children's views and experiences. There is a danger in taking an ethnographic approach whereby researchers make sense of children's behaviour through an adult lens. The filtering of information through our own experiences of childhood and its associated meanings can distort what children are telling us. Conversely, ethnographic researchers need to be mindful that by considering their research subjects as 'other' we dislocate children from all other aspects of social life. Ethnography needs to present not just the differences, but the similarities between and among the social worlds of children and adults (James et al., 1998).

To assume a knowledge of childhood is not necessarily a conscious act. It has much to do with the way in which children are constructed as vulnerable and powerless. As adults we often assume that we know best. However, ethnography can in fact empower children in the research process. It relies on children taking control over how researchers are included in their interactions and on researchers granting children their rightful position as 'experts'. In these ways children's experiences and views are given to us rather than extracted to fit into what we already think we know about what it means to be a child.

Ethnography, and participant observation in particular, require the researcher to work hard at ensuring children understand what is taking place and their freedom to opt out as well as into the research process. In using participant observation the researcher is often present over long periods of time. During this period children have the opportunity to shape how they manage the presence of researchers and the extent to which they allow them to take part. Participant observation by its very nature allows children to control the level of acceptance and involvement. The role of the researcher is therefore negotiated rather than imposed.

One problematic aspect of research into children's lives is these very terms. Homogeneity does not necessarily exist as a result of similar age categories and the generalizability of child-related research must be resisted. Rather there is a growing awareness that, despite an acknowledgement of the shared nature of 'childhood', sociology must be open to the possibility of many 'childhoods'. James, Jenks and Prout (1998) stress that this under-standing is a central tenet of the 'new' sociology of childhood.

Conclusions

Ethnography is in many ways one of the most challenging approaches to the study of children. It requires those who undertake this form of research to reflect not only on the data, but also on their use of self within the field. With specific regard to children, it requires us to suspend our sense of 'superior' knowledge and to learn the practices and perspectives of those under study. Furthermore it requires researchers to explore their own presentations of language and dress, their social practices, of listening and participating, and their ability to relate socially to those around them. For those of us who choose to embark on participatory research it may mean at times that we have to take personal risks: to sing, to tell jokes, to be questioned about our views or personal lives.

It must also be stressed that ethnography takes time. Children and young people must have control over the speed at which researchers are invited in to their world. Further time must be taken to fully understand the symbolic nature of the world under study and the strategies used by those within to shape and control it.

References

Agar, M. (1986). *Speaking of ethnography*. Beverley Hills, CA: Sage.

Alderson, P. (1993). *Children's consent to surgery*. Buckingham: Open University Press.

Backett, K. (1982). *Mothers and fathers: A study of the development and negotiation of parental behaviour*. London: Macmillan.

Becker, H. (1971). *Sociological work*. London: Allen Lane.

Becker, H.S., Greer, B., Hughes, E.C., & Strauss, A. (1961). *Boys in white*. Chicago: University of Chicago Press.

Brannen, J. & O'Brien, M. (1995). Childhood and the sociological gaze: Paradigms and paradoxes. *Sociology, 29*(4), 729–737.

Buckingham, D. (1994). Television and the definition of childhood. In B. Mayall (Ed.), *Children's childhoods: Observed and experienced* (pp. 79–96). London: Falmer Press.

Burgess, R. (1985). *Issues in educational research: Qualitative methods*. London: Falmer Press.

Corsaro, W. & Molinari, L. (2000). Entering and observing in children's worlds: A reflection on a longitudinal ethnography of early education in Italy. In A. Christensen & A. James (Eds.), *Research with children: Perspectives and practices* (pp. 179–200). London: Falmer Press.

Cottle, T. (1973). The life study: On mutual recognition and the subjective inquiry. *Urban Life and Culture, 2*, 344–360.

Delamont, S. (1984). The old girl network: Reflections on the fieldwork at St. Lukes. In R. Burgess (Ed.), *The research process in educational settings: Ten case studies* (pp. 1–14). London: Falmer Press.

Denzin, N.K. (1970). *The research act in sociology*. London: Butterworths.

Edwards, M. (1996). New approaches to children and development: Introduction and overview. *Journal of international development, 8*(6), 813–827.

Emond, R. (2000). *Survival of the skilful: An ethnographic study of two groups of young people in residential care*. Unpublished doctoral thesis, University of Stirling.

Ennew, J. (1994). *Street and working children: A guide to planning* (Development Manual 4). London: Save the Children.

Fielding, N. (1981). *The National Front*. London: Routledge and Kegan Paul.

Fielding, N. (1993). Ethnography. In N. Gilbert (Ed.), *Researching social life* (pp. 154–171). London: Sage.

Fine, G.A. & Sandstrom, K.L. (1988). *Knowing children: Participant observation with minors* (Sage University Paper Series on Qualitative Research Methods, 15). Beverly Hills, CA: Sage.

Goffman, E. (1968). *Asylums: Essays on the social situation of mental patients and other inmates*. London: Peregrine.

Gouldner, A. (1971). *The coming crisis of western sociology*. London: Heinemann.

Grisso, T. (1992). Minor's assent to behavioural research without parental consent. In B. Stanley & J.E. Sieber (Eds.), *Social research on children and adolescents: Ethical issues* (pp. 109–127). Beverley Hills, CA: Sage.

Hammersley, M. & Atkison, P. (1995). *Ethnography: Principles in practice*. London: Routledge.

Hessler, M.H. (1992). *Social research methods*. St Paul, MI: West Publishing.

Hey, V. (1997). *The company she keeps: An ethnography of girls' friendship groups*. Buckingham: Open University Press.

Jackson, S. & Scott, S. (2000). Childhood. In G. Payne, (Ed.), *Social divisions* (pp. 152–168). London: Macmillan.

James, A., Jenks, C., & Prout, A. (1998). *Theorizing childhood*. Cambridge: Polity Press.

Lee-Treweek, G. (2000). The insight of emotional danger: Research experiences in a home for older people. In G. Lee-Treweek & S. Linkogle (Eds.), *Danger in the field* (pp. 114–131). London: Routledge.

Leonard, D. (1990). In their own right: Children and sociology in the UK. In L. Chisolm, P. Buchner, H.-H. Kruger, & P. Brown (Eds.), *Childhood, youth and social change* (pp. 58–70). London: Falmer Press.

Lofland, J. & Lofland, L.H. (1984). *Analysing social settings* (2nd ed.). Belmont, CA: Wadsworth.

Mandell, N. (1991). The least adult role in studying children. In F. Waksler (Ed.), *Studying the social worlds of children* (pp. 38–59). London: Falmer Press.

May, T. (1993). *Social research: Issues, methods and process*. Buckingham: Open University Press.

Mayall, B. (1994). *Children's childhoods: Observed and experienced*. London: Falmer Press.

McCall, G. & Simmons, J. (1969). *Issues in participant observation*. New York: Addison-Wesley.

Polsky, H. (1962). *Cottage six: The social system of delinquent boys in residential treatment*. New York: Wiley.

Punch, S. (1998). *Negotiating independence: Children and young people growing up in rural Bolivia*. Unpublished doctoral thesis, University of Leeds.

Qvortrup, J. (1994). Introduction. In J. Qvortrup, M. Bardy, G. Sgritta, & H. Wintersberger (Eds.), *Childhood matters: Social theory, practice and politics* (pp. 1–24). Aldershot: Avebury.

Schatzman, C. & Strauss, A.L. (1973). *Field Research: Strategies for a natural sociology*. New York: Prentice Hall.

Smith, D.E. (1981). *The everyday world as problematic: A feminist sociology*. Milton Keynes: Open University Press.

Solberg, A. (1996) The challenge of child research: From 'being' to 'doing'. In J. Brannen & M. O'Brien (Eds.), *Children in families: Research and policy*. London: Falmer Press.

Stanley, B. & Sieber, J.E. (Eds.) (1992). *Social research on children and adolescents: Ethical issues*. Newbury Park, CA: Sage.

Stanley, L. & Wise, S. (1983). *Breaking out: Feminist consciousness and feminist research*. London: Routledge and Kegan Paul.

Thorne, B. (1993). *Gender play: Girls and boys in school.* Buckingham: Open University Press.

Thornton, S. (1995). *Club cultures: Music, media and subcultural capital.* Oxford: Polity Press.

Walsker, F.C. (Ed.) (1991). *Studying the social worlds of children.* London: Falmer Press.

Whyte, W.F. (1955). *Street Corner Society: The Social Structure of an Italian Slum.* Chicago: University of Chicago Press.

Williamson, H. & Butler, I. (1995). 'No one ever listens to us': Interviewing children and young people. In C. Cloke & M. Davies (Eds.), *Participation and empowerment in child protection* (pp. 61–79). Chichester: Wiley.

Willis, P. (1977). *Learning to labour.* London: Saxon House.

The Generation and Analysis of Text

8 Exploring Meaning in Interviews with Children

Helen L. Westcott and Karen S. Littleton

One of the main myths we wish to dispel in this chapter is that interviewing is an easy research method, and that all we have to do as researchers is to talk to children and they will talk to us. A host of practical and ethical problems concerning interviewing are hidden by the unquestioning assumption that interviewing is a straightforward task: for example, arranging access to children and negotiating 'gatekeepers'; obtaining consent from children and carers; confidentiality; ethical dilemmas (such as interviewing in child protection contexts), and so on. Perhaps more importantly, conceptual issues in interviewing are also hidden. Researchers are seldom explicit about how they perceive the interview context, what model of the child they assume or invoke, how they conceptualize the interviewer's role, and the processes by which they create meaning from what is said in interviews. In addressing fundamental issues such as these, the researcher will be moving towards conceptual clarity – and a more developed theoretical understanding – of the roles of the child and the interviewer in the context of the interview. It is easy to forget that children may rarely be spoken to, or seriously listened to, unless they have done something 'wrong'. Also, that far from being passive recipients of the adult's utterances, they are actively making sense of the interview situation for themselves, and possibly for others around them.

In this chapter we concentrate on the conceptual issues highlighted above, since we firmly believe that they must be addressed by researchers at the outset if the research interview is to be meaningful. We believe that children's perspectives are central to research, policy and practice in our own (and other) areas of work – namely forensic investigative interviewing and the psychology of education. We will be using examples from our experiences of one-to-one research interviews with children to illustrate arguments throughout the chapter. We do not cover practical or ethical issues per se; rather, we consider the practical implications of conceptual clarity. There are other resources in this volume and elsewhere to which readers can refer (for example, Christensen & James, 2000; Graue & Walsh, 1998; Memon & Bull, 1999; Stanley & Sieber, 1992; Westcott, 1996; Williamson & Butler, 1995). Further, this chapter is *not* a 'cookbook' on '*how* to interview'; for reasons we hope will become clear as the chapter develops, such an approach would be unproductive.

As a research method widely used in psychological and educational research, and one often used in applied settings, it is striking how often conceptual issues related to interviewing are left implicit, or unaddressed. Rarely is the researcher's orientation to the interview process clarified or 'problematized', in contrast to ethnomethodological or discursive approaches. In part, this is the result of the practical rather than theoretical development of interviewing as a research method. Nonetheless, addressing conceptual issues helps to prevent the researcher from inadvertently undermining children's competence in interview settings and beyond, as well as offering a framework within which to set up interviews and analyse responses. That is to say, conceptual issues do themselves have practical as well as theoretical implications.

It is also important to realize how research impacts upon children in wider society, and to recognize our responsibility as researchers not to 'theorize incompetent children' (Alderson, 1995; Light & Littleton, 1999; Säljö, 1997). As examples, in education, a young child who does not succeed on particular educational tasks or tests can be labeled as a 'failing child', a label which has a profound impact on his or her educational experience. In investigative interviewing, unthinking generalization of suggestibility research with pre-schoolers (for example, Ceci & Bruck, 1993) has led to many older child witnesses being unfairly perceived as inevitably suggestible by courtroom personnel. Thus it is important that conceptual clarity in the research interview is viewed as a requirement and not a luxury.

The Interview Context: The Model of the Child Underpinning the Interview

Researchers have conceptualized the child interviewee in a variety of different ways (see, for example, James, 1999; Woodhead & Faulkner, 2000), with varying implications for the manner in which the research question is approached, the findings are analysed, and the roles of the child and interviewer are conceived. The manner in which the power dynamics existing in interview settings are acknowledged or acted upon similarly varies depending upon the model of the child the researcher invokes. To take an example, traditionally, psychological research on investigative interviewing has come from the experimental paradigm, and typically from a cognitive-psychology approach (for example, Ceci & Bruck, 1995). One problem that arises from use of this paradigm in research is that the child is construed as a passive (powerless) participant or interviewee, and the fact that all situations are constructed – no matter how naturalistic they are – is overlooked. So, the focus has largely been on what information can be 'got' from children by the appropriate or inappropriate use of different questioning techniques, such as open-ended, closed, repeated and so on (see, for example, Poole & Lamb, 1998). How child witnesses perceive or contribute to the interview context is virtually unexplored (but see Wade & Westcott, 1997) within the overall aim not of creating understanding with children, but rather of 'revealing' it. To develop the example of questioning techniques above, this translates into a search for the 'right' question which will, seemingly automatically, produce the required response from the child (that is, detailed, accurate, and so on). Bruner (1984) distinguishes between a life as lived, experienced and told:

> A life lived is what actually happens. A life experienced consists of the images, feelings, sentiments, desires, thoughts and meanings known to the person whose life it is ... A life as told, a life history, is a narrative, influenced by the cultural conventions of telling, by the evidence, and by the social context. (p. 7)

Thus, the experimental paradigm ignores gaps between reality, experience and expression which occur in any interview. The 'life as told' by the child is inevitably what is available in the interview – yet typical research and practice guidance give the impression that the 'life as lived' is somehow present in the child for interviewers, if only they get the questions 'right'. This creates unrealistic expectations of both interviewer and child. Further, in ignoring the degree to which the child actively co-constructs the interview, experimental questioning research has consequently nothing to say about motivational factors which are so crucial in forensic settings, and has further contributed to the marginalization of children and young people in the planning process of genuine forensic interviews (since they are passive responders, they are seen as having little or nothing to contribute).

The Relationship between Context and Children's Competence

Lyon's (2002) work on children's understanding of the oath used in courts is a nice example of the need to ensure that the interview task has an appropriate context for children. Lyon and his colleagues postulated that the typical phrasing of the oath underestimates children's competence, and thus their credibility as witnesses. In a series of studies they made the oath-taking task more child centred by asking children to identify true and false statements, rather than provide abstract definitions of truth and lies; using examples which did not require the child to identify themselves or the adult authority figure as a 'liar'; clarifying certain language, for example, 'promise'. When the context of the task was made meaningful, even very young children's performances, taken as index of their competence, were dramatically improved.

The work of Waterman and colleagues (Waterman, Blades, & Spencer, 2002) on how and why children respond to nonsense questions is a further example of the importance of context, and of exploring children's explanations of their interview responses. Successive refinements were made to a famous experimental design that appeared to show that children were willing to answer even bizarre and unanswerable questions put to them by adults (Hughes & Grieve, 1980). Waterman and colleagues (2002) refinements revealed that, in fact, children do not answer all nonsensical questions, and that if the question is phrased in an open format (rather than requiring a simple 'yes' or 'no' answer) the majority of children indicate that they did not understand, or did not know the answer. Further, asking children to explain their answers when they did respond to nonsense questions showed that 'no' was often used to indicate that the child thought the question was silly.

This work is especially significant since the original Hughes and Grieve's study is often referred to as an example of children's incompetence in interview situations. It reveals the importance of adopting a sociocultural stance on the interview process. Researchers should not simply focus on the 'outcome' of the interview, but need to focus on the moment-to-moment co-constructive processes through which meaning is negotiated, renegotiated and contested. Thus, it seems obvious that children should be given the opportunity to explain their responses in interview situations, and also should be able to take the initiative as necessary to help them create a meaningful context with the interviewer. In so doing, they are an active participant in the interview process, thus the roles of 'teller and told' are shared and jointly created.

Joint Meaning-Making

The analyses of composite data prevalent in experimental interviewing research hide large individual differences in the 'performance' of children in interviews, and obscure the processes through which meaning is made (or not made) by the adult and child in the interview. Two examples from an unpublished experimental study of questioning by Westcott (1999) are relevant here. In this study, children viewed a five-minute videotape showing a young girl dropped off alone and early at school by her mother. She is later subject to an ambiguous approach by strangers, who arrive by car. Children were individually interviewed about the video and its contents. The first excerpt is from an 8-year-old girl who was overwhelmed by shyness in her interview with the author, to the extent that after her first few responses she provided virtually no information about the video:

Q: What happened on the video?

A: (.) Um (.) Mum and dad took her to school?

Q: Tell me everything you can remember.

A: (.) The little girl made a hopscotch (.) and then a lady and a man came in a car and said do you know where a road is or something is they asked her to get in the car and show her and she said no.

Q: That's great. What else can you tell me about the video?

A: She said no to going in the car and then a policeman turned the corner so the lady quickly jumped in the car and they drived off.

Q: Anything else?

A: (.)

Q: Anything else?

A: (.)

Q: Okay. Tell me about the girl on the video.

A: (.)

Q: What did she look like?

A: (.)

Q: Do you want to stop (girl's name)? Are you too nervous?

A: I'm nervous but I don't want to stop.

The second example comes from an 11-year-old boy, who, by contrast, was completely uninhibited, and highly imaginative, in his interview:

Q6:   What else can you tell me about the girl?

A6:   She was one of them girls that didn't have very much friends but she had a good imagination.

Q7:   And how do you know that?

A7:   She was the way she was playing by herself she was acting as if somebody else was playing with her …

Q11: Tell me about the mum in the video.

A11: The mum was one of them mums that if anything happens to the girl she'll um go straight down the school and have a go at the head teacher or something.

Q12: How do you know that?

A12: It's the way she was speaking to her 'oh darling' and all of this like mums do and stuff and she was very caring …

Q17: What else can you tell me about that woman?

A17: Um she was very cunning and she wasn't very intelligent.

Q18: What makes you think that?

A18: Well she just drove into school and it was pretty obvious that there was going to be teachers about or something but if she just drove to the park where there was children she could of just picked one up easily …

Q21: Tell me about the policeman.

A21: The policeman seemed very caring for all the children in the school and he wanted to do his job well and um he was very intelligent and he was very good at his job being a policeman.

Q22: How do you know that?

A22: Because as soon as the woman saw him he like chased after 'em …'

Q30. Okay, what was the mum wearing?

A30: Er, the mum was dressed all fancy something I can't really say what she was wearing.

Q31: What do you mean 'fancy something'?
A31: Um she was dressing like she was really posh and …
Q32: Why do you think she's posh? Describe it to me.
A32: Because all posh people wear long earrings speak very like [puts on accent] 'oh nice, really, nice, nice, lovely' and all of that, and she was like speaking sort of like that and she was acting quite weird when she came she was like all over the girl, studying her sort of thing …

Both these children raise awkward and difficult issues for researchers using an experimental paradigm, and are, for different reasons (shyness or confabulating), easily construed as incompetent or unreliable, and, in the case of the girl, likely to be characterized as an 'outlier' and excluded from the interview 'sample'. Similar problems evidently confront professional interviewers also, as the following quote from a police interviewer demonstrates:

'I said to him "have you got any concerns about anybody"? And he said "Yeah", and so I said, "Well, who's that?" and he said "Eric Cantona". He said he was worried that Eric Cantona would leave Manchester United. The whole interview was about Eric Cantona. That was his worry.' (Police interviewer in Davis, Hoyano, Keenan, Maitland, & Morgan, 1999: 23)

In all these examples, the 'problem' is seen as lying with the children, rather than with the paradigm, and the children's behaviour is readily attributed to psychological incompetence. As James (1999) explains, the methods of developmental psychology tend to:

define a researcher–child relationship in which children are objects of study, to be observed, tested and experimented on, where their feelings, behavior and beliefs are interpreted as evidence of relative competence against those standards prescribed for adults. (p. 234)

We need to guard against theorizing children's immaturity, when their responses in interview contexts reflect inexperience rather than immaturity:

some children are shy or hesitant, like some adults, but we also met confident fluent eight year olds. Adults tend to make more connections, and to reply in more detail at greater length than very young children. This difference is a matter of degree rather than of kind, and is perhaps less due to immaturity than to children's inexperience. When they are experienced they give mature replies. (Alderson, 1993: 71)

Rather than theorizing incompetence, then, we need to develop our understanding of the activity and responses of the child in context. We need to understand how the situations in which children are placed, and the meanings they ascribe to interviewer's questions, support or constrain their activity and performance. We also need to recognize that notions of 'competence' are problematic, and are informed by cultural beliefs and negotiated by participants in particular social, institutional and cultural contexts (Woodhead, Faulkner, & Littleton, 1999).

Thus a child's responses in an interview situation are fundamentally situated. It is not simply the case that some questions, situations or contexts are somehow 'fairer' than others and are therefore better at 'revealing' competence or understanding. The child's responses to an interviewer represent the 'tuning of particular persons to the particular demands and opportunities of a situation, and thus resides in the combination of person-in-situation, not "in the mind" alone' (Snow, 1994: 31). Moreover, interviews are psychological spaces requiring an 'attunement to the attunement of others' (Rommetveit, 1992). So, children's responses and reactions to the questions psychologists ask are crucially dependent upon the negotiation of the experimental or didactic contract (Grossen & Pochon, 1997), and the co-construction of meaning between interviewer and child.

Interviews are 'communication situations that are culturally rooted and whose meanings have to be constructed intersubjectively during the interaction' (Grossen & Pochon, 1997: 269). What is needed, then, is a detailed understanding of issues of negotiation and re-negotiation of meaning, subjectivity, intersubjectivity and social construction in the interview (Light & Littleton, 1999). This is because we are not engaged in the activity of discovering or uncovering the 'real' capabilities of the child. Rather, we are centrally involved in the business of constructing particular accounts and representations of the child and notions of competence (Woodhead et al., 1999).

This should lead the researcher to explore creative or 'challenging' responses for a greater understanding of the child's perspective, and at all times throughout the interview process to ask themselves: 'What is the child making of this?' Our own limited interpretations of what counts as good, correct or appropriate responses in interview settings mean that we often fail to recognize the creative responses children make in such situations. As an example, regarding the imaginative boy above, it is evident that in some circumstances such creativity is positively valued, for example in school creative writing tasks. However, in the experimental context his responses are viewed negatively as problematic, and indicate that the interviewer and child had not successfully negotiated a shared, co-constructed, meaningful context for their interaction. Consequently, this mismatch of meanings created problems for the researcher when she later came to interpret his responses. We are thus confronted with both the necessity and the difficulty of adopting the child's point of view regarding the task in hand, and the importance of attempting to understand their goals and frame of reference, as opposed to working with our own assumptions concerning what these are or should be (Light & Littleton, 1999).

The Role of Artefacts in Interviews

To focus solely on discourse processes neglects a further important sense in which meaning is created – namely, through our engagement with, and use of, tools and artefacts. As Goodman (1976) maintains, tools and artefacts are 'world making'. The choice of which artefact to use affects the structure of our activity (Scribner & Cole, 1981), thereby fundamentally transforming the cognitive and communicative requirements of our actions (Säljö, 1995: 90). The introduction of an object or artefact into an interview context can dramatically impact on the process of joint meaning-making, serving as an effective joint referent. Säljö (1997) presented a striking example of this when he demonstrated how, in interviews with children about their understanding of elementary astronomy, children were able to give much fuller, complex accounts when an artefact, a globe, was introduced into the interview context as a means of mediating and resourcing the joint discussion.

An alternative, less positive example, concerns the use of anatomical dolls in investigative interviews with suspected victims of child sexual abuse, a topic that has provoked fierce debate in forensic practice (for example, Boat & Everson, 1993). A lack of conceptual clarity as to why the dolls were being used (and especially the assumption by some that the dolls were 'diagnostic' tools for abuse) left some interviewers unaware of the possible deleterious effects of anatomical dolls on the child–interviewer interaction. For example, very young children struggle to grasp the symbolic representational function of the dolls used to represent them or the alleged perpetrator in the interview (DeLoache, 1995). Thus, the adult interviewers and children in these situations did not have a shared, meaningful remit for the introduction of the dolls in to the interview, with the adults believing the dolls meant something to the children that they did not.

Empowering Children, Enabling Competence

So far we have invoked a notion of agency as interpersonal and have acknowledged the need to understand the processes of joint meaning-making through careful analyses of discourse which focus on the continual, subtle, evolutionary process of negotiation and re-negotiation of meaning (Light & Littleton, 1999). However, it is also important to recognize that interactions are framed by, and therefore can only ever be fully understood within, the context of particular institutional structures and settings: discourse in any socially defined setting is nested within the wider sociocultural context (Valsiner, 1997).

Children's responses in interviews undertaken in educational settings are influenced by contextual systems which extend far beyond the immediate interaction between interviewer and participants, and are inseparable from how education is defined in our culture (Mercer & Fisher, 1992). As an example here, children in school are used to participating in IRF classroom discourse patterns. This means that they are used to teachers *initiating* (I) a discussion or interpersonal interaction, perhaps with a question. The child is then expected to *provide a response* (R) to this initiation, which in turn is commented on by the teacher and *feedback provided* (F). The IRF format of adult–child interaction in classrooms is well established and carries with it consequences for researchers working in classroom settings. Children have expectations regarding what is required of them when interacting with an adult in school contexts and their responses in interview contexts may well reflect these expectations. Making explicit reference to both the child's and interviewer's expectations again contributes to an interview that is meaningful to both adult and child, and in which the child is more likely to freely participate.

This is also likely to be true for interactions outside of education, where the school child is told he or she is to be 'interviewed'. In the absence of other guidance or discussion of what *this particular interaction is about*, the IRF communication pattern may naturally be assumed by the child to be operational and acceptable. It is the interviewer's responsibility to ensure that the child is aware if this is not the case – thereby contributing to the creation of a meaningful context for the interview interaction. Thus, for example, in a forensic interview – and in contrast to IRF – it is important that the child does not guess at a response, and only provides answers that he or she is confident about.

Indeed, much practical guidance on forensic interviewing contains advice on empowering children to challenge interviewers when they do not understand or agree with what they are saying (for example, Saywitz, Nathanson, Snyder & Lamphear, 1993). In the rapport or introductory phase the interviewer can explain and practise ground rules with the child, such as shouting out, 'I don't understand' or, 'Say that again in different words', or holding up a hand or small sign to indicate that the child wants to stop the interview. For young children, this can take the form of the interviewer making statements that the child is not in a position to answer, and dis-cussing with the child possibilities in responding. It is not at all clear, however, to what extent research interviewers use such techniques, and what strategies they adopt when a child does indeed take steps to clarify the context for themselves. One example of how *not* to respond in this situation comes from a study of the cross-examination questioning of suspected victims of sexual abuse (Westcott & Page, 2002):

> Q: Because I suggest, you see, that you have made up, you have pretended, you have imagined what you have been telling us via the videos today to do with rudeness.
> A: Is it because he told you that or …
> Q: I'm putting it firmly to you actually that for various reasons you have pretended: you pretended four years after that you say it happened, you went to the police, mummy told the police and you went along and I suggest you've pretended and I want you to think about that. You have pretended haven't you?
> A: No.
> (Female #3, 8 years)

The child's attempt to make sense of the lawyer's suggestion, by way of a clarifying question to the lawyer, is interrupted and ignored (here, deliberately, to serve the lawyer's purpose of maintaining control of the narrative). In so doing, the child is repositioned as incompetent. Although this is a strategic and deliberate intervention in the above example, inter-viewers may also unintentionally maintain such power imbalances through insensitive or clumsy approaches to questioning that exclude or marginalize children in the construction of accounts.

Even where current good practice is adhered to and ground rules are clearly explained and practised with children, it is clear that this is a process that remains centred on the adult interviewer's frame of reference and concerns. The ground rules that are intended to empower children to participate in the interview process are potentially disempowering when presented as 'givens' or conventions to be adopted by the child and adhered to. Nowhere do we see children and interviewers actively involved in co-constructing ground rules as a shared discursive framework for the interview.

Practical Implications of Conceptual Clarity

In this chapter we have endeavoured to raise conceptual issues that would-be interviewers need to address in order to successfully plan, carry out and analyse the findings from their research. We have also endeavoured to demonstrate that such conceptual issues do themselves have practical implications, both for the immediate research and for longer-term outcomes for the children involved. Interviewing as a research tool is often used in an atheoretical or 'aconceptual' manner, but this has few benefits for either the interviewer or the child. There are, however, many benefits in striving for conceptual clarity. Such clarity affords a clear conception of the function, nature and conduct of the interview, including each participant's role and how we construe the 'performance' and competence of both. Unambiguous objectives for the interview can be identified, including an appreciation of what may or may not be the appropriate use of resultant material. Issues of power and status should be considered and addressed explicitly. The processes involved in joint meaning-making can also be recognized – is the perspective of the adult dominant at the expense of the child's contribution? With these benefits in mind, we now highlight a few salient considerations for key stages in the interview process.

Before the interview

Before planning an interview, the researcher must consider the following questions:

1. Why choose an interview?
2. What are the benefits and disadvantages of an interview for the research question being studied?
3. How are the roles of the interviewer and child conceived?

We have argued in this chapter that an interview is not about 'unearthing things'; rather it is about constructing an account with a child. Further, we hope we have demonstrated that interviews are far from being a simple collection of questions and responses. Seen in this way, there are no doubt occasions when an interview designed to facilitate a co-constructed account with the child is not the most useful or most appropriate research tool. The type of information or response desired from the child must be a guiding factor.

Depending upon the model of the child favoured by the interviewer, then there will be different ethical implications to consider (for example, Hill, Chapter 4 of this volume; Stanley & Sieber, 1992; Thompson, 1990). As we have already noted, researchers have a responsibility to consider both the potential short- and long-term costs and benefits of participation in an interview for children. Although the welfare of participants in research interviews has predominantly been a concern of researchers working within feminist and constructionist approaches, experimental psychologists are belatedly evaluating their own practice more deeply in this respect. For example, an issue of the journal *Applied Cognitive Psychology* (Pezdek, 1998) was devoted to concerns raised about a particular interviewing technique ('the implanted memory paradigm') used in the investigation of child witnesses' 'false memories'.

Conducting the interview

Assuming that an interview is appropriate, then the researcher must consider *what factors facilitate 'constructing an account with the child'*. We would suggest that interviewers can usefully begin by trying to put themselves in the position of the child they are about to interview in order to take first steps towards creating a context that can be meaningful. Positive rapport as both an introductory phase to the interview, and as a style of questioning throughout, is essential, but, as we have noted above, this needs to be carefully thought out so that the child is empowered rather than merely subjected to a list of commands or instructions. The style of questioning itself is crucial: psychological research on investigative interviewing provides a number of useful lessons regarding the approach to questioning. Relevant research has recently been reviewed by Westcott, Davies, and Bull (2002). In brief, such research suggests that:

1. Open-ended question forms (for example, the 'Wh-' questions such as 'what?') encourage much longer responses from children with more detailed replies than focused or specific questions, regardless of child age.
2. Closed-questions that require single-word responses from children (especially 'Yes–No' question/response forms) should be avoided.
3. Children should not be questioned in a suggestive manner (for example, using questions which lead the child to the desired response).
4. Repeating questions in exactly the same form usually results in children changing their responses, as they think their first answer must somehow be wrong.

5. Interviewers should resist the temptation to interrupt the child, and should tolerate long pauses in children's narratives – it is important not to be frightened of silences, even in a methodology designed for talk.
6. Children's language or terminology should not be taken for granted.

The neglect of social skills, such as through eye contact, posture and general demeanour, can also have negative consequences for the interview (for example, a meaningful and comfortable context is not achieved), and consequently for the child's 'competence' and participation. One young man reflected on the investigative interview he had experienced due to suspected child sexual abuse, complaining that his interviewers were 'blunt' and 'rushed him':

> Not relieved, because of the way they were just like blunt or something. I couldn't say the whole story and I never did and I never will. (Wade & Westcott, 1997: 58)

Another young woman commented:

> I was just sort of shoved in the room and interviewed, really. I was introduced but I wasn't, I didn't really feel very comfortable at first ... I didn't want to speak to them because I didn't know anything about them and you know – complete strangers. I didn't know whether I could trust them or not. (Wade & Westcott, 1997: 55)

As both young people illustrate, trust is not a property automatically present in the interview situation, simply as a result of the adult's authority. Trust emerges through the interview process, and the researcher must give detailed consideration ahead of the interview as to how he or she may best establish a trusting relationship with the child.

In a review of studies of child witnesses talking about being interviewed, it was also evident that humour is highly valued by children (Wade & Westcott, 1997). Williamson and Butler (1995) also commented in a discussion of their interviewing approach with children and young people in care, that what the interviewees wanted was 'serious listening inside a funny shell – and researchers seeking in-depth views and information (are) no exception' (p. 77).

After the interview

In approaching the analysis of interview data there is always a tension concerning how far the analyst should add their own analytic interpretation, thereby extending children's accounts (for example, Burman, 1994; Parker, 1994). Some, such as Bearison (1991) feel that we should:

> Simply listen to the children speaking in their own voices about issues and events that are important to them. There is a great deal to be learned and

appropriated from their narratives. They teach us the value of listening to children on their own terms without judging them so that their internal voices will become louder in our time. (p. 26)

However, even following this approach, the researcher inevitably selects which extracts or voices to reproduce in their report. Taylor (2001) comments:

At the widest level, the issue here is who determines what language, especially talk, is 'about'. Should more weight be given to the interpretation of an outsider (the analyst) or an insider (the participant in the interaction)? (p. 12)

The theoretical stance of the researcher and their orientation to the construction of meaning will fundamentally affect the way in which interview material is used in analysis. This is perhaps best exemplified by discourse analytic approaches (for example, Yates, Taylor, & Wetherell, 2001).

Conclusions

Throughout this chapter we have argued that researchers should approach the interview as a co-constructive process of meaning-making, where notions of competence and issues of power are problematized. A recurrent theme has concerned both the necessity and the difficulty of building trust and successfully creating joint meaning with children: we are acutely aware that there is no such thing as 'the *perfect* interview'. However, we believe that greater conceptual clarity on the part of the researcher concerning issues such as the model of the child underpinning the interview can result in a *good* interview, where the child feels able to participate within a mutually negotiated and meaningful framework. It is thus essential to move beyond conducting 'researcher-centred' interviews that disempower children by focusing on *eliciting* responses from them. Instead, we need to empower children such that they can tell of their experiences, within the context of interviews that acknowledge the distinctions between life as lived, experienced and told. Further, there is a need for critical reflection on the methods we use to study children. As James (1999) asserts:

observation, participation and interviewing all entail implicit assumptions about children's competency ... tools of the trade they might be, but they are far from value free. (p. 244)

This is not to argue that interviews cannot be valuable and sensitive research tools. It does require of interviewers, however, that we look carefully at the contexts we create in interviews, with a view to maximizing the benefits of participation for both adult and child. Activities, experiences and skills children may have, which do not at first sight form part of an 'interview schedule', may significantly increase the meaningfulness of the interaction and research method. James (1999) provides an example from her own research of an insightful interchange between two young boys that developed during a drawing activity.

It has become apparent to us writing this chapter that interviewing typifies scholarly approaches that adapt methods devised for adults, rather than starting from 'where children are', and devising child-led methodologies. Again, James (1999) observes:

> recognizing children as people with abilities and capabilities different from, rather than simply less than, adults it may persuade us to be more adventurous in our methodology to find ways in which we can engage children in our research so our research *on* childhood can be effected through research *with* children. (p. 246, her emphasis)

Faced with the diversity among children as potential participants, and mindful of our own failings as interviewers, this spirit of adventure is essential if we are to understand context, competence and joint meaning-making in interviews with children.

Acknowledgement

The authors would like to thank all the children and adults who have participated in their research, and also Nicky Brace for her helpful comments on an earlier draft of this chapter.

Recommended Reading

Burman, E. (1994). Interviewing. In P. Banister, E. Burman, I. Parker, M. Taylor, & C. Tindall (Eds.), *Qualitative methods in psychology: A research guide* (pp. 49–71). Buckingham: The Open University Press.
Wade, A. & Westcott, H.L. (1997). No easy answers: children's perspectives on investigative interviews. In H.L. Westcott & J. Jones (Eds.), *Perspectives on the memorandum: Policy, practice and research in investigative interviewing* (pp. 51–65). Aldershot: Arena.
Westcott, H.L., Davies, G.M., & Bull, R.H.C. (2002). *Children's testimony: Psychological research and forensic practice.* Chichester: Wiley.

References

Alderson, P. (1993). *Children's consent to surgery.* Buckingham: Open University Press.
Alderson, P. (1995). *Listening to children: Children, ethics and social research.* London: Barnardo's.

Bearison, D.J. (1991). *'They never want to tell you': Children talk about cancer.* Cambridge, MA: Harvard University Press.

Boat, B.W. & Everson, M.D. (1993).The use of anatomical dolls in sexual abuse evaluations: current research and practice. In G.S. Goodman & B.L. Bottoms (Eds.), *Child victims, child witnesses: Understanding and improving testimony (pp. 47–69).* New York: Guilford Press.

Bruner, E.M. (1984). The opening up of anthropology. In E.M. Bruner (Ed.), *Text, play and story: The construction and reconstruction of self and society.* Washington, DC: The American Ethnological Society.

Burman, E. (1994). Interviewing. In P. Banister, E. Burman, I. Parker, M. Taylor, & C. Tindall (Eds.), *Qualitative methods in psychology: A research guide* (pp. 49–71). Buckingham: The Open University Press.

Ceci, S.J. & Bruck, M. (1993). Suggestibility of the child witness: A historical review and synthesis. *Psychological Bulletin, 113,* 403–439.

Ceci, S.J. & Bruck, M. (1995). *Jeopardy in the courtroom: A scientific analysis of children's testimony.* Washington, DC: American Psychological Association.

Christensen, P. & James, A. (2000). *Research with children: Perspectives and practices.* London: Falmer Press.

Davis, G., Hoyano, L., Keenan, C., Maitland, L., & Morgan, R. (1999). *An assessment of the admissibility and sufficiency of evidence in child abuse prosecutions.* London: Home Office.

DeLoache, J.S. (1995). The use of dolls in interviewing young children. In M.S. Zaragoza, J.R. Graham, G.C.N. Hall, R. Hirschman, & Y.S. Ben-Porath (Eds.), *Memory and testimony in the child witness* (pp. 160–178). Thousand Oaks, CA: Sage.

Goodman, N. (1976). *Languages of art.* Indianapolis, IN: Hackett.

Graue, M.E. & Walsh, D.J. (1998). *Studying children in context: Theories, methods and ethics.* Thousand Oaks, CA: Sage.

Grossen, M. & Pochon, L.C. (1997). Interactional perspectives on the use of the computer and on the technological development of a new tool: The case of word processing. In L. Resnick, R. Säljö, C. Pontecorvo, & B. Burge (Eds.), *Discourse, tools and reasoning: Essays on situated cognition* (pp. 265–287). Berlin and New York: Springer-Verlag.

Hughes, M. & Grieve, R. (1980). On asking children bizarre questions. *First Language, 1,* 149–160.

James, A. (1999). Researching children's social competence: Methods and models. In M. Woodhead, D. Faulkner, & K. Littleton (Eds.), *Making Sense of Social Development* (pp. 231–249). London: Routledge.

Light, P. & Littleton, K. (1999). *Social processes in children's learning.* Cambridge: Cambridge University Press.

Lyon, T. (2002). Child witnesses and the oath. In H.L.Westcott, G.M. Davies, & R.H.C. Bull (Eds.), *Children's testimony: A handbook of psychological research and forensic practice* (pp. 245–260). Chichester: Wiley.

Memon, A. & Bull, R.H.C. (1999). *Handbook of the psychology of interviewing.* Chichester: Wiley.

Mercer, N. & Fisher, E. (1992). How do teachers help children to learn? An analysis of teachers' interventions in computer-based activities. *Learning and Instruction, 2,* 339–55.

Parker, I. (1994). Qualitative research. In P. Banister, E. Burman, I. Parker, M. Taylor, & C. Tindall (Eds.), *Qualitative methods in psychology. A research guide* (pp. 1–16). Buckingham: The Open University Press.

Pezdek, K. (Ed.) (1998). *Applied Cognitive Psychology 12(3).*

Poole, D.A. & Lamb, M.E. (1998). *Investigative interviews of children: A guide for helping professionals.* Washington, DC: American Psychological Association.

Rommetveit, R. (1992). Outlines of a dialogically based social-cognitive approach to human cognition and communication. In A. Wold (Ed.), *The dialogical alternative: Towards a theory of language and mind* (pp. 19–44). Oslo: Scandinavian Press.

Säljö, R. (1995). Mental and physical artefacts in cognitive practices. In P. Reimann & H. Spada (Eds.), *Learning in humans and machines: Towards an interdisciplinary learning science* (pp. 83–96). Oxford: Pergamon Press.

Säljö, R. (1997). *Heavenly talk: Discourse, artefacts and children's understanding of elementary astronomy.* Seminar presentation, The Open University, Milton Keynes, November.

Saywitz, K., Nathanson, R., Snyder, L., & Lamphear, V. (1993). *Preparing children for the investigative and judicial process: Improving communication, memory and emotional resiliency.* Final report to the National Center on Child Abuse and Neglect (Grant No. 90CA1179).

Scribner, S. & Cole, M. (1981). *The psychology of literacy.* Cambridge, MA: Harvard University Press.

Snow, R. (1994). Abilities in academic tasks. In R. Sternberg & R. Wagner (Eds.), *Mind in context: Interactionist perspectives on human intelligence* (pp. 3–37). Cambridge: Cambridge University Press.

Stanley, B. & Sieber, J.E. (1992). *Social research on children and adolescents: Ethical issues.* Thousand Oaks, CA: Sage.

Taylor, S. (2001). Locating and conducting discourse analytic research. In S. Yates, S. Taylor, & M. Wetherell (Eds.), *Discourse as data: A guide for analysis* (pp. 5–48). London: Sage and The Open University.

Thompson, R.A. (1990). Vulnerability in research: A developmental perspective on research risk. *Child Development, 61,* 1–16.

Valsiner, J. (1997). Bounded indeterminacy in discourse processes. In C. Coll & D. Edwards (Eds.), *Teaching, learning and classroom discourse* (pp. 23–32). Madrid: Fundación Infancia y Aprendizaje.

Wade, A. & Westcott, H. L. (1997). No easy answers: Children's perspectives on investigative interviews. In H.L. Westcott & J. Jones (Eds.), *Perspectives on the memorandum: Policy, practice and research in investigative interviewing* (pp. 51–65). Aldershot: Arena.

Waterman, A., Blades, M., & Spencer, C. (2002). How and why do children respond to nonsensical questions? In H.L.Westcott, G.M. Davies, & R.H.C. Bull (Eds.), *Children's testimony: A handbook of psychological research and forensic practice* (pp. 147–159). Chichester: Wiley.

Westcott, H.L. (1996). Practising ethical and sensitive child protection research. *Practice, 8,* 25–32.

Westcott, H.L. (1999). *Questioning child witnesses: Questions about questioning research.* Unpublished manuscript.

Westcott, H.L. & Page, M. (2002). Cross-examination, sexual abuse and child witness identity. *Child Abuse Review, 11,* 137–152.

Westcott, H.L., Davies, G.M., & Bull, R.H.C. (2002). *Children's testimony: Psychological research and forensic practice.* Chichester: Wiley.

Williamson, H. & Butler, I. (1995). 'No one ever listens to us': Interviewing children and young people. In C. Cloke & M. Davies (Eds.), *Participation and empowerment in child protection* (pp. 61–79). London: Pitman Publishing.

Woodhead, M. & Faulkner, D. (2000). Subjects, objects or participants? Dilemmas of psychological research with children. In P. Christensen & A. James (Eds.), *Research with children: Perspectives and practices* (pp. 9–35). London: Falmer Press.

Woodhead, M., Faulkner, D., & Littleton, K. (1999). *Making sense of social development.* London: Routledge.

Yates, S., Taylor, S., & Wetherell, M. (2001). *Discourse as data: A guide for analysis.* London: Sage and The Open University.

9

Interviewing Children using an Interpretive Poetics

Annie G. Rogers, Mary Casey, Jennifer Ekert
and Jim Holland

A Relational Approach to Research with Children

The interpretive poetics method was created in the context of a particular research project and set of relationships. From 1992 to 1996, I worked with a team of doctoral students at Harvard on the design, data collection and analysis of a longitudinal research project: *'Telling all one's heart': A developmental study of children's relationships*. The phrase 'telling all one's heart' comes from an old definition of courage, 'the capacity to speak one's mind by telling all one's heart', a forgotten thirteenth-century meaning of the word (Rogers, 1993). The *'Telling all one's heart'*, study was undertaken to invite children, ages 5 to 14, into moments of courage by asking them to tell us about a range of relationships in their lives, from those that were supportive and loving, to relationships of ambivalence, difficulty, and disturbing pain.

In the course of this research with children, we drew on a relational approach in both data collection and in analysis of data. We began with the assumption that children have rich stories to tell, but will tell them only in relationships in which they are met with extraordinary honesty and respect. We did not think it was going to be possible for most children to speak candidly about their relationships in a single meeting. Children who participated in the study were interviewed individually two to three times annually and invited to remain in the project for three years. In the first interview, we did not use a prearranged protocol. We went to meet the children with drawing materials, cards, jokes, puppets, and ourselves, hoping first to form a relationship in which children could begin to trust us enough to tell us something real about their lives. The children were invited to play, speak and draw about their relationships at home, at school, and in their neighbourhoods. Interviewers followed the child's stories and play, rather than setting the agenda. In the second interview, we drew upon developmental materials (art materials and particular questions designed for specific age groups) to create an individually tailored interview based on the first interview. In the second interview, we wanted to explore more explicitly experiences of hurt or harm in relationships, because we discovered that if we did not ask these questions directly, the children told us only happy (and sometimes ambivalent) stories of relationships. In the third interview, the children were asked a series of questions about dreams, imagination and memory. If we had concerns about the wellbeing of a child based on ambiguous or confusing information, the interviewers went back for clarification from the child. There were several instances when we needed to speak with the principal about a harmful situation going on in school, or we needed to file a report about harm in the family with child protective services. In these instances, we stayed in touch with the child and let her or him know exactly what we were doing, so that children would not feel surprised and betrayed.

As we began to listen to the audiotaped interviews, looking at the verbatim transcripts and the children's drawings, we became aware of how difficult it is to understand children's ordinary, day-to-day experiences of courage, a concept of speaking that joins heart and mind, feeling and telling. We saw immediately that moments of courage in the interviews depended upon the child's relationship with the interviewer, and that even when this relationship initially appeared to be quite strong, the child's capacity to speak about a full range of relationships fluctuated quite dramatically. We were struck with the richness of the children's language and were reluctant to categorize these detailed conversations, even beginning with inductively derived categories. At the same time, we were aware of a poignant elusiveness in children's narratives when they began to speak about difficult and disturbing relationships in their lives, or when they evaded speaking directly about these relationships but spoke metaphorically about them nevertheless. Finding no method of analysis that traced both children's inarticulate knowledge of disturbing relationships and the richness of associations and metaphors in play and in speech, we set out to invent our own method.

Research on childhood has been based historically on two seriously limited methods: qualitative studies by scholars of various disciplines in which theory drives descriptions of children's lives, and survey studies where adults are asked about children's lives and the categories of response are constrained. Neither approach is conducive to discovering children's perceptions of their own particular life experiences. To date, open-ended interviews have been shown to be the most effective way to find out about experiences of childhood because the flexible face-to-face format of this method allows the researcher to follow up on vague, confusing, even contradictory information, sensitively and systematically. Additionally, interviewing has been used with great success in developmental research with children (Piaget, 1948; Selman & Hickey-Schultz, 1990). Interviewing has also been effective in helping children to discuss sensitive topics of real importance in their lives (Coles, 1990; Rogers, Casey, Holland, & Nakkula, 1997). While interviews are a highly flexible and adaptable way to explore sensitive experiences and to investigate developmental meanings of those experiences, offering a unique window into children's perceptions, interviewing methods present particular challenges to data analysis. Interviews commonly differ in style, length and content, even when interviewers have a common goal. One interviewer is not simply 'interchangeable' with another. Each interviewing relationship is unique, just as each child is an individual. Interview data have the unique potential of providing rich and highly illuminating material about children's perceptions of their lives, and there are interesting and innovative approaches to interview analysis, for instance, in this volume (see Westcott and Littleton (Chapter 8)). In creating our own method of analysis, my students and I felt the need for an approach that encouraged artistic writing and was flexible enough to include a wide range of children's stories, yet specific enough to establish clear guidelines for interpretation.

Interpretive Poetics:
A New Method of Textual Analysis

> Artistic form is congruent with the dynamic forms of our direct sensuous life: works of art are projections of 'felt life', as Henry James called it, into spatial, temporal, and poetic structures. They are images of feeling that formulate it for our conception. (Susanne Langer, 1942: 159)

In this section I describe a new method of textual analysis, interpretive poetics, then explain the philosophical foundations for the method. The interpretive poetics traces individual, subjective, and layered experiences of 'felt life' in interview narratives and written texts. In this chapter, I illustrate how it can be used in interviews with children. The interpretive poetics is an associative process whereby layers of meaning in narrative texts are interrogated and interpreted in a way that mirrors a sophisticated reading of a poem. The method is artistic, but also, crucially, raises questions about how interpretations are made, based on what textual evidence. The process of analysis relies on four related registers of interpretation: (a) story-threads; (b) a relational dance; (c) languages of the unsayable; and (d) woven and torn signifiers. Each interpretive reading reveals a fresh layer of meaning when applied in textual analysis. This layered process allows researchers to interpret a text using the registers in any sequence, as I show in detail in the second section of this chapter. The interpretive poetics is modeled on another relational method of interpretation, the Listener's Guide (Brown & Gilligan, 1992; Gilligan, Brown, & Rogers, 1990; Rogers, 1992; Rogers, Brown, & Tappan, 1993). This feminist method, which I used and elaborated with colleagues in previous research, employs multiple readings of texts and identifies the polyphonic nature of speech through various 'voice' readings. While the interpretive poetics does not rely on naming particular voices, it was inspired in part by the multiple, layered readings used in the Listener's Guide.

New ways of constructing the possibilities and limits of human understanding and meaning-making ground the interpretive poetics method philosophically. Taken together, these fundamentals – that knowledge is relational, understanding is largely metaphorical, the mind operates through a dynamic unconscious, and interpretations are inherently embodied – call for modes of inquiry that go beyond the available repertoire of qualitative methods.

Knowledge is relational

The ways we know the world, construct memories, tell and interpret stories are inescapably relational. Relational approaches to psychology and research begin with the premise that relationship is the central organizing principle of human experience (Gilligan, 1996). All knowledge is located within the sphere of social relatedness (Gergen & Gergen, 1984). Concretely, this means that analysis of narrative happens as a relational process on two levels – between the child and interviewer, and between the analyst and transcript – situated within the researcher's allegiance to children as experts on their own lives and contexts. Analysis is not merely an act of finding and synthesizing the meaning of a child's story. Rather, it is an iterative and interactive process that allows the researcher to make meaning around the story that emerges in an interview, with the understanding that the relationship developed between interviewer and child becomes the context that both invites and constrains that story. It is especially important to attend to the ways that power is negotiated in an interviewing relationship with a child, who is much less powerful and will read the relationship for signals about what to say and do. A relational understanding of a child's knowledge necessarily includes making it clear to a child we would like to learn from her or his experience and expertise on being a child.

Understanding is largely metaphorical

Various poetic or figurative processes shape human thought fundamentally. As linguists have documented, metaphors are not linguistic distortions of our literal experiences, but are basic schemes by which people conceptualize their experiences (Lakoff & Johnson, 1980). In *A poetics of mind*, Raymond Gibbs (1994) describes the language of everyday discourse, including inferences drawn from observation, as a continuous process of poetic thinking. In the field of cognitive science, researchers have established a link between neurological development and figurative processes:

> We acquire a large system of primary metaphors automatically and unconsciously simply by functioning in the most ordinary of ways in the everyday world from our earliest years. We have no choice in this. Because of the way neural connections are formed during the period of conflation [between subjective experiences and sensorimotor experiences], we all naturally think using hundreds of primary metaphors. (Lakoff & Johnson, 1999: 47)

In other words, children come into the world biologically and cognitively prepared to make sense of experiences metaphorically. All elaboration of thought draws on metaphors, making a compelling case for drawing centrally on figurative thought and its signifiers in data analysis.

The mind operates through a dynamic unconscious

Research in fields ranging from cognitive science to psychoanalytic psychology provides convincing evidence that most of human thought is unconscious, operating beneath the level of cognitive awareness, inaccessible to consciousness and happening too quickly to be observed. If thought is indeed mostly unconscious, how can we begin to tap into some of the implicit, indirect, unsaid, and unsayable knowledge that we hold? How can we come close to knowing our own minds, let alone the minds of children, who think differently from the way we do as adults?

Of course the very notion that we might know what is in a child's mind or head is ridiculous. However, we have learned from psychoanalytic psychology a great deal about how unconscious dynamic processes work in human relationships. For instance, Donald Winnicott (1958) describes three lines of communication that are created relationally in early childhood and continue to develop throughout life: the first form of communication is the child's relaxed subjectivity that is 'forever silent'; the second line is 'explicit' and is reflected in the child's capacity for negotiating understanding with another through language; and the third line of communication is an 'intermediate' line between the first and second lines, a way of bringing the inner world into contact with another's inner world through the use of shared symbols and gestures. Dynamic and relational unconscious processes between a child and his or her interviewer are most accessible to us through Winnicott's third line of communication, which depends on the intersubjective play of speech, gesture and metaphor.

The mind is inherently embodied

Children experience and interpret the world in ways that are inherently embodied. Although children share some common brain characteristics and developmental processes that affect how they perceive the world, construct memories and understand the world, the body is not universal, nor is it fixed in time. Children's bodies are both unique and shaped in critical ways through gender, racial, ethnic, and geographic and cultural characteristics. What is given genetically varies enormously. Children's bodies and minds develop and change over time and affect the ways they relate stories, especially in relation to adults. Cognitive science and neuroscience have repeatedly shown that the body and the mind are not separate entities (Edelman, 1992; Hobson, 1994). How and what children perceive depends on bodily states and feelings, which extend into how they use language, construct memories, and make meaning of living in a unique physical, relational and cultural world.

In summary, the interpretive poetics acknowledges human relationships as central to an understanding of embodied, unconscious, and metaphorical knowledge. This philosophical grounding predisposes the researcher to construct multiple meanings layered in children's stories, rather than to uncover a single set of themes or a single overriding interpretation of narrative data.

Four Registers of an Interpretive Poetics

There are four registers for analysing interview data that form the basis of our interpretive poetics: (a) finding story-threads; (b) tracing a relational dance; (c) identifying and interpreting languages of the unsayable; and

(d) listening for woven and torn signifiers. Putting these four registers together, the researcher follows the associative chronology of layered psychological processes. These registers, used in combination, provide a set of strategies that overlap in reading language, considering multiple perspectives, and taking soundings at several levels of interpretive depth. The logic of the four registers is complementary, and their use should be directed by research questions and emerging interpretations in an analytic process.

Story-threads

Finding distinct threads of stories in a narrative begins with reading interview transcripts or written texts with the goal of articulating several interpretive questions that link a researcher's broad questions to a child's particular story. The researcher begins with one question as a guide and creates what Seidman (1991) calls a crafted profile of the speaker using only text selected from the interview transcripts or written document. In the process of formulating several interpretive questions as bridges between a researcher's questions and a particular text, one creates multiple story-threads of that text. To fully appreciate this level of analysis in the interpretive poetics, it is important to acknowledge that no story is complete. Children's stories that are compelling, in fact, contain a sense of undisturbed mystery that defies naming (Rogers, 1995), and commonly have gaps and holes that reflect some process of censorship.

A relational dance

The changing dynamics of a research relationship with a child centrally inform the interpretive poetics analysis. This relationship is not only the context of the research, but also the medium for all that is learned. The relational dance that happens between an interviewer and a child inevitably invites and constrains what a child can know, what the researcher can know, and what they can know together. Using a layered process of analysis, the researcher reads, listens for, and reflects on three shifting relational moments: recognition, disconnection or an undoing of a recognition, and what follows after a retracted recognition or disconnection in interview transcripts. Interviewers also write about their experiences of meeting with a child, and this context helps us to understand what we can and cannot know about the child's experience (also see Behar, 1996).

Languages of the unsayable

In narrative research, interpretations are often carried out as if spoken words can be construed as representing another's experience. Silences are understood as pauses or refusals to speak about something particular when questioned. However, in listening to children (as well as adolescents and adults), we understood their *words* as revealing what they could consciously know and tell us (their experience), as well as marking unconscious and unsayable aspects of experience. Every sentence we speak is continually surrounded by, and lies between, what is not said and may be in fact, unsayable. In the interpretive poetics analysis, the researcher focuses on what is not said through what is said. We identify those negations, evasions, erasures, omissions, revisions, and silences that mark what is unspoken or unspeakable (Rogers, Casey, Nakkula, & Sheinberg, 1999). For example, if a child says, 'I ain't afraid of my teacher', in phrasing his sentence negatively he affirms his lack of fear, while raising the spectre of fear at the same time. But the feeling of fear remains unsayable, at least in that moment in the interview. If later, he says, 'Every time I go into that classroom, I am like, I'm always kinda nervous about what's going to happen', we hear this as a revision of the first statement. If asked, 'What do you mean by kinda nervous?' and the child shrugs a shoulder and says, 'Nothin', um I don't know', these words carry his silence about his feelings, as well as possibly conveying (without saying it) 'back off – don't push here'. These aspects of speech can be interpreted as various 'languages of the unsayable' (Budick & Iser, 1987). What is unsayable, when understood in this way, provides a more nuanced understanding of what a child actually says. Importantly, the goal of this analysis is not to speak the unsayable. This analysis intends to illustrate a doubling of meanings that mark a dynamic interplay between the not said and the said in moments of negation, evasion, revision, and silence in a particular interviewing relationship. This analysis of languages of the unsayable, with its specific focus on relational processes, is a particularly effective strategy for tracing the movement of a dynamic unconscious, making transparent the limits of what a child can hold in conscious awareness.

Woven and torn signifiers

The analysis of signifiers provides a powerful way to explore and understand figurative processes of thought in children's narratives. In the fourth register of analysis, we begin by listening for repeating and related words and metaphors that are woven into a story, or appear to be torn from the context of the narrative. In Wallace Stevens's words, the poetic in human thought, 'is never the thing, but the version of the thing' (1978: 332). Through an exploration of signifiers, it is possible to see how a particular child is constructing 'the version of the thing'. Language is not simply a representation of thought or experience, but is crucially a presentation of various linguistic relationships (Freeman, 1996; see also Bahktin, 1986). As human beings we are continually improvising with words to create experiences and meanings that at the same time elude us. Hearing contrasts in words and phrases that move in and out of one another as they braid through a story provides an initial map of psychological tensions and contradictions. An abrupt contrast in language may also create a tear in a story, leaving a gap where it was interrupted or radically revised. The use of figurative thought (which includes metaphors, changed words, word play and slips of the tongue) is often heightened around grappling with tensions and contradictions. Metaphors refer most fundamentally to something by the name of something else. Joel Dor explains Lacan's understanding that metaphors, and in fact *all* poetic or figurative forms of speech, function as substitutes for unconscious meanings, as signifiers of what cannot be known or said directly (Dor, 2000). In our analysis, substituted words and metaphors are crucial cues about how children construct experience in relation to particular tensions in language.

How to Use the Interpretive Poetics

In this section I illustrate the use of the interpretive poetics with a single child. The interpretive poetics can be used in a group analysis, and I comment lightly on comparisons to other children that we made, but focus here, for the sake of clarity, on just one child. My purpose is to show how it is possible to build an interpretation by layering the four registers of analysis. The interpretive poetics method can be used flexibly, in any order that is useful for a researcher. In this case, the sequence of analysis moved from story-threads, to languages of the unsayable, to woven and torn signifiers and finally to the relational dance of the interview.

In the first layer of analysis, *finding story-threads*, my students and I read for related yet distinct stories crafted in response to emergent interpretive questions. For example, we wanted to understand a range of children's relationships at home, at school, and in their neighbourhoods. Using crafted profiles, we created a series of distinct story-threads in relation to different versions of this basic question about relationships. Taken together, these profiles became multiples of a story of relationships that included the perspectives of the children about all their relationships. In response to the following broad research question, *'How do children describe a range of positive and negative relationships in their lives, at home, at school, and in their neighbourhoods?'*, we constructed stories from the children's interviews, rearranging texts to create these stories. In doing so, we removed the interviewer's part of the dialogue and placed words in brackets to fill in missing information. Finding story-threads highlights the voice and experience of the child.

In the following set of story-threads, Siyuan, a nine-year-old girl of Asian ancestry, speaks in her own words about a range of her relationships in her life:

> [I am] nine. I have two sisters. One is 12 and another is 7. I play games [with them]: Chess. Clue, Uno, Gin, Spit, that's it. My sister teaches me how to play cards. [My big sister is] sometimes wears her hair in a ponytail, and sometimes in a bun, and sometimes down. She does it herself. [When I play chess with her] I turn it into war. All the people go and bang into each other. She fights back. And she takes all her pawns and pushes them forward. And then I take all my people and then push them against them. Nobody [wins]. Then we just pick up all the people and put them back in the bag and close the board. When I'm bored I play the regular way. I let her collect all my valuable people and I only have my King

left and she has three pawns and she tries to get me. She always wins. I don't like it. Except for once. It was fun [getting] her. My little sister plays and watches TV. I don't play with her a lot. Because she always gets into a fight. I don't know [why]. Me and my big sister show her how to do long division and she can't do it ... My sisters, mm ... shared a big giant cushion with me, and we moved the bed around, sometimes it used to be where the TV was and my little sister would have her own private bed next to the big cushion, and me and my big sister would sleep on the cushion, and a dresser would be blocking the door that was near the way you come in. And once I couldn't sleep, so I climbed the poles that the hot water runs through and jumped down to where I slept ...

I like school sometimes. I like reading class. [I like reading] Paddingtun. He got his name by a train station. And he spells his name p-a-d-d-i-n-g-t-u-n. I draw sometimes. I don't like drawing people. We sometimes draw animals at art. We go to music at 9:55. Sometimes [I like it]. We're getting our recorders today or next week. [I have played] the piano since the first grade. My best friend is Tina. [We play] tag. [She is a] school friend. Tina is a little bit smaller than me. Dee-dee is also my friend. She's tall. [Nicole] asks me and my sisters to play in the park. We play four square or basketball, or hide-and-go-seek ...

When I was one to, or two to five or six, I lived on my grandmother's side [of the house we live in], in the room that my cousins used to live in. And when I was six to seven, I lived in what is now is the livingroom, and the livingroom was in the diningroom, before, because we used to eat in the kitchen next door. And now I live upstairs with my sisters and mom and dad. My grandmother brings us snacks. And sometimes we cook by ourselves. She teaches us and helps us do our homework. She teaches me how to read the next chapter because I only read one chapter and I don't know how to read the next one. She needs glasses, but my mother got glasses for her but she doesn't wear them. Because she doesn't want to. My dad is an engineer, a computer engineer. My mother is a programmer. She's, I don't know. I don't know [whether I'm close to her].

This new text captured a range of relationships in Siyuan's life, especially within her family. She spoke little about her relationships at school. As Siyuan told stories about her relationships, she adhered to the concrete realism of mid-childhood, creating details that may seem irrelevant from an adult point of view, but these details of play, place, and the rhythms of daily life are the very texture of Siyuan's stories. Looking at her storylines in relation to other children's stories allowed us to see patterns related to age and to gender.

After sorting through story-threads from crafted profiles for the group of children, we posed a second interpretive question, 'What are disturbing relationships or incidents that immediately affect the children, from the perspective of the children?' Initially we attempted to document what we saw as disturbing relationships, even if these might be denied or negated by a child, but then we decided to include what she or he experienced as disturbing and commented upon as negative or upsetting. Because the children commonly had difficulty speaking about these kinds of relationships in their lives, some aspects of their storytelling remained opaque and confusing. The following are story-threads of Siyuan's interviews of disturbing relationships, created as a series of crafted profiles:

I went to Toronto with my grandmother and while we were leaving we were going on a train to the airport and my grandmother put her – our luggage on me and my sister's – and, and she was going to get her luggage in, and she told us to sit in the train and wait for her. And while she was going to get her luggage, the whistle blew and it blew already three times and then the door started to close and then my grandmother yelled, 'Wait', and the driver's hand went out to open the door and she put her luggage through and then the door closed. And then he helped her open the door so she could get in and she got in ...

My big sister pushed me against the heater and I ran downstairs to my mother crying and my mother whacked my sister and my moth – my dad told me to lay down on the couch, and then when I got up from the couch, my sister saw some blood and then my dad looked in [or 'at'?] my head and saw a crack and my mother whacked my sister again and my dad called my aunt and my aunt went to Osco Drug and brought some sprays and my dad took a little can of blue spray and sprayed it on my head and he put a Band-Aid on my head and, mm, I had to stay home for two days ...

When we went to California to go to someone's, I think, wedding, and we were going to drop mm – people off to go to a movie, and my sister said 'Arachnaphobia', and I wanted to get a drink because I wanted to open the Coke in the coolers and then my grandmother said, 'No, no, no, wait 'til we get to a stop'. And I said, 'I'm thirsty, I'm thirsty, I'm thirsty', and mm – my grandmother hit me on the nose and my nose started bleeding.

Reading these experiences together as stories of disturbing relationships or memorable incidents highlights Siyuan's responses to being hurt and/or frightened. Putting these story-threads alongside those of other children her age, we were able to see clearly what kinds of relationships and incidents children found disturbing. It was unusual to hear multiple stories of being physically hurt by family members, and we were deeply concerned about these stories in Siyuan's interviews.

Children, and sometimes adolescents, find it extremely difficult to tell stories of mistreatment because they must believe in the goodness of their caretakers for psychological survival. We were concerned that Siyuan might be in danger, both physically and psychologically. In an effort to find out how serious and how common her injuries were, her interviewer, Elizabeth, attempted to get Siyuan to elaborate on the stories she'd told spontaneously. We found that we could make sense of their exchange most clearly through an analysis of *languages of the unsayable*.

At this level of analysis, a researcher reads for languages of negation, revision, smokescreen, and silence. *Language of negation* expresses an idea or feeling through the explicit negation of its opposite. *Language of revision*, or undoing knowledge, encompasses a range of instances, from the self-correction of details to explicit contradiction or denial. *Language of smokescreens* is more difficult to identify. A smokescreen distracts from the story the child has been telling, either through a change of topic or through a substituted story. What is said, the 'screen', becomes the figure, while the unsaid serves as the ground. *Language of silence* is the most elusive language. The mere absence of some information from an interview does not necessarily indicate a silence. Information is always absent from an interview, simply because some questions are not asked. More commonly, silences that follow a forbidden story or a fear of speaking take the form of shutting down and closing off communication.

As we read Elizabeth's dialogue with Siyuan, we heard revision and silence in Siyuan's responses. When a story is not sayable, utterance itself becomes an enactment of a process of forbidding speech. This was most evident when we returned to try to confirm stories of harm in interviews with the children, including Siyuan. Almost always the children altered or retracted their stories, as if they couldn't remember them, or could no longer speak honestly with us.

When Elizabeth attempted to clarify her own questions about whether or not Siyuan was harmed in her family, we heard a profound retraction of her stories. Siyuan had told Elizabeth about the heater incident, and about being hit by her grandmother. Elizabeth began, 'The last time you were telling me about a time your family took a trip to California'. Siyuan immediately started shaking her head no. 'No, you didn't tell me that?' Siyuan kept shaking her head no. Elizabeth persisted. 'Oh, what I remember is you mentioned a time when you took a trip to California, it may have been for a wedding, something like that?' Siyuan again shook her head, no. 'No. And I think you said something about being thirsty?' Siyuan just shook her head, no, 'No? And um, you said something about your grandmother hitting you in the nose. And it bled?' Siyuan was still, she paused, then again shook her head, no. 'No. Well when I was listening to the tape I realized that must have been pretty scary because you know sometimes scary things happen. Do you know what happened next?' Siyuan shook her head, no. 'No?'

Here Siyuan entered a long silence, broken only by shaking her head no in response to each of Elizabeth's questions, a negation of each of the stories she'd told earlier. But Elizabeth persisted in the face of denial and silence, as if Siyuan knew her stories but could no longer speak them. 'It made me concerned because it does sound scary, and I was wondering if there are other times you are hit.' Surprisingly, Siyuan nodded affirmatively. 'Can you tell me about one of those?' 'Mm – when I'm not supposed to do something.' 'Then what happens?' 'I get hit.' 'Where do you get hit?' 'On my hand.' 'On your hand. How does it work?' 'My mother hits me on the hand really, really hard.' 'Oh. What do you feel then?' ' Nothing.' 'Nothing, you don't feel at all angry or hurt?' 'No, because I always get hurt.' Elizabeth almost whispered, 'What do you mean?' And Siyuan told her this story:

> Mm, I play soccer, and sometimes the ball hits my face. Sometimes, someone kicks me in my leg, and sometimes they step on my toe. And, I always trip over some chairs and fall. And then sometimes I just fall off the stairs and I go tumbling down when I was young. And sometimes I trip over the stairs and sometimes I bang my head, and sometimes, I don't know, I get hurt by going down the stairs into the basement and then stepping on some wood and then I get a splinter on my foot. And sometimes I just kick something and it hurts.

We read and understood this story of accidental hurt as Siyuan's experience of herself, but also as a smokescreen for her more painful stories of physical hurt in her family. Elizabeth says sympathetically, 'So it sounds like you get a lot of bruises. Do you remember when this happens? Who you are with?' Siyuan shakes her head no again. Then she says, 'Mm. My sisters. And sometimes my grandmother, and sometimes my mother, and sometimes my dad.' Elizabeth muses, 'So do they get hurt too?' 'No.' 'It's just you.' Siyuan nods. 'Why is it just you?' 'Mm. Because I trip over things a lot.' 'What do they do when you trip over things?' 'Nothing.' There is a seven-second pause. Elizabeth asks, 'Do they ever ask, are you ok?' 'Mm. Sometimes.' 'And what do you say?' 'Yes, I'm ok.' 'Do you cry?' 'No. I just hop up and down ... because it feels better.' 'Because it feels better, ok. So, let me be clear, these accidents happen by yourself, no one hits or pushes you?' Siyuan shakes her head no. 'Like last time you mentioned how a sister pushed you into a radiator.' Siyuan shakes her head no. Elizabeth turns off the tape-recorder at this point.

Siyuan's attempts at communication shift back to silence and denial, and wisely Elizabeth turns off the recorder to give her a chance to speak more freely. What was at stake for this child in retracting her stories? How did she think about accidents and her family's role in physical hurt?

We then read Siyuan's interviews to identify *woven and torn signifiers* in Siyuan's stories. In this analysis the researcher searches for language contrasts, which often provide cues to contradictions and places of confusion. In language contrasts, children tend to resort to metaphors as signifiers, an inarticulate knowledge of something that has been contradictory or puzzling in their experience.

In Siyuan's interviews, we found an abrupt change in language that marked a tear in her stories, followed by metaphors of accidental harm woven into a new narrative she told. The first place of tearing was in her third interview, in a section in which we asked all the children about how they distinguished stories from dreams, and their own memories from others' memories. In a dialogue with Elizabeth, Siyuan abruptly recasts her story of the heater incident from her older sister's point of view, as an accident in which she 'tripped'. Siyuan ends this story in confusion about what really happened. We then compared the signifiers in this revised story of the heater incident with her story of her own accidents, which function as an explanation of Siyuan's experiences of physical harm in her final interview with Elizabeth.

Here is the first tear in the unity and coherence of Siyuan's narrative about her older sister pushing her into the radiator. Siyuan tells Elizabeth that her older sister insists that Siyuan's story of being pushed into the radiator was an instance in which she 'tripped'.

Elizabeth: Have you ever told a story and someone said, no – it didn't happen like that?
Siyuan: When I cracked my head, my sister said I – she pushed me and I fell and then I tripped, I think, against the heater. And that's how I cracked my head.
Elizabeth: So, is that how you remember it?
Siyuan: Mm. No. She pushed me against the heater.

Elizabeth: But she told people that you tripped?
Siyuan: She pushed me and then I tripped and then I fell against the heater.
Elizabeth: [softly:] Uh-huh? So how do you remember that?
             Mm … Mm … I don't know …

In this dialogue, Siyuan becomes confused about what actually happened, shifting from the action of being 'pushed' and making a substitution: 'I tripped', as she tells her sister's version of the story.

It is striking to us that what follows this account of 'I tripped' is a story of Siyuan's accidents as a substitute explanation for her experiences of physical hurt and harm. In this narrative, Siyuan describes a world of objects and obstacles that harm her. The objects in the narrative function figuratively as signifiers of her family's innocence and her own passively unlucky or clumsy behaviour: 'the ball hits my face … I always trip over some chairs and fall … I just fall off the stairs and I go tumbling down … I trip over the stairs and sometimes I bang my head … I get hurt by going down the stairs into the basement and then stepping on some wood and then I get a splinter on my foot.' We wondered – whose version and voice is this? Did Siyuan actually believe that she was simply and terribly clumsy? Or, was she terrified of the consequences of telling Elizabeth stories of harm within her family, even as she attempted to communicate that she was being hurt?

To answer these questions, we tried to understand Siyuan's relationship with Elizabeth and looked at the *relational dance* in the interviews. In this analysis the researcher seeks to understand what the interviewer could and could not understand about the child's experience, based on their relationship. Evidence includes looking at transcripts of interviews and the interviewer's reflections and impressions of the interviews. In tracing a shifting dance between an interviewer and a child, we focus on moments of recognition, moments of misunderstanding or an undoing of recognition, and what follows on from moments of misunderstanding (for instance, a tacit acceptance of a silence, a new recognition, resistance to re-visiting the topic, and so on).

In Elizabeth's interviews with Siyuan, we were impressed by how closely attuned Elizabeth was to Siyuan's feelings and stories throughout. Whenever Elizabeth misunderstood something, she found a way to clarify it and come to a new recognition with Siyuan. The length of this chapter precludes my presenting evidence of this relational dynamic in detail. The clearest evidence of Elizabeth's understanding of her relationship with Siyuan comes from Elizabeth's writing about what happened after she'd turned off the tape-recorder in the final interview:

I felt that I had very fragile footing, but that it was important to learn more about her falling. My world had narrowed so that only she existed, with the rest of the room and the noises outside having disappeared. Unlike with other parts of this interview and interviews past, she seemed more attentive, looking me in the eyes. I think she understood the importance of what I was asking, and felt the need to be careful. I asked her if she had ever broken a bone (I told her of how I had broken my left arm once). She said no, except for her head when her sister had pushed her into the heater. I asked how did she know her head was broken, and she replied that her finger could go inside. I asked if she had gone to the doctor in that case, and the answer was no. It was then that I became more concerned that she wasn't receiving proper medical treatment, so I asked if she had ever been to the doctor. The answer was yes, a few weeks earlier. Where does she get hurt when she falls? She pointed to her shins. I asked if there were bruises there now, and I asked if I could see, but she shook her head no. I asked if she was hurt anywhere else, and she pointed to a paper-cut on her finger. Again, I asked her about the trip to California. She said (or shook her head) that she did not remember it. But then, as an aside, I asked her how old she was when it happened. She said she was four. I asked her directly if she had ever been hit. When she said yes, on the hand by her mother, I felt somewhat relieved. But then she spoke rather spontaneously about always hurting herself. And it was at this point she held my gaze. I felt the room (the sight and sound of it) melt away, and all that mattered and all that existed was she and I. It seemed to me that she was trying to communicate something more than hurting herself, but that she could not use ordinary language.

Elizabeth felt that Siyuan was trying to communicate something about being hurt in which 'she could not use ordinary language'. In the language of gesture and metaphor, Siyuan looks directly at Elizabeth and draws a circle around what they can know together. Siyuan cannot tell Elizabeth that she is being harmed, so she tells another story, a smokescreen story of multiple accidents that also serves metaphorically as a way of saying, 'I am hurting. I am hurt now.'

We never fully understood Siyuan's story, and even as I revisit her transcripts now, I feel huge compassion for this child. She was unable to confirm or tell the stories she'd spontaneously told Elizabeth in her first interview. What is clear from her telling and retraction, however, is the fragility of telling, especially for a child. Siyuan wants Elizabeth to believe that she is a girl who is prone to accidents, and yet she provides details and limited confirmations (such as her age during the California trip) that do not allow Elizabeth to fully believe what has happened to Siyuan is purely accidental.

In summary, the four registers of the interpretive poetics analysis allowed us to explore our research questions in relation to Siyuan's particular stories, to hear what she could only say in languages of the unsayable, to name a smokescreen story and its signifiers, and finally to see clearly the limits of what we could understand about Siyuan's life. The analysis, undertaken in a group, depended upon evidence from the interview texts, the audiotapes, and Elizabeth's notes about her experience with Siyuan. We challenged one another with alternative interpretations and evidence before we came to the interpretations I have presented to illustrate this method of working.

Applications and Limitations of the Method

The interpretive poetics method is best suited to research projects that focus on psychological questions in which the researcher is interested not only in what participants say, but also in how experience is constructed and conveyed relationally. The method reveals a rich, in-depth understanding of individual children. Any of the four registers of analysis can be used separately or in various combinations. The method is flexible with respect to the order of analysis, as the reader could see in the illustration of Siyuan's interviews. It is also applicable to a wide range of projects, including, for example, narratives of people confronting mortality through illness (Pakos, 2000) and adolescents' understanding of moral inspiration in their lives (Casey, 2001). The interpretive poetics has also been used in an analysis of autobiographical novels, diaries, letters, and poems.

The interpretive poetics using the four registers does not lend itself to looking at large group patterns, however. Identifying story-threads across different participants through a single interpretive question is sometimes useful as a tool for looking at patterns of similarity and difference in relatively small groups. However, the in-depth analysis and the sheer amount of time it takes to analyse a single set of interviews makes the interpretive poetics method an unrealistic tool for large group analyses. The method was designed for small qualitative studies, and is most useful as a tool of analysis when the researcher is interested not only in what participants say, but also in how experience is constructed and conveyed relationally.

Acknowledgements

The Harvard students who were involved in the analyses described in this paper are Mary Casey, Jennifer Ekert, Jim Holland and Vicky Barrios.

I would like to thank the Milton Fund at the Harvard Medical School and the Spencer Foundation for supporting the *Telling all one's heart* research project and the students who served research apprenticeships with that project.

Recommended Reading

Rogers, A., Casey, M., Holland, J., Nakkula, V., & Sheinberg, N. (1999). An interpretive poetics of languages of the unsayable. In R. Josselson & A. Lieblich (Eds.), *The Narrative Study of Lives, 6* (pp. 77–106). Thousand Oaks: Sage.

Seidman, I. (1991). *Interviewing as qualitative research.* New York: Teachers College Press.

References

Bakhtin, M. (1986). *Speech genres and other late essays.* Austin, TX: University of Texas Press.

Behar, R. (1996). *The vulnerable observer: Anthropology that breaks your heart.* Boston, MA: Beacon Press.

Brown, L. & Gilligan, C. (1992). *Meeting at the crossroads: Women's psychology and girls' development.* Cambridge, MA: Harvard University Press.

Budick, S. & Iser, W. (1987). Introduction. In S. Budick & W. Iser (Eds.), *Languages of the unsayable: The play of negativity in literature and literary theory* (pp. xi–xvi). Stanford, CA: Stanford University Press.

Casey, M. (2001). *Heroes of the heart: Moral inspiration in the lives of racially diverse rural adolescents.* Unpublished doctoral dissertation. Available through Harvard University, Gutman Library, Cambridge, MA.

Coles, R. (1990). *The spiritual life of children.* Boston, MA: Houghton Mifflin.

Dor, J. (2000). *Introduction to the reading of Lacan: The unconscious structured like a language.* New York: Other Press.

Edelman, G. (1992). *Bright air, brilliant fire: On the matter of the mind.* New York: Basic Books.

Freeman, D. (1996). 'To take them at their word': Language data in the study of teachers' knowledge. *Harvard Educational Review, 66,* 732–761.

Gergen, K. & Gergen, M. (1984). *Historical social psychology.* Hillsdale, NJ: Erlbaum.

Gibbs, R. (1994). *The poetics of mind: Figurative thought, language and understanding.* Cambridge: Cambridge University Press.

Gilligan, C. (1996). The centrality of relationship in human development: A puzzle, some evidence, and a theory. In G. Noam & K. Fischer (Eds.), *Development and vulnerability in close relationships* (pp. 237–261). Hillsdale, NJ: Lawrence Erlbaum.

Gilligan, C., Brown, L., & Rogers, A. (1990). Psyche embedded: A place for body, relationships, and culture in personality theory. In A. Rabin et al., (Eds.), *Studying persons and lives* (pp. 86–147). New York: Springer.

Hobson, J. (1994). *The chemistry of conscious states.* Boston, MA: Little Brown.

Lakoff, G. & Johnson, M. (1980). *Metaphors we live by.* Chicago and London: Chicago University Press.

Lakoff, G. & Johnson, M. (1999). *Philosophy in the flesh: The embodied mind and its challenge to western thought.* Boston, MA: Basic Books.

Langer, S. (1942). *Philosophy in a new key.* Cambridge, MA: Harvard University Press.

Pakos, K. (2000). *'I don't know how I am': Expression, reception, and interpretation of illness narratives.* Unpublished qualifying paper. Available through Harvard University, Gutman Library, Cambridge, MA.

Piaget, J. (1948). *The moral judgement of the child* (M. Gabain, Trans.). Glencoe, IL: Free Press.

Rogers, A. (1992). Marguerite Sechehaye and Reneé: A feminist reading of two accounts of a treatment. *Qualitative Studies in Education, 5*(3), 245–251.

Rogers, A. (1993). Voice, play and a practice of courage in girls' and women's lives. *Harvard Educational Review, 63*(3), 265–295.

Rogers, A. (1995). *A shining affliction: A story of harm and healing in psychotherapy.* New York: Penguin/Viking.

Rogers, A., Brown, L., & Tappan, M. (1993). Loss in ego development in adolescent girls: regression or resistance? In R. Josselson & A. Lieblich (Eds.), *The narrative study of lives, 2* (pp. 1–36). Chicago: Sage.

Rogers, A., Casey, M., Holland, J., & Nakkula, V. (1997). Developmental research as an intervention in children's lives. In K. Vanderven (Ed.), *Journal of Youth and Care Work, 11,* 95–104.

Rogers, A., Casey, M., Holland, J., Nakkula, V., & Sheinberg, N. (1999). An interpretive poetics of languages of the unsayable. In R. Josselson & A. Lieblich (Eds.), *The narrative study of lives, 6* (pp. 77 106). Chicago: Sage.

Seidman, I. (1991). *Interviewing as qualitative research.* New York: Teachers' College Press.

Selman, R. & Hickey-Schultz, L. (1990). *Making a friend in youth: Developmental theory and pair therapy*. Chicago: University of Chicago Press.

Stevens, W. (1954). *Collected poems*. New York: Knopf.

Winnicott, D.W. (1958). The capacity to be alone. In *The maturational processes and the facilitating environment* (pp. 29–36). New York: International Universities Press.

10 Analysing Children's Accounts using Discourse Analysis

Pam Alldred and Erica Burman

Discourse analytic approaches to research depart from understandings of the individual and of the relation between language and knowledge provided by positivist and post-positivist approaches. This chapter sets out to show what this might mean for studying children's experiences through, for example, interview-based research, and how a discourse-analytic approach may bring into play conceptual resources that are particularly valuable for research with children. First and foremost, discursive approaches highlight the interpretative nature of any research, not only that with children. As a consequence, they challenge the conventional distinction between data collection and analysis, question the status of research accounts and encourage us to query taken-for-granted assumptions about distinctions between adults and children. Hence our emphasis here will be on the active and subjective involvement of researchers in hearing, interpreting and representing children's 'voices'.

The case has already been made for listening to children, as earlier chapters describe, however, we want to highlight processes involved in (to follow the aural metaphor) *hearing* what children say. We share the view that it matters 'that some people speak and that others are merely spoken' (Probyn, 1993: 72). Hence we present a particular discourse analytic approach as compatible with the aims that unite the authors of this book, 'of captur[ing] children's lived experiences of the world and the meanings they attach to those experiences from their own perspectives' (Hogan, 1998: 2). However, discursive approaches locate these meanings at a cultural, rather than an individual level. They therefore reframe the research enterprise as the production of a culturally situated account of cultural meanings and practices ('discourses'), often through the study of how particular individuals are able to draw on, or are positioned within, these discourses. 'Hearing children's voices' is an active, subjective process in contrast with the positivist depiction of data collection as a neutral process of gathering pre-existing facts that are unmediated by our perceptions and unchanged by our practices of description and representation.

In this chapter we highlight two aspects of a discourse analytic approach to describe what it can offer to research with children. The notion of discourse that we introduce points to the importance of context, and we highlight how discursive approaches insist on the contextualization of both the accounts children give researchers, and the accounts researchers give of these accounts in two key ways. First, a discursive approach to research with children studies the statements of particular children and their interlocutors in the context of cultural understandings of child*hood*. It seeks to understand what children say in relation to (a) what it was possible for them to say (Foucault, 1988); and (b) what it is possible for us (particular adult members of a particular culture) to hear them saying. Second, discursive work insists that analysis is similarly grounded in the context in which it is produced, hence the significance of the particular researcher in producing a particular analysis. This brings matters of interpretation to the fore. As researchers, we inevitably bring into the practice of research political, conceptual and ethical resources that any technical approach cannot in itself specify or provide. This means that, from the outset, we caution against either over-attributing political potential to features of discursive approaches, or on the other hand ignoring them. The discourse analytic approach discussed here is informed by feminist research and theory, which distinguishes it from more general approaches to discourse analysis (Wilkinson & Kitzinger, 1995). The features that we argue make this approach valuable for research with children relate to understandings of the individual (the subject) and of power. These derive from the post-structuralist-informed approach we employ. Post-structuralist ideas fuel useful challenges to prevailing models of language, representation, and (claims to) knowledge (Burman, 1990; Weedon, 1987). Indeed this starting point for discourse analysis has implications for the nature of research itself.

It is because discourse analytic research draws attention to processes of interpretation that we do not see the research interview as providing researchers with a clear 'window' through which children's experiences can be seen. Researchers themselves have to be brought into view within the frame of the research since, we argue, the interview is an inter-subjective process in a very particular social context (Mishler, 1986; Ribbens, 1989). Hence interpretation enters into both hearing and analysing what children say, and beyond this into how it is represented within research reports. This is why researcher reflexivity needs to go beyond the research dialogue (in the interview or any other 'data collection' exercise) to encompass the political judgements and subjective processes that enter into interpretative, authorial and editorial decisions about our representation of 'children's voices' (see also, for example, Marks, 1996).

Language, Subjectivity and Childhood

Discourse analysis, as its name suggests, is an approach to analysis, rather than to 'data collection'. Its epistemological stance runs counter to that of positivist and post-positivist approaches. As discourse analysts, we cannot offer a distinct method or set of techniques. Instead we invite readers into ways of viewing the interview, the analytic processes and the status of the accounts generated. This chapter focuses on describing the general features and implications of this critical epistemology, since there are profound implications for how research is understood. We therefore do not discuss 'age-appropriate' research methods or techniques that one would consciously alter with the age of the child. Indeed the points we identify as the potential contributions of discourse analysis to research with children are no more particular to research with children than with other participants. However, perhaps precisely because of this they have, in our view, particular relevance for children.

An approach that begins from a questioning of the conventional model of the individual is particularly valuable for those groups of people, such as children, who have historically been denied full subject status. It offers not simply inclusion for children in the category of the 'normal subject', but adds further weight to the critique of this (modernist) subject that has been developed from feminist, post-colonial, psychoanalytic and post-structuralist perspectives (see, for instance, Henriques, Hollway, Urwin, Venn, & Walkerdine, 1998; Rose, 1989). The idealized model of the subject, to which children have been compared and found lacking, has the irrational, like the emotional and traces of the unconscious, sanitized from it. Yet adult and child participants alike may 'interweave fact and fiction both consciously and unconsciously' (Mayall, 1994: 13) in their accounts, and we might use the more complex model of the subject this suggests to critique the narrow understandings of the normal subject in psychology and other modernist disciplines. Children's apparent deviation from the category of 'reliable informants' might not mark them out as special cases after all, and indeed could help us question presumptions about the subject and about interview accounts in general (Burman, 1997a, 1998). This modernist notion of subject-hood is culturally dominant and increasingly globally pervasive, its individualism being accelerated under neoliberal capitalism (Burman, 1995a, 1997b, 2001). Walkerdine (1988) showed how the value accorded to rationality means that those deemed less rational can be seen in a general sense as less 'civilized'. The superior presumption of 'development' in this modernist framework is used to warrant patronizing, controlling or colonial attitudes towards those viewed as more primitive, be they children or other (usually non-western, non-European) societies (Burman, 1994c, 1995a, 1995b, 1999). Feminist and post-structuralist thinking (for example, Burman, 1994a; Moi, 1985; Walkerdine, 1988) have highlighted the ways in which children and women have been viewed as differing from the ideal subject.

Furthermore, dominant western constructions of the child – as incomplete subject, at risk of being less rational, self-controlled or reflexive (Burman, 1994a) – can themselves be better evaluated via a discursive approach. This insists upon a reflexive framing of the 'object' of study so that the cultural 'taken-for-granteds' come under scrutiny. Thus the issues which discourse analysis raise about the status of accounts have particular significance for *adult* interpretations of children's experiences. Children's 'voices' cannot be heard outside of, or free from, cultural understandings of childhood and the cultural meanings assigned to their communication (for example, Alldred, 1998). What distinguishes childhood researchers influenced by social con-structionist or broadly post-structuralist approaches is the attention to the social construction of childhood alongside what particular actual children have said (Burman, 1992, 1994a; Lesnik-Oberstein, 1996; Stainton Rogers & Stainton Rogers, 1992). Being reflexive about analysis means stepping back from the tools and conceptual resources employed, including the categories invoked, and subjecting them to the same scrutiny.

Discursive approaches can inform analysis of material generated in a range of ways. While typically analyses are based on transcribed accounts of inter-view-based research[1], it is possible to analyse any type of verbal or visual text with this approach (see Parker & The Bolton Discourse Network, 1999, for analyses of material drawn from different media). The text need not neces-sarily be an account of speech by one person, or of a conversation between people, but could equally be a verbal account derived from the researcher's description of an object or a cultural practice, as we shall see later.

Discourses are frameworks of meaning produced in language. They oper-ate independent of the intentions of speakers or writers, as ideas that cohere and not only reflect the social world, but serve to construct it. Michel Foucault's work on the power of expert knowledge through individuals' own understandings is particularly relevant for examining the power of dis-courses of child, adult, individual, and so forth, and for the post-structuralist informed work described here. Drawing on Foucault, Ian Parker defines a discourse as 'a system of statements which constructs an object' (Parker, 1992: 5). Thus, psychological discourses of the self or of the nature of adult-hood compared with childhood become constitutive of our experience (Rose, 1989, 1993; Steedman, 1995). Notwithstanding the many varieties of 'discourse analysis'[2], common to all are three ideas: first, that language is structured so as to produce and constrain sets of meanings; second, that the social world can only be accessed and interpreted via language; and third, that this therefore means that it can only be studied via an approach that explores the work done by language. This is significant for the way research interviewing is understood, as we shall explore.

Discourse analysis is, then, an approach to interpreting verbal material that connects with critiques of the positivist empiricism and expert knowl-edge that characterized modernity. Its roots lie in the questioning of assump-tions about representation across the social sciences from the late 1960s onwards (Parker, 1989). For example, in psychology the ethogenic approach (Harré, 1979; Harré & Secord, 1972) that was the forerunner of discourse analysis saw interview accounts as pieces of a jigsaw, but this metaphor proved limited because it implied the picture could be completed. Instead, the notion of 'interpretive repertoires' (Potter & Wetherell, 1987) invites attention to both a range of possibilities and the sociocultural sourcing of individuals' accounts. Significantly, this allows for multiple and potentially contradictory accounts that do not have to be squared with each other, and is compatible with the idea that a person's account relates to a *perspective* rather than to their (unified) identity. People's utterances could be seen as functioning to create certain effects for them in the conversation (Billig, Condor, Edwards, Gane, Middleton, & Radley, 1988; Potter & Wetherell, 1987), rather than simply as reflecting 'their perspective' (as if this was unitary and static).

This attention to textuality, in terms of taking seriously the different forms of description available and provided, recognizes that different ways of describing something have different consequences for how we understand it. For example, whether a child is being 'naughty' or 'expressive' (see Walkerdine, 1998) illustrates how language constructs what it 'names' and therefore embodies as value judgements. This means that discourse-analytic work seeks neither to identify features intrinsic to children, at the expense of either differences between them or of their commonalities with adults, nor does it identify the accounts any particular child participants give as necessarily defining or entirely representing their individual 'perspectives'. Rather, every account generated is treated as partial – both in the sense of being incomplete (for within this framework there is no complete account) and motivated or shaped by individual social agendas.

From Analysing the (Isolated Deficient) Child to Children's Talk

Language can be seen as providing 'subject positions' for speakers to occupy rather than 'perspectives' (Henriques et al., 1998; Davies & Harré, 1990). As we speak, we are positioned and position ourselves in particular ways which serve certain functions. At another time or in a different context, we may occupy quite different subject positions. Acknowledging that the same person may be positioned differently at different times has profound implications. It challenges psychology's model of 'the subject' as unitary, stable and consistent, (including the notion of identity that usually underpins claims to hear children's – or others' – voices). It insists that contradictions and multiple subject positions are ordinary features of everyday life, not something marking out the pathological individual. Where psychology would conventionally attribute these differences between people to differences of their development or cognitive abilities – locating the difference within the individual – different accounts can instead be understood as drawing on differential linguistic resources made accessible through particular cultural practices. Clearly some subject positions wield more power than others, and are differentially available to people by virtue of their social and institutional positioning, with age and generational hierarchies being key limiting dimensions.

This move towards multiple, situationally constructed and constrained positions is significant for children, as for others for whom inconstancy or irrationality have been seen as marking their difference from the 'normal' subject. For example, when interviewing children about 'family', definitions of family that are logically distinct or even opposed can be interpreted without attributing this to faulty reasoning. In one study, (see O'Brien, Alldred, & Jones, 1996), children talking in focus groups contradicted themselves, at one point saying something like 'he's not my real dad, he's my step-dad', and at another defining a 'real' parent as one who's 'there for you', thereby prioritizing social relationships, especially of emotional support, over biological kinship. While the psychological model of the subject typically locates these contradictions inside the individual speaker's head, the discursive approach locates them culturally, whereby contradictions express features of the culture and indicate the multiplicity of discourses in circulation. Rather than seeing this logical inconsistency as caused by an individual child's limited cognitive ability to recognize the permanence of relations across location (that is, that he is still your dad even if you never see him), the 'confusion', if any, is cultural, reflecting how a multiplicity of accounts (or discourses) of 'family' coexist. Analysis of the group discussion transcript might further address the ways biological definitions of family can compete with social ones in claims to 'real family' status (as Edwards, Gillies, & Ribbens McCarthy, 1999 have explored in other interview material). Or it might examine the way different discourses of family construct different members, deploy different markers of membership and might be warranted in alternative ways – by appeals to truth ('it just is') or to experiential knowledge and subjective perspective ('in my family' or 'to me'). It might examine the meanings and values that are assumed and asserted, and make links between what was said in the discussion and what is going on at broader cultural levels.[3]

To limit analysis to a rational level about the technical definitions of family would clearly be absurd, because it understates both the generality of the issue – that adults as well as children negotiate these different understandings of family in relation to our own experiences and values – and the personal and emotional significance of the discourses, and of each specific social context in which it is discussed. Instead, a post-structuralist discursive approach focuses on the way discourses function for speakers in the discussion in relation to the cultural power they wield, for instance, through a conservative 'family values' discourse or a psychological discourse of 'what's normal' or 'what children need' (Burman, 1994a). Rather than rushing to attribute features of the account of family to children as a specific group (whether in relation to their cognitive limits, irrationality, lesser abilities, lesser articulacy or reflexivity), children's talk about family can be seen as illustrating the range of available discourses of family that in turn reveal some of our current cultural concerns. Thus the research could highlight what the children's discussion indicates about a culture, rather than about those particular children's psychologies or orientations. It might offer an analysis of a society's cultural or sub-cultural ways of making meaning, the processes by which ideology is maintained and also by which we, as individual subjects (including as researchers!), are produced and our senses of ourselves sustained. While individual, psychic processes are, of course, at play in the generation of accounts, discourse analysis in itself does not provide an interpretive framework for these. Indeed, accounts that claim to be able to do just this should be questioned. By not assuming that the accounts children give us simply tell us what is going on inside their minds, discursive approaches interrupt the temptation either to over-attribute to the particular individuals or to romanticize 'children's perspectives'.

Reflexivity and Representation: Being Explicit about Interpretive Claims about Children

Social/emotional dynamics are typically edited out of research accounts because conventional data processing and analysis stages have tended to mop up or ignore the messiness of people's accounts (for example, Alldred & Gillies, 2002). Including such 'messiness' might appear to further children's 'otherness' from the idealized subject. But deliberately framed to do so, this helps challenge the normativity of this sanitized area. A researcher might decide that taking the research dynamics as their focus for analysis serves children better by showing their insight and reflexivity, claiming for them a place within the conventional model of subjectivity.

For instance, we have each found that even young children can be reflexive and humourous about contradictions within their accounts (Burman, 1991, 1992; O'Brien et al., 1996). Seven-year-olds in the discussion group referred to earlier were sympathetic to each other where the personal implications of a particular discourse challenged each other's understandings of their own families. For instance, a child who began with a strong statement about the conventional family form allowed himself to be convinced otherwise by a girl who argued that her family was still a 'family' in spite of having 'no dad in it' (not just without a co-residential father). An equally powerful plea for social and emotional factors to be given primacy was made by a Muslim girl, with a family where biological and social roles did in fact overlap (O'Brien et al., 1996). Their open dialogue showed humility in letting someone 'change their mind', and empathy as they recognized how particular discourses of family might make people feel, and placed this above the 'face-saving' that sticking logically to their argument could offer.

Since social constructionist theory 'has warned that giving our "subject" a "voice" involves the fantasy that it is possible to have unmediated direct knowledge of experience (James & Prout, 1990)' (Marks, 1996: 115), an interview cannot be seen as an expression of the interviewee's own 'authentic voice', but as generated through such 'filters' as the participants' perceptions of the situation, the research focus, interview questions, likely audience and interpretation, as well as the structural constraints they face and their personal values and biographies. Discourse analysts therefore see children's accounts as reflecting any or all of these, and so potentially offering insight into relevant aspects of their perspective that inform their experience as children. However, they would also point out that the account might owe more to their being, say, a Londoner, black or a church-goer. That is, other aspects of their social identity may be more significant than their age in producing their perspective. Besides exploring what aspects of an interview account might be specific to them as particular children, discourse analysts keep a broader frame to look for what the accounts suggest about the human condition generally. The researcher's account of this introduces another layer, which we will discuss shortly.

Doing Discourse Analysis

We now describe a way of conducting discourse analysis that highlights the researcher's role in producing not only the analysis, but also the text. That is, identifying as interpretive those stages arising before what is usually identified as 'analysis'. The particular approach we outline here draws on Parker's work (1992, 1994). We then introduce some examples from our previous work to highlight how interpretative dilemmas that discourse analysts face echo those of feminists in using any discursive or deconstructive approach (see, for example, Burman, 1990).

Stage 1: Generating the text

For Parker (1992, 1994), the first stage of analysis is to turn the 'text' into a written form. Where research material has been elicited in an interview with a child, or similar verbal discussion, it usually comprises questions and responses that are typically tape-recorded and transcribed. The discourses employed can be examined in terms of how they function in the conversation. However, consumer artefacts can also be subject to the same kind of analysis, once they have been rendered a verbal text. Hence Parker (1994) takes the example of text from a children's toothpaste packet and shows how this cultural object reinscribes discourses of children, parents and health. He works with verbal features of the text, such as the 'directions for use', to explore the construction of the dutiful parent, and of the child's medicalized 'need' for toothpaste, and but also shows how visual elements of layout, fonts, colours and the reference to children's fictional characters (in this case Punch and Judy) can be analysed to show the way particular constructions of childhood are mobilized to lend the product the 'trustworthiness' associated with the 'good 'ole days' and 'traditional' childhoods. Thus he shows how visual elements (such as packaging) contribute to its meanings. So the starting point for analysis is the words, the textual account. Producing a verbal text is therefore the researcher's first task.

Acknowledging the process of production of the text to be analysed highlights some key features of a discourse analytic approach. In the case of a visual image, discursive approaches, as Parker puts it, 'bring into focus connotations that normally twinkle on the margins of our consciousness' (1994: 96). In the case of interviews, they trouble the idea that there can be literal representations. Discursive approaches therefore highlight the representational and interpretive character of all stages of the research processes, from defining a text (producing it, in the case of an interview transcript) and before any formal 'data analysis' begins. Mishler (1991) describes some of the decisions to be taken about representing the complexities of live social interaction – even a calm, polite, slightly formal interview conversation – in the two-dimensional form of a written account. Added to this is the recognition that hearing is an active process, and is already interpretive, always drawing on the meanings we already 'know'.

As anyone who has transcribed an interview or a lecture has found, transposing an auditory verbal account into a written one is not straightforward (Ochs, 1979; Stubbs, 1983; Tedlock, 1984). Not only might there be moments of indecipherability or ambiguity when re-playing the tape of an interview, there are decisions about selection regarding what constitutes legitimate material (does one transcribe the exchange with the person who 'interrupted' the interview, the offer of a cup of tea at the start, the discussion about research at the end, or all the 'innit' or 'y' know' utterances?). Deliberately adding (or withholding) punctuation involves decisions that alter the meaning of the same string of words, and moreover, might be done 'automatically' (this is discussed further in Alldred & Gillies, 2002).

Contrast, for instance, the word string 'yes no', which is surprisingly common at the start of a response, when punctuated 'Yes. No …' (meaning 'Yes' with an explanation following) as opposed to 'Yeh, no' (meaning 'No', but beginning with an affirming gesture to the previous speaker). The person transcribing is using his or her own understanding of the meanings intended, and is thereby already engaged in an interpretative process in the 'data generation' stage, before what is conventionally recognized as the analysis stage. On top of this, there are active processes of remembering (of our understandings at the time of nonverbal communication and of intended meanings) which are selective, loaded and interpretative – and which invoke the researcher's individual and cultural norms about memory and subjectivity in ways that we can perhaps only glimpse (Antze & Lambek, 1996). Multiple transcripts are thus possible from the same audio-taped interview (Mishler, 1991; Ochs, 1979). Rather than being an unproblematic starting point, an interview transcript is a new text, an artefact, that not only evidences the researcher's involvement in the interview dynamic, but is also produced by them (Denzin & Lincoln, 1994; Mishler, 1986).

'Data analysis', as Scheurich (1997) argues, 'is not the development of an accurate representation of the data, as the positivist approach assumes, but a creative interaction between the conscious/unconscious researcher and the decontextualized data which is assumed to represent reality, or at least, reality as interpreted by the interviewee' (p. 63). The researchers are already 'in the picture' that, within conventional research models, they think they are merely looking at. Objects of research scrutiny do not just land on our desks but are the product of our interests, and as researchers we define and delimit them albeit within conditions – political, cultural, economic, institutional, disciplinary, funding and departmental – not of our choosing. However, even in post-positivist research where the researcher is no longer seen as a neutral tool 'representing' the world, declarations about the researcher's subjectivity can imply that admitting their 'biases' allows them to be transcended (Bordo, 1989; Stanley & Wise, 1993). We insist that not only can such positionings not be wiped away, but that the researcher remains situated and the perspective particular even if it is these that are hegemonic for the period.

Stage 2: Making connections: elaborating the discourse

Once the object of study has been defined and a text produced, Parker suggests that the second stage of discourse analysis is to free associate as broadly as possible with the text: what meanings, associations and connotations could it have? It is the significance of the researcher in this elaboration of the text, as well as the first stage of analysis, that leads Parker (1992) and Burman (1994d) to suggest the value of working in a team. Working with others at this stage generates a broader range of associated meanings and helps researchers to notice the particularities of their own perspectives. Parker encourages us not to dismiss too quickly the quirky chains of association this might suggest because they can help to identify the meanings and associations that the interviewee may not necessarily have intended – and which the interviewer may be unlikely to notice because of his or her involvement in the interview conversation. These include drawing attention to banal conventions that mark assumed social hierarchies, as well as idiosyncratic engagements with or subversions of these. Teams doing feminist interpretive work have developed particular approaches to help each other consider their own investments in particular analyses (for example, Gordon, Holland, & LaHelma, 2000; Stephensen, Kippax, & Crawford, 1996).

Stage 3: Identifying objects and subjects:
what is a child?

The third stage Parker describes is the identification of 'objects' in the text (the transcript or section of transcript). As a starting point he suggests itemizing the nouns referred to. What sort of a world is constructed by this account? What are the explicit items and what are the implicit objects that are also called into being? This list of 'objects', as things that are 'described' or, as this approach argues, 'constructed', also contains implied relations between them. The relationship between, say, 'books' and 'learning' involves 'reading' or 'studying' or 'looking at'. As we 'fill in' these relationships, we are elaborating the discourses that are at work in the text. Before identifying the discourses that 'hold together' these objects by particular understandings of the world, he suggests we do the same thing for 'subjects'. That is, to list all the categories of person referred to or implied by the text. These can go beyond explicitly institutional identity categories such as teacher and pupil to include other (perhaps less formal) 'subject positions', such as 'good reader', 'swot', and any assumptions about them, such as, for instance, 'white westerner', 'owner of the book', or 'hard at study'. It might include those who are implicitly constructed in contrast to these subjects – 'disruptive pupils' or 'naughty boys'. Hence it becomes possible to explore to whom the text is addressed, and how the reader is positioned by assumptions structured around the particular array of subject positions that thereby work to persuade them to assume particular alliances.

Stage 4: Rights and roles: who can say what ...

The next stage involves thinking about what can be said from each of the different subject positions identified. Within the meanings made available by the text, differential rights to speak are designated. Teachers are allowed to identify 'good readers' in ways that children are not, and the rules that govern access to these discourses are a key way of examining the power that resides in the different subject positions identified. Different subject positions carry particular sets of rights and responsibilities. Children can, of course, refer to 'good readers', but with different effects and notably without a teacher's professional authority (though they can perhaps express their desire to draw on this). This highlights the importance of examining how what is said *functions* in the text.

Stage 5: ... and why: institutional links

One can then interrogate the text by exploring the different versions of the social world that coexist. What are the relationships between subjects in the text? And what are the implications for those who do not follow the rules implied? (They might appear silly, arrogant or irrational, for instance.) What penalties follow on from not adopting the subject positions and their consequential discursive rights and responsibilities? While these questions can be asked of the text as a whole (in terms of the total range of explicit subject positions available), they must also be asked of each specific discourse identified. The relationship between teacher and pupil embedded in the discourse of teacher authority involves not just responsibility for the pupil in *loco parentis*, but an authority that results from the teacher's claim to expert knowledge of (or 'about') the pupil. It may also embody elements of adult–child and age-related status hierarchies, and perhaps borrow from the discourse of parental authority over children that serves to further naturalize adult–child authority relations. This is the unpacking of sets of cultural meanings, and although it is one stage more abstracted from the text, both, remember, are artefacts.

Further considerations – for, by or about children: what's at stake?

Parker's (1992) version of discourse analysis identifies three further steps. Researchers should, he suggests, be concerned with how discourses relate to institutions, power and ideology (p. 17). Foucault's (1972) analysis of the relations between discourse and practice highlights the operation of power through language so that material practices are always invested with meaning. Speaking or writing – the deployment of texts – is also a 'practice,' which reproduces the material basis of an institution. Researchers should therefore examine the ways that 'discursive practices' work ideologically, in terms of sustaining or challenging institutions. Post-structuralist discourse-analytic approaches, in examining the relationship between children's own accounts and broader cultural understandings of children and childhood, do, of course, consider the social institutions of family and schooling, for instance. However, they also attend to the relations between these accounts and the research relationships and writing (and reading) practices that are structured by, and which sustain, academic institutions. Thus Carolyn Steedman's (1983) analysis of children's writing addressed both written accounts produced by children and also how these can only be understood in relation to the body of literature about children's writing, including writing for children (see also Steedman, 1995).

Analysis should therefore involve identifying institutions that are reinforced or undermined by a particular discourse (Parker, 1992: 18) by identifying who stands to benefit from, and who loses out from, use of the discourse and what relations of power are structured in, and reproduced by, particular discursive practices (Parker, 1992: 19). Not all versions of discourse analysis would share this concern with ideology, but it follows from the post-structuralist understanding of the constructive power of language that discourses or 'discursive practices' (practices arising from particular discursive representations) have political effects, and serve to produce and distribute power in particular ways (see, for instance, Weedon, 1987). This is not to imagine that some discourses are ideological, while others are true, or to accept the idea that some people are victims of false consciousness. Rather it is an important reminder to attend to the power relations and political effects of discourses both within and beyond the interview setting.

Clearly, the process will vary with the type of text plus the aim and focus of the analysis, however, Table 10.1 is offered as a summary of the steps described above and breaks them down for further simplicity.

Interpreting Children's Accounts – Some Claims and Cautions

Analysis is a subjective and (spatially and temporally) particular process whereby sets of cultural meanings are generated from personally and politically (and academically) situated locations. Meanings are 'not fixed by reference to positivist constructions of a simple, unmediated and directly observable reality', but 'by the intersection of multiple relations (too multiple to name) which reflect and produce structures of regulation (age, gender, class, "race", sexuality, etc.) constituting social realities' (Burman, 1992: 57).

Table 10.1 Conducting discourse analysis: A summary of analytic stages drawn from Parker (1992, 1994) and Burman (1992, 1996)

1. Produce a written text (e.g., transcript), and reflect on processes involved in its production.
2. 'Free associate' with the text. Consider surprising and unsurprising connections and reflect upon the perspectives from which they derive.
3. Identify 'objects' constructed by elaborating the nouns in the text. Consider the meanings and values implied.
4. Examine the relations between objects.
5. Explore to whom the text is addressed and how the reader is positioned.
6. Identify the different subject positions within the text and elaborate the rights and responsibilities that accompany each. Consider what can be said from each position and how this might function.
7. Examine the relations between subjects.
8. Examine the understandings that form connections between and among subjects and objects. Consider whether there are alternative versions of these relationships (discourses) in the text.
9. Consider the values and institutions that are reinforced or undermined by these discourses.
10. Consider who gains and who loses within each discourse, and map any relations of hierarchy, including of knowledge or authority.
11. Consider whether these discourses allude to alternative accounts and what this suggests about how they function culturally.
12. Reflect upon the political values and relations (discourses) that enabled articulation of the last three stages, and the personal investments in these perspectives and this particular analysis.

To state that both the 'hearing' and the 'analysis' of what children say are active processes of interpretation raises complex questions about epistemology, including who counts as a 'knower', that highlight the significance of the researcher. Particularizing both the account given by interviewee *and* the account of this account given by the researcher changes the nature of the claims made for the published research 'findings'. For when research accounts are not seen as definitive statements of 'knowledge', they may be subject to scrutiny and to contestation, (including by competing claims to represent children's views), which undermine the seeming omnipotence of the researcher implied in conventional models of research. Recognizing that *hearing* children's accounts is an interpretative process directs our attention to some of the cultural taken-for-granted, including the implicit common-sense, as well as technical, parameters of our analysis. Recognizing analysis as an active,partial, particular process can help us to lay bare some of the conceptual/analytic/theoretical tools we use, and perhaps some of the everyday ones too. Research can and should be reflecting upon the world in which it itself takes place.

While arguing that not only do children's accounts rely on socially available and context-specific meanings, but so also does their analysis and representation by researchers, discursive approaches provide little guidance in determining specific interpretive matters. Instead, researchers' personal interpretations and political judgements emerge as crucial to the determination of interpretive emphasis and ambiguity. This is why questions of reliability are eschewed in post-structuralist informed work in favour of reflexivity, which attempts to account for how a particular analysis was arrived at. Once it is accepted that interpretation can only ever be particular, this then means that there is no intrinsic value (such as claims to general 'truth') in common accounts (such as repeated measures notions of reliability). They might usefully aid the identification of hegemonic readings, as might team-working (although individual researchers are viewed as being just as competent to do this as cultural members whose perspective is no more or less valid than the next person's), but this is not to fix with certainty a definitive meaning of a child's utterance. We argue that a feminist perspective can and should inform analysis in terms of content and interview dynamic, because as Burman (1992) explains:

> One of the places where feminist and post-structuralist concerns meet is in affirming reflexivity, both as structured within research relationships (no longer colluding in the sanitization of subjectivity, identification and emotion from research encounters) and within the theory-method relation. (p. 47)

The analysis and presentation of data are areas where the people researched have least power (Mayall, 1999). Processes of analysis, writing and reporting privilege the researcher's own perspective, since in producing an account we have interpretive, authorial and editorial authority, even where the 'content' is attributed to children. Enabling children to be (recognized as) active in the interview dynamic is one thing, but surrendering some of our control by allowing them to be party to the selection, interpretation or representation of their accounts is quite another, especially where we view responsibility for the politics of the research findings as remaining with the researcher. Reflexivity needs to extend to processes occurring within the academy, not just within the field (Probyn, 1993). Therefore feminist researchers try to discuss what we bring to the research relationship in terms of interview dynamics and the interpretation of the accounts where personal and political aspects of ourselves, which are formed through our current and historically constituted positions, inform the meaning we make.

Thus discursive approaches to the analysis of children's accounts generated through interviews might aim to recognize the culturally available meanings they rely upon, including those that constrain children's access to these meanings, or which differentiate between specific categories of children on the basis of their social positionings (for example, gendered, classed, racialized positions), as well as the particularities of an individual child's perspectives and experiences. Discursive approaches encourage analyses that connect the microlevel (including within the particular interview dynamic and local cultures of meaning), with the macrolevel of broader social conditions and meanings (including what could not have been said from the subject position of child interviewee).

Refusing Meanings

Paradoxically, if discourse analysis has particular value for the analysis of interviews with children, this is not because of something intrinsic to the approach, but rather because of what it refuses to provide. By refusing to supply the researcher with guaranteed stable meanings, the researcher has to acknowledge his or her own role with the processes of interpretation that give rise to these meanings. In order to warrant a particular analysis, we have to make explicit something of how and why we constructed its meaning in that way. Sometimes the seemingly self-evident nature of a particular interpretation can make it hard to justify – indeed sometimes it is hard to identify the process as 'interpretation', because the meaning of something can be so commonplace as to be 'obvious'. However, this might precisely be an opportunity to generate particular insights about cultural defaults and dominant meanings such as the differences between adults and children. Reflecting on the (personal and political) resources that inform our analysis can at least help to avoid reifying a particular analysis to imply that a given interpretation is inevitable and would necessarily be shared by another researcher. However, this need not lead to a relativist view that all interpretations are equally viable or valuable. Attending to the power relations conferred by structural research practices and subject positions elaborated within discourses not only highlights previously unacknowledged diversities of meaning, but also limits the possible range of interpretation. Not only are the frameworks and political commitment the researcher brings to analysis significant, but the relations these produce for researcher and researched, as well as the dynamics produced in the interview itself, must be scrutinized.

Including reflection on the research process in the 'findings' disrupts the notion that research interviews provide a 'clear window' onto children's experiences (Alldred & Gillies, 2002; Marks, 1996). Researchers can admit a situated analysis by making processes of interpretation as visible as possible, and avoiding the passive language conventions that imply that themes or discourses 'emerge' from the text in any immediate or disembodied way. However, research reflexivity should not replace a 'view from nowhere' with a 'dream of everywhere', but rather it should admit and explore the implications of the view from somewhere quite particular indeed (Bordo, 1990: 142; Haraway, 1990). For example, Erica has argued that attending to the power relations which are structured and reproduced in over-determined ways (as in the age–researcher conflation within the adult–child, researcher–researched relation) can fix the potential variety of interpretations of an interview exchange (Burman, 1992).

Language, Gender and Power

In this extract from a corpus of interviews conducted with individual children in primary schools (from Burman, 1992: 52), Erica has invited a boy she is calling Ravi to ask questions of her:

Ravi	Erica
D'you park and put your bicycle in the other hall?	Well at the moment it's just outside here.
Parked? Outside there?	Yes in the corridor because it's wet outside.
Sometimes it can get stolen.	Yes.
Somebody may come in and he just get it and take it with them	Have you ever had a bicycle stolen?
Yeh. I had a bike stolen but I found it again ...	

What struck Erica in later reading of this transcript was the vague and ambiguous character of Ravi's statements. His use of the indefinite temporal qualifier 'sometimes', the impersonal pronoun 'it' and the passive infinitive 'get stolen' all manage to convey nothing specific about number or person and so suggest maximum indeterminacy. Through offering several alternative readings of the exchange, Erica shows how, while multiple interpretations are possible, 'analyzing the power relationship within which it occurred fixes that proliferation of meanings. Indeed, the indeterminacy is only apparent when the text is taken out of its (linguistic and wider discursive) context' (1992: 53).

First, the statement might be interpreted as friendly advice: 'Be careful. Sometimes ...', although this cannot account for the failure of place or object specification. Second, it could be interpreted as an implicit threat ('if you don't do *x* ...') encoded in the (apparent) observation 'something might happen to (your) bicycle.' Here, within the genre of the gangster movie at least, 'sometimes' conveys a generalized menace. However, Erica notes how the context did not lend itself to this interpretation: 'If my interviewee had been double or treble his age (and height), and had reacted to the interview with hostility, and had said this with rather different intonation, and so on, then I might have interpreted it as a threat' (1992: 52–53). In a third reading, the as yet unspecified 'it' can be understood as specifically conceived for Ravi, with the 'sometimes' operating as a way of generalizing or shifting the object which 'it' refers to from Erica's bicycle to his own. The indefiniteness of 'sometimes' permits a transition of topic to the loss that Ravi goes on to discuss without making the shift too abrupt or rude a challenge to Erica's conversational control.

Hence Ravi's 'Sometimes it can get stolen' and its uncertainty with respect to whose bicycle is or has been stolen was interpreted by Erica as offering an area he wanted to talk about. The uncertainty therefore was not about Ravi's knowledge of his topic (as a typical 'competence'-based developmental psychological inquiry might assume), but rather was about the context of speaking, where it indicated an implicit request to suspend the terms of the conversation, the role play set up by Erica, (or suggests Ravi's recognition that he was deviating from it). This interpretation mobilizes an understanding of adult–children relations in which age and authority are not only confounded, but also emphasized by the research relationship. Rather than indicating some conceptual or linguistic – or even conversational – deficit, then, this third reading illustrates both the deep connections between knowledge and power and Ravi's conversational skill in negotiating this. Hence, this analysis shows how texts beyond those under study must be drawn on to inform analysis and indeed will be, whether or not this is consciously recognized and acknowledged. Power relations, such as exist between adults and children, researchers and researched are not merely a consideration during reflexive analysis, but can be seen to have entered into the production as well as the interpretation of discourse.

Beyond the Objectification of Children: Putting the Researcher in the Picture

A post-structuralist informed approach to discourse alters the status attributed to a research account. First, we have written here in terms of 'eliciting' or generating accounts to highlight the active work of the researcher in generating interviewee accounts, usually via practices of questioning, and emphasized its joint construction in the discursive exchange and in the particular dynamic between researcher(s) and participant(s). Second, we have referred to the statements made in interviews as 'accounts' to ward off assumptions that these are representative in some essential way or define the participant's perspective. We have used the verb 'to hear' to acknowledge the active role of the researcher in attending, listening and making meaning of what the interviewee says – and 'making meaning' reminds us that this process is one of active interpretation. It is therefore culturally and historically specific and thus incomplete, particular and to some degree subjective. Meanings are grounded in the context of this particular form of social interaction (Mishler, 1986), which might include how children view the researcher, understand social research itself (Edwards & Alldred, 1999), and also how the particular topic is introduced and participation negotiated with children (David et al., 2001), as well as in relation to the broader social context of audiences such as social policymakers.

Discursive approaches problematize the assumption of literal representation or direct communication that conventionally frames researchers' accounts of interviews. For children's accounts in particular, the temptation to attribute authenticity to the accounts is bolstered by romantic discourses of childhood (illustrated in Wordsworth's 'out of the mouths of babes') and the association with the natural that is the flip-side of the attribution of 'civilized' rationality to (certain) adults. Broader social relations cannot be factored out of the research encounter, even if the interview process is consciously designed to critique the power relations it perpetuates. Researchers replicate structures of privilege through their proximity to institutions of knowledge, and this leads some (such as Patai, 1991) to argue that ethical research is simply not possible in an unjust world. Taking up a position as one who knows, in relation to those who are oppressed, is fraught with ethical problems that are not assuaged by good intentions (see, for example, Gillies & Alldred, 2002), and some of the colonial practices maintained in the name of saving children are a case in point (see Burman, 1994c, 1999). At the very least, this requires that we focus on the potential losses as well as the gains of particular approaches to research, or, indeed, involvement in research at all.

There are general issues of representation in and by research that feminists have queried (see Wilkinson & Kitzinger, 1996) and these have specific resonance in relation to children. In providing a research 'voice' for a particular group, we should recognize how we may simultaneously reinforce their construction as alien or 'other', and take our own (or the dominant cultural perspective) as central. Representing another can thereby inadvertently reproduce the very disempowerment it seeks to rectify (Opie, 1992; Reay, 1996). So while we share the democratizing impulse that lies behind wanting to use research to hear children's voices, we believe we must guard against the risk that, by drawing attention to them as a particular social group, we construct children as 'little aliens' (James, Jenks, & Prout, 1998), somehow essentially different from adults. We therefore hold in tension the benefits of extending subjecthood (through the status of research interviewee) to children, with a critique of the normativity of such subjecthood. Such reflection prevents us from assuming that our work is bound to be liberating (Marks, 1996) or even that an empowering experience for participants guarantees a progressive impact of research in terms of its cultural politics. Indeed, we must evaluate what particular representations mean for the participants, and for their social group in general (see Alldred & Gillies, 2002).

From 'Giving Voice' to Textualizing Representational Practices

Discourses of 'giving voice' would seem to offer a way of treating children as active subjects and recognizing that they may have distinct perspectives on the world. Or, rather, that dominant understandings might be adult-centric. However, this need not rely on an identity-based approach which assumes that a particular viewpoint follows from a particular identity (Bordo, 1990; Butler, 1990; Riley, 1988; Spivak, 1988), thereby reifying childhood as a universal state. Rather, researchers should assert the particularity of the accounts elicited and be wary of research rhetoric that implies that a reading claims to be representative (see, for example, Fraser & Nicholson, 1990; Henwood, Griffin, & Phoenix, 1998). Similarly, in seeking to recognize the subjective perspectives of those who are researched, we must also recognize the particularity of the researcher, rather than allowing their perspective or ours to remain naturalized in the research account (Probyn, 1993; Stanley & Wise, 1993; Ticeneto Clough, 1992).

In placing children's voices in 'the public sphere', we need to examine the broader context of meanings brought into play. We need to ask through what cultural understandings of children are the words of any child 'heard', and how our account of them will be heard. Does it, in the specific context and debate, serve the interests of children to present them as having a distinct perspective? Or does it serve children better to show that their perspectives are not fundamentally different from adults' or even that differences between them are regarded as significant? It also means admitting who makes such decisions.

Responsibility for interpretation and political decision making can be owned but not guaranteed. In addition, when doing research with and about children, we require them to make themselves understood in adult terms or to speak to adult agendas (for example, Alldred, 1998, after Grossberg, 1989). What are the particular implications of Patai's (1991) concern, given that researchers representing children's views do so within a power relation in which the researcher–researched relationship is confounded with the adult–child hierarchy (Burman, 1992)? Given the double-edged nature of offering children some of the rewards of full (research) subject status (such as their representation through research), researchers must use their political judgement about how and when to (claim to) represent children (Alldred, 1998). This is not a question to which a method can provide an answer (Burman, 1990).

We hope to have conveyed something of the possibilities of discourse-analytic work in research with child participants. It can offer detailed descriptions of the relations of meaning and power within particular cultural understandings, but cannot offer generalizable findings or indications of the frequency with which particular discourses are employed, except insofar as it takes seriously the impact of enduring social divisions on specific social interactions.[4] We have tried to disentangle what the approach itself can offer ethical research practice, and what researchers themselves must bring to it in terms of political awareness and a commitment to social justice. A researcher's political and personal values come into play via his or her reflexive self-positioning within the research frame and are necessary in order to warrant particular interpretations and in order to problematize unexamined assumptions about the contribution of research to struggles for social justice.

While discourse analysis can be employed to analyse what children say, it rejects some of the theoretical underpinnings of the voice-as-perspective approach. So we end here by reiterating our caution against assuming that the political advantages for children in having their voice heard through research are self-evident or straightforward.[5] Rather than either upholding or deconstructing the subject of the 'voice' discourse, a discursive approach can help us think through what is at stake in adopting or critiquing it within particular sites of intervention.

Notes

1. We will not describe the interview process here, but see Burman (1994d) and, for a wide-ranging discussion of issues raised in qualitative social research, see Ribbens and Edwards (1998). The general points such texts make about reflecting on research practice have particular implications in relation to children, for instance, a concern with how participants are contacted raises issues of whether parents or teachers act as gatekeepers, making or limiting decisions for children or re/presenting the research to them in particular ways, affecting the context in which the research topic has meaning (see Burman, 1991, 1992; David, Edwards, & Alldred, 2001).
2. These range from conversational analysis and psycho-linguistic approaches in psychology to post-structuralist approaches to cultural objects and practices in cultural studies (see Fairclough, 1989; Parker and The Bolton Discourse Network, 1999; Wood & Kroger, 2000).
3. For instance in the legal system, which increasingly recognizes the complexity of contemporary family forms and that parental and adult sexual partnership roles do not always overlap (Alldred, 1999).
4. See Parker and Burman (1993) on the problems of discourse analysis, and Burman (1990) on the limitations and political noncomittal nature of post-structuralist approaches.
5. As Hogan (1998) and others have noted, hearing children's views is not only a concern in academic research, but increasingly in practitioner domains such as health (though notably not in education, see Monk, 2002) as service-user feedback (for example, Davie, Upton, & Varma, 1996). This reflects the extending consumer ethos, in which empowerment packages are sold as individual consumer rights, that forms part of the broader cultural context for 'hearing children's voices', and the conditions that make this view of research possible; including the political discourse of rights, of voice-as-empowerment as well as legislative frameworks on children's rights (see also Burman, 1996). This broader reflection on how a society views its children (and discourses in which children and adults are united, such as in that of consumers) is what Parker (1992) is advocating as the consideration of institutional contexts of research within the analysis of discourse.

Recommended Reading

Burman, E. (1994). Interviewing. In P. Banister, E. Burman, I. Parker, M. Taylor, & C. Tindall (Eds.), *Qualitative methods in psychology: A research guide* (pp. 49–71). Buckingham. Open University Press.

Burman, E. & Parker, I. (Eds.) (1993). *Discourse analytic research: Repertoires and readings of texts in action.* London: Routledge.

Parker, I. (1994). Discourse Analysis. In P. Banister, E. Burman, I. Parker, M. Taylor, & C. Tindall (Eds.), *Qualitative methods in psychology: A research guide* (pp. 92–107). Buckingham: Open University Press.

References

Alldred, P. (1998). Ethnography and discourse analysis: Dilemmas in representing the voices of children. In J. Ribbens & R. Edwards (Eds.), *Feminist dilemmas in qualitative research: Public knowledge and private lives* (pp. 147–170). London: Sage.

Alldred, P. (1999). *'Fit to parent'? Psychology, knowledge and popular debate.* Unpublished doctoral dissertation, University of East London.

Alldred, P. & Gillies, V. (2002). Eliciting research accounts: Producing modern subjects? In M. Mauthner, M. Birch, J. Jessop, & T. Millar (Eds.), *Ethics in qualitative research* (pp. 146–165). London: Sage.

Antze, P. & Lambek, M. (Eds.) (1996). *Tense past: Cultural essays in trauma and memory.* New York: Routledge.

Billig, M., Condor, S., Edwards, D., Gane, M., Middleton, D., & Radley, A.R. (1988). *Ideological dilemmas: A social psychology of everyday thinking.* London: Sage.

Bordo, S. (1989). Bringing body to theory. In D. Welton (Ed.), *Body and flesh: A philosophical reader* (pp. 84–97). Oxford: Blackwell.

Bordo, S. (1990). Feminism, postmodernism, and gender-scepticism. In L.J. Nicholson (Ed.), *Feminism/Postmodernism* (pp. 133–156). New York: Routledge.

Burman, E. (1990). Differing with deconstruction: A feminist critique. In I. Parker & J. Shotter (Eds.), *Deconstructing social psychology* (pp. 208–220). London: Routledge.

Burman, E. (1991). Power, gender and developmental psychology. *Feminism & Psychology*, 1(1), 141–153.

Burman, E. (1992). Feminism and discourse in developmental psychology: Power, subjectivity and interpretation. *Feminism & Psychology*, 2(1), 45–60.

Burman, E. (1994). *Deconstructing developmental psychology.* London: Routledge.

Burman, E. (1994c). Innocents abroad: Projecting western fantasies of childhood onto the iconography of emergencies. *Disasters: Journal of Disaster Studies and Management*, 18(3), 238–253.

Burman, E. (1994d). Interviewing. In P. Banister, E. Burman, I. Parker, M. Taylor, & C. Tindall (Eds.), *Qualitative methods in psychology: A research guide* (pp. 49–71). Buckingham: Open University Press.

Burman, E. (1995a). Developing differences: Gender, childhood and economic development. *Children & Society*, 9(3), 122–142.

Burman, E. (1995b). The abnormal distribution of development: Child development and policies for southern women. *Gender, Place and Culture*, 2(1), 21–36.

Burman, E. (1996). Constructing and deconstructing childhood: Images of children and charity appeals. In J. Haworth (Ed.), *Psychological Research* (pp. 170–194). London: Routledge.

Burman, E. (1997a). Telling stories: Psychologists, children and the production of 'false memories'. *Theory and Psychology*, 7(3), 291–309.

Burman, E. (1997b). Developmental psychology and its discontents. In D. Fox & I. Prilltensky (Eds.), *Introduction to critical psychology* (pp. 134–149). London: Sage.

Burman, E. (1998). Children, false memories and disciplinary alliances: Tensions between developmental psychology and psychoanalysis. *Psychoanalysis and Contemporary Thought*, 21(3), 307–333.

Burman, E. (1999). Appealing and appalling children. *Psychoanalytic Studies*, 1(3), 285–302.

Burman, E. (2001). Beyond the baby and the bathwater: Post-dualist developmental psychology. *European Early Childhood Education Research Journal*, 9(1), 5–22.

Butler, J. (1990). *Gender trouble: Feminism and the subversion of identity.* London: Routledge.

Christensen, P. & James, A. (2000). *Research with children: Perspectives and practices.* London: Falmer Press.

David, M., Edwards, R., & Alldred, P. (2001). Children and school-based research: 'Informed consent' or 'educated consent'? *British Educational Research Journal*, 27(3), 347–365.

Davie, R., Upton, G. & Varma, V. (Eds.) (1996). *The voice of the child: A handbook for professions.* London: Falmer Press.

Davies, B. & Harré, R. (1990). Positioning: the discursive production of selves. *Journal for the Theory of Social Behaviour*, 20(1), 43–63.

Denzin, N. & Lincoln, Y. (1994). Introduction: Entering the field of qualitative research. In N. Denzin & Y. Lincoln (Eds.), *Handbook of qualitative research.* Thousand Oaks, CA: Sage.

Edwards, R. & Alldred, P. (1999). Children and young people's views of social research: The case of research on home-school relations. *Childhood, 6,* 261–281.

Edwards, R., Gillies, V., & Ribbens McCarthy, J. (1999). Biological parents and social families: Legal discourses and everyday understandings of the position of step-parents. *International Journal of Law, Policy and the Family, 13,* 78–105.

Fairclough, N. (1989). *Language and power.* London: Longman.

Foucault, M. (1972). *The archaeology of knowledge.* London: Routledge.

Foucault, M. (1988). Technologies of the self. In L.H. Martin, H. Gutman, & P.H. Hutton (Eds.), *Technologies of the self: A seminar with Michel Foucault* (pp. 16–49). London: Tavistock.

Fraser, N. & Nicholson, L. (1990). Social criticism without philosophy. In L. Nicholson (Ed.), *Feminism/Postmodernism* (pp. 19–38). New York: Routledge.

Gordon, T., Holland, J., & LaHelma, E. (2000). *Making spaces: Citizenship and difference in schools.* London: Macmillan.

Grossberg, L. (1989). On the road with three ethnographers. *Journal of Communication Inquiry, 13*(2), 23–26.

Haraway, D. (1990). A manifesto for cyborgs: Science, technology and socialist feminism in the 1980s. In L. Nicholson (Ed.), *Feminism/Postmodernism* (pp. 190–233). New York: Routledge.

Harré, R. (1979). *Social being: A theory for individual psychology.* Oxford: Basil Blackwell.

Harré, R. & Secord, P. (1972). *The explanation of social behaviour.* Oxford: Basil Blackwell.

Henriques, J., Hollway, W., Urwin, C., Venn, C., & Walkerdine, V. (1998). *Changing the subject: Psychology, social regulation and subjectivity* (2nd ed.). London: Routledge.

Henwood, K., Griffin, C., & Phoenix, A. (Eds.) (1998). *Standpoints and differences: Essays in the practice of feminist psychology.* London: Sage.

Hogan, D. (1998). Valuing the child in research: Historical and current influences on research methodology with children. In D. Hogan & R. Gilligan (Eds.), *Researching children's experiences: Qualitative approaches* (pp. 1–9). Dublin: The Children's Research Centre, Trinity College.

James, A. & Prout, A. (Eds.) (1990). *Constructing and reconstructing childhood: Contemporary issues in the sociological study of childhood.* London: Falmer Press.

James, A., Jenks, C., & Prout, A. (1998). *Theorising childhood.* Cambridge: Polity Press.

Lesnik-Oberstein. K. (Ed.) (1996). *Children in culture: Approaches to childhood.* London: Macmillan.

Marks, D. (1996). Constructing a narrative: Moral discourse and young people's experience of exclusion. In E. Burman, G. Aitken, P. Alldred, R. Allwood, T. Billington, B. Goldberg, A.J. Gordo-Lopez, C. Heenan, D. Marks, & S. Warner *Psychology, discourse, practice: From regulation to resistance* (pp. 114–130). London: Taylor and Francis.

Mayall, B. (1994). (Ed.). *Children's childhoods: Observed and experienced.* London: Falmer Press.

Mayall, B. (1999). Children and childhood. In S. Hood, B. Mayall, & S. Oliver (Eds.), *Critical issues in social research: Power and prejudice (pp. 10–24).* Buckingham: Open University Press.

Mishler, E.G. (1986). *Research interviewing: Context and narrative.* London: Harvard University Press.

Mishler, E.G. (1991). Representing discourse: the rhetoric of transcription. *Journal of Narrative and Life History*, 1(4), 255–280.

Moi, T. (1985). *Sexual/Textual politics: Feminist literary theory*. London: Routledge.

Monk, D. (2002). Children's rights in education – making sense of contradictions. *Child and Family Law Quarterly*, 14(1), 45–56.

O'Brien, M., Alldred, P., & Jones, D. (1996). Children's constructions of family and kinship. In J. Brannen & M. O'Brien (Eds.), *Children in families: Research and policy* (pp. 84–100). London: Falmer Press.

Ochs, E. (1979). Transcription as theory. In E. Ochs & B. Schieffelin (Eds.), *Developmental pragmatics* (pp. 43–72). New York: Academic Press.

Opie, A. (1992) Qualitative research, appropriation of the 'Other' and empowerment. *Feminist Review*, 40, 52–69.

Parker, I. (1989). *The crisis in modern social psychology, and how to end it*. London: Routledge.

Parker, I. (1992). *Discourse dynamics: Critical analysis for social and individual psychology*. London: Routledge.

Parker, I. (1994). Discourse Analysis. In P. Banister, E. Burman, I. Parker, M. Taylor, & C. Tindall (Eds.), *Qualitative methods in psychology: A research guide* (pp. 92–107). Buckingham: Open University Press.

Parker, I. & Burman, E. (1993). Against discursive imperialism, empiricism and constructionism: thirty two problems with discourse analysis. In E. Burman & I. Parker (Eds.), *Discourse analytic research: Repertoires and readings of texts in action* (pp. 155–172). London: Routledge.

Parker, I. & The Bolton Discourse Network. (1999). *Critical textwork*. Buckingham: Open University Press.

Patai, D. (1991). US academics and third world women: Is ethical practice possible? In S. Berger Gluck & D. Patai (Eds.), *Women's words: The feminist practice of oral history* (pp. 137–153). London: Routledge.

Potter, J. & Wetherell, M. (1987). *Discourse and social psychology: Beyond attitudes and behaviour*. London: Sage.

Probyn, E. (1993). *Sexing the self: Gendered positions in cultural studies*. London: Routledge.

Reay, D. (1996). Insider perspectives or stealing the words out of women's mouths: interpretation in the research process. *Feminist Review*, 53, 57–73.

Ribbens, J. (1989). Interviewing: an 'unnatural' situation. *Women's Studies International Forum*, 12, 579–592.

Ribbens, J. & Edwards, R. (1998). (Eds.), *Feminist dilemmas in qualitative research: Public knowledge and private lives*. London: Sage.

Riley, D. (1988). *Am I that name?* London: Verso.

Rose, N. (1989). *Governing the soul: The shaping of the private self*. London: Routledge.

Rose, N. (1993). *Inventing ourselves*. London: Routledge.

Scheurich, J. (1997). *Research method in the postmodern*. London: Falmer Press.

Spivak, G. Chakravorty (1988). *The post-colonial critic*. New York: Routledge.

Stainton Rogers, R. & Stainton Rogers, W. (1992). *Stories of childhood: Shifting agendas of child concern*. Lewes: Harvester Wheatsheaf.

Stanley, L. & Wise, S. (1993). *Breaking out again: Feminist ontology and epistemology*. London: Routledge.

Steedman, C. (1983). *The tidy house: Little girls' writing*. London: Virago.

Steedman, C. (1995). *Strange dislocations*. London: Virago.

Stephenson, N., Kippax, S., & Crawford, J. (1996). You and I and she: memory-work and the construction of the self. In S. Wilkinson (Ed.), *Feminist social psychologies: International perspectives* (pp. 182–200) Buckingham: Open University Press.

Stubbs, M. (1983). *Discourse analysis: The sociolinguistic analysis of natural language.* Oxford: Blackwell.

Tedlock, D. (1984). *The spoken word and the work of interpretation.* Philadelphia, PA: University of Pennsylvania Press.

Ticeneto Clough, P. (1992). *The ends of ethnography: From realism to social criticism.* New York: Sage.

Urwin, C. (1985). The persuasion of normal development. In S. Steedman, C. Urwin, & V. Walkerdine (Eds.), *Language, gender and childhood* (pp. 164–202) London: Routledge.

Walkerdine, V. (1988). *The mastery of reason.* London: Routledge.

Walkerdine, V. (1990). *Schoolgirl fictions.* London: Verso.

Walkerdine, V. (1998). Developmental psychology and child-centred pedagogy. In J. Henriques, W. Hollway, C. Urwin, C. Venn, & V. Walkerdine, (Eds.), *Changing the subject: Psychology, social regulation and subjectivity* (pp. 153–202). London: Routledge.

Weedon, C. (1987). *Feminist practice and post-structuralist theory.* Cambridge: Blackwell.

Wilkinson, S. & Kitzinger, C. (Eds.) (1995). *Feminism and discourse: Psychological perspectives.* London: Sage.

Wilkinson, S. & Kitzinger, C. (Eds.) (1996). *Representing the other.* London: Sage.

Wood, L.A. & Kroger, R.O. (2000). *Doing discourse analysis: Methods for studying action in talk and text.* London: Sage.

Narrative Analysis of Children's Experience

Susan Engel

Why study children's stories?

This chapter describes work in which children's narratives are explored for the insight that they offer into children's experience of their worlds. The concept that children will tell us about their thoughts and experiences has gone out of fashion. Come to think of it, it may never have been in fashion. Until the turn of the last century scientists didn't seriously consider that children had any thoughts or experiences worth knowing about. Then Jean Piaget showed that children not only had thoughts and experiences worth knowing about, but that these thoughts and experiences were different from the thoughts and feelings of adults. But by that time, social scientists had fallen in love with the possibilities of experimentation. The explosion of ingenious experiments that yielded insights about how children construct knowledge, how they plan, remember, solve problems, and learn information has revolutionized our understanding of human development. It is not always clear that it has yielded equally rich information about children, per se. An unexpected and often unnoticed side effect has been that our understanding of what and how children think and feel about themselves and their world has not kept pace with our understanding of various influences on their development. Happily, one source of change in this regard has come from the fairly recent and intense interest in children's narratives.

The current scientific interest in narrative development grew out of a model embedded in the information processing/artificial intelligence boom of the 1970s. Schank and Abelson's *Scripts, plans, goals and understanding* (1977) laid the foundation for a focus on the way that children might organize knowledge of their daily life. Schank and Abelson argued that people organize experience in the form of mental scripts. These scripts revolve around goal-based events (going out to lunch, getting ready for school, birthday parties) that include people, places and events. Nelson's influential work on children's script knowledge (1986, 1989) was inspired by Schank and Abelson. Early on, Nelson's theory was based on the assumption that the form of knowledge in children's minds mapped onto the form of events (for example, children's mental representations matched the way things in the real world unfolded). The first research Nelson did was deceptively simple. Interested in the fact that children seemed to have such difficulty answering questions such as, 'What did you eat for breakfast this morning?' Nelson changed the question a little. Instead children were asked, for instance, 'What do you eat for breakfast?'. While children of 2, 3, and sometimes 4, could not answer the first question they could usually answer the second, and offered a kind of breakfast script ('Well, I have cereal and toast, and sometimes I have juice'). Nelson argued that this was evidence for the primacy of generalized representations of experience. She claimed that children's particular memories grow out of more general scripts that they have formed about events. The script metaphor also clearly implied that these events are organized around goals and people, two heavily socialized and meaning-laden entities. As her research program unfolded, the shared meanings of scripts became a more salient aspect of the theory (Nelson, 1989).

Over time two things became clear: (a) the scripts that children were using to organize their knowledge were actually constructed by the child – these constructions were imbued with meanings, many of those meanings derived from social interactions and the child's culture; and (b) the verbal scripts that children produced to represent their knowledge about experience and the world were stories as much as they were scripts. These constructions had as much to tell us about the development of narrative as they did about the development of event knowledge and the kinds of logic and concepts that might emerge from such event knowledge.

Nelson's work led to a surge of interest in the possibilities inherent in asking children to talk about their day. One such collection of studies is described in a book she edited, *Narratives from the crib* (1989) in which a group of diverse research psychologists analysed the pre-sleep monologues of one toddler, Emily. Taken together, the chapters show how a child's talk about his or her experience can reveal different layers of information about how the child thinks. Other research showed that children's general descriptions (scripts) of well-rehearsed events (breakfast, going to nursery school, birthday parties) lay the foundation for their memory of more specific instances of those events (a particular birthday party at which something exciting happened, for instance). An underlying theme of the script/narrative research was that stories do not merely convey special fantasies or the representation of unusual feelings or experiences, but also provide a fundamental intra- and interpersonal process through which children make sense of themselves in the world. In other words young children tell stories about their experience all the time, for a wide range of psychological purposes. Storytelling is pervasive. In recent years researchers have learned a great deal about how children come to tell stories, and about how those stories change as a function of development. In the next section of this chapter, I try to summarize what we have learned about children's narratives, then I talk about what it has taught us about children, and finally I discuss the kinds of things we might yet learn about children from their stories.

How Narrative Ability Develops: Through Reminiscing

Children begin participating in, and listening to, stories some time before they can tell stories on their own. Children as young as 16 months listen attentively as their parents recount what they have done, what they will do, or repeat a favourite made up story (possibly from a story book). Toddlers' early contributions may simply be a nod of the head, or the repetition of one of the parents' phrases. Often their early contributions simply serve to keep the parent telling (or repeating) the story. Take for example the following segment of conversation between a 24-month-old and her mother. The little girl is sitting at the kitchen table having a snack:

C: Mommy, tell about when, about when, Casey went on the big slide.
M: Ok. Well, Casey and Sara were at the park. And Casey wanted to go down the big kids' slide, and Sara said it was too dangerous. But Casey said *I wanna go down.*
C: Down. Then?
M: So Sara helped Casey up the steps, and when Casey got to the top, she was *so* high, and then, what did Casey do?
C: What she did?
M: Casey came down so fast, and Sara was scared, but not you, right? You weren't one bit scared.

Casey initiates the story, demonstrating the early and powerful interest children have in stories, particularly ones that relate their own experiences. None of Casey's contributions to this narrative are original or autonomous, but both serve to keep the mother telling the story. Elsewhere I have offered examples in which it is clear that the child wants the mother to say the same story over and over again so that the child has a chance to internalize it. Often over the course of several repetitions the child will begin doing more and more of the narrative work, contributing details, adding new elements, and offering perspective (Engel, 1995).

Stories told by toddlers and their parents are typically collaborative. Early development consists of the child taking on a more active and autonomous role in the narrative. So, for instance, children between the ages of 18 months and 28 months might add one word to an adult's account of the past. By the time children are 3-years-old, they are able to contribute novel information, structured in sentences that fit into the overall narrative. During their fourth year, most children are able to tell a story to an interested listener, on their own, however rudimentary, or elliptical. The following story told by a 3-year-old to his grandfather is an example of a simple and incomplete story, that nevertheless demonstrates a host of narrative skills.

I got a bike. Mommy got me a big bike. And I got a helmet. But I couldn't– I couldn't. I didn't know how to wear the helmet!

In this example, the little boy tells a story that includes two people, or characters, actions, and objects. There is a high point (not knowing how to wear the helmet) but no resolution to the high point. The boy also shows that he has a clear sense of audience. He has chosen a sympathetic and interested listener, whom he knows – his mommy. He is both impressing his audience and requesting sympathy, two interpersonal functions often served by the stories young children tell family members (Burger & Miller, 1999; Miller & Sperry, 1988). In the next example, a 4-year-old dictates to an adult:

> Little Worm and Big Worm were playing tag and then it started raining so they went home.

This story, in contrast to the bicycle helmet story, is imaginary. It too contains characters, action, a high point, and a kind of resolution (they went home). This example illustrates the fact that by 4 children are able and willing to tell a wide variety of types of stories, to a range of audiences, for a range of purposes. Alison Preece tape-recorded the stories three children told to one another on the way to and from school each day for a period of eighteen months, while they were in kindergarten and first grade. She identified fourteen types of stories. Most common was the personal anecdote. Fairly rare was a fantasy story, though the few that were told were quite elaborate and fully constructed both in terms of content, story structure, and grammar (Preece, 1987).

Not surprisingly, as children get older their narratives look more and more like the narratives of the adults with whom they live (both in their family and in their community). McCabe has diagrammed the developmental shifts in young children's stories in the following way. Toddlers can tell stories, most often of personal experiences. They are likely to include only one event. Next, they are likely to have two events or episodes in their story. Next comes what McCabe calls the 'leap frog' approach, which is to add several episodes, often in some kind of logical or narrative relationship to one another, but to mix up the order such that the audience can't always detect the logic or chronology of events (McCabe, 1997). McCabe claims that by 4-years-old most children are able to tell stories that have a logical order of causal events, a problem and its resolution, and a beginning and an end.

One thing these researchers have tended to agree on is that children's stories become increasingly conventional in all aspects of their presentation. The stories of school-aged children look more and more like the stories of adults. But the adults they are usually being compared to are non-artists, certainly not novelists. When children are compared to novelists the developmental trajectory looks somewhat different. Perhaps the most powerful characteristic of many memoirs and autobiographies of childhood is an emphasis on vivid sensation. The writers who recall their childhood describe sounds, smells, textures, and images in detail, recapturing the intensity of experience and the sensitivity to detail that seems to be a feature of the child's response to the world. Children, it would seem, respond with intense absorption and awe to events that seem humdrum and regular to older people. Young children use play, gesture and stories to transform ordinary experiences into something out of the ordinary, by expanding them in dimension, detail or interpretation.

A 5-year-old child is watching his mother peel a cucumber for dinner. He begins to try to cut a cucumber himself, using a butter knife, and says: 'My harmless inside heart turned green. I stabbed myself by accident and my heart rotted because it could no longer live without being in me.' At the same time young children can take for granted spectacles or events that seem full of import to the adult. In Jerome Bruner's discussion of the toddler's efforts to decipher the canonical from the non-canonical, he suggests that children explore, play and transform the usual and the unusual (Bruner, 1990). This is the writer's task as well, which makes the writers exploration of childhood particularly powerful.

A further striking characteristic of childhood portrayed by adult writers is a quality of dis-synchrony of time and space. One event takes up a huge place in the mind, and another long span of time takes up almost no time at all. Nabakov devotes ten pages to describing the way he and his brother disappointed their mother on Christmas morning, and gives one paragraph to a world war (Nabokov, 1967). Clearly some of this is a function of the memory process itself that must collapse great periods of time in order to have enough room to concentrate on the events and details that are important, no matter how small. But it is not merely a characteristic imposed by the memory process. Children, we now know, do have a strangely jumbled sense of time and space. Meaning dominates over chronology. Elsewhere, I have talked about why this leads to young children writing autobiographies in which sequence, place and time serve the meaning of the event rather than mirroring an objective reality. For instance a 7-year-old boy writing a life story describes his parents' divorce with no commentary or interpretation. But the very next sentence says: 'In the bath I was afraid I'd get sucked down the drain' (Engel, 1995).

In general, as children enter their middle childhood years, they become less avid story tellers. More of the time they are telling stories on command from an adult (in a school setting for instance). This may or may not explain why their stories become less idiosyncratic, more complete, and often less expressive.

The Other Foundation of Narrative: Play

Some time before children begin participating in their parents' stories (both factual and fictional) they begin engaging in symbolic play. In its simplest form, this involves using something (an object or gesture, for example) to represent something else. This kind of symbolization involves transforming reality, and is a pervasive and powerful process in early childhood, linked among other things to: the acquisition of grammar (Bruner, 1985), an understanding of events (Lucariello & Nelson, 1985), the development of imagination (Harris & Kavanaugh, 1993), the differentiation between symbol, symbol user, and audience (Werner, 1948; Werner & Kaplan, 1963) the appearance reality distinction (Flavell, 1983; Piaget, 1954) and an understanding of the mental states of others (Harris & Kavanaugh, 1993). These first symbolic transformations can be quite simple, involving no more than one action: for instance, when a child takes an object such as a spoon and uses it like a sword, or takes a wooden block and pushes it along the floor making the sounds of a truck. But during the second and third year of life many children begin to enact long rambling sequences involving language, gesture and the use of objects in non-literal ways. Often these play sequences are story-like:

> He-Man sees his enemy. He smashes him [sound effects of fighting], I'll never die He Man. Oh yeah? Take that and that [more sound effects]. He's gonna throw him down. Cyclops thinks he's dead.

This episode of play contains the elements of a rudimentary story: a protagonist, a series of actions, a problem and an ending, if not a solution to the problem. Often these sequences are accompanied by language that is itself story-like. For instance: 'The friends were walking in the woods. They didn't know it was getting to be night time … ' (accompanying the manipulation of small dolls). The relationship between language and play can shift. Early on, the language is sporadic and amplifies or augments the play. Sometimes the language may narrate or describe the action as it unfolds. As children get older, they are more and more likely to put the weight of their play into the language – they plan the sequence describing what will happen, who is who, what the denouement will be. Children often spend a great deal of time and mental energy using narrative language to plan a play sequence, then devoting only cursory energy and time to the acting out of the narrative. This represents a transitional point between gestural and narrative play.

Among 4- and 5-year-olds, these play sequences are often collaborative and so is the language that supports, elaborates and directs the play. In one study, my students and I were interested in the ways in which 4- and 5-year-olds used narrative to create and maintain intimacy. We tape-recorded friends and non-friends in a free play area of a day-care centre, finding that friends have a whole range of linguistic devices within the narrative dialogue structure that help not only build a story, but build a relationship. The following example shows the ways in which children who play together construct stories together:

John: Hey Nicole! Let's pretend, um, that, um, that a storm began again and then a big …
Carrie: No, no we're not, we're not playing!
Nikki: Yeah, we're not playing that. The storm, the storm said it's never gonna come 'gain.
John: Oh. Wait. Know what? Right as … the other side of the world they're having a storm.

In this example, there is some negotiation of who gets to help build the narrative. But the social dynamics of the threesome also influences the narrative that gets developed, and keeps the narrative in flux, causing the main event, the storm, to change location.

In the next example, two young friends are creating a story as they play with some small figures, but this exchange also leads them to discuss the boundary between fact and fiction:

Erik: And Adam, um pretend I was pulling a rope and then you were pulling it and, and then and then and then I let go of it and then you went flying and then hurt yourself.
Adam: Except I didn't really hurt myself?
Erik: Yes you did.
Adam: No I didn't.

In this case the children negotiate not only what goes into the story, but also the boundary between fiction and reality. Stories like this are a symbolic enactment of the child's forays back and forth across the border between what is imagined and what is real. These transitions can be made through pure dialogue (a child or children telling a story) or as the narrations of ongoing play action. In both cases, they reflect the way in which the child's narrative is never a static or finished text as it sometimes is for the more mature storyteller.

As children get older it is not only the form of the narrative that changes, but also the interpersonal context in which narratives unfold. Research on toddlers and their mothers shows that telling stories with a parent is a compelling activity for young children (Miller & Sperry, 1988). Individual differences suggest that mother-child pairs vary in how much and what kind of reminiscing they do. The interdependence between speakers manifested in these data also shows that early on shared experience and shared ways of conveying that experience are important to the young storyteller. In other words, making up stories, and creating stories out of recollected experience are not simply solitary or intrapersonal activities, but are fed by, and feed, relationships. People do not only collaborate and share everyday literal experience, it seems, but in fact at least some of the time, take great delight in sharing fictive worlds.

The Uses of Narrative

Research in the past twenty years has provided us with a sense of how children's narratives change as a function of age. But we have also learned that children's stories are shaped as much by the purpose they are serving as they are by the age of the storyteller. For instance, a 3-year-old sitting at dinner, impressing his parents (and reliving) his fall off of the slide at day care that day will tell a different kind of story from the child co-narrating an imaginary fight between two action figures as he sits on the floor of his bedroom with a same-aged peer. These two stories serve different purposes, unfold in different interpersonal contexts, and contain quite different formal characteristics.

One of the insights from the analyses of Emily's pre-sleep narratives was that Emily was telling those night-time stories to herself as a way of solving a variety of puzzles. We now have data that show children use storytelling for the following purposes: to solve emotional and cognitive puzzles; to establish and maintain friendships; to construct and communicate a sense of self; to recast events in ways that are satisfying; and to participate in the culture. This variety of functions has implications for how data are collected.

Children are not likely to tell the kind of story to a researcher that they might tell to an intimate friend as a way of reaffirming intimacy, for instance. The child's sensitivity to context raises major questions about how typical the narratives elicited by a researcher can be. We need to discover more about how the production of narrative at the request of, or in the company of, a stranger or researcher differs from the production of narrative with familiar adults and children. While laboratory settings, and specific kinds of elicitation, can be very useful for shedding light on some aspects of narrative development, naturalistic data collection is necessary for learning about certain things. At the end of the chapter I will return to the question of how to collect and analyse different kinds of narrative data.

Researchers have begun to appreciate how closely tied the form of a story is to the function it is serving. We also know that children can be highly attuned to the responses of their audience. The stories of pre-schoolers, like those of toddlers, reflect interpersonal processes as well as intrapersonal cognitive processes.

When toddlers construct stories with their parents, the input of each partner shapes the story. Recordings of these kinds of conversations show that some parent–child couples are highly attuned to one another during these collaborations. Subsequent research has shown that some pre-schoolers are also quite attuned to the interest and input of their same age peers as partners in telling stories about the past. Take the following conversation, for example, between two boys at a day-care centre:

T: Last night me and my dad went fishin'.
M: You went what?
T: *Fishing.* We went fishing.
M: You did? Did you catch a shark?
T: Yeah. I mean no. It was a ... But it was all bloody!

He opens the story with a clear interest in sharing experience, interesting and impressing his friend. Very quickly his listener signals that he wants some excitement in the story (was it a shark?). Tony feels tied to the truth since he has begun this as a personal narrative. But he still wants to fulfill his audience's request, so he puts in a different kind of excitement, by adding a description of the blood.

The characteristics of a child's story must be understood in terms of the context in which the story is created. A challenge in good narrative analysis is to apply at least two levels of analysis, one to the text itself (the story, the conversation, and so on) and another to the process through which the text was created. These two analyses should, optimally, address one another empirically or theoretically.

Often, as said earlier, the function of telling a particular story in a particular setting is to solve some kind of emotional or cognitive puzzle. Identifying these puzzles is one goal of research, complicated by the fact that the story-teller is not always or even often aware of what their concern is, what puzzle they are tackling. The interesting thing about narratives is that they embody, symbolize and communicate thoughts of the teller, but the teller is not necessarily aware of what is in their own story. So while these stories tell us about the puzzles that shape the child's daily experience that does not mean he or she consciously experiences these puzzles as puzzles.

Focusing on different aspects of narrative

To some extent the differences in researchers' views of what develops and when are determined by the specific narrative model the researcher has in mind. Some, such as Nancy Stein (1986), have looked at the structural components of a child's narratives as evidence of their developing cognitive capacities. Others have looked at the content of the child's stories and probed for evidence of the storyteller's fantasies and concerns (Coles, 1989; Paley, 1990; Stern, 1989). Other researchers have focussed on the way in which children acquire narrative skills as evidence of their changing aesthetics, and their increasing participation in their culture (McCabe, 1997).

The model of telos or endpoint a researcher uses will determine their ana-lytic criteria (what counts as a story) and will also shape the kinds of develop-mental processes they identify (how children become more accurate, more logical, more aesthetically sophisticated, less stylistically flexible, less idio-syncratic, less interested).

What have we Learned about Children?

We have learned quite a lot in the last twenty years about how children's narratives change as they get older, and we have good evidence about some of the reasons why they change. We know a fair amount about what does and does not vary across individuals and cultures.

That leaves us with the questions: what has this research taught us about children, and what could it still teach us? We have learned that children are avid storytellers and story listeners from an early age. On the one hand, it seems fairly evident that narrative is a universal and ubiquitous form in which people construct, represent and share experience. On the other hand, equally compelling is the evidence that shows how deep cultural narratives are, how powerful stories are as a socializing agent, and, conversely, how much they reveal about the values and habits of mind of a given culture or community.

Our study of the stories children tell, and how those stories change with development, has told us a lot about how they think about the world, how they go about making order in the world. They look for a sequence that makes sense, particularly when the story is about remembered events. They also look to put themselves at the centre, just as adults do.

A story is a way of understanding oneself-in-the-world. Emily's monologues in particular are a dramatic example of how essential it is to children to make sense of their lives and how powerful a tool narrative is in this effort to make sense. McCabe (1997) has explained that her choice of personal narratives as a source of data was a result of the observation that often, when children are asked to tell fictions, they produce copies of stories they have already heard. This converges with other research that shows how alert children are to the stories they hear, and how eager they are to adopt appealing genres and subject matter. They rehearse the stories of others as much as they rehearse their own stories. Rehearsal serves a problem-solving function – it allows the child to master something. When Emily rehearses her day over and over she is mastering a cognitive puzzle (which things caused which things, what came first?) or an emotional puzzle (Why do I have to go to sleep by myself? How do I feel about my younger brother Stephen?). When children repeat known stories they are solving a different kind of puzzle – What matters in this community? Who are good guys? Who are bad guys? What kind of story gets the attention of others? What are the dramas and plights that are important to those around me?

Perhaps the most interesting thing we have learned about children's experience from their stories is the part still least understood, which is the ways in which they move back and forth between the literal and the nonliteral, the real world and the imaginary, what is and what could be, and the ways in which they either need or love to play with those boundaries, at least in their stories.

The Story Shapes Experience and Experience Shapes the Story

As the early narrative monologue of Emily suggests, storytelling is a deeply social activity, but an equally powerful private activity. Children tell stories when alone, they tell stories that have private meanings, and they use stories as much for their internal thoughts and feelings as they do to communicate. As Halliday (1975) said, children use language to communicate and to think. Children's stories help them to think, particularly the kinds of thinking that are less socially derived and directed and stories help them to organize and articulate their experience.

Bruner, among others, has argued that it's not that easy to tease apart the structure of stories children are learning, from the structure of thinking and experience that they are building and/or acquiring (Bruner, 1985). In other words, one can look at the problem in two different ways. One way to view it is that children are learning new ways of telling stories, and the changes in their stories reflect their competence with various forms, and their expanded repertoires of forms. The other way to view it is to assume that the kinds of narratives we construct shape and determine the kinds of mental experiences we have, and that change in the kinds and range of stories children tell reflects a changing range of mental representations that children have. So, for instance, a young child tells a simple, somewhat elliptical story of a past event: 'A fish nibbled my toe. Schuyler laughed his head right off. It tickled.' In contrast, consider the way this 10-year-old writes about his summer holiday:

> Last year my family went to North Carolina for a summer vacation. It was very fun. The best part was getting to swim in the ocean, and have picnics on the beach. They had these boards you could rent for $10.00 and me and my sister Angie went boogie boarding. We weren't too good at it, but it was really great.

Should the researcher assume that this little boy experienced his summer vacation in the bland and conventional form of his narrative? Does his narrative style at this point in his life shape or affect the way he re-experiences that memory? Similarly, does the younger child have such a direct and crystal clear experience of his summer escapade? His story has little to frame it temporally, little embellishment, which serves to highlight the salient or charged details of the experience.

As described above, much has been learned in recent years about the ways in which children enter in to a community of storytellers through their storytelling. We have also seen that stories are one central means through which children develop a range of thinking skills that lie at the heart of everyday cognition. Stories enable children to work out sequencing, causation, temporal and spatial perspective, distinctions between what is in their mind and what is in the mind of a listener (or a character in a story), and seem to provide the basis for more abstract forms of mental organization such as concepts. The stories children tell about their day-to-day experience, as well as their memories of specific and special experiences (a fall from a tree, a family vacation, an adventure with their dog) reveal the ways in which they are organizing experience.

Where to Go Next

Clearly narrative researchers need to refine understanding of the long-term effects of early individual differences in narrative ability and proclivity, to identify the experiences and influences that seem to facilitate narrative skill, and to understand the full range of cultural differences in narrative construction as well as the meanings of those differences in various real-life settings. All of these directions concern the traditional territory of contemporary developmental psychology: children's behaviours (often seen as abilities) and what influences those abilities. There is a second equally rich direction in which narrative research can go. I hope to have shown in this chapter that narratives are an invaluable source of insight into what children think and feel, and also how they think and feel. What we have learned so far is that children create text in much the same way they create play scenarios. Within a given narrative, children employ a series of forms, and often move from one topic to another, or one approach to the topic. This shifting indicates the dynamic nature of their attempts to understand the world, and their interest in establishing (and manipulating) boundaries between spheres of reality. Their narratives suggest that they experience the world dynamically and in open-ended ways.

It may well be that some of the shifting and meandering in children's narratives stems from their lack of narrative tools, and their tendency to forget the requirements of an audience (though often enough when they need to they are extremely attuned to the audience). But it may also be true because part of what is so compelling to young children about creating a story is not the presentation of a piece of text to be admired, but the pleasures of creating the text.

Some guidelines for doing narrative research

Though much has already been learned about how and why children tell stories, there is more to be learned. How then should we go about learning it? While some questions require finely tuned and carefully controlled experiments (for instance, learning just what kinds of mental states children can understand in stories, and what kinds of logic children can and cannot employ in constructing a story) many questions require a different empirical approach. The research and themes referred to in this chapter point us in a few specific directions. The form and content of children's stories are tied to the context in which they tell stories and the purposes for which they are telling them. The story a child tells to impress a peer is different from the one he or she will tell to an unknown adult who asks to be told a story. This means that researchers need to do a lot of fieldwork, trying to record the stories children spontaneously tell. They also need to think carefully about how to elicit stories when that is called for. What does the child think the purpose of telling the story is? What does he or she make of her listener? For example, the question 'Tell me a story about something that has happened to you', is likely to elicit a different narrative from the question, 'What's the worst thing that has ever happened to you?' While the second question constrains the type of story you will hear it also will probably lead to a more authentic, communicatively oriented answer than the first. It is more like the questions people actually ask one another in real situations involving friend-making and friend-maintenance.

In a recent study we wanted to find out what kinds of stories children know and can tell about the lives of their friends (Engel & Li, 2004). We found that the kinds of information they share with one another over a snack are quite different than the information they offer a researcher about the same material (and in this case the researcher was a youthful looking college student). While they exchange small snippets of gossip about one another when they think no one is listening, 7- and 10-year-olds are less inclined to communicate anything but the most banal stories when they are talking to an investigator. This means that a researcher might try a much slower, more casual warm-up before asking the target questions. The more the child thinks the investigator is sincerely interested in finding out about the friend (rather than eliciting a performance from the child) the more authentic the narrative is apt to be.

One also has to think carefully about the kinds of prompts to be used. On the one hand, experimental convention tells us that the same protocol (set of questions and prompts) should be used across subjects to ensure comparability of answers. On the other hand, we now know that narrative production is extraordinarily sensitive to audience, context, participation and perceived purpose of the task. This means that the researcher may want to use a more open-ended, 'naturalistic' questioning technique to elicit stories from young children. The antidote to the comparability question is to analyse the interviewers' questions when analysing the data. So for instance, in our recent study of young children's stories about one another, when looking at length and richness of stories elicited we also looked at number and kind of prompts used, to see if differences in interview technique might account for differences in narrative (Engel, 2004).

We see a big difference between the question, 'Can you tell me a story about … ?' and 'Tell me the life story of (yourself, your friend, your sister).' Both of these requests, however, cue the child to take a narrative stance towards the task. We have seen that children as young as 6 are able to take a narrative stance, and that even at age 2, children are learning from reminiscing with others that storytelling entails a certain linguistic and paralinguistic stance (for instance, that reminiscing begins with a tag such as 'Remember when' and that storytelling begins with a tag such as 'Once upon a time'). Both of these requests, however, ('Tell me a story', and 'Tell me the life story of …') are different from asking a child to write a story on the one hand, or analysing the stories they tell informally within conversations, on the other.

One endpoint of storytelling is story writing. Yet this is clearly a different task from talking with a friend, or making up stories as one plays or even just daydreams. It involves a kind of deliberateness and revision that spoken stories do not have. It is hard to know just how to compare the written stories of a 9-year-old with the spoken stories of a 4-year-old. When comparing the written stories of 6-year-olds with those of 14-year-olds, for instance, one also has to take into account the child's comfort level with writing. One solution we have devised to make the life stories of younger children more comparable to the life stories of older children is to take dictation from younger children, show them what they have said, and invite them to make revisions. In doing this, we are making the textual, formal aspect of the process salient to them, so that they view their own autobiographies or stories as text in somewhat the same way as do the older children who are writing their stories.

Another difference, of course, between written stories and told stories, is that all the performative and dialogic aspects of told stories are missing or invisible (hard to trace) in written stories. *If* the process of storytelling is important, one has to videotape or at least audiotape the storytelling activity. For instance, if one is interested, as I have been in recent years, by the ways in which children go back and forth between spheres of reality, capturing the whole process is essential. Our research has shown that there are important differences between the stories children tell at a snack table, while building blocks, and when sitting quietly across the table from a researcher. Clearly asking children to write alone at a table is going to elicit a different kind of material from when the same children are telling stories with good friends while eating daily snacks at child care.

On the other end of the continuum from the formal setting, are those stories children tell when they do not necessarily even know they are telling stories. These can be collected in naturalistic settings (with tape-recorders and so on, in schools, homes, and playgrounds). But an interviewer can also engage children in conversations that lead the child to tell stories about his or her experience, without necessarily framing the process as a storytelling activity. Here there are two questions: how does one elicit stories in a casual conversation and how does one analyse such data? The first involves getting children to talk about their lives the way you would anyone you genuinely want to get to know or are curious about. It allows researchers to adapt their questions and manner to the specific child or setting in which they are collecting the narratives. This seems essential since the narratives people construct (especially children) in everyday life are so responsive to the expectations and feedback of his or her conversational partner or audience. It also allows researchers to adapt their approach to the specific cultural conventions of any given community (see Shirley Brice-Heath (1983) for a rich discussion of this topic).

There obviously is no one way to collect narrative data, but the purpose of a given study should be clear enough to direct whether written or spoken narratives are included. In relation to the analysis of data, it is important to develop criteria for identifying separate narratives within conversation. For instance, a child might begin talking about what they like to do best at school, and then slide into a story about 'this really fun game' he or she plays with their best friend. This might, in turn, lead him or her to tell a story about one particular time he or she played the game and what happened. Where is the story? When does it begin and where does it end? These are the questions the researcher must address. In our work we define a story as the depiction of an event. There has to be some sense of specific place and time (even if only evoked or implied rather than stated explicitly). There has to be some action or drama (however limited in scope). There has to be some clear beginning and ending statements. We always use a second coder to establish inter-coder reliability because interpretation is inherent in the task. When we are analysing conversations between people that include narratives, we count number of turns as well as length of narratives, and the number of turns begins with the first response to any utterance that begins the narrative and ends with the last relevant and contiguous utterance.

Because collaboration and co-construction are prevalent in storytelling, we have often used the technique of mapping out the story across speakers. When looking at the stories of young children this allows you to go back and assign responsibility for various components of the story to different speakers, and at the same time to characterize the narrative as a jointly produced text.

Analyses of stories can be at one of several levels, described below.

Content

What is the story about? Stories can easily be sorted into autobiographical and fictional. Many stories combine these two genres, and it is often difficult to decipher what segments are 'true' and which are made up. But most stories are told as if they are either actual or made up. Within these genres, children can talk about a wide variety of issues. They can tell about their families, their friends, their own adventures, their bedrooms and possessions, their pets, or their own favourite stories (from books, television, the movies).

Though one might think of theme as a different category, stories can revolve around themes that are content based: terrible things that have happened, special occasions, adventures. Very often when asked to tell about his or her life a child will string together a series of events that share a common theme.

Form

How is the story put together? One can use several approaches including, but not limited to: establishing a series of prototypes that represent different styles or developmental levels and then assigning each story to one type; identifying types of links and measuring the frequency of each type of link in each story; characterizing the stories by genres. Children under about the age of 8 often combine several genres within a story. The story transforms in theme, style and content as it goes along. This is evidence of how dynamic the process of storytelling is. We need to know more about how children use and blend these different forms. Do certain forms express one kind of content, and other forms another kind of content? Are certain forms more prevalent at one developmental stage or another? For example, in my analysis of one little girl's story about Vietnam (Engel, 1997), I showed how the author used dialogue, epistolary, and first-person fictional narrative interlaced with actual autobiographical information to tell a story about two sisters on opposite sides of a war. In order to do that, I identified the different literary forms used in the text, and then showed how one led to the other. In this case I argued that the meaning of the story (sibling rivalry) led to such a creative use of literary techniques.

Underlying meanings

What are the conscious and unconscious themes, puzzles, and constructions of the world conveyed in the content, form, and process of the story and its telling? One of the dilemmas facing contemporary narrative researchers is how to deal with what they may intuit is the underlying meaning of the story. Cognitive and linguistic researchers are often loathe to make the kinds of interpretations more clinically oriented psychologists would be interested in. One way to deal with the fuzziness of interpretations is through inter-coder reliability. If several coders identify the same general underlying meaning (sibling rivalry, for instance) one is on slightly stronger ground in making a claim about the meaning of the story. In my opinion, avoiding these interpretations leaves us with an incomplete understanding of narrative development, since expressing levels of meaning is such an important function of narrative. Another way to handle this problem, is to elicit or collect stories from children, and then ask other potential audiences (peers, teachers, people who are parents) to interpret them. This is what is meant, in part, by 'perlocutionary effect', as described below.

Perlocutionary effect

Borrowing from J.L. Austin's groundbreaking work, *How to do things with words* (1962), this kind of analysis assumes that the effect of a story on its listener is as important to know about as the intention of the speaker, or the content of the text. What does someone (an adult, another child) hear, feel, see or think when he or she hears the subject's story?

Intra- and interpersonal function

What is the story doing for the child (for example, solving a puzzle, ordering experience, making upsetting material feel safer, gaining mastery, experimenting with boundaries, making a friend, impressing others, gaining attention, gaining admittance, and so on)? For instance, in the story of Tony and his shark fishing, it is clear that he is fulfilling several functions in the story including sharing experience as a way of making and/or keeping a friend, presenting himself as an adventurer, and getting a rise out of his friend by telling exciting/gory details. Again, as with other category systems described here, establishing inter-coder reliability is an essential tool in making sure there is some solidity to the interpretations.

Aesthetic devices

What kinds of aesthetic devices are in the child's story? These devices might include, for example, ellipsis, alliteration, re-ordering of events, switches in level of detail and focus, switches in narrative voice, and omissions.

Movement across categories

Finally, it is the case that stories change their form and function in the course of telling. For example, they may lie at the boundary between social and private or move between these spheres. Shifts between spheres and the crossing of boundaries in the process of storytelling need to be more fully explored. One way to do this is to code stories for genre or story form, and then simply count the number of times the story shifts back and forth between the various forms used. Another way would be to identify types of shifts themselves, and then code for those types (for instance, sudden shifts in form, from dialogue to narration, mid-sentence shifts from one style to another, and shifts that occur slowly across a whole story such that the story begins as one kind of story and ends as another). It may be that younger children shift more readily between spheres of experience and/or genres.

In conclusion, children can tell us a lot about their lives, and about how they experience their lives, through their stories. But it is clear that a story reflects a dynamic process, one which is influenced by a myriad of forces. Those who elicit, record, and analyse such stories need to be acutely aware of the ways in which their methods shape their findings.

Recommended Reading

Engel, S. (1995). *The stories children tell*. New York: W.H. Freeman.
Nelson, K. (Ed.). (1989). *Narratives from the crib*. Cambridge, MA: Harvard University Press.

References

Austin, J.L. (1962). *How to do things with words*. Oxford: Clarendon Press.
Brice-Heath S.B. (1983). *Ways with words: Language, life and classrooms*. Cambridge: Cambridge University Press.
Bruner, J. (1985). *Actual minds, possible worlds*. Cambridge, MA: Harvard University Press.
Bruner, J. (1990). *Acts of meaning*. Cambridge, MA: Harvard University Press.
Bruner, J. & Lucariello, J. (1989). Monologue as narrative recreation of the world. In K. Nelson (Ed.), *Narratives from the crib* (pp. 73–97). Cambridge, MA: Harvard University Press.

Burger, L.K. & Miller, P.J. (1999). Early talk about the past revisited: Affect in working-class and middle-class children's co-narrations. *Journal of Child Language, 26*(1), 133–162.

Coles, R. (1989). *The call of stories*. New York: Houghton-Mifflin.

Engel, S. (1995). *The stories children tell*. New York: W.H. Freeman.

Engel, S. (1997). How to read the work of child authors. *Journal of Narratives and Life History, 7*, 229–235.

Engel, S. & Li, A. (2004). Narratives, gossip and shared experience: what young children know about the lives of others. In R. Fivush, J. Hudson, & P. Bauer (Eds.), *The mediated mind*. Hillsdale, NJ: Lawrence Erlbaum.

Flavell, J. (1983). The development of knowledge about the appearance–reality distinction. *Monographs of The Society of Research in Child Development, 51*(212).

Halliday, M.A.K. (1975). *Learning how to mean*. London: Edwin Arnold.

Harris, P.L. & Kavanaugh, R.D. (1993). Young children's understanding of pretense. *Monographs of the Society for Research in Child Development, 58*(231).

Lucariello, J. & Nelson, K. (1985). Slot-filler categories as memory organizers for young children. *Developmental Psychology, 21*, 272–282.

Mcabe, A. (1997). Developmental and cross-cultural aspects of children's narration. In M. Bamberg (Ed.), *Narrative development: Six approaches* (pp. 137–174). Hillsdale, NJ: Lawrence Erlbaum.

Miller, P.J. & Sperry, L.L. (1988). Early talk about the past: The origins of conversational stories of personal experience. *Journal of Children's Language, 15*, 293–316.

Nabakov, V. (1967). *Speak, memory*. New York: Random House.

Nelson, K. (1986). *Event knowledge: Structure and function in development*. Hillsdale, NJ: Lawrence Erlbaum Associates.

Nelson, K. (Ed.). (1989). *Narratives from the crib*. Cambridge, MA: Harvard University Press.

Paley, V. (1990). *The boy who would be helicopter*. Cambridge, MA: Harvard University Press.

Piaget, J. (1954). *The construction of reality in the child*. New York: Basic Books.

Preece, A. (1987). The range of narrative forms conversationally produced by young children. *Journal of Child Language, 14*, 353–373.

Schank, R. & Abelson, R. (1977). *Scripts, plans, goals and understanding*. Hillsdale, NJ: Lawrence Erlbaum.

Stein, N. (1986). *A model of story telling skills*. Boston University Conference on Language, October.

Stern, D. (1989). Crib monologues from a psychoanalytic perspective. In K. Nelson (Ed.), *Narratives from the crib* (pp. 309–319). Cambridge, MA: Harvard University Press.

Werner, H. (1948). *Comparative psychology of mental development*. New York: International Universities Press.

Werner, H. & Kaplan, B. (1963). *Symbol formation*. New York: Wiley.

12 Phenomenological Approaches to Research with Children

Tom Danaher and Marc Briod

Approaching Lived Experience: Theory in Tradition

After a century of tradition and transformations, phenomenology, as method, has proven itself to be an agreeable host to a variety of social science disciplines (see, for example, Natanson, 1973; Embree et al. (n.d.) 1). According to an old witticism, though, this history has created as many phenomenological methods as there are phenomenologists. The authors hope to dispel some of that sentiment, through a retracing of necessary theory and a presentation of two instances of our own work. However, old criticisms may endure, for 'the method' is malleable, sensitive to subject matter, and the researcher's presence is evident and essential. Phenomenology remains research in the first person, one that describes from the explicit life-world experiences of individual *I*s, the shared structures of meaning implicit in the *we*.

Unlike predominate methods of natural and social science, there are no formal procedures or pre-established rules that must be applied universally. The unity of phenomenology is found, instead, in the manner that method is conceived in such close relation to the subject matter: meaningful experience. Supporting a unifying double movement between person and life-world, there follows a distinct attitude and methodological orientation that both outline and limit phenomenological research:

1   The researcher develops a guiding question or concern in the light of lived experiences that are seriously interesting and commit us to better understand the experiencer's life-world.
2   When investigating experience as lived, preconceptions, assumptions, and beliefs are either set aside or brought into the open.
3   Themes or meanings essential to the experience are both intuitively (passively) and imaginatively (actively) discovered.
4   A narrative and descriptive general structure of the experiential phenomenon is offered (following van Manen, 1990: 30).

Since the issue at hand is the phenomenological research of children, an additional point needs to be made concerning 'research in the first person'. Access to children – 'childhood' – rests upon a radical empirical fact: 'To be human means that one is or was once a child. The experience of being or having been a child is known to every person as an essential condition of his or her existence' (Briod, 1989: 115). The experiential threshold to a child-as-child is discovered through remembering and re-imagining childhood's *life-world*: the world as directly meant and immediately experienced. But this avenue of research is largely closed to adult understanding until an effort is made to attend to methods that open us, as researchers, simultaneously to the subject matter and to the child we once were.

Adults, and the phenomenological attitude

Standing against reflective methods is an adult's everyday participation in what phenomenology terms the *natural attitude*: the shared assumptions of common thoughts, opinions, and beliefs in everyday living. Regardless of diversity in cultural and natural backgrounds, a human commonality is assumed and acted upon, unreflectively, at the mundane levels of daily existence, in eating, dressing, working, playing, relaxing. Not that we all eat or dress the same way, but we all participate in ordinary forms of domestic and community living. In the natural attitude, adults assume intimate acquaintance with immediately recognizable objects, situations, and contexts that are fundamental and practical to life-world pursuits. Children, for example, are initially perceived as small – and that is usually the end of it. But to children, adults are inevitably the 'big people', but this signifies something else entirely. As 5-year-old Wally tried to explain in a conversation with his kindergarten teacher, the author Vivian Paley, 'people [that is, children] don't feel the same as grown-ups' (Paley, 1998: 4). The wealth of such 'obvious' and often overlooked viewpoints provides our experiential data.

Children, especially the younger ones, inhabit a world fresh and relatively unfamiliar, a world inviting their exploration and discovery. It is this world-opening quality of anticipation and expectation – their sense of wonder – that distinguishes some of children's most defining experiences. Phenomenology's task is to capture in everyday language distinctive qualities in a child's emerging world, qualities that may not be remembered, or seem quite foreign to adults. To accomplish this aim research investigates those experiences of wonder and intentional meaning that are at the core of concrete existence, and provides the experiential 'stuff' for all that is truly empirical. A phenomenological study of children aims to clarify, describe and interpret their unique forms of 'intentionality' that constitute a child's way of attending to the world. A sound beginning asks the questions: What is it like to *be* a child? What does it mean to live in the special manner of a child?

Generally, the explanatory power of quantitative research has required elaborating on the variations of empirical data concerning children's nature, culture, and developmental progress. Resulting differences and similarities are recorded, quantified, and compared, often in association with the almost requisite categories of age, 'stages', ethnicity, socioeconomics, and so on. But phenomenologists do not prejudice the freshness and 'whole cloth' of lived experience by deciding understanding in advance using preconceived categories. Further, unexamined assumptions in the natural attitude encompass not only the practical, but the intellectual world too, in which such constructs as 'developmental', 'scientific', and 'childhood' were created in the first place. Thus, every seemingly 'natural' category promotes a categorical mode of thinking, and this phenomenological method seeks to *bracket*: to set aside.

The purpose of such an understanding, then, is not to categorize and explain children's behaviour and experience. Rather, it is to thematize (that is, to structure meanings) through descriptive methods, and so strengthen our sense of what it means to *be* a child, to live in the world *as* a child. Unfortunately, research studies in phenomenology, though widespread, are grounded in unfamiliar (to most schooled in empiricism), even alien, philosophical traditions. Orientation to the methods later presented, however, is unavoidably tied to a grasp of the history.

Phenomenology and the Human Science Tradition

Phenomenology 'as a rigorous discipline' was inaugurated by Edmund Husserl (1859–1938) at the beginning of the twentieth century. Following the highly influential Immanuel Kant, and a radicalized René Descartes, Husserl's overarching plan was to found a philosophy and method for an indubitable reflective inquiry into mind, or consciousness. Philosophical phenomenology was to secure its own self-evidence through the 'scientific' study of consciousness as 'intentionality'. It would further ground and reconcile a variety of more empirical phenomenologies related to psychology, sociology, history and other fields of human science. Although Husserl's prodigious and meticulous efforts toward a grand design never achieved the heights of his vision, his original thinking has remained to this day a worldwide touchstone for phenomenological methodology.

Husserl is originally connected to the wider movement of human science research through the early influence of Franz Brentano (1838–1917). Prior to the full formulation of his own thinking, Husserl found in Brentano's lectures on 'descriptive psychology' the pivotal insight that consciousness is never an empty vessel for thought, but always 'intends' an 'object'. Consciousness is never simply vacuous awareness, but an awareness *of*, the minding of something, a mental posture (attitude) toward some meaningful phenomenon. Husserl assumed Brentano's conception and developed the notion of many-layered intentionality (Spiegelberg, 1982: 97). In Husserl's hands, intentionality provided the 'initial set of tools to develop his phenomenology of consciousness' (Moran, 2000: 118). This step allowed him to overcome the split between person and world – between subjective and objective thinking – and to investigate the perceptions and experiences of the intersubjective life-world (*Lebenswelt*).

The wide-ranging life-philosophy of Wilhelm Dilthey (1833–1911) also played a significant role in the development of phenomenology. Part of Dilthey's importance was his contribution to some of the (still resonating) early debates about the nature and validity of a 'science' of human beings (Polkinghorne, 1983: Chap. 1). These discussions centred on the need for a separate epistemology and methodology for human sciences (*Geisteswissenschaften*) in order to go beyond the limitations of natural science methods. Dilthey argued that human life can neither be investigated nor understood as a reduction to physical or biological causal systems subject to universal laws of nature (Polkinghorne, 1983: 25). His argument held that the proper study for human sciences should be 'life experience'. He called for an *interpretative method* that would explicate the already organized and meaningful expressions of individual and social life, including their cultural and historical contexts (Polkinghorne, 1983: 26–27).

For Husserl, reflective access to any human realm was directly through an intentional analysis of consciousness. Dilthey's fundamental notion of 'understanding' (*Verstehen*), on the other hand, was to include 'cultural systems, social organizations, and systems of scientific or philosophical concepts', as well as 'expressions of life – literature and art, social life, and the course of history' (Polkinghorne, 1983: 221, 223). The stage was set, then, for a period of dispersion, foment, and development between the world wars. Colleagues and students pursued new directions of phenomenological investigation, often under the broadened banner of 'human science'.

Arguably the most profound new voice in phenomenology and human science arrived with the publication in 1927 of Martin Heidegger's *Being and Time*. Heidegger (1889–1976) was Husserl's younger colleague and the magnum opus retained the distinctive signs of the phenomenological method of 'showing' or laying bare, of making explicit. But phenomenology, 'understood correctly', was to be a disclosure of the existential modes of being human at the most fundamental level – a study of what it *means* to be a human being, not just a study of the consciousness or knowing. With his interpretation of human existence as a global 'fact', being-in-the-world, Heidegger provided phenomenology with his fundamental ontology of 'being-in-the-world'.

These philosophers and their students (many prominent in their own right) began the broad movement known today as continental thought and research. In the years surrounding World War II, it expanded through the existentialism of Jean-Paul Sartre, Maurice Merleau-Ponty, Victor Frankl, and others. In sociology, Alfred Schutz and later Thomas Luckmann (1967) developed a phenomenology of the social construction of the life-world. Moreover, what had been mainly a Germanic philosophic enterprise widened as translations began to appear, and important figures such as Frankl, Schutz, Aron Gurwisch, and Hannah Arendt emigrated, establishing continental thought abroad. In Holland, F.J.J. Buytendijk was instrumental in founding the Utrecht School, initiating inquiry into pedagogy and phenomenology. In France, the still highly influential Merleau-Ponty (see, for example, Silverman, 1988) had lectured at the Sorbonne on children and phenomenological psychology in 'friendly' debate with Jean Piaget (see Rojcewicz, 1987). Continental thought had also incorporated a 'linguistic turn', with Hans Gadamer (1975) and Paul Ricoeur (1978), whose hermeneutic interests in narrative research helped to deepen the ties between phenomenology and the broader tradition of interpretive human science. This opened the way to more recent studies about children and 'folk psychology or pedagogy' by American researchers such as Jerome Bruner, (1990, 1996), Katherine Nelson (1996) and others, who rely heavily upon anecdotal or narrative forms of phenomenological data.

Phenomenology and human science exist in universities worldwide (see, Center for Advanced Research in Phenomenology (n.d.)) in the realm created by this expanding tradition. Which thread of such traditions is relevant to a project at hand, however, depends on a researcher's own interest, subject matter, and personal fund of knowledge. Within this domain, though, 'privileged access to meanings is not numbers, but rather perception, cognition, and language' (von Ekartsberg, 1986: 2). Rather than remove research from life-world access, phenomenology and human science would 'probe into the meanings, structures, and limits of thought itself, within the ongoing concerns, needs, desires, values, principles, concepts, language, and texts of everyday experience' (Silverman, 1988: 6).

Phenomenology, language, and children's experience

A phenomenology of children relies mainly upon data given through language, as the primary carrier of experience and meaning. For this reason, it is, of course, of very limited use as method to researchers of infancy. Like a frustrated parent who can only guess what the baby feels or 'means' when it is crying, the researcher must wait for language.

Some phenomenologists, most notably Maurice Merleau-Ponty (1964: 161–169), have suggested that the visual panoply of artistic media can provide nonverbal ways for describing experience and grasping its essential meanings. It has long been acknowledged that children's drawings, movements, singing and playing (the latter as a kind of 'mixed media' version of children's experience) could all be fruitfully explored in phenomenological studies (for example, Werner, 1956). Children's movements, their expressive bodies-in-action, could be interpretively re-understood. With reference to Merleau-Ponty, Susan Langer and Ricoeur, dance therapist Ilene Serlin describes how three levels of relational movement could, in fact, be interpreted (1996).

The fact remains, however, that nonverbal expressions of experience eventually call for interpretation, some sort of translation into the 'lingua franca' of meaningful words. The scope of this chapter must remain limited to the more traditional view of phenomenology as a research enterprise that relies upon verbal and written data.

Orientations to Method

In a traditional division, children's life-worlds may be approached phenomenologically by means of essentialist, existentialist, and hermeneutic inquiry (Polkinghorne, 1983: 201). As an introduction, the first and last methods will be discussed, for method may also be divided by emphasis: *descriptive* and *interpretive*. In simplest contrast, the first seeks to intuitively structure data, delaying open interpretation, and the latter emphasizes interpretation throughout.

The descriptive phenomenological approach

The essentialist orientation, associated with Husserl's 'rigorous discipline', aims at understanding essences, or typical structures inhering in the themes of daily experience. From this perspective, empirical events and the world of causality are placed in phenomenological suspension (set aside) as merely contingent. The particularities in descriptions (data) that could be imagined as being otherwise in a different context are considered superfluous (inessential). Thus, it may be irrelevant whether a child's 'sense of belonging' or 'feeling shy' takes place in a schoolyard, on a camping trip, or in a home. Typical thematic structures or *essences* are descriptions, embedded in concrete examples of how – in what way – significance, meaning, or making sense, occurs.

The methodical suspension of empirical belief introduces the *phenomenological reduction*: the initial stance allowing the reflective thematization that separates phenomenology from the level of ordinary description (Ricoeur, 1978: 75–76). Description must begin 'not in terms of what we already know or presume to know', but rather with what presents itself to the researcher, 'exactly as it presents itself' (von Ekartsberg, 1986: 5).

An emphasis on imagined possibilities introduces *imaginary variation*, the meticulous consideration of descriptive data through which the researcher imaginatively peels away the empirically contingent – again, the essentially superfluous. Its purpose is to disclose a *general structure* of invariant qualities in descriptive and narrative data.

THE LAYERS OF INTENTIONALITY

Considering phenomenology inevitably leads to the necessary concept of *intentionality*. Phenomenologically, all thinking, whether it is imagining, remembering, or reflecting, is oriented in the double movement, that is to say, invited by, and intended toward, its object. The same is true for perceiving, feeling and bodily action: love is invited by its object, yet intends or gives to it as well; grasping (literal or figurative) is both a reaching for something with the intention 'in order to …' and a responding to something. With the powerful notion of intentionality, the researcher of lived experience commands an idea of the structure of person-and-world 'that indicates the inseparable connectedness of the human being and the world' (van Manen, 1990: 181).

Intentionality may be specific, as in a particular relation of love or hate. It may also be diffuse, as in an overall sense of joy, wellbeing, or even depression. And it is (by definition), in no way confined to the present as if it were merely some static form of awareness. There is, for instance, the temporal element introduced by the 'in order to ... '. Intentionality both provides and assumes a very different sense of the future through present action which, when carried through, creates and confirms a past intention or 'intentional past' (see, for example, van den Berg, 1972: 79–83). A subject's feelings, also, disclose a situated relation with others in a 'felt' world. Always experienced in the present, it is felt as a 'presence to' the world and others. Overall, intentionality represents the primary, unmediated, and complex experience that constitutes meaning and significance in our consciousness of the life-world.

Phenomenological researchers cannot and should not try to avoid their own intentionalities. The phenomenon chosen, the questions asked, and the subjects approached, are all intentional acts. One can never become a neutral 'positing power' of rationally imposed understanding. Instead, phenomenological investigation must employ 'the hidden art of imagination' in unity with its best efforts at both meaning and understanding others (Merleau-Ponty, 1996: xvii).

Hermeneutics: The interpretative approach

A phenomenologist may choose to emphasize the undeniably interpretive aspects of research in order to disclose the experiential meanings implicit in descriptive, or narrative, data. Hermeneutic accounts are renderings of coherent meanings by a reader of a literary text, and deliberately incorporate his or her subjective life perspective with the text's disclosure of meaning. But these studies can involve interpretive readings of people (or 'life-texts') as well. A person's narrated life-world can be 'read' or disclosed in much the same way as a literary text. Such readings require not only descriptive skills, but also the interpretive skills needed to unpack or uncover the meanings of experience, always from the perspective of the interpreter's own life-world, cultural circumstances, and personal fund of knowledge.

For the study of children, hermeneutic phenomenology is not the inquiry into essences of a child's life-world, but the disclosure of meanings that are uncovered in the light of the phenomenologist's life-history and personal childhood. It is a look at children in light of such remembering. And memories, though largely obscured by the passage of time, can be rearticulated in autobiographical reflections and anecdotes. This is not an indulgence in a 'subjective bias', but an effective way to awaken the awareness of actual childhood. Such awakening can animate our observations and descriptions of today's children, living in ways similar to ours in some respects, yet different in others.

DATA, QUESTIONING, AND THE HERMENEUTIC CIRCLE

Anecdotal stories, then, need to be written out. These are the data from which a fuller phenomenological interpretation proceeds. To separate a narrative, as before, 'from the level of ordinary description', one must do more than simply record children's verbal expressions. The range and power of adult language should be utilized to communicate and interpret the sense and contextual situation. Hermeneutic phenomenologists commonly select from diverse accounts those few that are rich enough to exemplify characteristic or existential qualities of lived experience.

Phenomenologists often speak of a *hermeneutic circle*. In part, this circle (or spiral) refers to the relationship between question and data. There are several degrees of ambivalence about this relationship, because we can never be certain whether a question arises from unexamined intentions or the data at hand, or whether an applied question will frame the way we come to understand the subject matter. There is, also, no single correct procedure for linking the anecdotal data, interpretation, and phenomenological questions. In general, though, it is helpful to collect and become familiar with a variety of written accounts before attempting to refine or even formulate a research question.

The motive in proceeding from anecdotes to questions is that there is no way to know in advance what meaningful themes may intuitively emerge from the data. Conversely, it is always possible to define a question 'up front', in a more essentialist manner, then utilize method with data to explicate a predetermined theme. The advantage of proceeding from data to questions is the possible uninfluenced attentiveness to the full flow and texture of experience. On the other hand, the essentialist is more openly methodical with stages of explication, therefore more accessible to inter-subjective review, counter-example, and at more points in the process. Even though hermeneutic efforts seem more authentic and natural when we proceed from data to questions (probably not to the unfamiliar reader), the hermeneutic circle requires that we explore in both directions.

The issue of validity (reliability and generalizability)

Researchers in phenomenology remain, for the most part, within the onto-logical and epistemological stances developed in the continental descriptive and interpretive traditions. Since insight into experience is the goal, valid evidence is constituted by the representation in descriptive and narrative form, of a general(izable) structure of meaning. As crucial and specific as the concepts surrounding validity are to empirical fact-based science, it should not be surprising that such questions have a different relevance in phenom-enolgy. Steinar Kvale relates how he, as a 'moderate post-modern qualitative researcher', came to terms with validity (1996: 230). For him, 'the under-standing of verification starts in the lived world and daily language where issues of reliable observation, of generalization from one case to another, of valid arguments, are part of everyday social interaction' (1996: 231). From this beginning he finds that:

> Ideally, the quality of the craftsmanship results in products with knowledge claims so powerful and convincing in their own right that they, so to say, carry the

validation with them, like a strong piece of art. In such cases, the research procedures would be transparent and the results evident, in the conclusions of the study intrinsically convincing as true, beautiful, and good ... Valid research would in this sense be research that makes questions of validity superfluous. (1996: 252)

Such research speaks to *possible* meanings of phenomena, as opposed to the specifics concerning the manipulation and prediction of empirical events. Phenomenological intent, in contrast, is the meaningful explication of the implicit, and validation of 'results' does not, therefore, correspond to the procedures of an empirical theoretical framework.

In the end, such research must guarantee its own validity in its own language, in its: (a) *vividness*, describing the feeling of genuiness; (b) *accuracy*, making writing believable, enabling readers, also, to 'see' what it is like; (c) *richness*, the depth of description, the sensual-aesthetic dimension; (d) *elegance*, unifying the essential description in simple and economical expression (Polkinghorne, 1983: 46). As a researcher discovers relevant voices or places within the historical tradition of human science, he or she must also search for a voice, text, or attitude with which to feel at home regarding the issue of validity.

Researching Pre-schoolers' Lived Experience: Two Methods

The context of data and thematic questions

The following narrative anecdote was written by a graduate student in an early childhood education seminar. The participants (all pre-school teachers) were encouraged to keep journals about daily life in their classrooms, especially experiences of pedagogical interest. Each week a variety of these anecdotes were shared and discussed.

The first phase of the research involved gathering topical anecdotes. As the semester progressed, entries tended to describe children who expressed special interest in their own sense of self or personal identity. As new examples arose for discussion, our rather free form of inquiry became more explicit, until we posed the same question to every anecdote: What is it like, or what does it mean, for a young child to experience a changed sense of selfhood or personal identity? We then formulated a narrower version of this theme: What is it like for young children to move in or out of alternate, or pretend, identity?

Here, then, is an exemplary anecdote from the graduate seminar, 'April'. The numbering is for ease of reference in the first of the two applied methods, and denotes transitions in meaning (for a range of similar methods, see Giorgi, 1985). Though numbering is unavoidably the choice of the researcher, it is not arbitrary. Transitions should be recognizable to the reader, and thus valid.

Narrative anecdote: 'April'

1. Brittani is ducking in and out among several groups of children in my class. She spies Dylan buckling into his aviator jacket. 'Oh, Michaelangelo, I see you have new clothes. I really like them a lot. Do you like mine?' She pirouettes with the grace of a future ballerina.
2. Dylan mumbles 'yeah' without glancing up.
3. 'I'm April' announces Brittani. (In the Ninja Turtle TV series, April is the young girl who is the contact between the underground turtles and the real world – a powerful figure indeed.) 'Let's get Marvin for Ninja Turtles.'
4. Marvin wants to finish his puzzle but Brittani is not to be dissuaded. 'You be Raphael,' she assigns imperiously, 'I'm April, you know.' Marvin abandons the puzzle and dons a cape.
5. The children spend the remainder of free play acting out various segments of the 'Teenage Mutant Ninja Turtle' episodes, with Brittani orchestrating their play in true Spielberg fashion.
6. After cleanup, we are sitting in a circle ready for attendance. When I call out Brittani's name, there is no response. Marvin giggles, Todd stares, and all the children look her way. She smiles impishly. I raise my head and look at her expectantly. No response. Then 'April's here!' she suddenly announces. I smile. 'April was here during free play when you were pretending. Now it's time for Brittani to join us.' Brittani purses her lips and stares at me.
7. 'Is Brittani Jessica here?' I ask with a smile. The addition of her middle name is meant to appease. It does. Her face brightens at this concession on my part. 'I'm here,' she cheerfully acknowledges.
8. Just then, Dr. B., the principal, enters our room. 'Good morning,' she addresses us with a smile. 'Hi, Dr. B.,' greets Brittani. 'You can call me April.'

Essential explication of meaningful segments

The text should be read and re-read for a sense of the whole. Only after this first effort should constituent and thematic segments be identified. The segments are allowed, intuitively, their own coalescence and re-languaged in a way that captures and presents nuances of meaning in a systematic form.

1a. B's already imagined project opens with her graceful, bodily interaction among playmates in a familiar place.
1b. B reaches out to a single and solitary D. In a friendly speech setting, B is looking, complimenting while inviting compliments, and asking D about style and dress.
2. D's answer is verbally affirmative toward B, but is bodily ambivalent, and hesitant about meeting her look.
3a. Within a shared myth-like story of apparently familiar characters, B confirms her project to D, announcing her role as the powerful 'April'.
3b. Still as B, she asks D's help in enlisting M.
4a. B meets with resistance from the third possible character, M, also engaged in solitary activity.

4b. B's insistence is reinforced by a restatement of her role as April.

4c. M, in the face of B's persistence, joins B and D, and assumes his assigned role and necessary style for play.

5. Within the allotted time, the children perform their roles, with B directing her imagined project.

6a. With playtime over, and as the day's structured activities move on, the assembled children are accounted for and addressed by the teacher, name by name.

6b. After an expectant pause, B suddenly announces that she is continuing to inhabit the role of April.

6c. B's smiling refusal is accompanied by the other children's attentive (knowing) reactions to the standoff.

6d. In the face of 'time to join us', B maintains her stance with an expression of stare and silence.

6e. In smiling refusal, B will not participate in the naming process on the teacher' terms.

7a. Returning B's smile, the teacher confirms that April was present at the socially appropriate time, but disconfirms her continuing presence.

7b. Still in a smiling manner, the teacher wins B back to the official school naming routine with the addition of her middle name to her first.

7c. B's refusal is appeased by the teacher's further acknowledgement of her original first and middle names.

7d. A 'brightened' B cheerfully accepts the compromise with her name as a way out of the standoff with authority. The sudden appearance of a second powerful adult is seized upon by B in order to reintroduce herself as April.

From a combined back and forth reading of the segments and original text, a reduced essential structure is disclosed by the elimination of inessential data in imaginative variation. The movement is from the particulars of the situation of the text to a more typified (general) and possibly more psychologically languaged understanding of the phenomenon.

DESCRIBING THE SITUATED STRUCTURE

Within an accustomed place and period of time, B intends her imaginative project: getting her playmates to join her in assuming fictional identities and names. With graceful movement and social inquiry, B interacts, inviting familiar others to join in a re-creation of fictional identities from already known stories and style. B assumes an identity of acknowledged power, enlisting one, then another, of the solitarily engaged playmates to recreate out episodes of the stories. When the teacher ends the allotted playtime – and with it the pretend identities – B alone among the attendant children refuses to acknowledge the required change: her 'return' to B. This results in a somewhat confrontational standoff, then a disconfirmation of her imagined self by the teacher. B is testing the implicit strength, in a smiling, but staring continuation of the pretend identity. She is appeased, though, by additional kind attention and confirmation, and she ends the standoff by accepting individualized attention to her original name. A change in the situation – a second adult, a visitor – prompts her to introduce and test her fictional identity anew.

FROM SITUATED EXAMPLES TO A GENERAL STRUCTURE

For a full phenomenological study, several anecdotal examples would be required in order to thematically combine single-situated structures to a general narrative structure of the phenomenon in question: the meaning of children's pretend personal identities. The aim is to disclose a general or essential structure across examples, valid and consistent from situation to situation. The present example, though phenomenologically explicated, is situated in a particular place, with particular children and adults. In a full study, thematic comparisons, contradictions, and coincidences of meaning would be presented in systematic form.

A SECOND ANECDOTE: 'DREW AND CHRISTOPHER'

> Drew and Christopher are playing in the block area, arranging small boards around a table to enclose it. Drew says, 'This is our doghouse, right Christo?' Christopher replies, 'I'm not Christo, I'm a big doberman.' Drew crawls in the house, growls, and says, 'I'm the biggest and this is the only house, and I'm a German shepherd dog, okay Christo?' Chris gets on all fours and paws the air with his hands. Drew laughs and paws the air, then hits Chris on the head with a board. As Chris starts to cry and the teacher walks over, Drew crawls in the doghouse. He yells out, 'I didn't do it! The dog did it!' Chris stops crying and says, 'You can't hit me, Drew, even the dog can't. I'm not your friend now.' He walks away with the teacher who applies a cold compress to his head. Then he goes back to Drew, who is stacking blocks. The teacher asks, 'What happened, Drew?' 'I didn't do it. The dog did, so I'm taking the house away.'

The same method of explication used for Brittani's experience of changing identities would need to be repeated for the 'Drew and Christopher' example. Space will not permit lengthy application, but the new data already suggest thematic content that further essentialist investigation might describe. For instance, in each example the children could be understood as testing their roles and negotiating power, both among themselves and in the presence of an intervening adult authority.

The second narrative, however, involving two boys and sudden violence 'hijacks' the reader's attention. Our inquiry is tempted into categories of previous knowledge: role-playing, gender, 'animal' aggressiveness, 'acting out', and the like. We are intimately familiar, we immediately recognize the situation – but this describes the natural attitude. We must begin again, strictly, with such categorical thinking set aside. The method and data, only, must inform the guiding concern: possible meanings in changing identities.

Imagining variations of the situation, the anomalous laughing violence certainly might have been otherwise. The violence, though phenomenal in its own right, is contingent and an inessential quality to this research. More importantly, an integral phenomenon then 'shows itself' in the data that is more subtle and germane than any 'role testing' or 'negotiating power'. By re-imagining childhood we can remember that there was, at times, terrible importance to pretending in play. An intangible subjective 'fact' offers meaning to 'what it was like'. The protocols of playing are sometimes serious stuff.

Drew asks Christopher directly for recognition, or confirmation of a pretend world and identity, '"right Christo … okay Christo?"' The reply, '"I'm not Christo,"' is, perhaps, disconfirming of a fragile, but important, imagined identity. Perhaps, Christopher's refusal to answer from, or even acknowledge his human identity to Drew – 'to step out of his role' – offends precious protocol, or is too frightening for the necessary play atmosphere, which must be ended. Such intuitions may not be the case, more examples must shed light. But if mistaken, we are phenomenologically so, the inquiry remains true to the method, rather than being tempted into explanatory natural attitude categories.

With the addition of a third and fourth example, the thematic issue would become still more systematically explicated. Each *situated structure* would be read in light of every other example, so that a more nuanced *general structure* could emerge: a 'final' narrative composite of invariant, essential, and thematic meaning.

The hermeneutic phenomenological approach to narrative data

The author of the 'April' anecdote suggests that she moved with 'the grace of a future ballerina', took 'imperious' action, and wore an 'impish' smile. Such metaphorical, adjectival, or adverbial terms bring interpretive colour to the reported incident, infusing description with unmediated perceptual impressions. This 'quality' of the original narrative data may then translate, in turn, directly to descriptive language in later interpretation. Metaphors and action language in general, though, should be considered carefully in research. It may call for psychological review (for example, for signs of distorted reporting), because a weakness of the method is the temptation to import 'colour' where none exists. 'The grace of a future ballerina', for instance, though conceivable in a pre-schooler, may be exaggeration. Whereas the essentialist simply substituted 'gracefully', and moved on toward essence; within hermeneutics, 'future ballerina' language should never be passed over. It has something to say. Carefully considered, it may well be, or not, a significant moment in the narrator's full and sensitive reading of the experience.

Rich description must capture not only the words and actions of others, but their intentions, emotions, or other embodied expressions as well – expressions that may provide important intuitions to an overall sense and meaning of the experience for each participant. Since sensitive readings of children's experience are so crucial to hermeneutic phenomenology, a researcher-as-fully-concerned-party might best be able to generate interpretive data. That is, one of those whose subjectivities are vitally engaged, whose lives are intertwined with children in a pedagogical way, such as parents, caregivers, teachers, and therapists. Their experience, caring attitude, and daily closeness, in itself, can attune them to the nuanced qualities essential to meaningful data. As a result, such researchers are in a strong position to offer colourful interpretive language incorporating key meanings in children's experience, rather than lifeless accounts of what merely 'was said' or 'took place'. Accordingly, they may be able to see beyond children's immediate presence to the world, to anticipated futures, and felt pasts, thus paying special heed to the difficult temporal qualities that add dimension and meaning to researching children's intentionalities.

EXTENDED HERMENEUTIC READINGS THROUGH IMAGINATIVE VARIATION

For our graduate seminar, continued discussions and rereadings of 'April' suggested several distinct, yet overlapping issues. Initially, we noted that our 'take' on the narrative events was necessarily more removed, seemingly less authentic than the author's original account because of her direct pedagogical concern – helping children acquire 'appropriate' social demeanour in the classroom. We, however, were in a position to reflect on each step in the story, and thus imagine different possibilities in the actions and decisions of the moment. Second, we realized that the author's original description was an already 'nuanced' interpretation in itself, expressed in fresh and immediate descriptive language. Lastly, we noticed how each reader of the anecdote, despite our detached perspective, nonetheless gave necessarily varied interpretive insights throughout. Here, for example, is a commentary from a student in the seminar:

> Brittani is anxious to be the leader, and very insistent that she has a good idea here. She is direct about what she wants others to do, reflecting the strength of the April character. Her role as this character must be convincing since the boys follow her direction. Perhaps she likes the feeling the role of April gives her, and isn't ready to let it go even though the time period has ended. Not wanting to let go made her hesitate about the name Brittani and try to hang on a bit longer to the April character. The teacher, adding the middle name, brought her back to the real classroom with something extra added. She's a bit put out about leaving the April character until the teacher uses her middle name, which is kind of special. However, the April character must mean a lot to her, since she tells the principal, 'You can call me April'.

THE PHENOMENOLOGICAL REDUCTION IN PRACTICE

Here we must restate the function of the phenomenological reduction in suspending belief in direct empirical claims. This student's interpretation contains a phenomenological misstep. Although we feel we know what the student meant, Brittani was not brought back to 'the real classroom'. This is the student's preconception. Brittani, instead, was enticed away from her pretend identity. In the natural attitude there is, indeed, a 'real world' that claims our attendance and belief, that brings us back from reflection and imagination, but researchers must stay very close to description. In the original anecdote, the classroom was described simply as a rather vague container ('my ... classroom', and 'our room'). The meaningful interactions occurred within. The researcher's mistake, in an otherwise accurate interpretation, was in using the word 'real'. Thereby, 'true' reality is ascribed to the everyday classroom of the natural attitude, while Brittani's imaginative play is reduced to something less, to a 'nothing but ... '. Inquiry into the significance of Brittani's lived sense of self and personal identity becomes biased.

Phenomenological method intends the disclosure of meaning and significance only, with the intention of formal and thematic description. An important methodological distinction must be made between searching for meanings and searching for 'real' truths. Phenomenological methodology should be clear about this. Phenomenological research is not an inquiry into an assumed empirical world resulting in theoretical explanation, for it is only experiential description and explication that count.

VALIDATION THROUGH INTERSUBJECTIVE AGREEMENT:
COLLABORATIVE RESULTS

Considering and discarding varied possibilities led to a final stage in reflection: our interpretations began to converge on a collaborative understanding of B's way of experiencing herself and her personal identity. We agreed that we were seeing a sense of self at play. Brittani was experimenting; by changing her name and identity she was moving in and out of a personally chosen character role. This playful way of controlling changes in persona did not occur all at once, but in five distinct phases or 'moves'. The members of the research seminar all contributed to the following descriptive interpretation:

1   *The roaming*: B was looking around, checking things out in a purposeful way, as if she were taking the pulse of the room before choosing her playmates. She apparently wanted to play, but only on her own terms.
2   *The new identity*: By assigning roles to other children, B. was deciding what to play and with whom. She obviously liked pretending to be someone else, especially the feeling of the 'April' identity. As 'April', she was very direct about what she wanted others to do. She was especially convincing to the boys. Clearly, she had the ability to draw others into her play, with her very competent language skills. She seemed to be the creative one that others enjoyed following. But what does this tendency to direct others portend for B? Is it the early sign of a good leader, or could it be the beginning of a young dictator? It is interesting that she chose the name of April for herself, the only girl in the television cartoon. In choosing the name, did she recognize the power of this imaginary person? Did she choose it for its gender?
3   *The refusal*: B obviously decided to try to stay as April. She was not ready to let go of the name, and tried to hang on a bit longer. Even in the face of a gentle challenge, she was reluctant to give up her powerful role. She gained too much enjoyment from carrying her pretend name into an everyday social situation. But perhaps she wanted to go further by

experimenting with controlling others and attempting to dictate how the teacher would call her name. She certainly didn't like it when the teacher would not play it her way. Was she enjoying manipulative power?

4   *The compromise*: B responded to the teacher's compromise with initiative, an elaboration on her real identity. She accepted the teacher's concession with one of her own. She was able to give in to the teacher's insistence on the social significance of her name, and responded. Her original name now became a little more special and individualized. She had reached a compromise with the teacher while showing meaningful cooperation.

5   *The reverting*: The first chance she got, she became 'April' again. Or rather, she was still 'April', even after the compromise initiative. Clearly, this character meant a lot to her. When she saw the chance to recruit another player and get her power back, she immediately resumed her fictional identity. She found an unwitting collaborator for her play in Dr. B. (the most 'powerful' person in the school!), and seemed quite satisfied to again be able to assert her control.

By distinguishing these five phases, we begin to understand that B's changing sense of self was not founded on a single, univocal expression of 'who she was'. Rather, in an experiential cycle, she purposefully shifted from Brittani to April, then back to Brittani, and finally, to April again. Each turn depended upon immediate changes in her engagements with the others. During the cycles, she sought to control responses to her shifting identity, with varying degrees of success. She seemed most successful with the suggestible and acquiescing boys, and least so with her literal-minded teacher. Somewhat surprisingly, she seized the first opportunity to discard her 'real' name when the school principal unwittingly walked into the unfolding drama.

Essentially the meaning of Brittani's experience was in her 'compromise' in every experiential encounter in the classroom. 'Compromise', not as a dilution or diminution, but in the sense that her willful (and willing) intentions encountered and engaged those of the other children, of the teacher, and (one supposes) of the principal. For Brittani, as for everyone else who was directly or indirectly involved, hers was a 'lesson'. She was already learning that her social identity and status are relational. This meaning to identity is explicated here as a function of an intersubjective relation with every involved personae, real or imagined.

The contemporary need for studies of children's life-worlds

Why pursue a phenomenological study of children? And for whom? A concluding answer to these questions calls for a different sort of interpretive appraisal of circumstances affecting children and families. As the demand for comprehensive social administration has been expanding, so have the requirements for child care, education, health, and other human services. Parents' time and energy have been increasingly absorbed at the workplace, and within a few generations, an economic and cultural shift has altered relations to children. Now early childhood educators and other caregivers are routinely expected to assume functions that were traditionally the parents' domain. These changes have necessarily affected family life and, therefore, the life-world experience of children: their routine ways of relating to adults, parents, and to each other, as well as the manner in which adults relate to and see (or fail to see) them.

Contemporary specialized, even fragmented, social response lacks the deeper vision of what a 'childhood' is or can be. Despite its best intentions, many of the global and integrative functions of family and community are replaced with piecemeal professional services that can, indeed, lose sight of the whole and individual child. One way to soften the impact of these changes, in our opinion, is to open the study of children's life-worlds to a broader readership. Research studies about children need not be exclusively for, or in the language of, professionals. Phenomenological images of children's lived-experience, in its everyday language, can be read and interpreted by a wider range of concerned adults, including parents.

With the decreasing presence of parents at home, to name just one exigency, there is a place for research into how children experience, for instance, 'absence'. In examples such as this, researchers have an obligation to broaden people's horizons about the life-worlds of children, and to invite more adults into taking longer and deeper looks at what being a child means. The moral effort required of us is to re-humanize our relationships with children by connecting us to a radically qualitative and humanistic vision of children's life-worlds. The moral conviction behind this kind of research is that a deepened sense of children will translate into social relations among adults and children that are more humane for all. The hope is for more reflective parenting and child care, as well as to higher quality health, pedagogy, and education.

Postscript: Further Studies

Unfortunately, the founding 'great works' are notoriously difficult texts. And there is no such thing as an out-of-date book, as the website of the Simon Silverman Phenomenology Center (n.d.) proclaims. Thus, the sheer amount of unfamiliar material can be overwhelming to the most determined. In the face of all this, Max van Manen's current *Researching Lived Experience* (1990) offers (students or professionals) an understandable, yet detailed, introduction to pedagogical methods from the continental tradition, with practical examples, and a comprehensive glossary of human science terminology. Many dissertations in this field may also serve to introduce and exemplify approaches through particular topics (see, for example, van Manen's phenomenologyonline (n.d.)). Centres of human science research (listed at online addresses) have been, in addition, traditional and welcoming forums for the voices of 'minorities' and women's experiential writings. Not surprisingly, research is currently being done at universities and degree programs linked to websites in North America: Duquesne University, Pittsburgh, PA; the University of Dallas, Houston, TX; Saybrook Graduate School, San Francisco, CA; The State University of West Georgia, Carrollton, GA; the University of Alberta, Edmonton, Canada.

Recommended Reading

Giorgi, A. (1985). *Phenomenology and psychological research.* Pittsburgh, PA: Duquesne University Press.
Polkinghorne, D. (1983). *Methodology for the human sciences.* Albany, NY: State University of New York Press.
van Manen, M. (1990). *Researching lived experience.* NY: SUNY Press.

References

Briod, M. (1989). A phenomenological approach to childhood development. In R. Valle & S. Halling (Eds.), *Existential-phenomenological perspectives in psychology: Exploring the breadth of human experience* (pp. 115–126). Norwell, MA: Kluwer Academic and Plenum Publishers.
Bruner, J. (1990). *Acts of meaning.* Boston, MA: Harvard University Press.
Bruner, J. (1996). *The culture of education.* Boston, MA: Harvard University Press.
Center for Advanced Research in Phenomenology. (n.d.) http://www.phenomenolo-gycenter.org Accessed 10 October 2004.
Embree, L., et al. (Eds.) (n.d.) *Encyclopedia of phenomenology.* http://www.wordtrade.com/Philosophy/encyphen.htm Accessed 10 October 2004.
Giorgi, A. (1985). *Phenomenology and psychological research.* Pittsburgh, PA: Duquesne University Press.
Giorgi, A. (1989). Some theoretical and practical issues regarding the psychological phenomenological method. *The Saybrook Review, 7,* 71–85.
Kvale, S. (1996). *InterViews.* Thousand Oaks, CA: Sage.
Luckmann, T. (1967). with Berger, P. in *The social construction of reality: A treatise in the sociology of knowledge.* New York: Anchor Books.
Merleau-Ponty, M. (1964). Eye and mind. (C. Dallery, trans.). In J. Wild, (Ed.), *The primacy of perception.* Evanston, IL: Northwestern University Press.
Merleau-Ponty, M. (1996). *The phenomenology of perception.* (C. Smith, Trans.). London, New York: Routledge.
Moran, D. (2000). *An introduction to phenomenology.* London, New York: Routledge.
Natthanson, M. (1973). *Phenomenology and the social sciences* (Vol. I). Evanston, IL: Northwestern University Press.
Nelson, K. (1996). *Language in cognitive development: The emergence of the mediated mind.* New York: Cambridge University Press.
Paley, V. (1998). *Wally's Stories: Conversations in the kindergarten.* Cambridge, MA: Harvard University Press.
Polkinghorne, D. (1983). *Methodology for the human sciences.* Albany, NY: SUNY Press.
Ricoeur, P. (1978). *The philosophy of Paul Ricoeur.* C. Reagan & D. Stewart (Eds.). Boston, MA: Beacon Press.

Rojcewicz, R. (1987). Merleau-Ponty and cognitive child psychology. *The Journal of Phenomenological Psychology, 18,* 201–222.

Serlin, I. (1996). Kinesthetic imagining. *The Journal of Humanistic Psychology, 36*(2), 25–33.

Silverman, H. (1988). *Philosophy and non-philosophy since Merleau-Ponty.* New York: Routledge.

Simon Silverman Phenomenology Center. (n.d.) Retrieved from http://www.duq.edu/library/silver2.htm. Pittsburgh, PA: Duquesne University.

Spiegelberg, H. (1982). *The phenomenological movement: A historical introduction.* Boston, MA: Martinus Nijhoff Publishers.

van den Berg, J. (1972). *A different existence.* Pittsburgh, PA: Duquesne University Press.

van Manen, M. (1990). *Researching lived experience.* New York: SUNY Press.

van Manen, M. (n.d.) phenomenologyonline. Retrieved from http://www.ualberta.ca/~vanmanen/.Edmonton: University of Alberta.

von Ekartsberg, R. (1986). *Life-world experience.* Lanham, MD, London: University Press of America.

Werner, H. (1956). On physiognomic perception. In G. Ketes (Ed.), *The New Landscape.* Chigago: Theobald Press.

13 Exploring Children's Views through Focus Groups

Eilis Hennessy and Caroline Heary

Background

A focus group is a discussion involving a small number of participants, led by a moderator, which seeks to gain an insight into the participants' experiences, attitudes and/or perceptions. The origins of the focus group are typically traced to Bogardus (1926), who advocated the use of group interviews because of their ability to stimulate people to present points that might be neglected in individual interviews and because they are cheaper and quicker to conduct than individual interviews. However, the group interviews described by Bogardus (1926) seem to have been primarily information gathering sessions and the large numbers of individuals present (at times as many as forty-five) would have made it impossible to explore complex or sensitive topics in any depth.

The origins of the principles that guide the running of most focus groups in sociological and psychological enquiry today owe much to the pioneering work of Merton and Kendall (1955). They described the uses of their 'focused interview' as a means of understanding and interpreting the results of quantitative research. Crucially they described the characteristics of the focused interview as: (a) involving a small number of individuals who have something in common; (b) gathering data on the subjective experiences of the participants; and (c) led by a moderator who guides discussion on the topics of interest. In contrast to the ways in which focus groups have been used in recent publications, Merton and Kendall (1955) saw the primary aim of the 'focused interview' as hypothesis testing. In its origins, therefore, the 'focused interview' was conceptualized as deriving from the natural science approach that was dominant in psychology at the time.

Much of the development of the focus group format in the 1970s and 1980s took place in applied settings, particularly market research. By the mid-1980s, however, social scientists, particularly within sociology and education, were taking an interest in the method which they believed had the potential to contribute to their discipline as a qualitative research method. This view of the value of the focus group seems to be shared by most recent authors on the topic (for example, Krueger, 1996; Morgan, 1996; Vaughn, Schumm, &

Sinagub, 1996). The focus group, therefore, is currently characterized as a qualitative research method.

The last ten years have seen a considerable rise in the number of publications in which focus groups were used with children and teenagers. The largest number of studies are broadly within the field of health psychology and health education, however they have also been used in many other fields of research, for example, social work (Charlesworth & Rodwell, 1997), sociology (Wight, 1994), market research (McDonald & Topper, 1988), school counselling (McMahon & Patton, 1997), education (Lewis, 1992), child psychiatry (MacMullin & Odeh, 1999), children with special needs (Morningstar, Turnbull, & Turnbull, 1995; Rinne, 1997), and anthropology (Agar & MacDonald, 1995). Within these disciplines focus groups have been used to different ends and at different stages of the research process, for example, in order to explore children's ideas and values, develop and adapt questionnaires for children, and develop educational programmes.

Although focus groups have been used most often to gather information on children's views or perspectives, they are also useful when children's experiences are of interest to researchers. For example, Garley, Gallop, Johnston and Pipitone (1997) used focus groups to gather information about the experiences of children and adolescents living with a parent who was mentally ill. Kisker (1985) collected information on adolescents' sexual experiences and Hunter and Chandler (1999) used focus groups with high-risk young people to discuss essays which group members had written about their lives. The findings of all three studies suggest that focus groups were an effective way of gathering this data despite the sensitive nature of the topics.

Advantages and Disadvantages of using Focus Groups with Children

Focus groups have long been viewed as having advantages over interviews for gathering certain types of qualitative data. For example, Vaughn et al. (1996) claim that the support offered to individuals within a focus group allows the participants greater openness in their responses. Lewis (1992) points out that, unlike an interview, a focus group does not have to be terminated when an individual does not respond. Further advantages outlined by Basch (1987) can be summarized as follows: reduced pressure on individuals to respond to every question; flexibility to be used alone or in combination with other research methods; reduced cost over interviews with the same number of individuals.

In addition to these advantages, there are reasons that make focus groups particularly suitable for use with children. Thus, Mauthner (1997) argues that focus groups create a safe peer environment and replicate the type of small group settings that children are familiar with from their classroom work. The peer support provided in the small group setting may also help to redress the power imbalance between adult and child that exists in one-to-one interviews. Hill, Laybourn and Borland (1996) argue that children may be encouraged to give their opinions when they hear others do so and their memory may be jogged by the contributions of other participants. This effect has also been noted by the present authors in their study of children's perceptions of the causes of psychological problems. In the excerpt from the study that follows, a group of six 14-year-old boys is discussing the possible causes of the behaviour of a fictional boy (Frank), which has just been described in a short vignette. The group discussion is moderated by the first author (E.H.)

> Alan: It's probably a social insecurity problem eh … once again one that you would have had since birth and I tend to agree with Jim in saying that his upbringing would not have helped. I mean there are parents and parents. And Frank [the fictional child in the vignette] has probably got the type of parents who pay him absolutely no attention, he's maybe … maybe they're quite often out at work so Frank seeks attention and channels that into his dreadful behaviour.
>
> Oscar: Yeah, I think attention seeking is …
>
> Paddy: Too much attention.
>
> E.H.: And do you think it would be because of a lack of attention at home or do you think it's more likely to arise from something that's going on in school?
>
> Oscar: It could be at home because that's the first place you look, that's the first place you're taught, you know and then maybe at school he looks for attention at school because he doesn't get it at home.
>
> Chris: Maybe he gets too much attention at home and he lashes out because he's sick of everyone always talking to him and wondering how he is and stuff.
>
> Oscar: Maybe he gets lots of attention at home and he expects the same kind of attention at school …

Although all the comments in this excerpt refer to attention seeking as a possible cause of the behaviour, each boy's view differs slightly. In this way the group context has provided a much richer account of the nature of attention seeking than would have been possible from a series of interviews.

Finally, Levine and Zimmerman (1996) suggest that an important advantage of using focus groups with children is that the method acknowledges the participants as experts. Thus, a child participating in a focus group should not feel that he or she is being questioned by an adult but rather that he or she is sharing experiences with a group of peers. In contrast to an individual interview, the adult's role should be one of facilitating and encouraging the discussion rather than formally leading it. Indeed, the method might well be suited to facilitating a greater involvement by children in the research process, with children leading focus groups on topics they have chosen. The authors are not, however, aware of any such work at present.

Of course, focus groups are not appropriate for all uses and Basch (1987) argues that one of the major limitations of focus groups is that they are not useful for testing hypotheses in a traditional experimental design. This view contrasts with the view of early researchers (for example, Merton & Kendall, 1955) but is consistent with current theory and practice guiding the uses of focus groups. Basch (1987) also argues that focus groups are not appropriate for drawing inferences about larger populations or for statistical testing, which requires quantitative findings.

Interpersonal interaction is generally seen as an advantage of focus groups, however, it is important to consider the role of group processes in determining the nature of that interaction and to recognize that such interactions are not necessarily positive. For example, there is always the possibility that intimidation within the group may inhibit some individuals from making a contribution (Lewis, 1992). There is also a possibility that an individual's expressed opinion may be influenced by a desire to fit in with other group members. Thus, Wight (1994) reported that 16-year-old boys taking part in focus groups tended to exaggerate their use of sexist obscenities in line with the norms of masculinity that were dominant in the group.

Although not systematically researched in relation to focus groups, individual characteristics of the participating children and their relationships with one another will be powerful determinants of the group dynamic. Thus the personal qualities of the participating children, such as their levels of shyness or confidence, their age and whether or not they know the other participants, are all likely to influence the discussion. Based on their research with primary school children Hill et al. (1996) suggest that individual interviews may be better for encouraging diffident children who might have concerns about speaking in a group. However, Mayall (2000) suggests that having a friend present can be supportive and enabling and may assist children who would feel very shy if they were alone.

Focus groups can be run successfully with children as young as 8 years but it may be best to use playful group activities rather than conversation with younger age groups to facilitate their participation (Clark, 1996; Hill et al., 1996). Older children and adolescents are unlikely to have difficulties with the conversational demands of the group and therefore the method is typically most appropriate for this age group.

Although focus groups are generally perceived as more economical (with time and money) than a series of individual interviews (Basch, 1987; Morgan, 1997), there may be difficulties about getting all the participants together in the same place at the same time that do not arise for researchers who are using individual interviews. Thus, the authors had to abandon the use of focus groups in favour of individual interviews in a children's hospital because of difficulties involved in organizing groups of children due to hospital schedules and restrictions based on children's illnesses.

Ethics in Focus Group Research

Involving children in focus group discussions gives rise to ethical issues that are not confronted by researchers using other research methods (Hill, 1998). These issues arise from two aspects of the focus group: (a) the fact that disclosures by participants are shared with all group members and not just the researcher; and (b) intense group discussion may give rise to stress or distress in individual participants. Both of these issues should be considered by the moderator when planning the groups and it is his or her responsibility (in addition to the usual requirements of establishing consent/assent for participation) to take all necessary steps to safeguard the participants in the groups. Although there are few guidelines available for running focus groups with children, suggestions from work with adult participants serve as a useful starting point. In relation to the first of these issues, Smith (1995) suggests that all participants be requested not to disclose group discussion to non-participants and also suggests that the researcher should alert participants to the possibility that such disclosure may occur. Hill (1998) advises that the moderator tell children that it is alright to say something very general about the topics discussed but not to give details and not to identify what any individual has said. This type of information from the moderator can form part of the introduction and could also include information on what will be done with the researcher's notes and tape recordings of proceedings.

The possibility that group discussion can give rise to strong emotional reactions is another important issue for consideration when running focus groups. In a group situation, it will not be possible for the moderator to guarantee that participants will not be upset or offended by one another's comments. Smith (1995) offers a number of suggestions for running focus groups on sensitive topics. These include the need for the moderator to monitor stress levels of participants and to be prepared to intervene when necessary, the importance of having small groups, and the value of debriefing sessions in which participants can discuss their reactions to the discussion. He also emphasizes the importance of having a co-leader with clinical experience present whenever the focus group is dealing with a sensitive topic in order to adequately monitor the 'comfort level' of the participants. While Smith's (1995) suggestions relate to running focus groups with adult participants, they are equally applicable to research with children.

While these ethical concerns are relevant to all research in which focus groups are used, they are particularly pertinent when the topics being discussed are sensitive in nature. Thus, researchers organizing focus groups to discuss topics such as parental separation/divorce or sexual behaviour would need to pay particular attention to these issues. Because of the risks of disclosure of personal information outside the group setting, special attention should be given to the composition of such groups. For example, it may be possible to ensure that children do not know one another and are unlikely to meet again because they do not live near one another. Such precautions would minimize the risk of disclosure within a group becoming widely known in the child's neighbourhood or among their immediate peer groups.

Running a Focus Group

Group composition factors

A number of factors need to be considered when planning the composition of focus groups with children. These include group size, age, gender and other variables relevant to the topic of discussion. In relation to group size, the typical recommendation is that it should contain no fewer than five children and no more than eight (Charlesworth & Rodwell, 1997; Greenbaum, 1988; Vaughn et al., 1996). The danger with groups smaller than this is that they may become parallel interviews, while larger groups may make it more difficult for the moderator to maintain the focus of the discussion.

With regard to other aspects of group composition, the general rule appears to be 'homogeneity is best'; however, most recommendations are based on the experiences of authors as opposed to the systematic investigation of factors that impede or facilitate productive group discussions. In order to control for developmental differences, many authors recommend that the participants in a single group should be within a two-year age span (Charlesworth & Rodwell, 1997; Greenbaum, 1988; Spethmann, 1992). Large age discrepancies are likely to create an imbalance within the group in terms of needs and abilities and, as a result, may upset the group dynamic. In addition, some authors only recommend the use of focus groups with children over six years, as the expressive language and social interaction skills of younger children may not be sophisticated enough to engage in the group process (Clark, 1996; Greenbaum, 1988; Vaughn et al., 1996). Evidence relating to the value of using focus groups with younger children is limited and contradictory (Charlesworth & Rodwell, 1997; Klein et al., 1992; Turner, Mayall, & Mauthner, 1995).

Many authors recommend that, with children and teenagers, single-sex focus groups work best (Mauthner, 1997; Spethmann, 1992; Vaughn et al., 1996). Greenbaum (1988) argues that younger children often dislike members of the opposite sex while teenagers may show high levels of interest in the opposite sex and this may detract from the flow of discussion. During early and middle childhood, there is substantial research evidence that children are most likely to play in single-sex groups (Maccoby, 1998) and this might provide one reason to consider single-sex groups when working with children this age. However, when children know one another well, as in Hill et al.'s (1996) research, mixed groups may work equally well. The researcher should certainly consider single-sex groups if the topic of the research is sensitive or if participants are likely to feel uncomfortable talking about their experiences because members of the opposite sex are present.

Planning a focus group also requires some consideration of the maximum length of the discussion. Vaughn et al. (1996) recommend that focus groups for children under 10 years should be less than forty-five minutes long and for children between 10 and 14 years they recommend a limit of one hour. These times should serve as guidance only. The moderator should be prepared to terminate discussion early if children appear bored or tired and may prolong the session if children appear engaged and eager to contribute.

A final consideration when planning the composition of a focus group is whether to include children who know one another (such as groups of friends or classmates) or children who are unfamiliar with one another. The section on ethics above has already indicated some circumstances when groups of 'strangers' may be most appropriate. The final decision on composition should be based on consideration of factors such as the topic to be discussed and the age group of the children. Whatever composition is chosen, the researcher should remember that when children are meeting for the first time, they may wish to get to know the other participants before they are prepared to contribute. Because of this, a group composed of 'strangers' may take longer for discussion and the exchange of views to get started. In contrast, children from the same class in school know one another well and their interactions with each other will be a function of their relationship in the classroom and playground.

The role of the moderator

The success of the focus group discussion and the quality of the data obtained will be strongly influenced by the skills of the moderator and his or her ability to stimulate and maintain discussion among the participants. The moderator has three major functions, the first of which is to make the group feel comfortable and at ease. In order to do this the moderator should try to communicate with the group participants using language they understand and should acknowledge the value of each child's contributions. Including activities that will engage children's attention can also be an important part of ensuring that the participants feel comfortable within the group.

In addition, the moderator should set him or herself apart from other authority figures and emphasize that his or her role is not to judge or discipline the children, but to listen to stories about their experiences and to understand their feelings. There are many ways in which the moderator can try to do this but some suggestions include using his or her first name and ensuring that he or she has the same seating arrangements as the children. Children may also feel more comfortable when discussing some topics if they can readily identify with the moderator, for example, because of his or her race, accent or gender. Whenever possible, consideration should be given to matching the moderator and the group, particularly if the moderator's race, accent or gender is likely to be relevant to the group discussion. For example, a group of children from a minority ethnic group might feel more comfortable talking about their experiences of racial identity or harassment if the moderator of the group is from the same ethnic group. A group of teenagers might feel more comfortable discussing their life experiences if the moderator appears close to them in age rather than close to the age of their parents or teachers.

The second function of the moderator is to keep the group discussion focused on the topic of interest and to ensure that all children have the opportunity to contribute. This does not mean that the moderator must work rigidly through the interview with a series of carefully prepared questions. With young children, the moderator must welcome contributions on topics that are important to the participants, including their jokes and their stories about recent events, even if these do not appear to be closely linked to the research question. The following section of transcript from the authors' work illustrates the way in which younger children (in this case 8-year-old girls) will bring their own stories to the group discussion. The short section immediately follows the moderator's reading of a vignette to the girls, who are clearly reminded of the behaviour of other members of their class. After a few comments, however, one of the participants suggests that they return to the original discussion and the participants are happy to accept the suggestion:

May: He's always like that, Roger [a boy in their class] he's always like that, scratching himself.
Jane: When we're playing the tin whistle Roger has to play it sometimes at a different time and he's always going like that [scratching].
Sara: He's always scratching. He doesn't like playing the tin whistle.
C.H.: Oh yeah.
May: I love it but I hate when it gets to high D.
Sara: Will we get back to the stories now?
C.H.: Yeah will we?
Group: Yeah.

Clark (1996) argues that when children are having fun it will be easier to keep them focused on the interview topic. Telling jokes and stories can help to keep a sense of fun in the group. Allowing the children's ideas to dominate for at least part of the discussion also conveys to the group that the adult is not controlling all the topics of discussion.

At all times the moderator needs to monitor the contributions of children and to ensure that shy or reticent children are encouraged to contribute and the more vocal participants are not allowed to dominate the discussion. To achieve this balance when the group discussion is very lively, it may be necessary to ask the children to help to ensure that each member of the group gets a chance to make a contribution without interruption. For example, all children could be given a coloured card before the discussion starts which they can display when they wish to contribute. Then the moderator, or one of the children, can call each person displaying a card in turn. This system ensures that everyone who wishes to speak gets a chance.

Finally, the moderator must try to enhance the clarity of the children's contributions by seeking clarification when responses seem ambiguous or when there are contributions from the same child that appear contradictory. The purpose of seeking such clarification is to ensure that the moderator has an accurate account of the child's views. For example, in the section of transcript that follows, the group is discussing why a child might display challenging behaviour in a classroom. Sam (11-years-old) makes a suggestion and the moderator (E.H.) seeks clarification of the phrase to ensure she understands what it means to him:

E.H.: Okay, any other ideas?
Sam: Not being brought up well.
E.H.: Okay, Sam. What would that mean, not to be brought up well?
Sam: If your parents don't really care about you, just let you do whatever you do.

Sam's response to the request for clarification provided the researchers with much more useful and detailed information than his original contribution.

When asking a child to explain potentially contradictory contributions, it is important to acknowledge that what appears contradictory to an adult may not be so to a child and the moderator should not seek consistency. However, seeking clarification can help to ensure the accuracy of the adult's perceptions of the child's knowledge and experiences. Whenever possible, it is best to phrase the question using the same words as the child and to reflect them back as a means of stimulating further conversation. At other times the moderator may need to attend to a child's nonverbal behaviour or tone of voice to interpret exactly what is meant.

While each individual contribution is important, the moderator may also need to find out whether there is consensus or divergence among the group on an issue. In these circumstances, it may be useful to ask the children if they have any different ideas or if their ideas are the same as those already expressed. Sometimes it can appear that there is consensus in the group when there is not. This is illustrated in the following section of transcript taken from the authors' study mentioned earlier. In this section of the transcript the moderator (E.H.) checks to see if everyone agrees, even though the initial reaction of the 8-year-old boys suggested complete agreement among group members. At this point, Mark indicates his disagreement with the group and he is soon joined by Jack.

E.H.: Who thinks he could just decide to stop [reference to inappropriate behaviour]?
[Many members of the group put their hands up.]
E.H.: So you all think he could just decide to stop?
Mark: No, not all of us.
E.H.: Mark, you don't think he could just decide to stop?
Mark: Not if he kept on watching fighting games programme on tele[vision].
E.H.: So if he kept watching them he wouldn't be able to stop?
Mark: Yeah.
Jack: Or he could watch wrestling and try to do it on his friends.

Finally, it is useful if the moderator uses the children's names when addressing them or when acknowledging their contribution in order to facilitate accurate transcription. Otherwise, the process of identifying each individual's contribution during transcription can prove very difficult.

Recording the group discussion

There are two alternatives to recording the group discussion: audiotaping and videotaping. The most common method of recording is with audiotapes. Although videotapes capture the nonverbal behaviours of the participants, the presence of a camera may be intrusive and may affect spontaneity (Krueger, 1994). When an audiotape is used, an assistant moderator should be present at the discussion to take notes on the emerging themes and overall group dynamic. This may include taking notes on the nonverbal behaviours of the individuals, the emotional climate, the enthusiasm of the participants and the reactions of the individuals to the issues discussed and the questions asked. This information can provide important details that will enhance understanding of the discussion when it is transcribed. It also allows one to record details of the actual process of communication. For example, hesitance among individuals, consensus within the group (for example, when individuals nod in agreement) and details regarding patterns of interaction among the participants. Most qualitative data analysis packages allow these notes to be inserted alongside the appropriate place in the text to assist with the interpretation of statements.

Arranging the location/seating

Children are likely to feel most comfortable when they are in a familiar environment and whenever possible, children's familiarity with the location and ease of access should be considered when the groups are being planned. Schools are often the first locations considered by researchers and resource rooms, halls or empty classrooms can be suitably arranged for focus groups. However, there are circumstances when a school might not be an appropriate location. For example, if the researcher wished to understand children's experiences of truanting and their reasons for not going to school then the school environment would not be conducive to a free discussion.

Consideration should also be given to the seating arrangements prior to the actual discussion. For younger children, sitting on the floor can contribute to a relaxed and informal atmosphere. If the children are to be seated, appropriately sized chairs should ideally be arranged around a circular table. The table can serve as a support or prop and may make children or adolescents feel less self-conscious. Whatever the seating arrangements, it is important that all participants should be able to establish eye contact with one another and the moderator. Krueger (1994) suggests that, ideally, the more dominant participants should be seated at the side of the moderator and those individuals who are shy should be placed directly across from the moderator so as to facilitate maximum eye-contact. With children, however, it may be more important to encourage them to choose their own seating arrangements so that they can sit close to a friend with whom they feel comfortable. Allowing children the freedom to choose their own seating arrangement can also help to distinguish between the adult–child relationship of the classroom and the focus group.

Introducing the group

Given the unfamiliarity of children with focus groups, it is essential to state clearly at the outset the purpose of the group discussion and provide children with an opportunity to ask questions. The amount of detail provided will depend on the ages and abilities of the children participating. If the interviews are to be audiotaped or videotaped, it is important to explain to children why this is necessary and to obtain their permission in order to do so. The format and nature of the group discussion should then be explained. This should involve explaining that (a) there are no right or wrong answers to the questions asked, that this is not a test, and that the aim of the discussion is to understand children's ideas on a specific topic; (b) children's answers will be confidential except in exceptional circumstances (for example, disclosure of abuse); (c) children should not discuss what others have said once they leave the room; and (d) only one individual should speak at a time and each individual's comments should be respected.

Using 'ice-breakers'

In the opening ten or fifteen minutes of the focus groups it is important to put the children at ease and set the stage for later involvement. A variety of ice-breakers may be used during this warm-up session. This may involve something simple such as allowing the children to listen to themselves speaking on the tape (an activity that the second author found very useful with children between the ages of 7 and 9 years). Younger children often enjoy making and wearing their own name badges and this will also help the moderator to remember the participants' names. Each participant, including the moderator, could then share some information about him or herself (for example, age, interests and so on). Activities like these help to make all participants feel relaxed and gives everyone a chance to practice saying something to the group.

Before introducing the topic of interest to the researcher it is a good idea to have the children engage in further 'ice-breaking' activities. The choice of activity should depend on the way in which the group discussion has been organized. If the core tasks of the focus group will involve physical activities (for example, sorting objects or role play games) then it can be useful to begin with games that involve moving around the room. However, if the core tasks are based around discussion or visual images then this should be reflected in the 'ice-breaking' activities. For example, Charlesworth and Rodwell (1997) used a paper and pencil pie chart and asked the children general questions in order to initiate a free flow of communication. Examples of these questions included: 'Who is your favourite singer? 'What is your favourite TV show?' Ensuring some continuity between 'ice-breakers' and the main discussion/activity avoids potential difficulty with transition from one type of activity to another.

Structuring the questions

The focus group should begin with more general questions and proceed in a sequential manner to the more specific topics. The initial opening questions are intended to foster conversation and interaction (Krueger, 1994) and to allow the participants to reflect on the topic of concern. Krueger (1994) recommends avoiding questions that imply 'yes' or 'no' answers and 'why' questions, as they may make individuals feel defensive or put pressure on them to rationalize their attitudes or behaviours. A less directive approach is to ask people 'what' or 'how' they feel about the object of discussion. The final questions that the moderator asks also have a critical role to play. The moderator or the assistant moderator may choose to summarize the main issues that arose during the interview and then check with the participants if this is an accurate summary or if anything important was missing. It may also be valuable to use this time to ask the participants to rank order the issues that they consider most important.

Using activities and supplementary materials

Given the importance of maintaining children's concentration and interest throughout the discussion, flexibility and creativity are essential when running focus groups. A variety of exercises and activities have been used by researchers to stimulate discussion. One of the most creative approaches adopted to date is evident in the work of Hill et al. (1996). These authors used a variety of developmentally appropriate techniques to explore children's emotional experiences and wellbeing. These included brainstorming, visual prompts, role play, self completion instruments and artwork. Other research protocols have included the use of colour slides that were relevant to the topics of discussion (Doswell & Vandestienne, 1996; Houghton, Durkin, & Carroll, 1995). Sentence-completion techniques have also proved an effective means for maintaining attention on the discussion topic. Each individual has to complete the task and subsequently discuss their ideas with the group. This exercise can be used to stimulate deeper discussion while also functioning as a means of involving all participants in the overall process (Greenbaum, 1988).

Analysing Focus Group Data

There are many different ways to analyse focus group data (for example, see Bertrand, Brown, & Ward, 1992; Clark, Marsh, Davis, Igoe, & Stember, 1996; Krueger, 1994; Vaughn et al., 1996) and the final method chosen will reflect the nature and purposes of the study. Systematic and thorough data analysis for academic research relies on full transcripts of the discussion with additional notes about the emotional tone of the group from the assistant moderator. The steps that follow are based on suggestions from a number of expert sources and on our own experiences of analysing data from focus groups run with children and adolescents.

1. Most experts advise an initial reading of the transcript combined with recollection of the discussion in order to identify and summarize major themes emerging (Krueger, 1994; Vaughn et al., 1996). This process is greatly facilitated if the transcript is read as soon as possible after the group discussion to ensure that the emotional tone of the discussion is remembered by the researcher.

2. The next stage in the analytic process is referred to by Vaughn et al. (1996) as 'unitizing the data'. This process involves finding the units of information that will be the basis for defining categories. Vaughn et al. (1996) describe this as a time-consuming process because adult participants may give long and detailed contributions to the group discussion. Our experience of working with transcripts of focus groups with children is that their contributions are typically short, thus making the process of identifying units considerably simpler. Because the units will subsequently be grouped together in categories, it is important to develop a coding system for the units that will allow them to be linked back to specific participants in specified groups.

3. The next stage in the analytic process is the categorization of the units (Bertrand et al., 1992; Krueger, 1994; Vaughn et al., 1996). This stage involves grouping the units according to common features. If the researcher is using a qualitative data analysis package, this task is considerably simplified; however, there are many other ways in which the categorization can be completed. Vaughn et al. (1996) advise cutting out the units from the typed transcript and placing them in envelopes representing the emerging categories. Bertrand et al. (1992) describe an alternative system in which each emerging category is given a colour or number code and this is then written in the margin of the transcript beside the appropriate unit. One of the advantages of this system is that it is not possible to lose track of the source of individual units. An alternative system used by the current authors involves 'cutting' and 'pasting' units from the transcripts into new files representing the emerging categories. Regardless of the method used, it is important throughout this process of categorization to periodically review the categories for overlap and completeness (Vaughn et al., 1996). Thus some units which were initially placed in a 'miscellaneous' category may begin to emerge as categories in their own right. At the end of the process it should be possible to define each category in a way that can be used by another researcher.

4. The final stage of the analysis involves returning to the themes that were identified in the first stage (Vaughn et al., 1996). The categories should now be compared with the themes that were initially identified in order to determine whether they support them. If the categories do not support them, the themes may need to be re-evaluated. The categories should also be examined for consistency with the theory guiding the research.

Ensuring Quality in Focus Group Data and Analysis

The task of ensuring that good quality data are collected and that analysis is rigorous and systematic is common to researchers using quantitative and qualitative methods. Whereas the methods of establishing reliability and validity of quantitative data have received widespread attention and are widely documented, much less has been written about the issues in qualitative research. Recently, however, the issue has been addressed in a number of publications (Elliott, Fischer, & Rennie, 1999; Krueger, 1993; Merrick, 1999). In this section we do not attempt to provide an exhaustive account of all possible approaches to the question of the quality of focus group research data, but rather to provide some illustrations of approaches adopted by researchers who have used focus groups with children.

Stanton et al. (1993) used a form of triangulation by comparing data obtained in focus groups with data obtained from individuals in a pile-sorting technique. Pile-sorting requires individuals to organize cards with phrases or pictures into clusters or categories based on a perceived shared dimension. The authors found that the pile-sorts revealed support for most of the views expressed in the group discussions. However, the sorts also found some interpretations that were not revealed in focus group discussions.

The issue of credibility (similar to aspects of reliability) is addressed by Kidd, Townley, Cole, McKnight and Piercy (1997), who explored the role of children in potentially dangerous farm chores. In their study, credibility was established by comparing information from focus groups about children's involvement in farm work with data on paediatric injuries on farms in the area. Another form of credibility checking employed by the authors involved presenting each focus group with some themes that had emerged from previous groups for clarification.

Checks of coding consistency or inter-rater reliability are among the more common methods used by researchers to establish credibility. Thus, Kidd et al. (1997) randomly selected 10 per cent of the data bits per transcript and compared coding using a kappa coefficient. Morningstar et al. (1995) used a consensus method with two researchers who compared their identification and classification of relevant data units. Where they disagreed they discussed their perspectives until they reached a consensus.

There are also a number of possible approaches to establishing internal credibility (see Elliott et al., 1999). For example Clark et al. (1996) verified the researchers' interpretation of the focus group discussion on perceptions of health risk by comparing the issues which emerged from a matrix analysis of the transcripts with the total amount of time the teenagers had spent talking about each of the risk factors.

Reporting on Focus Groups

Because the goal of the focus group is to establish the perspectives of the participants it is very important that the researchers give enough detail about the participants and the context in which their views were given. Thus it is important to provide details such as the age range of participants in each group, whether the groups were mixed- or single-sex, whether the children were friends, acquaintances or strangers, the size of each group and the setting of the discussion (for example, school, youth club and so on). In addition, it may also be important to explain the defining criteria for admission to the group discussion and the length of the discussion which took place. Providing this information allows the reader to place the children's views in an appropriate context, so it is unfortunate that it has been omitted from so many publications (Heary & Hennessy, 2002).

Conclusions

Focus groups are a versatile method of gathering qualitative data with children from as young as 8-years-old through to adolescence. A skilful moderator should be able to use the dynamic of the group discussion to help children to give open and honest answers in a supportive environment. Indeed, the presence of a supportive peer group may make the focus group more appropriate than the individual interview for use with children, in some circumstances. As the method becomes more widely accepted in research with children, it is likely to receive greater attention from researchers and to be used in an even greater variety of research projects.

Recommended Reading

Heary, C. & Hennessy, E. (2002). The use of focus group interviews in pediatric health care research. *Journal of Pediatric Psychology, 27,* 47–57.
Hill, M., Laybourn, A., & Borland, M. (1996). Engaging with primary-aged children about their emotions and well-being: Methodological considerations. *Children and Society, 10,* 129–144.
Krueger, R.A. (1994). *Focus groups: A practical guide for applied research.* London: Sage.
Morgan, D.L. (1997). *Focus groups as qualitative research.* London: Sage.

References

Agar, M. & MacDonald, J. (1995). Focus groups and ethnography. *Human Organization, 54,* 78–86.
Basch, C.E. (1987). Focus group interview: An underutilized research technique for improving theory and practice in health education. *Health Education Quarterly, 14,* 411–448.
Bertrand, J.T., Brown, J.E., & Ward, V.M. (1992). Techniques for analyzing focus groups. *Evaluation Review, 16,* 198–209.
Bogardus, E.S. (1926). The group interview. *Journal of Applied Sociology, 10,* 372–382.
Charlesworth, L.W. & Rodwell, M.K. (1997). Focus groups with children: A resource for sexual abuse prevention program evaluation. *Child Abuse and Neglect, 21,* 1205–1216.
Clark, C.D. (1996). Interviewing children in qualitative research: A show and tell. *Canadian Journal of Market Research, 15,* 74–79.
Clark, L., Marsh, G.W., Davis, M., Igoe, J., & Stember, M. (1996). Adolescent health promotion in a low-income, urban environment. *Family and Community Health, 19,* 1–13.

Doswell, W.M. & Vandestienne, G. (1996). The use of focus groups to examine pubertal concerns in preteen girls: Initial findings and implications for practice and research. *Issues in Comprehensive Pediatric Nursing, 19,* 103–120.

Elliott, R., Fischer, C.T., & Rennie, D.L. (1999). Evolving guidelines for publication of qualitative research studies in psychology and related fields. *British Journal of Clinical Psychology, 38,* 215–229.

Garley, D., Gallop, R., Johnston, N., & Pipitone, J. (1997). Children of the mentally ill: A qualitative focus group approach. *Journal of Psychiatric and Mental Health Nursing, 4,* 97–103.

Greenbaum, T.L. (1988). *The practical handbook and guide to focus group research.* Lexington, MA: Lexington Books.

Heary, C. & Hennessy, E. (2002). The use of focus group interviews in pediatric health care research. *Journal of Pediatric Psychology, 27,* 47–57.

Hill, M. (1998). Ethical issues in qualitative methodology with children. In D. Hogan & R. Gilligan (Eds.), *Researching children's experiences: Qualitative approaches* (pp. 11–22). Dublin: The Children's Research Centre, Trinity College.

Hill, M., Laybourn, A., & Borland, M. (1996). Engaging with primary-aged children about their emotions and well-being: Methodological considerations. *Children and Society, 10,* 129–144.

Houghton, S., Durkin, K., & Carroll, A. (1995). Children and adolescents' awareness of the physical and mental health risk of tattooing: a focus group study. *Adolescence, 30,* 971–988.

Hunter, A.J., & Chandler, G.E. (1999). Adolescent resilience. *Image: Journal of Nursing Scholarship, 31,* 243–247.

Kidd, P., Townley, K., Cole, H., McKnight, R., & Piercy, L. (1997). The process of chore teaching: Implications for farm youth injury. *Family and Community Health, 19,* 78–89.

Kisker, E.E. (1985). Teenagers talk about sex, pregnancy and contraception. *Family Planning Perspectives, 17,* 83–91.

Klein, J.D., Forehand, B., Oliveri, J., Patterson, C.J., Kupersmidt, J.B., & Strecher, V. (1992). Candy cigarettes: Do they encourage children's smoking? *Pediatrics, 89,* 27–31.

Krueger, R.A. (1993). Quality control in focus group research. In D.L. Morgan (Ed.), *Successful focus groups: Advancing the state of the art* (pp. 65–88). London: Sage.

Krueger, R.A. (1994). *Focus groups: A practical guide for applied research.* London: Sage.

Krueger, R.A. (1996). Group dynamics and focus groups. In B. Spilker (Ed.), *Quality of life and pharmacoeconomics in clinical trials* (2nd ed., pp. 397–402). Philadelphia, PA: Lippincott-Raven.

Levine, I.S. & Zimmerman, J.D. (1996). Using qualitative data to inform public policy: Evaluating 'Choose to defuse'. *American Journal of Orthopsychiatry, 66,* 363–377.

Lewis, A. (1992). Group child interviews as a research tool. *British Educational Research Journal, 18,* 413–421.

Maccoby, E.E. (1998). *The two sexes: Growing up apart, coming together.* Cambridge, MA: Belknap Press.

MacMullin, C. & Odeh, J. (1999). What is worrying children in the Gaza Strip? *Child Psychiatry and Human Development, 30,* 55–69.

Mauthner, M. (1997). Methodological aspects of collecting data from children: Lessons from three research projects. *Children & Society, 11,* 16–28.

Mayall, B. (2000). Conversations with children: Working with generational issues. In P. Christensen & A. James (Eds.), *Research with children: Perspectives and practices* (pp. 120–135). London: Falmer Press.

McDonald, W.J. & Topper, G.E. (1988). Focus-group research with children: A structural approach. *Applied Marketing Research, 28,* 3–11.

McMahon, M. & Patton, W. (1997). Gender differences in children and adolescents' perceptions of influences on their career development. *The School Counsellor, 44*, 368–376.

Merrick, E. (1999). An exploration of quality in qualitative research: Are 'reliability' and 'validity' relevant? In M. Kopola & L.A. Suzuki (Eds.), *Using qualitative methods in psychology* (pp. 25–36). London: Sage.

Merton, R.K. & Kendall, P.L. (1955). The focused interview. In P.F. Lazarsfeld & M. Rosenberg (Eds.), *The language of social research* (pp. 477–491). New York: The Free Press.

Morgan, D.L. (1996). Focus groups. *Annual Review of Sociology, 22*, 129–152.

Morgan, D.L. (1997). *Focus groups as qualitative research.* London: Sage.

Morningstar, M.E., Turnbull, A.P., & Turnbull, H.R. (1995). What do students with disabilities tell us about the importance of family involvement in the transition from school to adult life? *Exceptional Children, 62*, 249–260.

Rinne, M.G. (1997). Potential barriers to implementing a bilingual/bicultural program for deaf children. *Sign Language Studies, 93*, 327–355.

Smith, M.W. (1995). Ethics in focus groups: a few concerns. *Qualitative Health Research, 5*, 478–486.

Spethmann, B. (1992). Focus groups key to reaching kids. *Advertising Age*, 10 February (S-1 & S-24).

Stanton, B.F., Aronson, R., Borgatti, S., Galbraith, J., Feigelman, S., & the AIDS Youth Research Team (1993). Urban adolescent high-risk sexual behavior: Corroboration of focus group discussions through pile-sorting. *AIDS Education and Prevention, 5*, 162–174.

Turner, S., Mayall, B., & Mauthner, M. (1995). One big rush: Dinner-time at school. *Health Education Journal, 54*, 18–27.

Vaughn, S., Schumm, J.S., & Sinagub, J. (1996). *Focus group interviews in education and psychology.* London: Sage.

Wight, D. (1994). Boys' thoughts and talks about sex in a working-class locality of Glasgow. *Sociological Review, 42*, 703–737.

14 Creative Methodologies in Participatory Research with Children

Angela Veale

An increased emphasis on children's rights and citizenship has resulted in sustained attention to children's participation in research. 'Participation' has the status of a new orthodoxy in many areas of social research (Heeks, 1999). In researching with children, there is an excitement of discovery about participatory research and methods. It is an integral part of a reconceptualization of 'childhood' which recognizes that children have their own 'child cultures' and that power, status, social and economic differentials between children, as between adults, result in a multiplicity of 'childhoods' that need to be understood (Dawes, 2000). There is also increased awareness of children's agency and ways in which children actively contribute to family and community coping strategies in circumstances of extreme hardship (Hinton, 2000). This has led to a critical examination of traditional research methods and a search for methods that can serve as tools or frames for children's experiences to be articulated in the research process.

Systematic attention to participatory approaches in research with children began to emerge through the 1990s, prompted in part by increasing awareness about child participation rights (Ennew & Boyden, 1997). In brief, participatory research has its roots in liberation theology, Friereian pedagogy and analytical tools, and development works such as participatory rural appraisal methods (Chambers, 1997). A core principle of participatory research is the generation of knowledge (rather than its 'extraction') through a merging of academic with local knowledge to provide oppressed people with tools for analysing their life condition. The research process should be experienced as transformative, based on principles of social justice, non-hierarchical relationships and reciprocal learning between participants and researchers (Fals-Borda, 2001). Children and young people have traditionally been positioned passively in research and have lacked the opportunity to analyse and represent their position, often at a cost. Ennew (1994) pointed out that portrayals of street children as abandoned have not been of service to street children or their families. Dawes (2000) argues that, in contexts of political violence, representations of young people as traumatized, 'lost' or damaged can undermine local coping strategies. Participatory researchers argue that they have a responsibility to work with people to define their own reality and challenge imposed knowledge.

Creative methods are those that draw on inventive and imaginative processes, such as in storytelling, drama and drawing. They can serve as constructivist tools to assist research participants to describe and analyse their experiences and give meaning to them. The creative methods outlined in this chapter arose from an examination of innovations in research methodologies used in participatory research. Participatory methods are those that facilitate the process of knowledge production, as opposed to knowledge 'gathering', as is the case with methods such as individual interviews, surveys or checklists. According to Chambers, methods should shift the traditional balance from 'closed to open, from individual to group, from verbal to visual, from measuring to comparing' (1997: 104). The aim is to facilitate reflection, debate, argument, dissent and consensus, to stimulate the articulation of multiple voices and positions, and, through the process, to lay the foundations for empowerment. Participatory methods that have been used in community settings include matrix development, 'problem trees', and timeline analysis as a means of analysing community problems and identifying solutions (Chambers, 1997). Another example is official history, which can be reclaimed and reanalysed by oppressed groups through a focus on family archives, oral tradition and collective memory (Fals-Borda, 2001). Drama (Cornwall, 1996), ethnodrama (Mienczakowski & Morgan, 2001), photography and community arts (Lykes, 1994, 2001) have also served as creative analytical tools. Fals-Borda (2001) argues that participatory research promotes a 'logos–mythos technique' which is about the combination of scientific rigor and critical analysis with imagination and creativity as a means of coming to an interpretation of people's worlds within their cultural frames (p. 30).

In the same way, participatory research is not reducible to methodological devices alone (Chambers, 1997); creative methods can be used within or outside of a participatory paradigm. They are examples of qualitative methods which have the advantage over many traditional methods of engaging participants in knowledge production, and involving their participation in the interpretation and analysis of that knowledge. As such, these methods may be useful in a wide range of qualitative research.

In this chapter, I present examples of how creative methodologies were used with children as part of a larger participatory research project with a community in Rwanda. The project was initiated by the unaccompanied children's team (UAC) of a non-governmental organization responsible for the reintegration of over 30,000 children to their communities of origin. As a result of genocide and the loss of large numbers of men in communities, traditional child support systems were in disarray, social relations politicized and fragmented, discourses of ethnicity and divisions silenced. The project sought to engage with a rural community in a participatory process to describe the reality for children and members of the Sector, to reflect on the impact of violence on social relations as it impacted on children, and to give voice to the barriers or constraints to collective responsibility for 'vulnerable' children's wellbeing. The project objective was to pilot the use of community education as a tool to mobilize Rwandan communities for the psycho-social support of vulnerable children. The full concept of participatory research was worked out through the community education program. The work with children and youth served the more specific function of engaging them in an analysis and articulation of their perspectives on the lives of children in the community. This chapter examines the strengths and challenges of using creative methods in this context.

Fitting creative methods into the research process

For ethical reasons in this project, we sought methods that would avoid asking children for their personal story since we wished to explore the situation of reintegrated children without forcing the family and community to label individual children as 'orphan', 'fostered' or 'not of the family'. Methods such as individual interviews or personal narratives were therefore inappropriate. Instead we sought methods that were participative and non-directive, whereby ownership and control of material generated would be within the hands of the research participants. We were also aware that the research entailed exploring social relations in a highly specific and emergent context: a rural Rwandan community post-genocide. We sought methods that were dynamic and could be responsive to a 'grappling' with understanding that we felt communities were experiencing within themselves. It was at this point that we began to explore the possibility of working through games and creative methods.

To some extent, the microprocess we engaged in is matched by changing trends with social research in general. According to Flick (2002), social research is moving towards the oral, to the analysis of particular cases and activities in their local, historically bound context. She argues the role of methods increasingly is to analyse how people construct knowledge and engage in 'world making' in their everyday lives. In this context, creative methods can offer tools to engage research participants in an active process of producing externalized representations or symbolic worlds that can function as visual or text-based data. These data do not conform to narrow definitions of reality and truth but open how people organize and represent their experiences for exploration. (See Flick, 2002: 29–37 for a fuller discussion of the construction and understanding of texts and the relationship between text and reality.)

For the above reasons, we decided to develop a collective, workshop-style methodology, appropriating some ideas from Freirian tools of development education (Freire, 1970), participatory rural appraisal methods (Chambers, 1997), participatory research (Lykes, 2001) and liberation theatre (Boal, 1995). Core methods with children and adults were community mapping and drama. In addition, a wider variety of methods were used in children's workshops that incorporated activities engaged in spontaneously by children, such as storytelling and drawing.

In thinking about the composition of the workshops, the team considered which children associate together spontaneously. This led to reflection on local power and status differentials between children. Would it inhibit the participation of non-schooled children to be in workshops with school-going children? Would non-schooled children be comfortable with drawing? The team decided to include schooled and non-schooled children in the same group, while different activities could be ongoing at the same time if desired. Should workshops be mixed gender? If so, would this impact on the participation of girls, given cultural expectations and practices? In working with adolescents, it was felt separate workshops for girls and boys would maximize the participation of girls. The final set of children's workshops comprised: children 7–12; boys 13–17; girls 13–17; reunified children 7–12; reunified children 13–17; children in child-headed households.

The research team comprised of six members of the unaccompanied children's program of an international non-governmental organization who had worked together for 3–4 years, had developed innovative child-centred tracing methodologies and were highly experienced. The research process took place over a six-week period in the context of established relations with the community. An introductory community meeting was attended by about 300 adults. Following this, a community meeting was held with children and young people and about 400 children attended. All of the children wanted to participate in the children's workshops, and a transparent system of random selection was devised. The facilitators outlined the overall objective of the project, namely for people 'to understand the everyday lives of children in Rwanda' and to explore how to support children in difficult circumstances.

Dialogue, Drama, Storytelling: Data Collection using Creative Methods

Social mapping

Each workshop began with a community mapping exercise. This is a visual technique from Participatory Rural Appraisal (PRA), which is used to identify economic and other resources in communities (Chambers, 1997). In PRA, paper is placed on the ground and stones, leaves, sticks, pens and crayons are used as 'markers' of resources. Chambers (1997) argues the ground is an equalizer. Educated and non-educated, facilitators and participants work on the same level. We adapted the method for use as a psycho-social tool. The objective was to focus on understanding local constructs of 'vulnerable children' and to undertake a situated analysis of who supports vulnerable children and how such support functions. It also attempted to identify who are the important people in the community as a means of developing a 'sociogram' of social relations in children's worlds.

In their respective workshops, child and adult participants were asked to identify (a) categories of vulnerable children in the sector; (b) important people for children in the sector; and (c) people that help children when they experience difficulties and the kind of help they give. Participants named different categories of 'vulnerable' children, sometimes identifying particular children and placing stones or using the marker to indicate where children lived. It was evident that there was a high degree of awareness of children experiencing difficulties. Children in altered family structures which were the result of the genocide were identified as most vulnerable. This included child-headed households as a result of genocide and children living alone because a parent was dead and the other parent in jail on charges of genocide, children spontaneously fostered by relatives or neighbours, reunified children with relatives and homeless children. The discussion explored understandings of 'orphan' children. Understandings differed according to the profile of workshop participants. The local authorities and 'educated' group (for example, social workers, non-government organization staff, and respected community members) had definitions similar to UNICEF's definition of the orphan as a child that has lost one or both parents. Women and general community members also considered that 'A child of a prostitute is taken to be an orphan.' Children had the most fluid definition, less tied to formal definitions and more descriptive of the conditions the child experienced. They included 'children without the protection of their parents and without assistance for their problems', 'children who were living in another family when their own parents were still alive, then after the death of parents, the children were chased away', and 'children separated from their parents in the displacement during the genocide.' When asked to identify children that may be in similar circumstances to 'orphans', children identified children in poor families and 'Wandering children when the family is unable to feed them. A parent can chase away a child and a neighbour rescues him or her. A child can miss clothes and someone takes him or her to work so that the child can have something to wear.' Children's definitions gave rich situated detail on children's situations.

A ranking exercise was used to rank order the most needy to less needy groups of children, and to analyse the reasons for the ordering. The analysis forced children to reflect deeply on other children's experiences. Adolescents, especially, were highly sensitive to the challenges experienced by children, especially boys and girls of their age who now were heads of households. In the workshop with children in child-headed households, they found the social mapping exercise emotionally difficult as they were forced to confront their isolation in the community. The facilitators wanted to stop the exercise, but the children said they found it helpful because they now knew each other, that their feelings of isolation, burden and constant survival anxiety were also felt by other children in similar circumstances. Through the mapping, they got to know each others' houses and could visit. The following excerpt gives an example of the social mapping process.

Social Mapping – 'Who Helps You'

Child-headed households mentioned their brothers and sisters, paternal aunts and uncles, a cousin, a godparent, grandmother, and occasionally neighbours as people who helped them. Three participants became upset during this exercise and started crying as they talked of being supported by 'no one'. Children were asked to describe how people help them.

Child:	*My paternal aunt. By providing me with food to take to my people who are jailed.*
Child:	*Paternal uncle. He provides me with food.*
Child:	*My brother. He cares for me. He buys food.*
Child:	*My paternal uncle. He used to help me to care for the baby left behind when my parents passed away and now he intervenes by paying school fees. My maternal aunt cultivates for me. She likes to bring food to my jailed people.*
Child:	*No one ... Only those I beg to intervene.*
Child:	*No one. We just wait for God to intervene. My elder sibling.*
Child:	*None. When for instance it is a problem of the shortage of food, I just lie down and pass the night with an empty stomach.*
Child:	*My sister. We share tasks at home.*
Facilitator:	*Pick up a rock and map on the map those people you feel are important to you.*
Child:	*For me, there is no one.*
Children:	*We know our peers ... Will we also mark those that do not come to visit?*
Facilitator:	*Add on the list those that visit you.*
Child:	*None.*

Mapping served both as a descriptive and analytical tool. It provided an overview of the experiences of children in the community. The map provided visual evidence of the collective knowledge in each group of the extreme survival issues faced by some children. By doing the same exercise with groups positioned differently in the community, such as local authorities, women, educated people, and children, multiple constructions of children's experiences emerged. These considerably enriched 'official' knowledge. Importantly, it brought to light categories of children that were invisible to policy makers, such as children in child-headed households because a parent was jailed as a 'genocidaire'. This high-lighted embedded politicized constructions of 'vulnerability' as linked to genocide survivors, rendering children of perpetrators outside aid dis-courses (Veale & Dona, 2002). Children and adults conducted the analysis as they answered the questions of the facilitators. Children's analysis focused on those whom children could call on for different types of support (neighbours for food, local authorities to sort out conflict with a neighbour). Adults analysed the barriers to collective support for children, which they identified as linked to poverty and the complex political and social impact of the genocide on relations in the sector. Thus, through the analysis, sociocultural and ethnopolitical dynamics impacting on children began to emerge.

This method generated visual data, a 'map' of the community, that could be analysed through determining the features and people that were included and also those that were excluded. It generated simple numeric data in the form of ranking scales, and verbal data, which were recorded using a prepared documentation sheet. This textual material was analysed thematically. Technically, this method must probe for particularities to be effective. Who helps? Specifically, how do they help? The task of mapping, while non-directive, provided focus, thus addressing potential problems of diffuseness. However, participants did get stuck on irrelevant detail, such as the exact physical boundary of the sector, or the location of one place with respect to another. This needed sensitive facilitation.

An issue in this exercise is how to define 'community', a term with multiple interpretations. We used the physical boundary of a sector, which is the smallest administrative unit in Rwanda, tightly defined, and clearly understood even by young children. In piloting this method, we found that different maps emerged when a question, 'Who are the important people in this sector?' was rephrased to 'Who are the important people for children in this sector?' This yielded information that more specifically addressed our research question. It highlights the need to understand, with participants, what 'community' is being defined through the exercise.

Storygames

While social mapping provided an overview of children's experiences, another method, storygames, gave deeper insight into children's constructions of their world. Storygames are an open 'story' in which each child is invited to give a line of a story. The story goes from child to child until it reaches its natural completion. In the study, it was noted that the approach was similar to a game traditionally played by Rwandan children. For ethical reasons, we had sought methods that did not ask children for 'your story', and methods which avoided structuring the content of children's material in any way. Storygames functioned as a 'frame' to support children's meaning and children participated readily. Facilitators had to keep the story moving from child to child as some children enthusiastically took control of a section. Stories reflected children's everyday lives, household responsibilities, school. In the workshop with reunified children aged 7–12 years and 13–17 years, children's first stories were structured around experiences that occurred during the genocide and its aftermath.

Stories of genocide

[One boy chooses to tells his own story.] I am from Gikongoro. We came here by running away. When we reached here people were going to kill us. My grandmother was killed and I survived. I was lost in a house but Rekeraho found me and then I stayed with him. Since then I have had no problem. (Reunified children's group aged 7–12)

[Each line contributed by different children.] We ran away and lost our parents. – I was hungry. – I was separated from my parents. – We found a child. – Other's died. – There were a lot of bullets shot. – We moved by running. – They brought us into an orphanage. – We met nice people. – When we reached home a child died, – was found, – was buried. – We experienced terrible things. – We met those who carried us. – They brought us back home. (Reunified children's group aged 13–17 years)

The 'wandering child'

There lived a child … He went away from home – he became a wandering child – he left his parents – left home – his young brothers remained alone at home – they went to look for him – they found him – they brought him back – they punished him – refused to settle down – he went away – they couldn't get him – they went to look for him – they found him again – they beat him – he sat down – he went back – they made an announcement in church but couldn't find him – they later found him – he decided not to run away again. He began to help them in home duties – now he is upright child – if he would do so again he would be punished. (Boys and girls aged 7–12 years)

'Being beaten': Punishment and rebuking

I went to fetch water. I met someone. He beat me. (7–12-year-olds)

Parents sent me to fetch water – I delayed on the way home, – when I reached home I was beaten, – I broke a Jerrycan, – they beat me, – they repaired it, – I ran, – I was angry, – they refused me food, – I ran as fast as I could, when I was beaten I threatened others who had come to fetch water, – Mom asked me the reason I was beaten, – I said because I was late, – I went to my grandmother, – they found me there, – they brought me back home and forbid me to return there.

Facilitator: The story with which we started, what is it about?
Children: It is about threatening the child, to be beaten for nothing.
(Girls 13–17 years)

In this context, the storygame yielded some harrowing 'stories' of events that have now stamped the identity of Rwanda. Yet through the collective telling, the stories were brought into a public forum. The sense of a 'game' may have been protective for children as the stories were produced without apparent distress. These storygames support assertions that in contexts of widespread political violence, 'trauma' is not a pathology solely located and isolated in individuals, but suffering and traumatic memories are part of a socially distributed reality. According to Summerfield (1999), 'It is simplistic to regard victims as mere passive receptacles of negative psychological effects which can be judged "present" or "absent" ... suffering arises from, and is resolved in, a social context, shaped by the meanings and understandings applied to events' (pp. 1453–1454). The storygame method dramatically highlighted how children pooled their individual memories, fantasies and meaning to give rise to a cohesive narrative that did not arise from any individual 'head', but from their collective, shared understanding.

Children's storygames were taped, transcribed and then translated. A problem with this method is that there are no established analytic procedures for interpreting storygames. They can simply be retold as 'stories' and analysed for their content. A discourse analytic approach could also be used to explore the interpretative repertoires used in their constructions. Importantly, storygames are likely to draw heavily on culturally situated storyframes such as popular TV or film characters, 'happy ever after' stories, 'evil stepmother' stories or 'child overcoming odds to emerge as a hero' stories. This does not render them meaningless and devoid of content; Bruner (1990) notes this is also a feature of autobiography where the narrative of a life story draws on larger scale 'life' as the teller draws on easily recognizable and universal genres, for example, the tale of the victim. In our research, a number of stories had the structure of a child who behaved badly, was punished, reformed and then became the best or most loved child. These stories have elements of a cultural frame found in Rwandan proverbs which values good and respectful behaviour for children (Donà, Kalinganaire, & Muramusta, 2001). It was clear that stories are constituted culturally and are also culturally bound.

Drawings

A method that can offer insight into children's individual experiences is the use of drawing as a research tool. Children's drawings are increasingly being used as a means of researching children's experiences. Traditionally in psychology, drawing has been used widely in clinical work and as a standardized assessment tool of cognitive and emotional functioning through the 'draw-a-man' technique (Goodenough, 1926; Koppitz, 1968). The 'draw-a-man' test has also been used in non-Western cultures (Aptekar, 1988). A number of researchers have recognized the potential contribution of drawing as a research process that offers a representation of children's worldview (Golomb, 1992).

Vygotsky (1935, 1978) posits that from about 7 years, children begin to master the symbolic meaning of drawing and that drawing can serve as a cultural tool, in the same way as signs and language, for the mediation and transmission of experience. Drawings can be communicative but also in their production, pictures are 'discovered' (Andersson, 1994). It is this capacity of drawing to bring something into meaning that is of interest in child research.

In spite of this, much research with children's drawings has taken a quantitative approach. Andersson (1994) examined the content and meaning of children's social worlds. His methodology invited children to draw 'My future family'. He undertook a cross-cultural comparative analysis of sociocultural values by looking at drawing strategies like size scaling, detailing, centrality and social distance as indicators of sociocultural variation. A quantitative analytical approach has been common in other interesting research using children's drawings. Research with war-affected children in Croatia found children's experience of war was not reflected in the analysis of the size and placement of emotive topics in their drawings (Jolley & Vulic-Prtoric, 2001). Research on living and coping with ongoing violence in South Africa and Northern Ireland used structured rating indices to assess drawings (Rudenberg, Jansen, & Fridjhon, 2001). An evaluation of 'favourite kind of day' drawings from physically maltreated and non-maltreated children analysed inclement weather, size, and movement of weather as variables (Veltman & Browne, 2000). Research on the drawings of Honduran street children asked children to draw a picture of an ideal person engaged in an activity and to write comments. The analysis compared standard scoring systems with one developed by the authors to examine indicators of the children's social environment, personal aspirations, and cultural values (DiCarlo, Gibbons, Kaminsky, Wright, & Stiles, 2000).

In our research, we were interested in the interpretative potential of drawings. We experimented with using children's drawing in different ways. We developed a set of drawings representing generic categories of people, including an old man and old woman, a man and a woman with a baby on her back, boys and girls of different ages and a baby, and asked children to 'make a story'. This method was not particularly successful. Younger children seemed to find it hard to combine the different drawings into a narrative and a lot of time was spent identifying what the drawing represented. A university student, a friend of one of the team, had developed the drawings. Children quickly picked up on social cues that the facilitation team had not seen. For example, the drawing of the 'mother' figure showed a woman in nice clothes. Children spent time discussing how she was obviously a rich woman off to market. Thus, no story emerged as the drawing of this figure was discontinuous with the others and children didn't make relationships between them.

Free drawing was used in mixed age group workshops, as some younger children became bored with the discussion around social mapping and wandered away. The facilitator gave children paper, crayons and pencils and left them to draw by themselves. When they had finished their picture, the facilitators sat with each child individually and invited children to talk about their drawing. The following gives examples of how children's analysis of the drawings gave insight into their experiences.

Free drawings

A 15-year-old boy drew a picture of himself, a tree and a car. In describing the car, he said it was important because 'it brings wood from the forest to the cachot in the Commune office and prisoners use the wood to cook.' His father was a prisoner and that is why the car is useful. He also drew a mug. He explained it was a cup of water and that water is cheaper than food, and when they don't have food, he takes water only.

A 15-year-old girl drew her cousin ('she helps me fetch water, look for wood, we talk about everything'); and her small brother ('we understand each other. We are of the same blood'); and trees ('they give us wood'). She commented that she didn't draw her relatives, as they don't do anything for them.

Importantly, children referred to the people they chose not to depict in their drawings. These were relatives that offered them no support.

A second way of using drawings was the use of happy/sad drawings. This involved using a drawing of a happy girl/boy and a sad girl/boy and asking children to discuss what the child might be thinking. A similar methodology was used by Woodhead (1999) in his 'Children's Perspectives Protocol' for researching child labour. The drawings evoked different things for different groups of children and the discussion reflected the different realities of the groups. Older boys discussed the possibility why a boy might be sad; the loneliness of looking after animals on your own, feeling overworked or hungry.

Workshop with boys aged 13–17 years

Facilitator: *I would like you to observe these pictures. What is this one?*
Child: *It is a boy around 13 years.*
Facilitator: *How do you find him?*
Child: *He is sad.*
Facilitator: *What do you think he is thinking about?*
Child: *He has been under the hot sun, so he is taking some rest in the shade.*
Child: *He was looking after cows.*
Child: *He is lonely.*
Child: *He has been beaten.*
Child: *He is sad because he may not have got any food.*
Child: *To be overworked while others are sitting at home cross hands, doing nothing.*

In workshops with reunified children, there was reference to the identity of the child 'not of the family' as different to that of the others. The children in the 13–17-year-old group of reunified youth defined themselves with respect to other children in the community as those that do not have parents.

Workshop with reunified children aged 7–12 years

Facilitator: *Why is this child happy and this child sad?*
Child: *This one is sad because they shout at him.*
Child: *The child is sad because he is doing everything at home alone, and the other children in the same family aren't doing anything. They play everytime.*
Child: *The other is happy because they like him, they look after him, he doesn't do many things. They buy clothes for him. When he makes a mistake and they tell the parents, they don't punish him.*
Facilitator: *Why is one liked and the other not liked?*
Child: *That one is liked because he is their own child. The other one is someone who has been reunified to that family.*
(Reunified children aged 7–12 years)

F: *What category of child is happy like this kid.*
C: *Those that have parents.*
F: *Who are sad?*
C: *They are those that don't have parents, they that are fostered, because they are cared for as if they were not children, like telling them to go to fetch water in heavy containers that they can hardly carry.*
(Boys 13–17 years)

In the group of 7–12-year-olds, children associated being happy like the child in the picture with being 'liked' and being 'sad' with 'not being liked'. 'Being liked' was associated with being a child of the family and 'not being liked' was linked with 'not being of the family'. Being sad was also linked with being shouted at, doing everything at home alone and working while others were playing. Being happy, on the contrary, was associated with being well looked after, with being given clothes and not being punished. What emerged through the discussion was that in the everyday distribution of work, punishment and discipline in the home, reunified children were sensitive to making associations between perceived fairness and unfairness and love, acceptance and belonging. Further exploration of the dimension 'liked' and 'not liked' showed children also included the behaviour of the child as an influential factor; the child that behaved 'in a good way' was liked and the child that 'doesn't behave well' was not liked, irrespective of their relationship to the family. Developmental differences were evident in the responses of the younger and older children. While younger children tended to 'split' their experiences of guardians into dichotomous categories of good/bad, linked to feelings of belonging/not belonging and perceived fairness/unfairness, older children recognized that guardians were not in a position to give children what they wanted, not from 'bad will' but 'because they don't have it'. These multiple analyses gave insight into the complex psychological issues inherent in reintegration and fostering.

Drawings were also used in a comparative analysis exercise. Inspired by repertory grid analysis, this involved taking the different categories of 'vulnerable children' that emerged in the social mapping exercises and developing drawings to represent each one. These were placed opposite each other in different combinations, and child and adult participants were asked to say 'what is the same' and 'what is different' about the children represented in these two pictures. Systematically, pictures were paired against each other. A prepared documentation sheet was used to record verbal answers. This brought forth a complex analysis of issues surrounding children's position in extended families, the impact of the genocide on patrilinear traditional care structures, and the situation of children who experienced the breakdown of these structures. This was challenging for participants to think about because this knowledge was not previously verbalized, and it was also a learning experience for the facilitators. It highlighted constructions of children's lives in different types of family structures and the complexity of issues around education, work, family love and a sense of belonging.

Free drawings yielded visual data but it was the verbal material recorded as children gave their interpretation of their drawings that provided the data for interpretation – words about pictures. Images can be data, however, many children have little experience of drawing or are unconfident in the medium and a one-off drawing, without a verbal account of the meaning the child wishes to portray, may not be useful as a visual image in itself. As in research using photography, free drawings as images might work most effectively if children have the opportunity to become comfortable with this medium of expression, and it may not suit all children. Free drawings may also suffer from diffuseness if children are unclear about the research objective. They may also fail if children do not trust the research process and wish to passively resist revealing personal material. The drawings in the examples here were produced in the context of the workshops which were about helping us 'to understand the lives of children' in the sector. In this context, children generated drawings they were happy to communicate about and the method worked in creating a methodological frame which children could fill with their own meaning.

The use of drawings in the comparative analysis exercise provided a means of moving the research process forward from general category identification to analysing the specific dimensions in which vulnerable children's lives were similar or differed. The validity or otherwise of this method lies in the appropriateness of the categories used for contrasting cases. In the research described here, these categories were generated through the social mapping. Participants filled in a prepared matrix with 'similarities' and 'differences' as columns, and the pairs of drawings compared as rows. This was how the data were presented in a final form and the method thus yielded the analysis.

Drama

A final method used for accessing interpretative repertories was the use of drama. Drama has been infrequently used in psychological research. It is common as a constructivist tool in psychotherapy, such as in working with post-traumatic stress disorder (PTSD) (Johnson, 2000), as a way of exploring alternative possibilities (Smith & Nylund, 1997) and in learning (Broström, 1999). Drama has been used in participatory health research (for example, Cornwall, 1996), in psycho-social community-based participatory research on the impact of violence on communities (Lykes, 2001), and in research with street children (Donald, Wallis, & Cockburn, 1997).

We wanted to explore how reflection on the situation of children could be mobilized to get participants to think about collective support for children. We adapted principles of Boalian liberation theatre to use drama to invite child and adult participants in their separate workshops to generate stories of child vulnerability and to select 'actors' to act out the stories, with a crisis, and to find a resolution through the drama (Boal, 1995). The facilitators instructed participants not to enact a real live situation but to develop a 'story'. The facilitators 'workshopped' the method themselves, with the organization staff as an 'audience'. They experimented with freeze-framing the action mid-way through the story, to focus on actors and their situations, motives, feelings at that moment and consequences of behaviour. However, these interruptions were found to be frustrating. It was decided that, after delivery, participants would be invited to discuss the story and re-enact part of the story from critical or 'crisis' moments in the development of a situation. This provided a forum for exploring alternative strategies of action. In practice, where participants were asked to re-enact a 'scene' to explore alternative solutions to a situation through the drama, the participants spontaneously introduced new characters and changed actors. However, sometimes the generation and enactment of the play took so long there was only time for discussion without re-enactment. The discussion explored the thoughts, motivations and actions of the characters represented.

Children's dramas

'An unhappy' child who feels overworked and made to work alone has a fight with his 'father'. The boy demands money, and the 'father' complains he is a lazy and demanding child. The boy announces he will leave for Kigali to get money. The boy ran away from home. (Reunified children 7–12 years)

A fostered child who started missing school and began wandering in the community. In the drama, children selected a 'neighbour' to advise the child to return to his foster family. The child stopped wandering, returned home and became the best in his class. (Reunified children 13–17 years)

> An orphan boy in a child-headed household became stubborn, began stealing people's property and spent the day wandering in the community. His sisters ask the local authorities to intervene. The local authorities threatened to punish him. He promised to stop stealing and to participate fully in his work at home. (Children aged 7–12 years)
>
> One orphan boy persuades the other boy to steal from his parents so they can get money to go to Kigali. They leave for Kigali but life is tough and they return home. The father calls on neighbours and local authorities to punish his son. The boy is punished and he asks to be forgiven. (Boys 13–17 years)
>
> An adolescent girl whose group of friends tries to persuade her to go to Kigali. A neighbour hears of her plan and tells her that to remain here and go to school; in Kigali she could only become a prostitute. The neighbour asked her where she would get money to go to Kigali and she replied she would have to steal it. In discussion, children said, if she would not change her mind, neighbour, relatives and the local authorities should be involved in advising the child not to go. (Girls aged 13–17 years)

Drama offers a tool for getting at shared symbolic systems and understanding. In a context such as Rwanda where meaning is fragmented, dichotomized and in disarray, drama offered a tool for communication, shared discovery and possibly transformation. It is challenging to think about it in Vygotskian terms; the process is almost like a reversal of original learning in that, through drama, intramental, internalized images, experiences and fantasy are brought back out into the intermental where they can be analysed, explored, agreed or disagreed with. Bruner (1990) argues that, 'Psychology … must be organized around those meaning-making and meaning-using processes that connect man to culture' (p. 12) so that 'meaning is rendered public and shared' (p. 13). This may also offer a methodology that addresses critiques, in post-conflict contexts, of individualistic psychological interventions uninformed by cultural repertoires (Dawes, 2000; Summerfield, 1999).

In an examination of role-play as a research methodology in situations where it would be ethically inappropriate to use an experimental methodology, Yardley (1995) explored the relationship between the 'as-ifness' or make-believe aspect of role-play and actuality. She argued that role-play offers a frame within which possibilities can be explored, actors can reach forwards and backwards in time and explore their beliefs about real consequentially. A similar argument can be made for drama. However, she argued, the method can only really be effective when there is a suppression of the conditionality of role-play, so as to 'experience' inside the frame. For this reason, she argued, debriefing is ethically important, to facilitate participants to cross back into reality and out of a role. We noted a related difficulty in that, while participants were instructed that their drama was to be a story or make-believe, fantasy and reality could become mixed. In one case, what began as fantasy began to take the shape of a particular situation in the community. When the facilitators noted this, they intervened to give instructions that the drama was to be make-believe and not based on a real situation. The relationship between 'as-ifness' and reality in drama is highly complex, as it both constitutes the method (that meaning and social practices are being reconstructed through drama) and impinges on the method (instructions 'not to portray real people') and needs technical facilitation.

Technically, Yardley (1995) argues that there are three principles that are important in making role-play effective as a research method, and these also have relevance to drama. These are particularizing, the explicit detailing of the scene; presencing, the here and now quality of the experience, such as 'This is such a place', 'You are'; and personalization, or 'the process through which the inductor draws on and makes explicit use of individual participants' personal experience and meaning systems' (p. 117). The difference between role-play and drama, however, is most vividly related to this latter quality. In role-play, the researcher constructs the episode for simulation, the social context, and sets the parameters on the situation. In drama, the 'actors' construct the situation; the method is a tool for exploring what it is that actors 'know' and representations of their meaning systems. Gebauer and Wulf (1995) suggest a concept of mimesis as something that 'makes it possible for individuals to step out of themselves, to draw the outer world into their inner world, and to lend expression to their interiority' (1995, pp. 2–3). Drama facilitates this type of mimetic process.

As with storygames, analytic procedures for interpreting drama are not established. An additional difficulty with drama is the question of what constitutes the data. Is it the visual data, including spatial and nonverbal data, the transcribed verbal material, the drama itself or also the discussions that went into producing the drama and the follow-up discussion analysing the material? Also, does drama have the problem shared by other visual methods of selecting what is foregrounded in the drama? What is left out? It shares the issue faced by storygames of drawing upon familiar narrative genres.

We used children's dramas as transcribed text and then we examined their content or simply recounted the stories contained in them. We focused on sub-texts of the movement of children or their circulation in the community as a solution to crisis, either from one family to another or to the street. This drew our attention to processes that are not yet well understood in much child-oriented post-war literature. Drama transcripts are suited to various forms of qualitative analysis such as themal or discourse analysis.

Applications

Social mapping, storygames, drawing and drama were chosen as methods in the context of an ethically sensitive research project examining the situation of vulnerable children in a rural Rwandan community. These methods may have useful applications in other ethically sensitive research with children or in situations where children are unused to formal question and answer exchanges.

It is likely these methods can be used with any groups of children or young people. However, children who are highly socially anxious may feel uncomfortable and prefer individually focused methodologies. Developmental factors may also be influential in choosing the appropriateness of a method; for example, storytelling worked well with younger children, but was less suited to working with adolescents; drama worked better with older children and young people as they were more spontaneously expansive. Broström (1999) has successfully used drama games for educational purposes with children as young as 6 years, so drama can be used with young children but may need greater expansive support.

The methods used here are examples of collective methods. Collective methods can have their theoretical base in participatory research principles which aim to facilitate a group with shared meanings, interests or experiences to access and analyse those experiences. As such, collective methods are particularly suited to working with groups that have some common experiences or worldview, such as children from minority cultures. O'Connor (2000), for example, used the construction of a drama as a method with adolescents attending a program for youth with learning disabilities, and they used the drama to portray their experiences of being labelled by the broader society. Collective methods are also useful in research that wishes to access polyphonic expression as they stimulate the appearance of multiple voices, allowing for consensual, dissenting and conflicting perspectives to emerge and exist.

Limitations of the Methods

Conversely, as collective methods, these methods are unsuited for working with groups composed of individuals from very diverse backgrounds with few shared meanings. They are also unsuited to empirical research describing children's individual experiences. Collective methods also need ongoing reflection with respect to group processes and their relation to broader political, cultural and social realities. According to Heeks (1999), participative groups and processes tend to reproduce their political and cultural contexts. Collective methods can hide inequitable participation. Therefore 'low status' children (for whatever reasons status/power are ranked by the group, such as socioeconomic status, gender, ethnicity, popularity) may not participate equally with 'high status' children in the research. Collective methods can also generate false consensus, and take for granted ongoing consent. Some children may engage passively with the methods and therefore not participate fully. This can be linked to motivational and trust issues, and may be a form of withdrawing consent.

Conclusions

In creative methods, perhaps more so than in traditional methodologies such as individual interviews or even semi-structured focus group discussions, the success of the method hinges on being able to stimulate children to engage with the process. Ideally, the principles and process of participatory research (PR), where ownership of the research process lies with the participants, and thus has the possibility to be intrinsically motivating, may provide a paradigm for child research. In the project reported here, our team assumption was that responsibility for transformation and action was situated with *adults* in the community and ownership and responsibility for the outcome of the community education process lay with them. The operationalization of participatory principles in the methodology with children was limited. In part, this was a deliberate decision. As the research was ongoing, we asked some questions. First, through child research and its methods who is (should) be empowered? What are the *consequences* of empowerment? Where is *responsibility for change* situated? As we engaged in the creative methods outlined here, we had questions about ethical responsibilities. If, through a participative research process, children's engage-ment in description, reflection and analysis is experienced as transformative and empowering (as the PR approach demands), could it potentially bring children and youth into conflict with authority figures in a way that could be harmful for them if not followed through and supported, for example, with staff from children's centres or with guardians? Second, is it the case that for some issues, full participation and ownership of the research process may be appropriate with children but for others, *where children do not control the resources*, where responsibility should lie elsewhere, (for example, with adults), could operationalizing participative research place too big a burden of expectation and responsibility for children to shoulder? We used creative methods as constructivist tools to access children's shared meanings. Our final analysis revolved around a sense that it was necessary to engage children and young people in fuller and more authentic participation in the research process than we succeeded in here, and to attempt to operationalize the principles of a participatory paradigm. In work with children, perhaps more so than with adults, there is a complex relationship between issues of power, control, responsibility and ethics in the research approach and methodology, and questions about 'participation' in child research continue to pose challenges.

Acknowledgements

The author acknowledges the collaboration of Reiseal Ní Cheallacháir, Alice Mutabasi, Jacqueline Nzaramba and all the staff of Concern Rwanda's Unaccompanied Children's Program. Funding support for this work was received from the International Famine Centre, UCC.

Recommended Reading

Flick, U. (2002). *An introduction to qualitative research*. London: Sage.
Reason, P. & Bradbury, H. (Eds.). (2001). *Handbook of action research: Participative inquiry and practice* (pp. 27–37). London: Sage.

Rudenberg, S., Jansen, P., & Fridjhon, P. (2001). Living and coping with ongoing violence: A cross-national analysis of children's drawings using structured rating indices. *Childhood: A Global Journal of Child Research*, 8(1), 31–55.

References

Andersson, S. (1994). *Social scaling and children's graphic strategies: A comparative study of children's drawings in three cultures*. Linköping: Linköping Studies in Arts and Science.

Aptekar, L. (1988). *Street children of Cali*. Durham, NC: Duke University Press.

Boal, A. (1995). *The rainbow of desire: The Boal method of theatre and therapy*. London: Routledge.

Broström, S. (1999). Drama games with 6-year-old children: Possibilities and limitations. In Y. Engeström, R. Miettinen, & L. Punamäki (Eds.), *Perspectives on activity theory* (pp. 250–263). New York: Cambridge University Press.

Bruner, J. (1990). *Acts of meaning*. Cambridge, MA: Harvard University Press.

Chambers, R. (1997). *Whose reality county: Putting the first last*. London: Intermediate Technology Publications.

Cleaver, F. (1999). Paradoxes of participation: Questioning participatory approaches to development. *Journal of International Development, 11*, 597–612.

Cornwall, A. (1996). Towards participatory practice: Participatory rural appraisal (PRA) and the participatory process. In K. de Korrie & M. Martin (Eds.), *Participatory action research in health: Issues and experiences* (pp. 94–107). London: Zed Books.

Dawes, A. (2000). Cultural diversity and childhood adversity: Implications for community level interventions with children in difficult circumstances. Paper presented to *Children in Adversity: An International Consultation on Ways to Reinforce the Coping Ability and Resilience of Children in Situations of Hardship*. Refugee Studies Program, Oxford, UK, September.

DiCarlo, M.A., Gibbons, J., Kaminsky, D., Wright, J., & Stiles, D. (2000). Street children's drawings: Windows into their life circumstances and aspirations. *International Social Work, 43*(1), 107–120.

Donà, G., Kalinganire, C., & Muramutsa, F. (2001). *The Rwandan experience of fostering separated children*. London: Save the Children.

Donald, D., Wallis, J., & Cockburn, A. (1997). An exploration of meanings: Tendencies towards developmental risk and resilience in a group of South African ex-street children. *School Psychology International, 18*(2), 137–154.

Ennew, J. (1994). Parentless friends: a cross cultural examination of networks among street children and youth. In F. Nestman & K. Husselman (Eds.), *Social networks and social supports in childhood and adolescence* (pp. 409–26). Berlin: De Gruyter.

Ennew, J. & Boyden, J. (1997). *Children in focus: A manual for participatory action research with children*. Stockholm: Swedish Save the Children.

Fals-Borda, O. (2001). Participatory (action) research in social theory: Origins and challenges. In P. Reason & H. Bradbury (Eds.), *Handbook of action research: Participative inquiry and practice* (pp. 27–37). London: Sage.

Flick, U. (2002). *An introduction to qualitative research*. London: Sage.

Freire, P. (1970). *Pedagogy of the oppressed*. New York: Herder and Herder.

Gebauer, G. & Wulf, C. (1995). *Mimesis: Culture, art, society*. Berkeley, CA: University of California Press.

Golomb, C. (1992). *The child's creation of the pictorial world*. Los Angeles: University of California Press.

Goodenough, F. (1926). *Measurement of intelligence by drawings*. New York: Harcourt, Brace and World.

Heeks, R. (1999). *The tyranny of participation in information systems: Learning from development projects* (Development Informatics Working Paper Series, Working Paper No. 4). Manchester: University of Manchester, Institute for Development Policy and Management.

Hinton, R. (2000). Seen but not heard: Refugee children and models for intervention. In C. Panter-Brick & M. Smith (Eds.), *Abandoned children* (pp. 199–212). Cambridge: Cambridge University Press.

Johnson, D. (2000). Creative therapies. In E. Foa, T. Keane, & M. Friedman (Eds.), *Effective treatments for PTSD: Practice guidelines from the International Society for Traumatic Stress Studies* (pp. 302–314). New York: The Guilford Press.

Jolley, R. & Vulic-Prtoric, A. (2001). Croatian children's experience of war is not reflected in the size and placement of emotive topics in their drawings. *British Journal of Clinical Psychology, 40*(1), 107–110.

Koppitz, E. (1968). *Psychological evaluation of children's human figure drawings*. New York: Grune & Stratton.

Lykes, M.B. (1994). Terror, silencing and children: International multidisciplinary colloboration with Guatemalan Maya Communities. *Social Science and Medicine, 38*(4), 543–552.

Lykes, M.B. (2001). Creative arts and photography in participatory action research in Guatemala. In P. Reason & H. Bradbury (Eds.), *Handbook of action research: Participative inquiry and practice* (pp. 365–371). London: Sage.

Mienczakowski, J. & Morgan S. (2001). Ethnodrama: Constructing participatory experiential and compelling action research through performance. In P. Reason & H. Bradbury (Eds.), *Handbook of action research: Participative inquiry and practice* (pp. 220–227). London: Sage.

O'Connor, D. (2000). *Renegotiating 'Rehab': A study with people with learning difficulties*. Unpublished thesis presented for Higher Diploma in Psychology, University College Cork, Ireland.

Rudenberg, S., Jansen, P., & Fridjhon, P. (2001). Living and coping with ongoing violence: A cross-national analysis of children's drawings using structured rating indices. *Childhood: A Global Journal of Child Research, 8*(1), 31–55.

Smith, C. & Nylund, D. (1997). *Narrative therapies with children and adolescents*. New York: The Guilford Press.

Summerfield, D. (1999). A critique of seven assumptions behind psychological trauma programs in war affected areas. *Social Science and Medicine, 48*, 1449–1462.

Veale, A. & Dona, D. (2002). Psychosocial interventions and children's rights: Beyond clinical discourses. *Peace and Conflict: Journal of Peace Psychology, 8*(2), 47–62.

Veltman, M. & Browne, K. (2000). An evaluation of favorite kind of day drawings from physically maltreated and non-maltreated children. *Child Abuse & Neglect, 24*(10), 1249–1255.

Vygotsky, L.S. (1978 [1935]). *Mind in Society: The development of higher psychological processes*. M. Cole, V. John-Steiner, S. Scribner, & E. Souberman (Eds.), Cambridge, MA: Harvard University Press.

Woodhead, M. (1999). Combating child labour: Listen to what the children say. *Childhood: A Global Journal of Child Research, 6*(1), 27–49.

Yardley, K. (1995). Role Play. In J. Smith, R. Harré & L. Van Langenhove (Eds.), *Rethinking methods in psychology* (pp. 106–121). London: Sage.

Index

friendships, 89–91
  with participants, 131
Frønes, I., 48, 54
funding, 66
Furedi, F., 53

Gadamer, H., 221
Galbraith, J., 17
Gallop, R., 237
Gane, M., 179
Garbarino, J., 16, 35, 62, 64
Garley, D., 237
Gaskins, S., 108
gatekeepers, 70–1, 78
Gebauer, G., 268
gender, 3, 54, 55, 110–11
generalization, 136, 224–5
generational order, 55–6
Gergen, K. and Gergen, M., 161
gestalt movement, 33
Gibbons, J., 262
Gibbs, R.W., 10, 161
Giddens, A., 2, 50
Giesecke, H., 49
gifts, 71
Giles, A., 70
Gillies, V., 180, 181, 189, 192
Gilligan, C., 160, 161
Giorgi, A., 225
Glantz, L.H., 61
Glendenning, C., 62, 70
globalization, 54
Goenjian, A.R., 76
Goffman, E., 108, 124
Goldhaber, D.E., 104
Golomb, C., 261
Göncü, A., 108
Goodenough, F., 261
Goodey, C., 68, 69, 71
Goodman, N., 147
Gordon, B., 35
Gordon, T., 184
Gottman, J.M., 90, 95, 97
Gouldner, A., 126
'grand theories' of child
    development, 31, 32
Graue, M.E., 65
Gray, J., 28, 102
Greenbaum, T.L., 241, 247
Greene, S., 1–21, 9, 24, 25, 31, 38, 115
Grieg, A., 13, 77
Grieve, R., 9, 144
Griffin, C., 192
Grisso, T., 127
Grodin, M.A., 61
Grossberg, L., 193

Grossen, M., 147
group methods see focus groups
Guba, E.G., 31, 79, 103, 104
Gurwisch, A., 220

Haight, W.L., 108
Halfar, C., 108
Hall, B.L., 63
Hall, G. Stanley, 31
Halliday, M.A.K., 208
Hammersley, M., 124, 128
Harach, L., 24, 102
Haraway, D., 189
Hardman, C., 42
Harker, R., 18, 68
Harkness, S., 108
  harm, 65, 72–4
  emotional, 73–4
  protection from, 73–4, 80
Harré, R., 178, 179
Harris, J.R., 10
Harris, P.L., 203, 204
Hart, B., 108
Hart, R., 73
Hart, S., 30, 35
Hastrup, K., 50
Heary, C., 236–52, 250
Heeks, R., 253, 269
Heidegger, M., 220
helping, 92
Hembrook, H., 34
Hendrick, H., 30
Hennessy, E., 236–52, 250
Henriques, J., 177, 179
Henriques, W., 5
Henwood, K., 192
Heptinstall, E., 70
hermeneutic circle, 224
hermeneutic phenomenology, 223–4,
    229–32
Herych, E., 77
Hessler, M.H., 124, 127
Hey, V., 124
Hickey-Schultz, L., 159
Hill, M., 1–21, 61–86, 237, 239, 240,
    241, 247
Hillman, M., 52
Hinde, R.A., 107
Hinton, R., 253
historical origins of research, 29–33
history, official, 254
Hobson, J., 162
Hodges, K., 27
Hogan, D., 8, 15, 22–41, 102–22, 175
Holland, J., 159, 184
Holloway, I., 70, 72